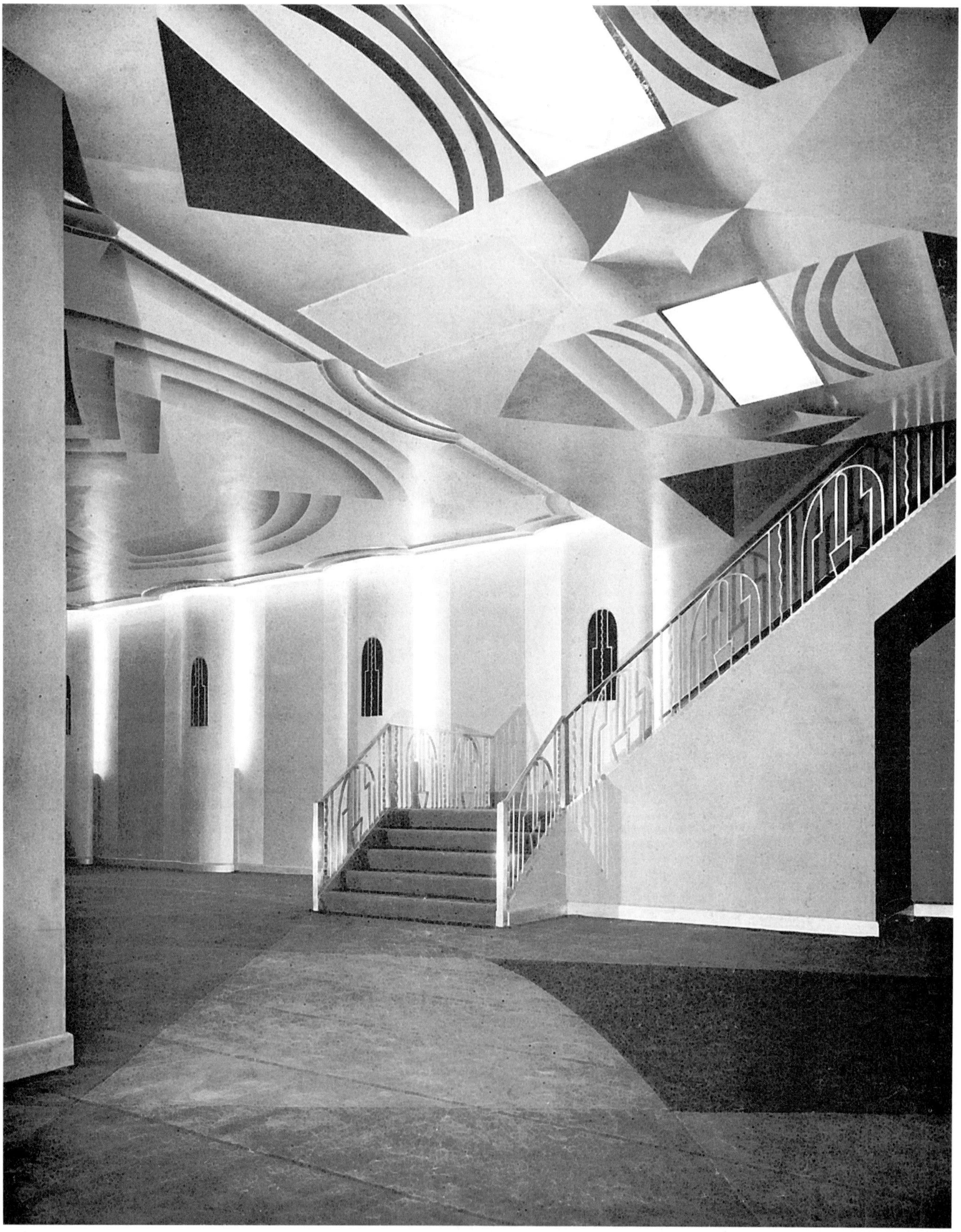

The main foyer of the ballroom, Hotel St. George, Brooklyn. See also page 129.

# AMERICAN ART DECO
## AN ILLUSTRATED SURVEY

Edited by
R. L. Leonard
and
C. A. Glassgold

DOVER PUBLICATIONS, INC.
Mineola, New York

*Bibliographical Note*

This Dover edition, first published in 2004, is an unabridged republication of the work originally published in 1931 as the *Annual of American Design 1931 by the American Union of Decorative Artists and Craftsmen* by Ives Washburn, New York.

*Library of Congress Cataloging-in-Publication Data*

Annual of American design
American art deco : an illustrated survey / edited by R.L. Leonard and C.A. Glassgold.
p. cm.
"An unabridged republication of the work originally published in 1931 under title: Annual of American design 1931 by the American Union of Decorative Artists and Craftsmen"—T.p. verso.
ISBN 0-486-43374-9 (pbk.)
1. Decoration and ornament—Art deco. 2. Decoration and ornament—United States. 3. Design—United States—History—20th century. I. Leonard, R. L. (Robert Leo), b. 1879. II. Glassgold, C. Adolph. III. Title.

NK1396.A76A53 2004
745.4'0973'09041—dc22

2003068767

Manufactured in the United States of America
Dover Publications, Inc., 31 East 2nd Street, Mineola, N.Y. 11501

# CONTENTS

# LIST OF ILLUSTRATIONS

## THE SHOP



## THE HOME



## TEXTILES



## NEW MATERIALS



## INDUSTRIAL DESIGN

## ARCHITECTURE



## HALLS, WALLS AND FITTINGS



## GRAPHIC ARTS IN ADVERTISING



## COMMERCIAL PHOTOGRAPHY

A C K N O W L E D G E M E N T

Thanks are due to Dr. M. F. Agha, Art Director of Condé Nast Publications; Richard F. Bach, Director of Industrial Relations, Metropolitan Museum of Art; M. D. C. Crawford, Research Editor, Fairchild Publications; Hugh Ferriss and Lewis Mumford whose interest prompted them to write articles for this volume; and to Manuel Komroff for his editorial advice.

## LEWIS MUMFORD

# culture and machine art

Modern industrial design has advanced at a rapid pace during the last ten years. Its successes are no longer confined to objects which, like automobiles and airplanes, are themselves the product of new conditions. Modern design has also begun to conquer the traditional arts, and the feeling for abstract form, first expressed in our time in the works of Picasso, Bracque, Brancusi, Duchamps-Villon in Europe, or Stieglitz, Benton, and Storrs for example in the United States, has finally entered architecture and the decorative arts. Our china and glassware and rugs and chairs begin to show a common spirit: they exhibit the clean lines, the fine sense of fitness, and the exquisite proportions which must always be present in machine work, since lacking these characteristics, it has few other charms with which to seduce the eye or the mind.

One may say, I think, that the canons of machine design have been established: the success of any particular design now rests with the skill and personality of the designer: a tradition is already in existence.

But the problem of design does not end in the studio and the factory. It is plain that the victory which has been achieved in architecture by Wright, Gropius, Le Corbusier, and Mies van der Rohe, and which has been the product of a hundred almost anonymous designers in the industrial arts, has not yet been consolidated in society. Modern industrial design is based on the principle of conspicuous economy. Unfortunately, the bourgeois culture which dominates the Western World is founded, as our American economist, Thorstein Veblen described in his classic "Theory of the Leisure Class," on the principle of conspicuous waste. The aim of the arts, in this society, is not essentially to serve and enrich life, but to establish the pecuniary position of the patron. This aim is widespread: it is as notorious in the home of the most humble manual worker, who feels that lace curtains are "respectable," as it is on Park Avenue. In fact, a good part of what is called beauty in this society consists of objects which show, at first glance, their costly and luxurious character. The old-fashioned house was a species of private museum; and one of the chief occupations of the housewife was that of curator. If the poorer member of our society cannot achieve this kind of "beauty" at first hand, he demands it in some cheaper reproduction or caricature: America dyed catskin takes the place of ermine; and debased rococo furniture, built out of poorly seasoned wood and carved by the machine, simulates the luxury of the Renaissance.

Now the best industrial designs of today psychologically contradict the standards of this society. They are cheap; they are common; they fulfill their peculiar function; whereas, to satisfy the canons of conspicuous waste, an industrial design should look expensive, should seem unique, and besides performing more or less its essential function should increase the sense of power and self-importance of the owner. This confronts us with a real dilemma. Whatever the politics of a country may be, the machine is a communist! The whole social life and ritual of Western European countries, on the contrary, is built on gradations of financial caste and status; and the business of the industrial and decorative arts in the past has been to label gracefully these social distinctions. Incidentally, these arts have often achieved beauty of form, as incidentally they may also have performed certain functions: but a large animus behind these arts was show.

The machine has revolutionized this condition. By its aid, we now have at our command a store of power which, if properly used, will do away with industrial slavery and create, for every member of the community, an equal share in the essentials of life. The esthetics that goes with this system of production is necessarily different from that which fitted a purely handicraft regime: unless this esthetics is formulated and generally applied, the machine will have no rational and effective ends. In this new economy, there is still a place for individuality, for that is a constant attribute of a developed human personality; and I am far from looking forward to a time when, as Mr. Buckminster Fuller thinks, the whole world will live in his standard Dymaxion house, built on exactly the same design in Brooklyn as in Bombay. Nor do I think that standardization is tolerable without a considerable freedom of choice between standard patterns, and without a flexibility in production which will permit the free creation of new patterns. (The costly standardization of the Model T Ford is a warning, not a happy example!) But the individuality which can be achieved by machine design has precious little to do with social status and financial success. Hence, to put the problem in another way: What place is there in contemporary bourgeois society for our best and most typical industrial art? The answer is that there is very little place. Before modern industrial design can conquer every department of life we shall have to change our standards and attitudes. Industrial design has improved most swiftly in departments of the household, like the kitchen, where practical functions must be performed, and in the construction of cheap workers' houses, where the demands of economy were uppermost, whether the worker himself was pleased with this fact or not. With these two exceptions, the best modern designs, such as those of Djo Bourgeois, have been executed for that handful of the elite,, produced even by bourgeois society, who have oriented themselves deliberately to the modern world, and who have sought to eliminate in their personal lives the vestiges of a more sordid culture, bound by an undue respect for property, financial status, and the things that money can buy.

Our modern industrial esthetics, then, requires for its success, an ethical reorientation to life, and a corresponding change in many venerable habits and institutions. We can enjoy these new forms to the full only when we no longer ask them to satisfy irrelevant interests: the impulse to display oneself, the impulse to dominate one's fellows, the impulse to demand homage, not for what one is, but for what one has. For the lack of such a spiritual conversion, a good part of modern industrial art is so only in name, and in the fact that its eccentric forms and its extravagant gestures have no direct precedent in the art of Baroque or Medieval times. "Modernist" art, though it superficially may take its cue from machine forms and may cling to abstract geometrical patterns, satisfies none of the real conditions of good machine form: it is a luxury art, and the fact that it may be produced by the machine is only an unimportant accident.

If we cannot root out snobbery and caste-assertion, we should find some less offensive outlet for them than that which they now have in the industrial arts. For we stand, perhaps, on the threshold of a new age, and unless we understand the machine and use it to aid in the creation of appropriate standards and modes of life, we will be debased by it. Standardization at a high level will give us freedom and new opportunities for cultural expression. Standardization at a low level, with luxury and sensuous display as its main aim, will give us a culture even lower than that of the Carthaginians, for it will endow a vast servile population with the vices of its masters. Modern industrial design presents a sharp alternative. The road branches: we must make a choice.

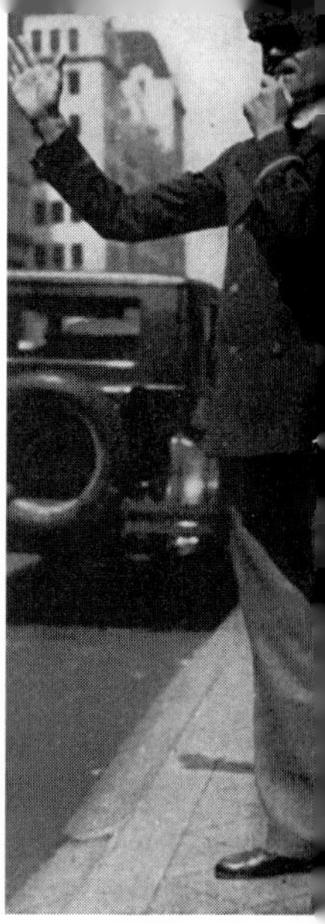

# K E M   W E B E R

# T H E   M O D E R N   S H O P

The modern American store with its necessary requirements is certainly not a place for superficially applied interior decoration nor is it the outlet for artistic temperament.
Its problem is not solved by standardized store equipment corporations who have made no basic change in their solutions for the last twenty years and who cannot consider the individual problems of a store because of their huge stock of standardized materials.
Successful merchandising today is dependent upon the ability of the retail merchant to keep pace with modern progress and to be thoroughly cognizant of the latest developments in relation to the merchandise he sells.
Public acceptance of a newly developed commodity depends upon the consideration and interest the retailer gives to it and upon his effort to awaken public recognition for its advantages.
Because of his position as a combination of servant and tutor to the public taste, the modern American retail merchant is becoming more and more an important factor in the cultural development of his country.
It is evident that American merchants have not awakened to the importance of keeping their stores esthetically in tune with the progress made in their products.
Theoretical and practical retail merchandising problems, merchandising efficiency, economy, buying and selling, advertising, etc.,—in fact all of the various phases of store operation are being discussed in conventions, in the trade press, and through professional merchandising advisors.
Innovations are being analyzed and compared, experimented with, and if successful employed everywhere.
This co-operative progress, however, has not included any question of esthetics.
The importance of public reaction towards appearance, the strong psychological influence of well balanced form and color is finding only occasional recognition here and there.
Its vital and direct influence on the success of retail merchandising establishments has never been fully accepted.
Store appearance and store designing, the necessity of attraction, practical store requirements, etc., are being "solved" through a stereotyped method of selling store equipment.
The retail merchant has a limited selection of typical store fronts and display windows which vary in type slightly, depending upon the merchandise to be sold.
There are more or less typical solutions for each of the various branches of merchandise which standardize appearance and which classify any departure as radicalism.
The particular locality of the store, its immediate environments, the individuality of the community and the people the store is to serve, the characteristic methods of operation, which in many cases have been responsible for its success—all of these are being continually submerged in favor of a standardized method of planning and "design."
Store designing has been divided into two functions.

First—store planning which incorporates all the practical requirements and which is based upon a traditional development of business activities.

The "bible" which is followed religiously is a book of knowledge in which is printed in black on white apparently unshakable proof that all stores must always be planned in a fashion which allows standardization to the manufacturer of store fixtures who wrote the bible.

Second—interior decoration which superimposes such forms, details, mouldings or colors on the store plan as happen to be the fashion of the time.

The latest introduction into the field of store designing is the method of employing a store architect who knows the "bible" by heart and in addition an artist designer to attend to the interior decoration.

The store architect knows and can definitely prove traditionally the correct sizes for the heights of a display case, or selling counter, or hosiery drawer. He knows the relation between the different departments and the Lamson tube system, and all other operating requirements according to the "bible."

The artist designer knows all about balance, and form and color and vistas.

The result is a COMPROMISE.

The modern American store has to be a definite departure from heretofore used methods of procedure.

Its design must be based upon the unbiased recognition of its particular purpose and functioning.

The design of such a store must be an effort to accept the machinery of modern merchandising as a basic factor and to develop out of it an expression esthetically beautiful.

Or to phrase this differently esthetic beauty has become an essential function of a modern merchandising machine.

This is not achieved by merely buying the store a new dress. It is only successful if the organization of all its essential parts and details is healthy, well proportioned, and well balanced.

Display, service, stock facilities, operating devices, accommodations for customers, air, light, comfort, efficiency, and all the many details necessary for modern methods of selling merchandise must be combined; and the esthetic beauty of the completed store depends upon the quality of these details and the understanding, restraint, and culture employed to formulate the entirety.

The esthetic beauty of any piece of machinery grows with the elimination of non-essentials.

It, therefore, depends upon the fineness of the individual parts necessary for its performance and the balance created through the combination of these parts into rhythmic entity.

Our recognition of beauty in commodities changes with the development of such commodities.

The Tudor wood panelings of old England were recognized as an esthetically beautiful design due to the acceptance and understanding of the necessity of putting wood panels into heavier wood frames.

The origin of this "design" was the technical necessity of securing proper performance out of the material used.

The present possibilities of plywood, the product of gluing together three or more layers of wood and changing the direction of the grain in each layer, open entirely new fields for design.

We can now make wood panels of any size without frames. We are not forced, therefore, to depend upon rectangular panels as a decoration and we can show the character of the beautiful graining of the wood itself to much greater advantage.

The elimination of non-essentials does not necessitate crudeness. In fact, proper consideration of the technical and esthetic possibilities of such simplification opens a vast untouched sphere of beauty which is ours to exploit and develop.

Advertisement—lettering—sign—electrical light effects—reflections—movements and other attractions hitherto superimposed upon the classical architectural efforts of our store fronts have now become the basis for store front design—copies of classical columns, pilasters, cornices and antique stone structure are replaced by designs evolved from modern steel and concrete construction, and advertising necessities are the means of enrichment, variation, and character.

The display window ceases to be the annoying open glass plate which interfered with the classical column to maintain its proportions, but becomes the joy and play for the constructive imagination of the modern Michael Angelo. He can design his solution for material, structure, and purpose heretofore unknown.

Escalators, elevators, tube systems, automatic selling devices, moving display, unlimited advantages of lighting, ventilating communication, now support and encourage the conceptions of the designer and instead of being hidden behind unsuitable solutions copied from bygone periods, become the basic features through his acceptance of the esthetic value in their functionings.

There is no more room in modern America for the superimposition of falsities under the fake smoke screen of medieval romanticism—there is no excuse for modernized medievalism, for old Spanish elevator cabs, old English wood paneling and Italian chandeliers with cardboard electric candles. This type of poor and ridiculous fake has been the backbone of draftsmen unable to conceive the beauty of modern progress, it has been used as empty chatter to cover this utter inability by the salesman for store fixture shops and by the business men who are afraid of the upward flight of young America.

Some outstanding examples have proven it to be good business to recognize the advantages and further and support an esthetic expression of modern progress in science—technique—and merchandising.

Those store owners, who have accepted the work and advice of such men as are capable of solving these problems, are known today as America's leading retail merchants.

The forming of an artistic self expression of our age is not a matter of temporary fashion, has nothing to do with bizarre, freakish and loud forms and color, but is a sincere recognition of the absolute necessity of discovering and accepting modern progress esthetically.

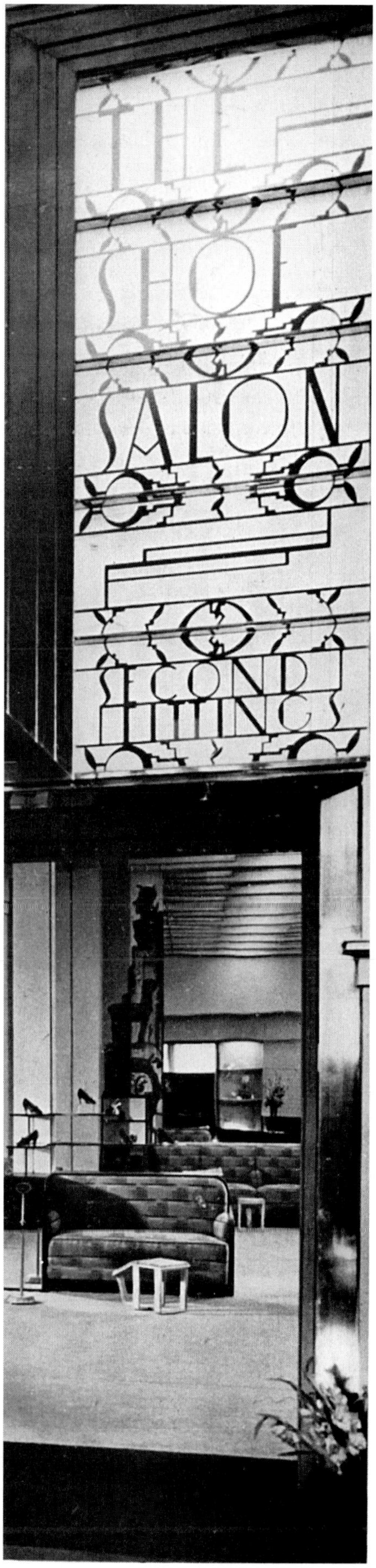

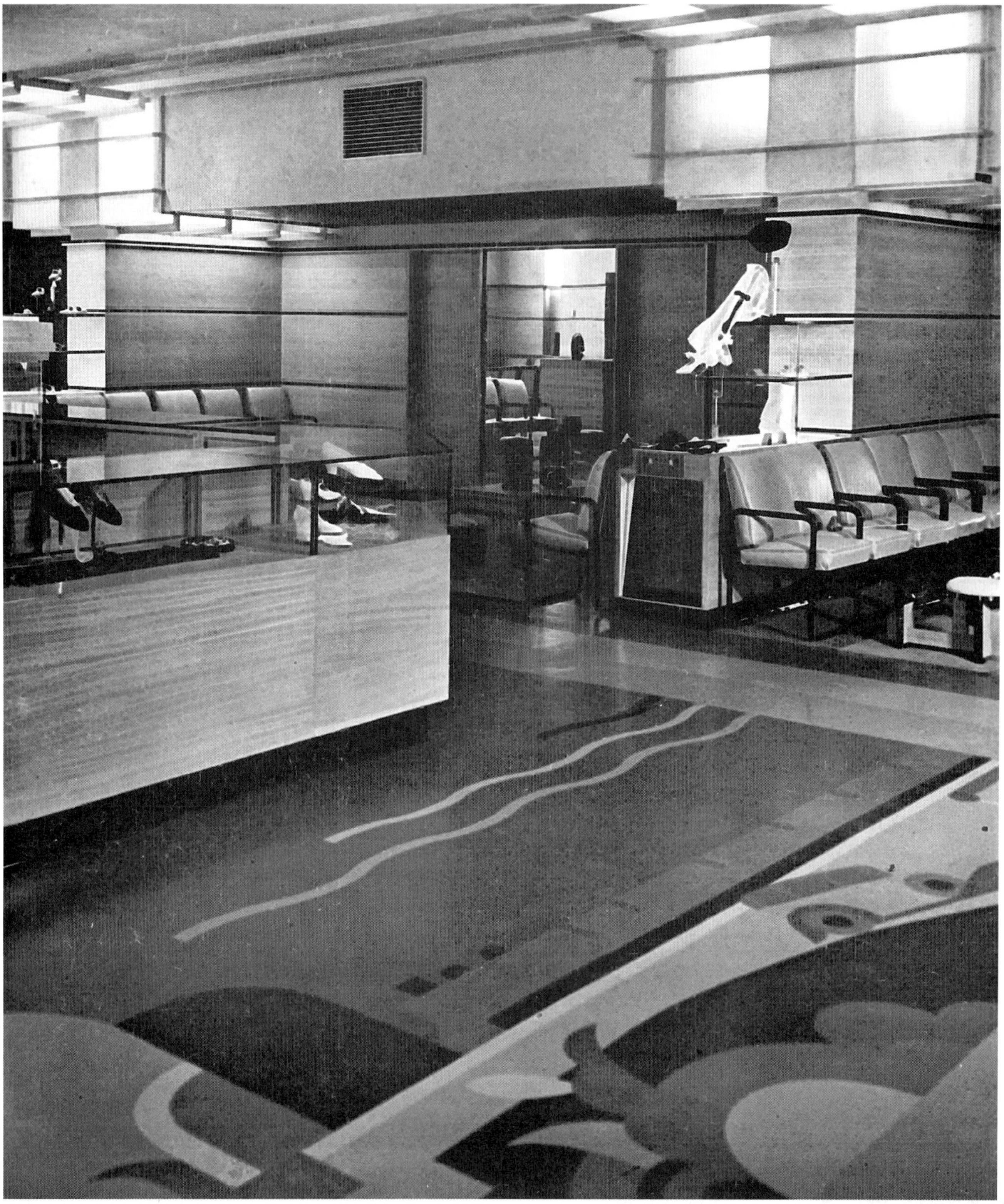

K E M W E B E R

Three views of the Sommer & Kaufmann Department Store, San Francisco. Above—Children's Department. Plaster walls in sage green and tan — Woodwork natural Philippine mahogany — Black metal tubing chairs covered in cream colored Nemoursa.

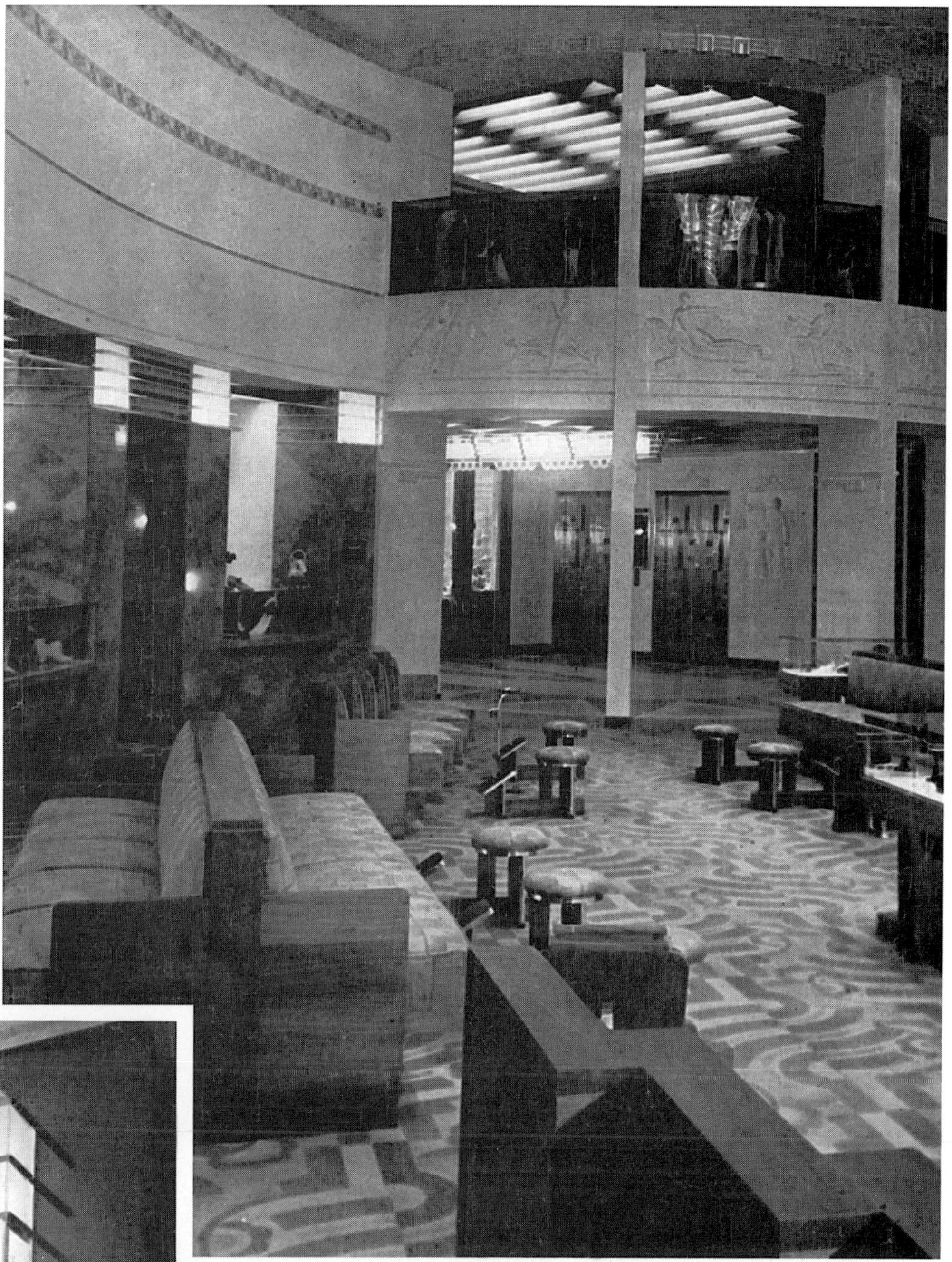

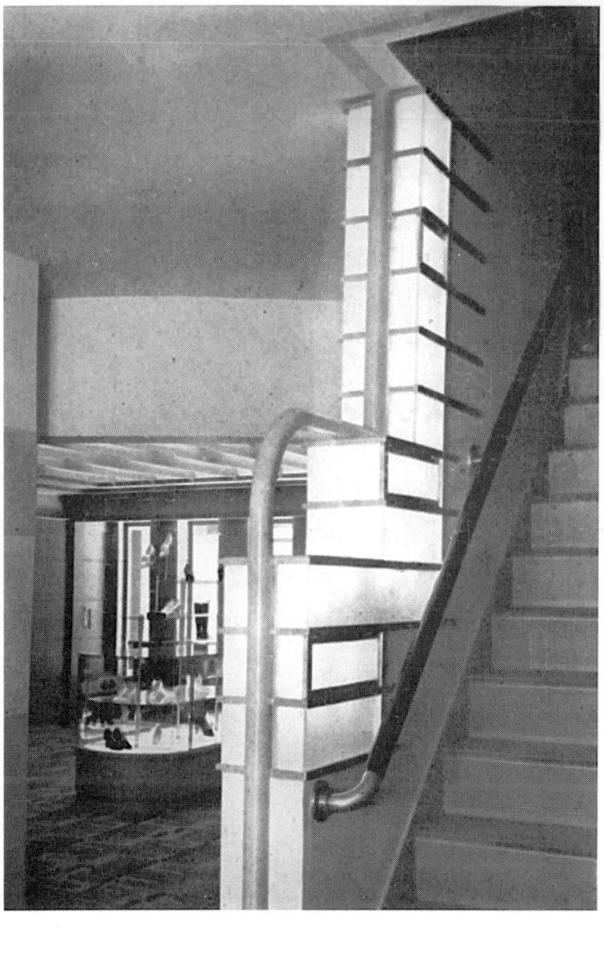

Main sales room and stairway to Mezzanine — Light diffused through sand blasted glass — Woodwork American black walnut executed by Pacific Manufacturing Company in light canary yellow — Marble of Napoleon Melange. Carpet and furniture executed by W. & J. Sloane in pink, beige, gray and yellow.

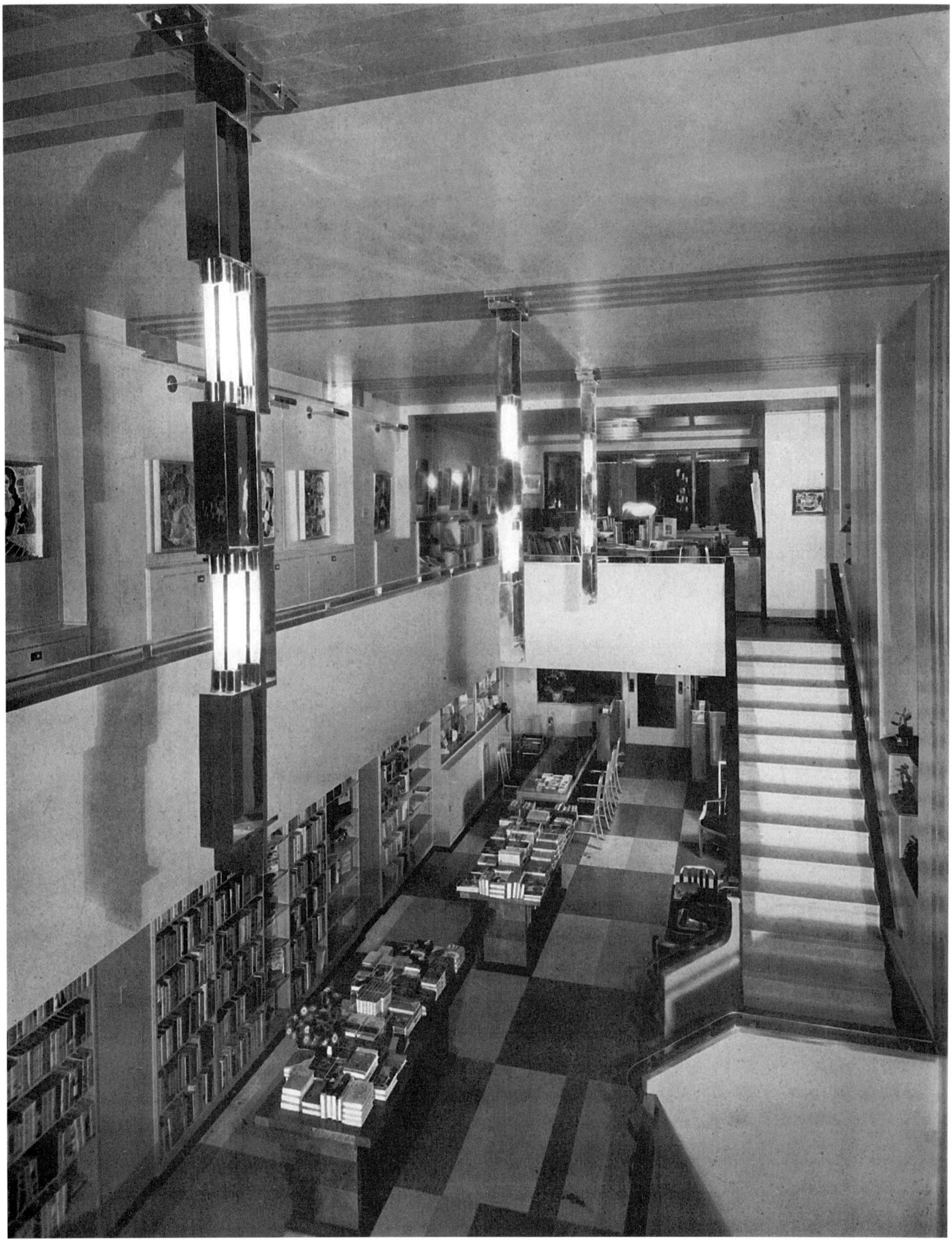

HOLABIRD & ROOT, architects
WINOLD REISS, designer

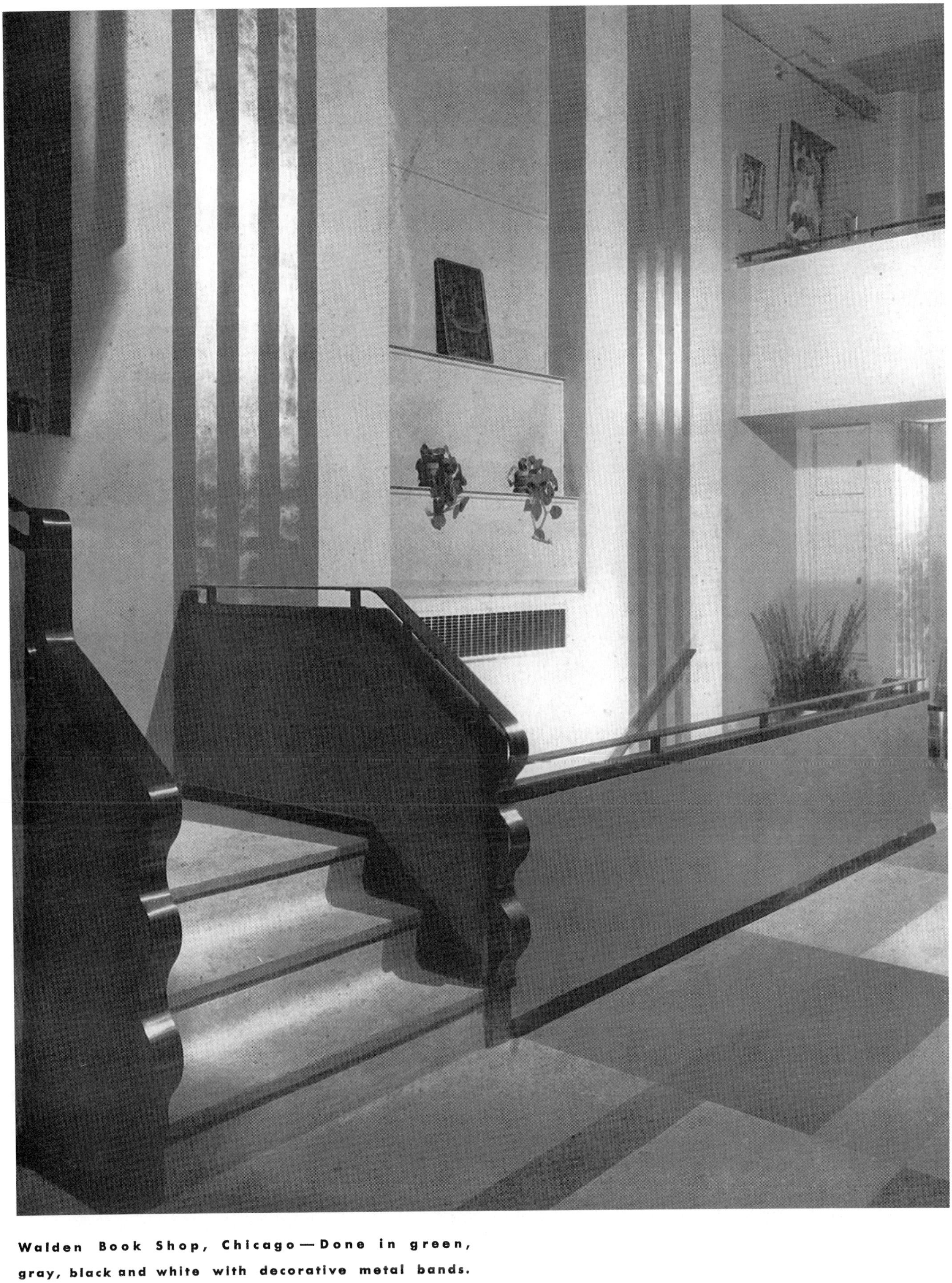

Walden Book Shop, Chicago—Done in green, gray, black and white with decorative metal bands.

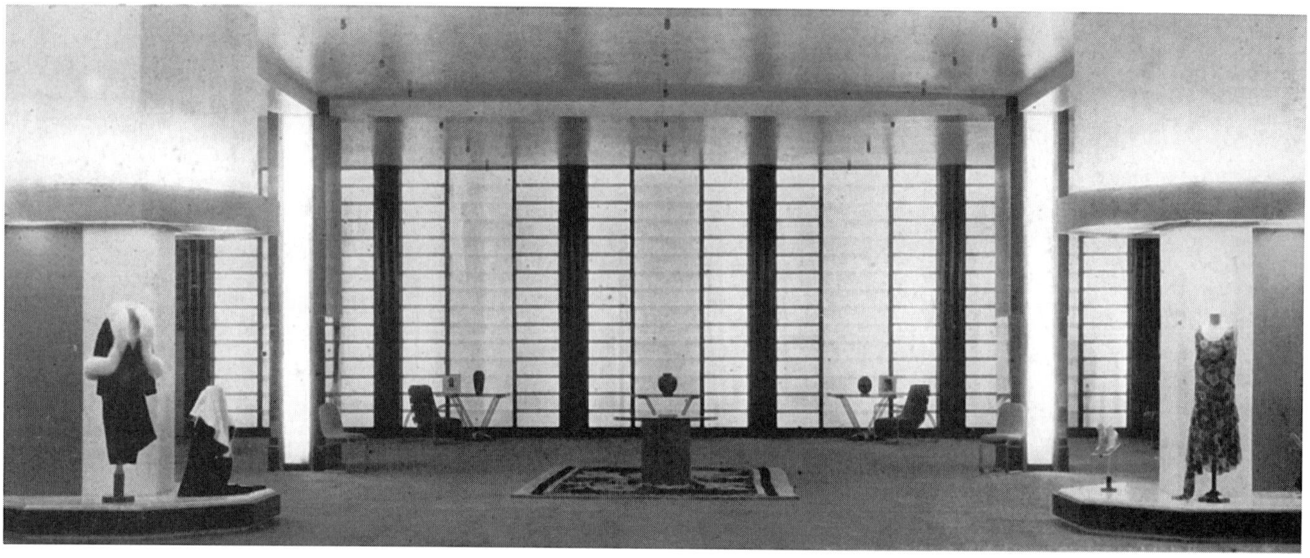

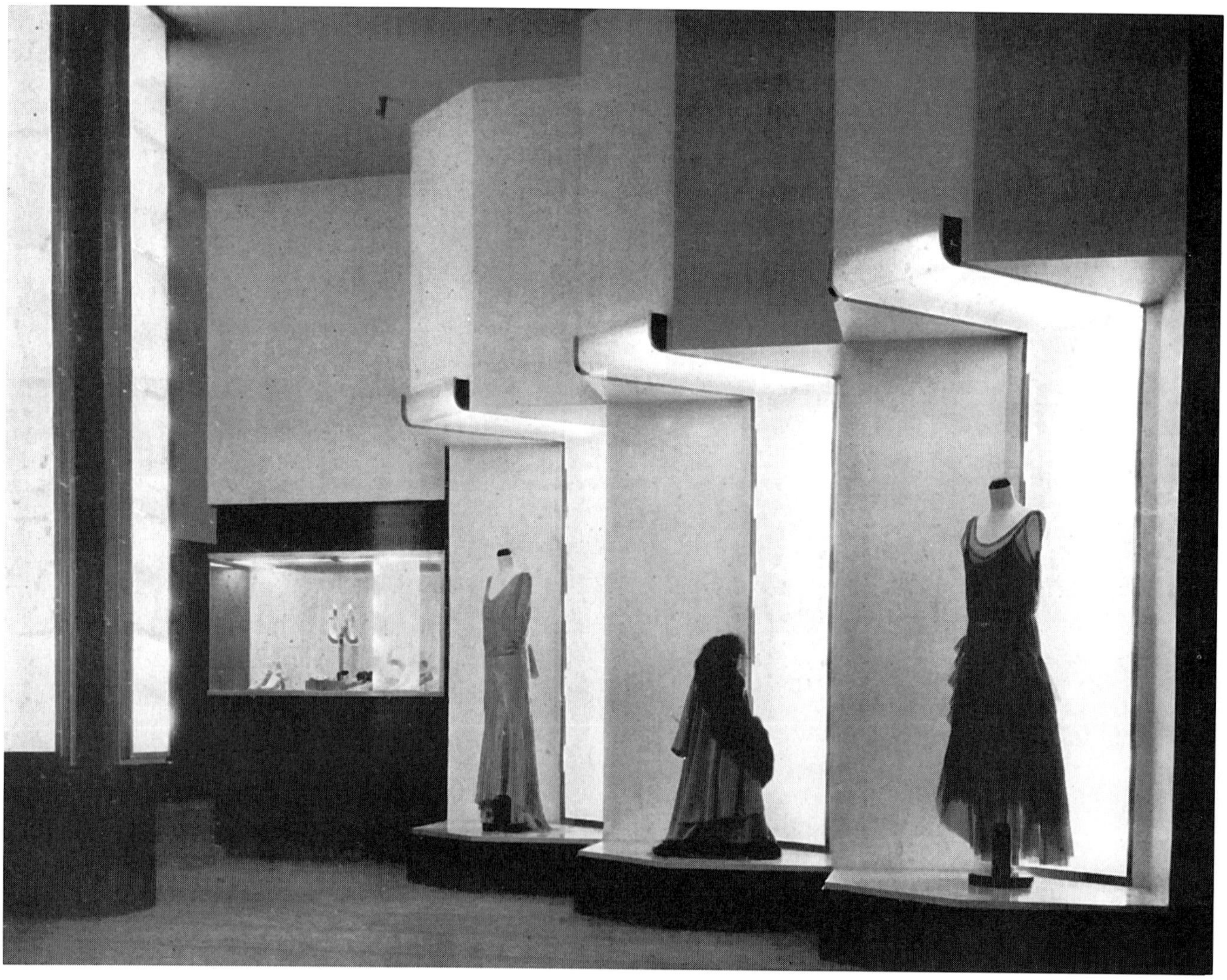

J. FRANKLIN WHITMAN, JR.,
and PERCIVAL GOODMAN

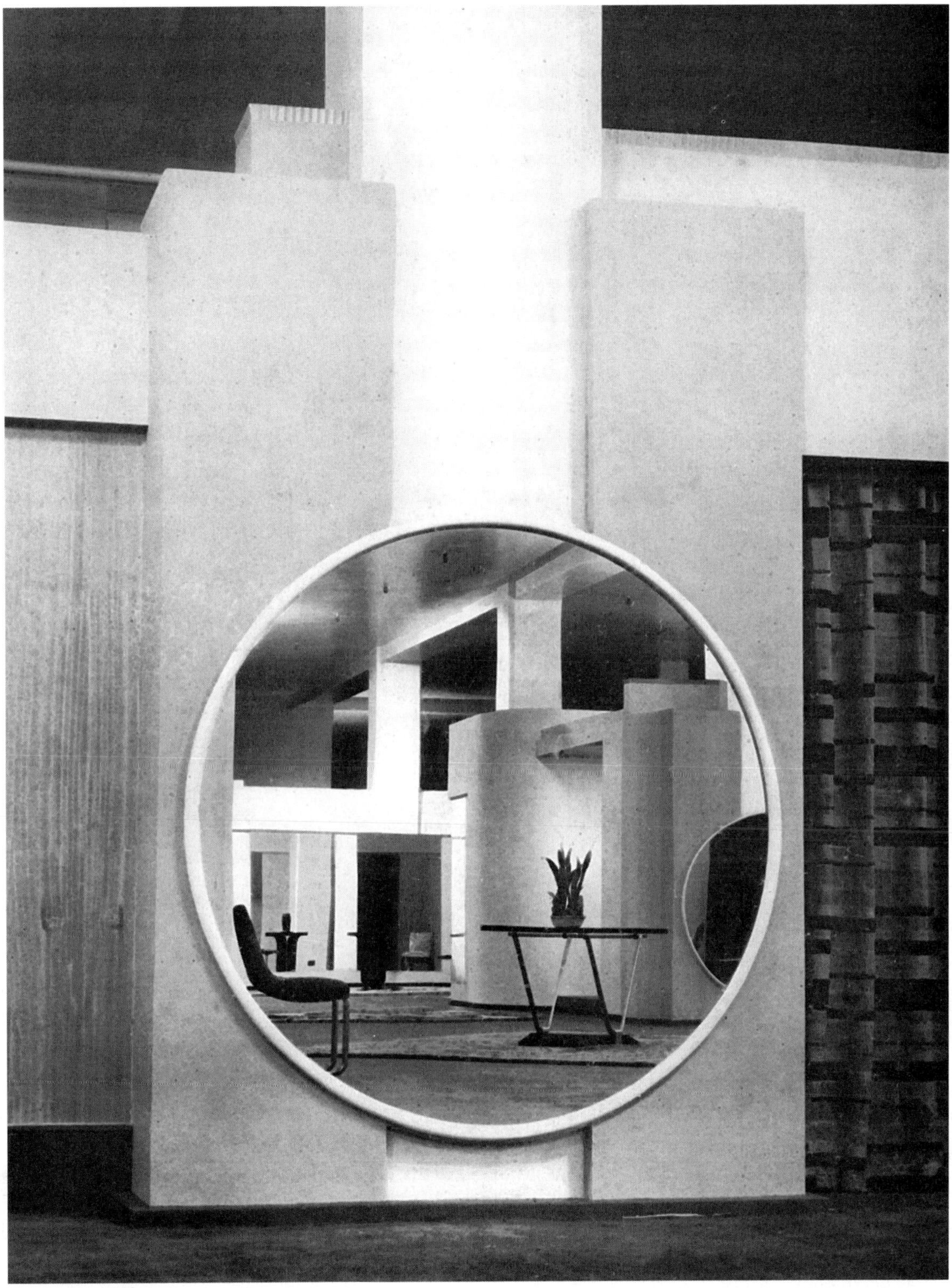

**Three views of the fifth floor in Saks and Company, Fifth Avenue Store, N. Y. C. Through changes in woods and colors the floor is sanctioned off into a number of special departments.**

**V A H A N   H A G O P I A N**

**Store front of London Shoe Co., N. Y. C. During and after alterations. Neon Lights — Metal lettering indirectly illuminated.**

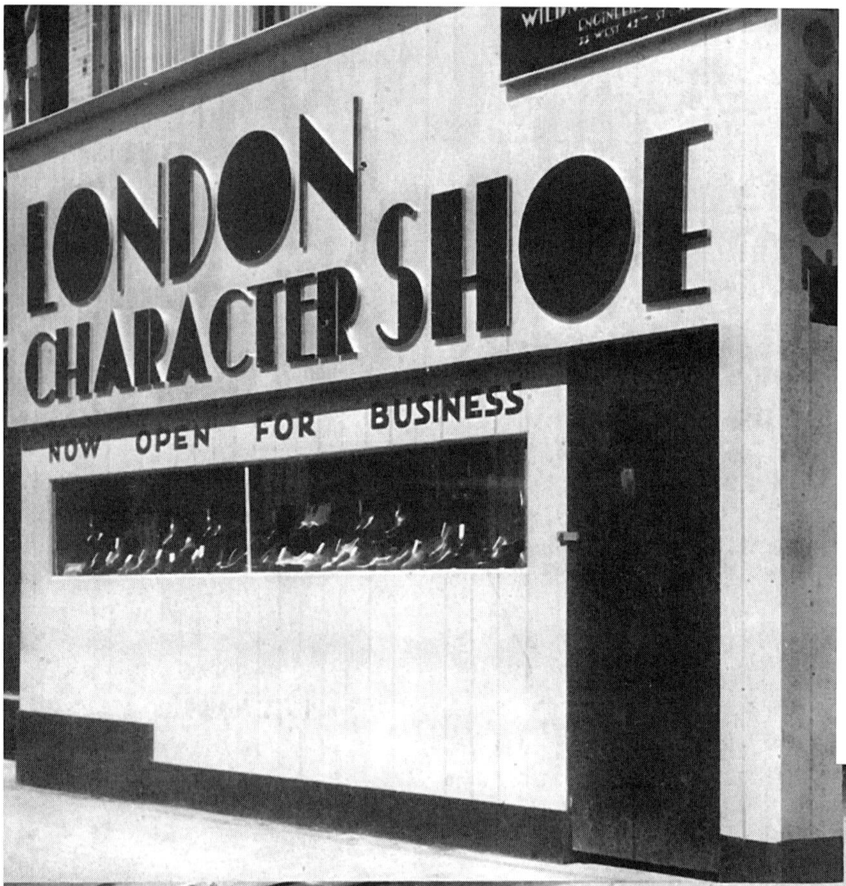


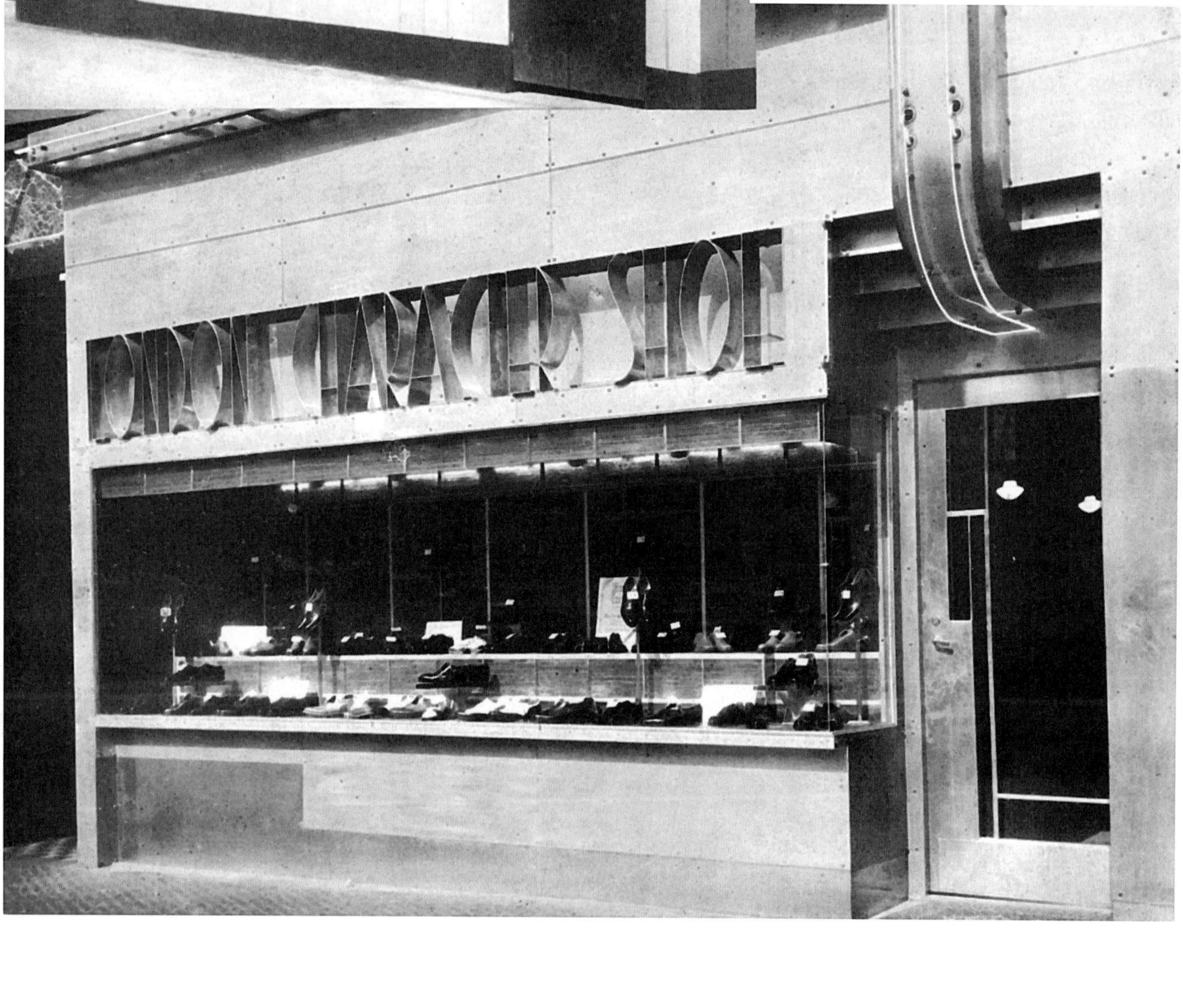

**J. R. DAVIDSON**
**Office front in Los Angeles**

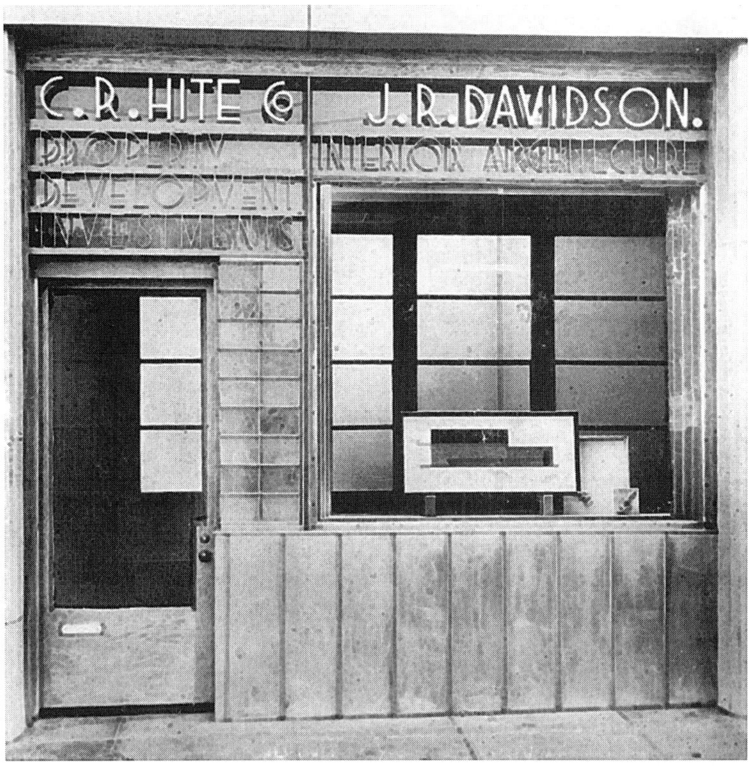


**THOMPSON & CHURCHILL**
**Belgian black marble, opal glass in chromium plate on store facade, N. Y. C.**

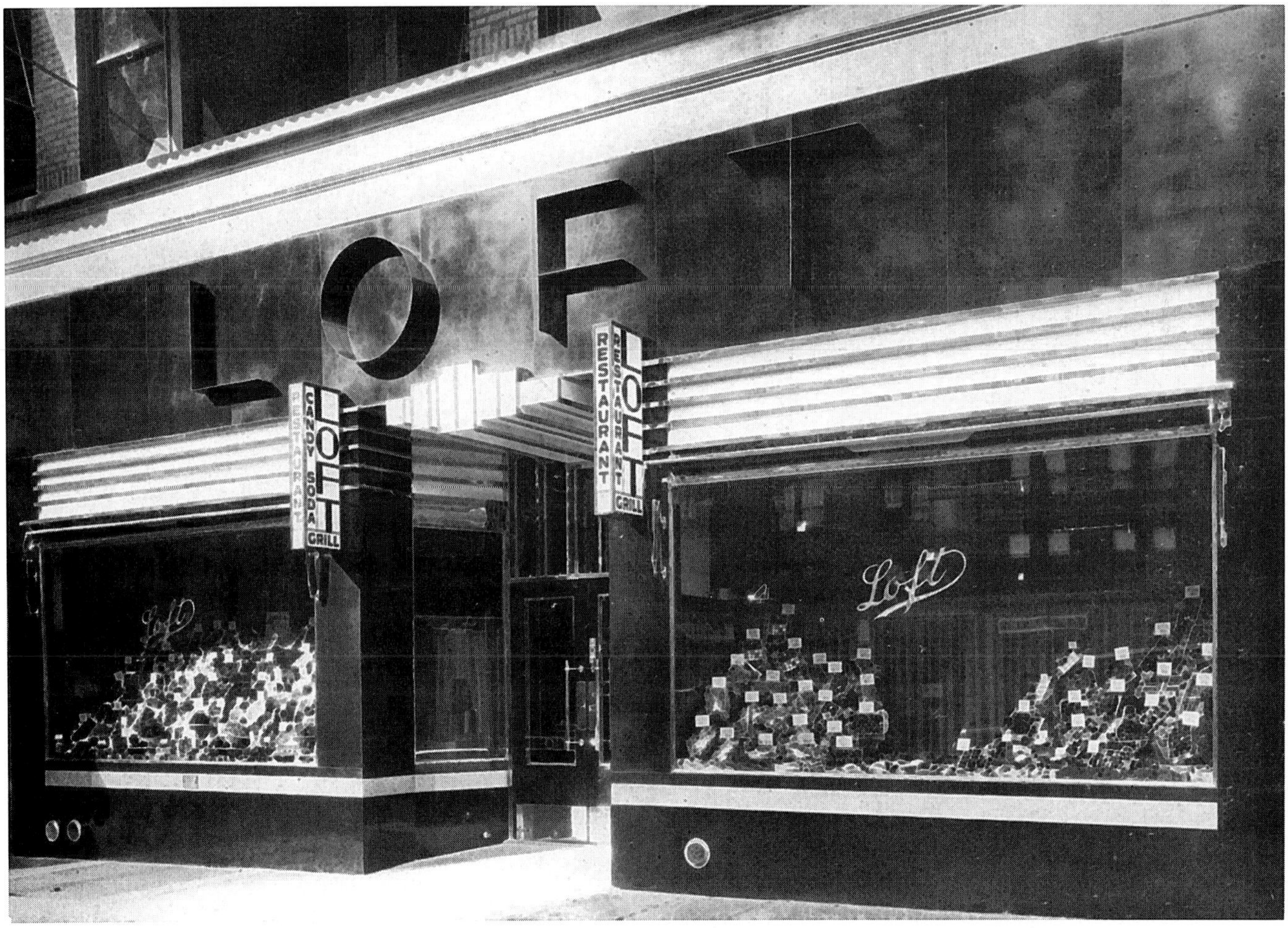

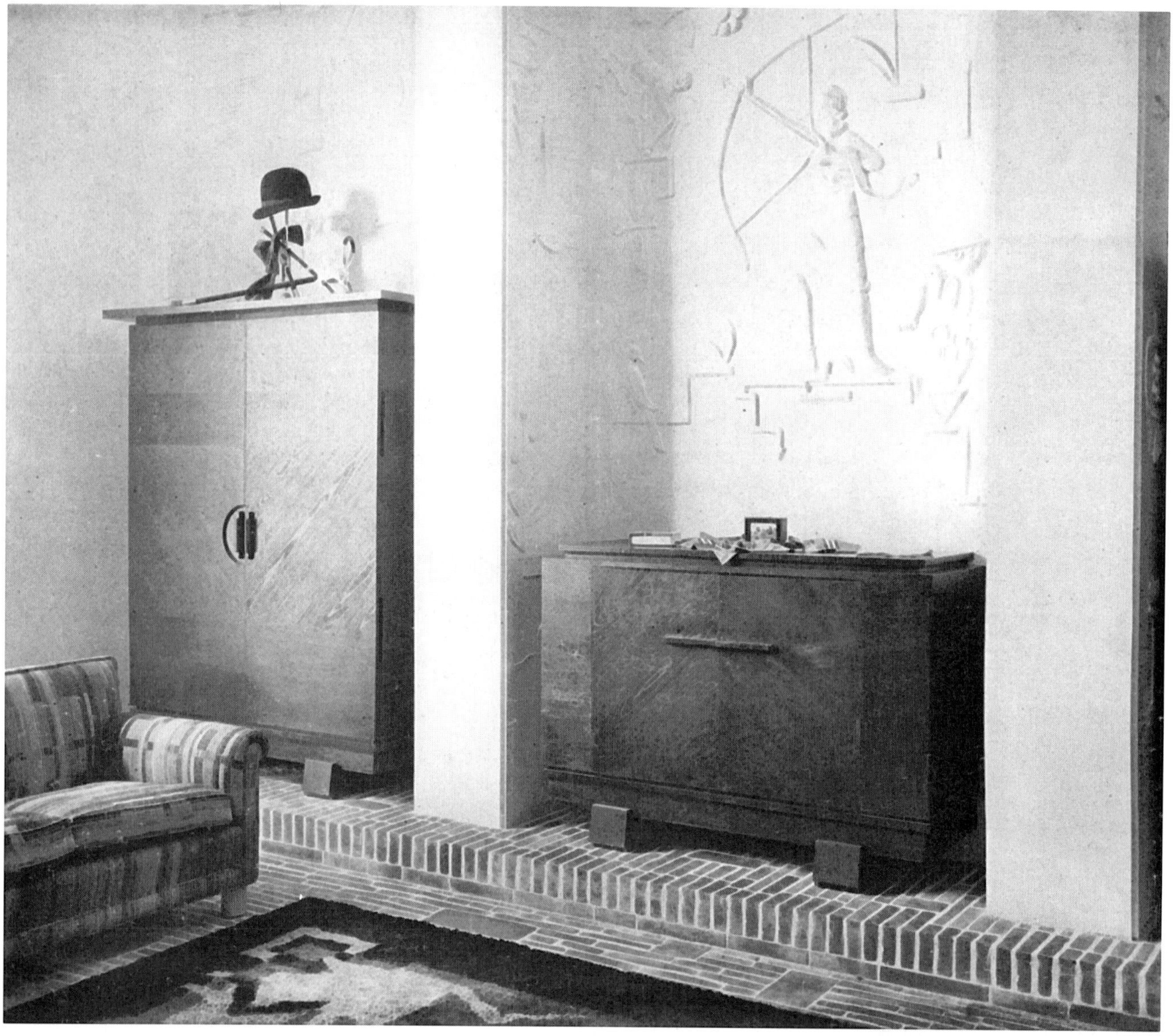

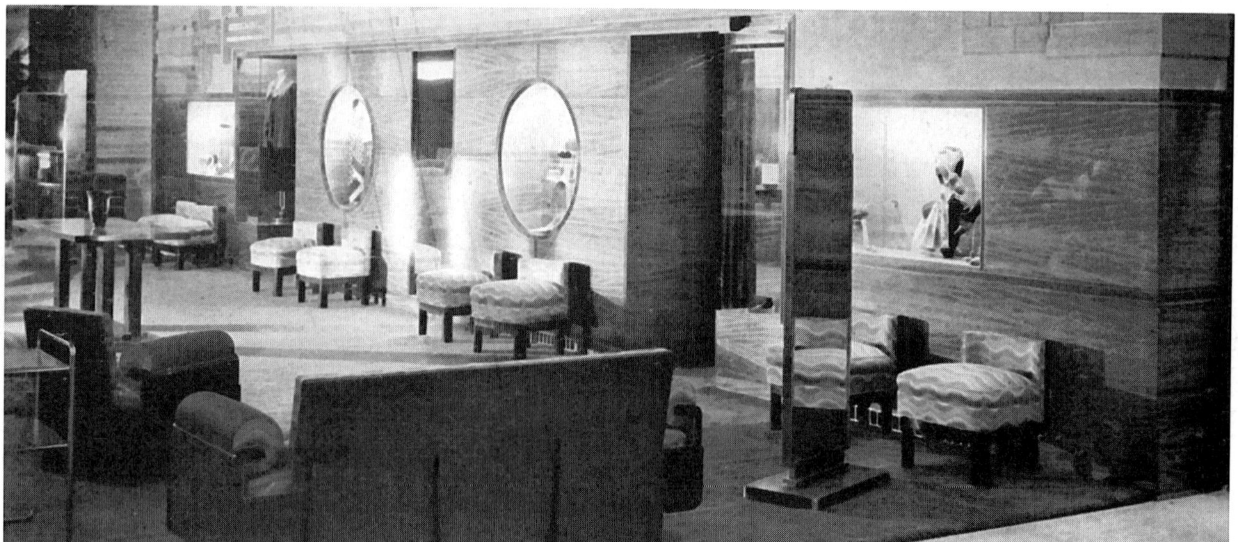

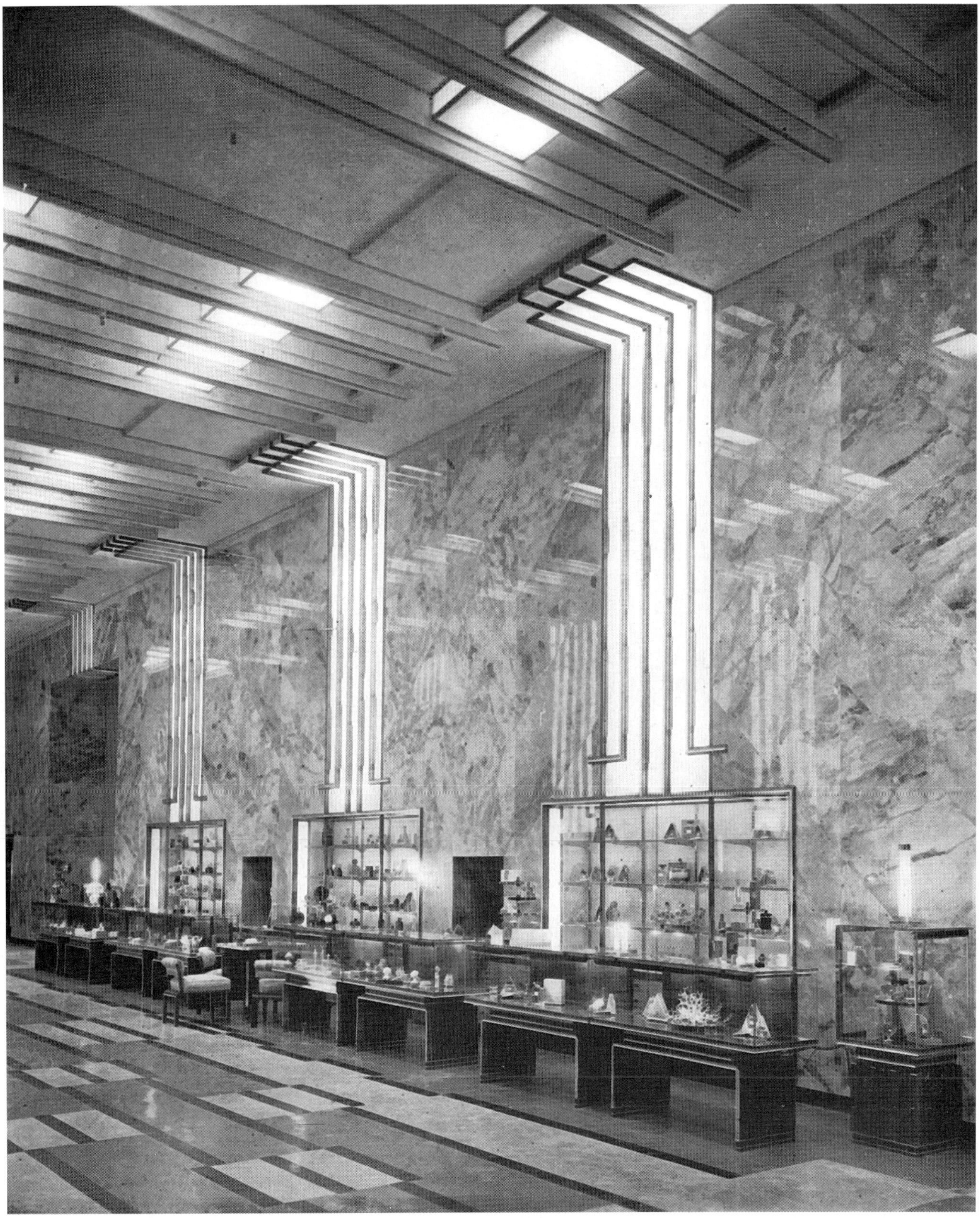

J O C K D. P E T E R S

Three views of the Bullock's Wilshire Department Store—Los Angeles, California — Riding Shop — Sportwear Department — Main Hall showing a part of Perfume Department.

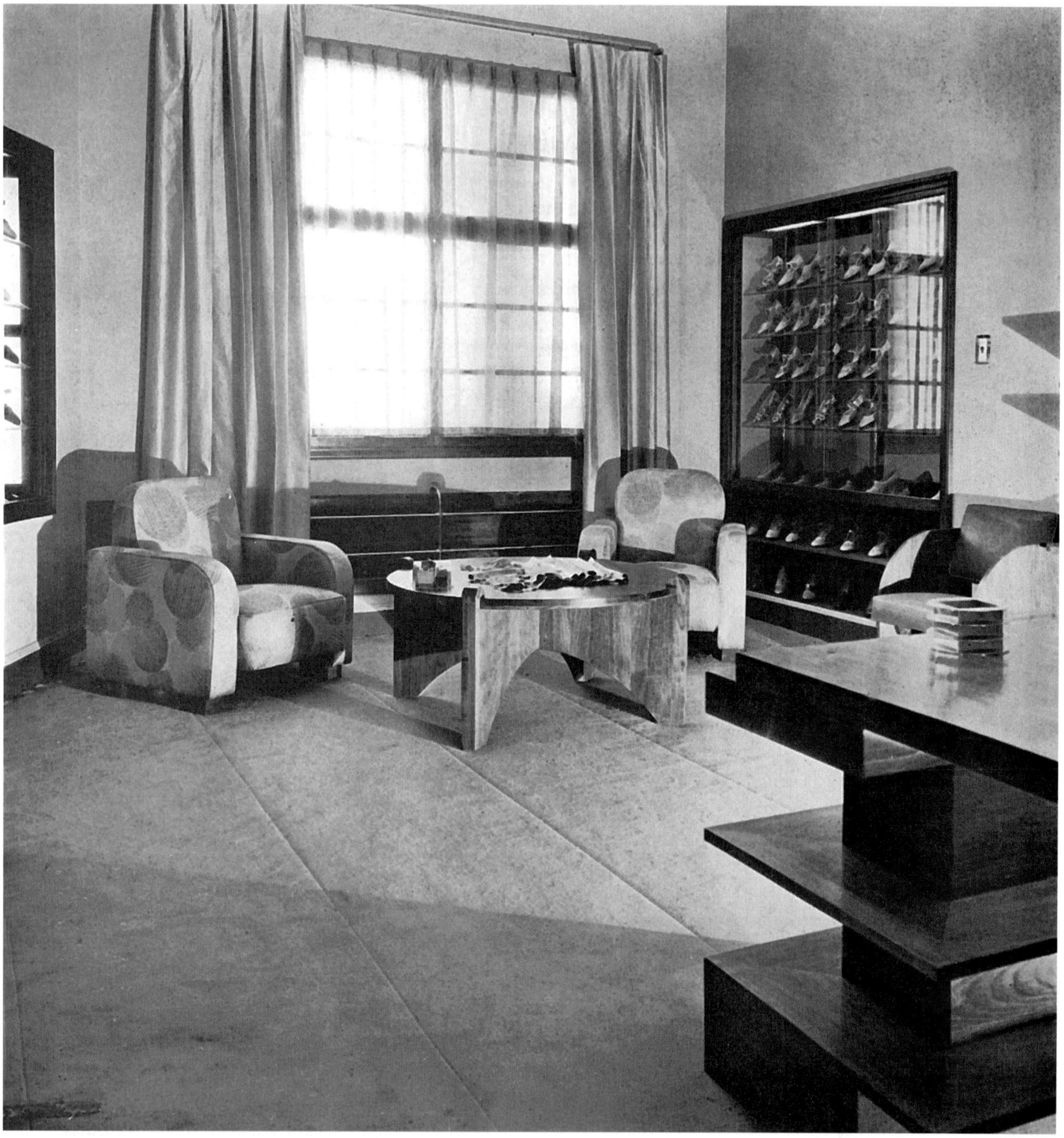

HOWE & LESCAZE
Showroom of Andrew Geller executed in gumwood. Color scheme — gray and blue.

**P. T. FRANKL**

# THE HOME of yesterday to-day and to-morrow

In centuries past, homes were built to last, if not forever, at least for coming generations. Domestic structures symbolized the stability and the continuity of family life. They were enduring monuments to good breeding, to respectability, to dynastic solidity. Homes were, moreover, the center of important social, industrial and educational activities. In the home were centered a great number of handicrafts essential to the business of living—industries such as weaving and the preparation and preservation of food stuffs among others. In the home also children were educated; and in the home—especially on the continent, even up to the present time—business and professional activities were often conducted. In brief, the home was a veritable community, embracing factory, school, and office. Gradually these secondary functions have been removed—an inevitable result of the industrial revolution and the advent of the machine age. With these radical changes a vast retinue of servants and retainers has dwindled until even among the well-to-do, mechanical devices are gradually supplanting domestics. Decidedly home is not what it used to be.

Yet even after the secondary functions of the home had been transferred to factories, schools and offices, after the machine age had wrought a profound revolution in the habits and tempo of life, men continued to erect imposing houses as a means of crowning their success in life. Many cities and towns in this country are lined with these grandiloquent and slightly ridiculous structures that today await the crowbar of the wrecker. In our dynamic era they are as obsolete as a dinosaur on a flying-field. They are obsolete today because they were built only to fulfill a vain wish to impress the community, the passerby and the public at large. The uniform curtains and draperies which one glimpesd at every window indicated that these mansions were decorated to impress someone outside looking in.

Machines have swept away the pretense as well as the oldtime sentimentality concerning home. Machines have projected us into a new world, a world of change. To live in this world of change requires flexibility and adaptibility. In this period in which everything of the past has been uprooted and much of it scrapped forever, it would indeed be foolish to expect or to hope that home should remain intact. Not without significance—nor irony, for the matter—comes the news that intransigeant architects in Europe are now publishing plans for the "dwelling machine," as they prefer to characterize the houses they are designing for the "minimal" families of the future. Homes often compressed into a single room, but adapted to various uses! To the sentimentalist there is something almost inhuman in the mechanized "boarding houses" recently exhibited by Walter Gropius. But to a generation which is born in a hospital, brought up in schools and summer camps, lives in apartment hotels, eats in restaurants (clubs), and leads a nomad existence in motor-car, airplane, ocean liners, or express trains there may be no pang of regret for the joys of home life which have never been experienced. It is difficult, even, to become sentimental over a city apartment, especially as we have become habituated to move from one to another every so often. Whereas in the past—even as late as the nineteenth century— the family home endured for three or four generations at least, today three or four homes are consumed by a single generation. We use up homes as we do clothes and motor-cars. We demand change in our living quarters; what delighted us last year aggravates us this.

Nowadays the home is assembled, as the motor-car is, out of machine-made parts— steel, glass, hardware, plumbing, wiring, heating equipment and refrigeration. Comfort and conveniences have been vastly increased. Due to the motor-car and better roads, there is no longer any insurmountable separation between country life and city life. We can combine the two in a fashion never possible before the advent of rapid transportation and good roads. With ever more complete conquest of drudgery, even the wife and mother have been liberated. Women are no longer confined to the home; and with this liberation another profound change has been realized. The home as the center of entertainment for large parties has lost its former prestige. The whole tendency has thus been one of liberation, of uprooting. The home is no longer the monument to conspicuous success it once was, exacting relentless toil from an army of servants and housekeepers to maintain its impressiveness. Comfort has supplanted ostentation; and convenient privacy is preferred to formal dignity. Those who still maintain homes on the large scale confess that more and more their houses resemble hotels.

In its beginning, some thirty years ago, the so-called "modern" decorative movement was essentially a continuation of the tradition of the past rather than a precursor of the spirit of today. That tradition was based upon individual handicraft. The designer and the cabinet-maker of the eighteenth and early nineteenth centuries were primarily concerned with the needs and tastes of some particular client. The modern decorators first worked for a small number of sympathetic clients who like themselves were tired of traditional period styles, yet were wealthy enough to build homes in the traditional grand manner. Superficially novel as the outward form of this school of decoration might have been, it was indeed no new departure but rather the last step in the old-fashioned way of doing things. And it must be confessed that much of the interior decoration that passes among the unknowing as the last word in modernism today is really the dying gasp of the grand manner of the eighteenth century. The outward form may differ, but the inner impulse remains the same.

True modernism is of a radically different nature. It aims to satisfy the needs of modern living and to express the spirit and the flexibility of modern life. It no longer holds aloft the banner of the defunct handicrafts and peasant arts, but acknowledges its allegiance to the benevolent despotism of the machine. It recognizes that the modern home is essentially a more or less harmonious assemblage of machine-made parts. This assembling excludes neither furniture, nor lighting fixtures, nor anything else. The parts are, so to speak, standardized. Looked at with an impartial eye, these parts are just so much merchandise. The apartment itself may be merely one of a series. Yet out of all this the art of living demands that we create some sort of individual expression. Contemporary art has demonstrated a spirit truly creative in the new vocabulary of artistic expression it has evolved out of new materials, new methods, and new combination of form and line. This achievement is all the more notable in that it has been attained without reliance upon the styles or decorative conventions.

Today we are in a transitional age. The accelerated tempo of contemporary living has swept away the home of the past; yet most of us still react to "memories vague of half - forgotten things nor true nor false, but sweet to think upon" concerning home sweet home. But it is well to recall that the rising generation will not be encumbered with such sentimental memories. The tradition of building for posterity, of leaving heirlooms of no intrinsic value, will have disappeared. So in the creation of furniture and interiors there will be no attempt to build for the next generation. The beauty will lie rather in the free expressiveness of the gesture than in the permanence of the created object. Instead of sobbing over our lost servitude, we will exult in the sense of liberation from things and from the heavy responsibility of a pompous household. We will no more dream of handing down undesired heirlooms than we would think of handing down a pair of outworn shoes. Furniture and furnishing will be manufactured as scientifically and as efficiently and withal with as great variety, as motor cars or airplanes are today. The moving into a new home will no longer entail the weeding out of the old and the retention of inharmonious pieces which beg to be kept on for sentimental reasons. We shall no more think of moving them into a new home than we would an old ice-box into kitchen equipped with the last word in refrigeration. We shall be able to discard our old home as we discard an old suit of clothes, and emerge into a new milieu to enjoy the sense of rejuvenation and refreshment it alone can bring to our spirit.

If this modern movement means anything significant, it must mean not a mere subservience to a demand for novelty by the irresponsible and the sophisticated, but an effort, through the agency of the machine, to make available for the masses what is now the luxury of the few. It will, let us hope, remove from the realm of luxury what should be any every day requirement. Whatever we lose in this process, its compensations far overbalance the passing of the old family home. For we may be just as happy, if not happier, in casting off the reminders of the past as in dragging with us forever these reproachful fetiches.

The home of yesterday is gone forever; the home of today is passing; the home of tomorrow we can dimly foresee. One thing seems certain: the artist of today must be more concerned with meeting the unformulated demands of the new home than in seeking to perpetuate the senescent standards of the past. No less than his colleague the architect, it is the duty of the creative designer to study the trends of our current change and to work in terms of the reconstruction that is imminent in the basic structure of American homes. Good design must be as much a commonplace in the American home of tomorrow as perfect plumbing and heating are today. There is no reason why beauty in furnishing should remain any more of a luxury than efficient illumination. It should result automatically out of an awakened demand, and should entail no financial sacrifice. Our problem is to demonstrate that efficient planning and effective design are as essential to health as bodily well-being.

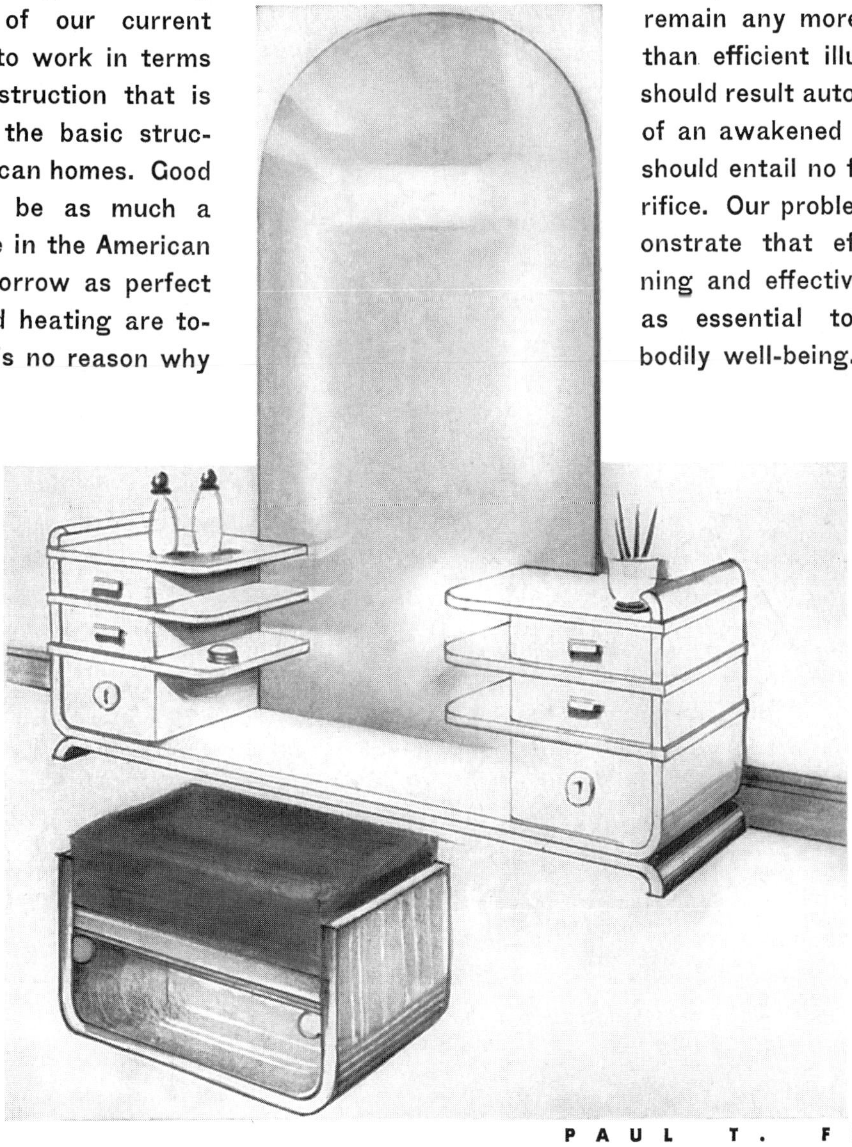

P A U L  T .  F R A N K L

**Dressing table in natural maple, vermilion.**

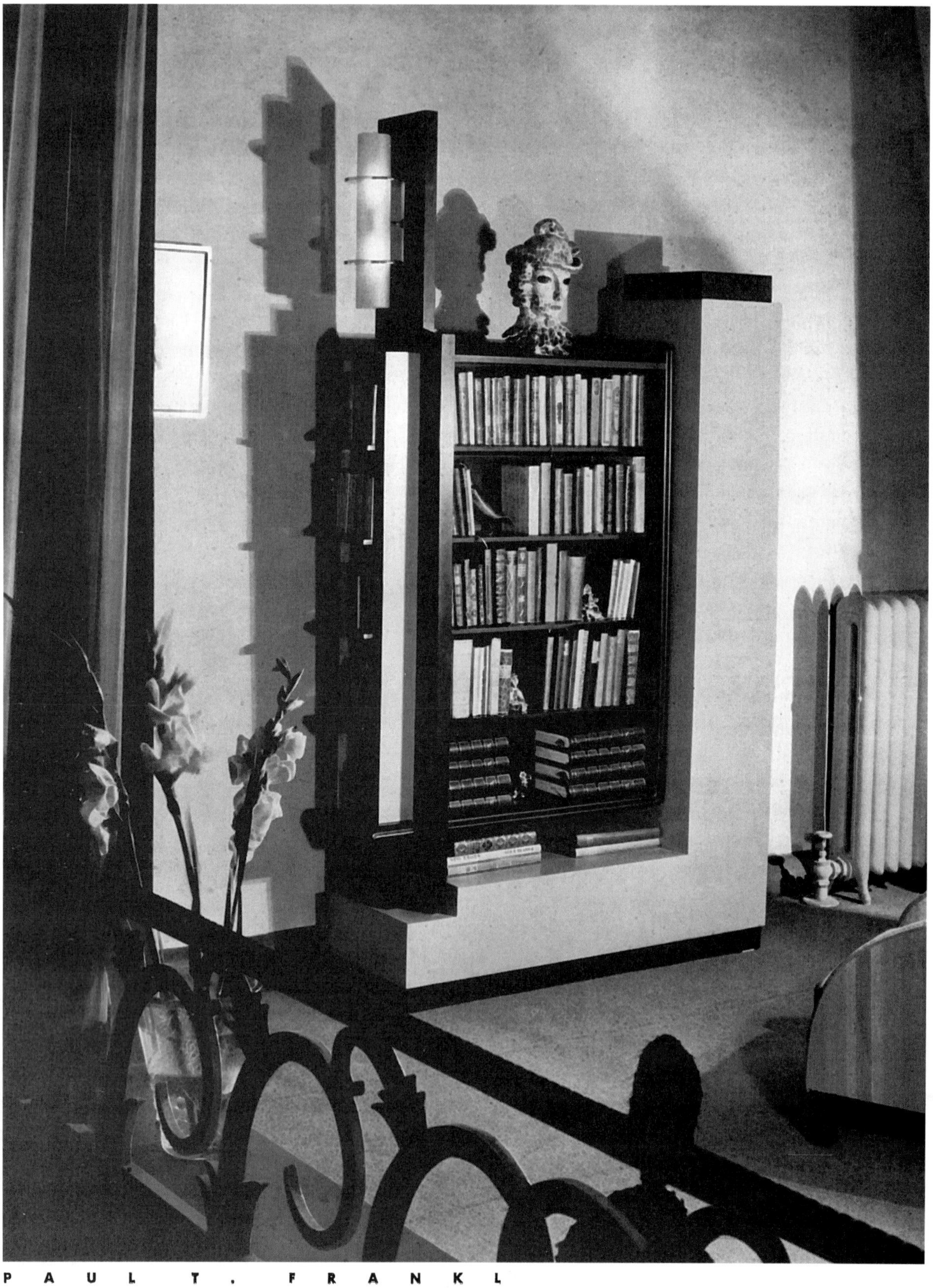

PAUL T. FRANKL

Bookcase in two tones of lacquer.

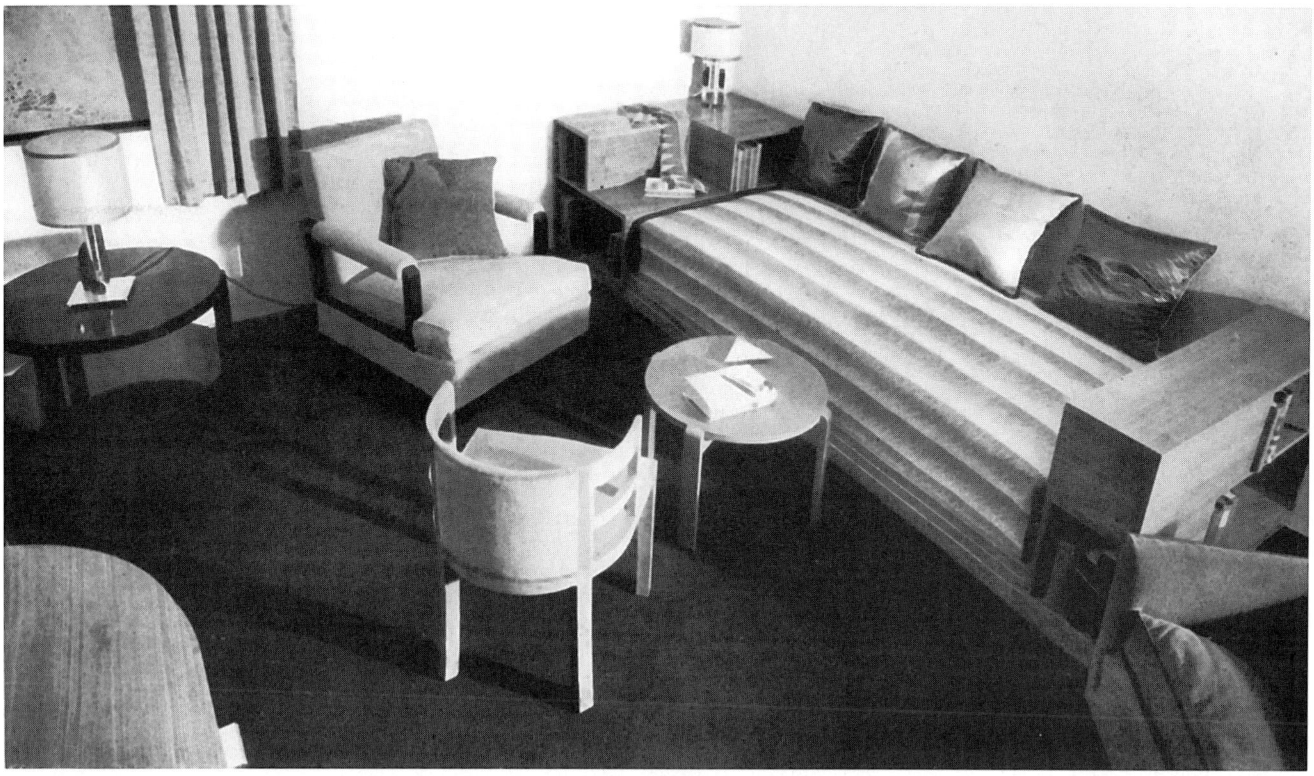

WILLIS S. HARRISON
Combination bed room and den — French walnut with orange and brown upholstery.

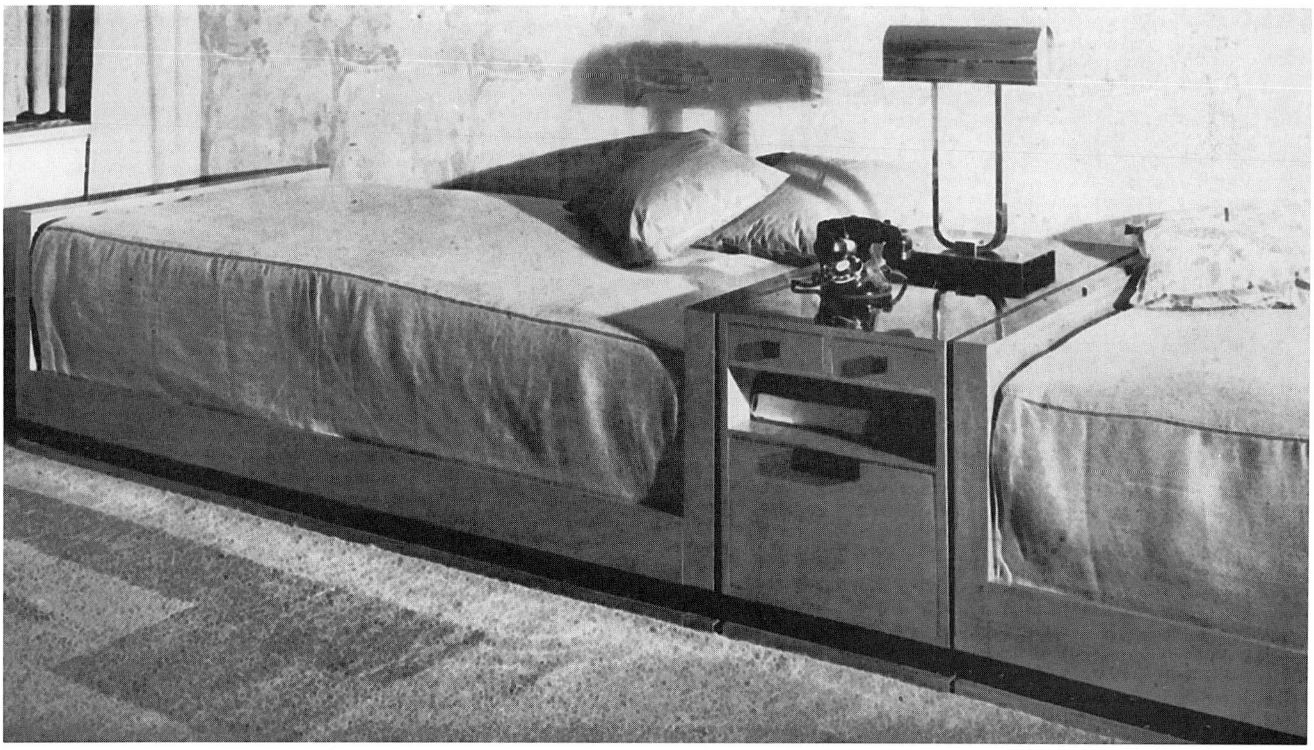

GILBERT ROHDE
Concealed boards in head ends of bed rise to form back rests.

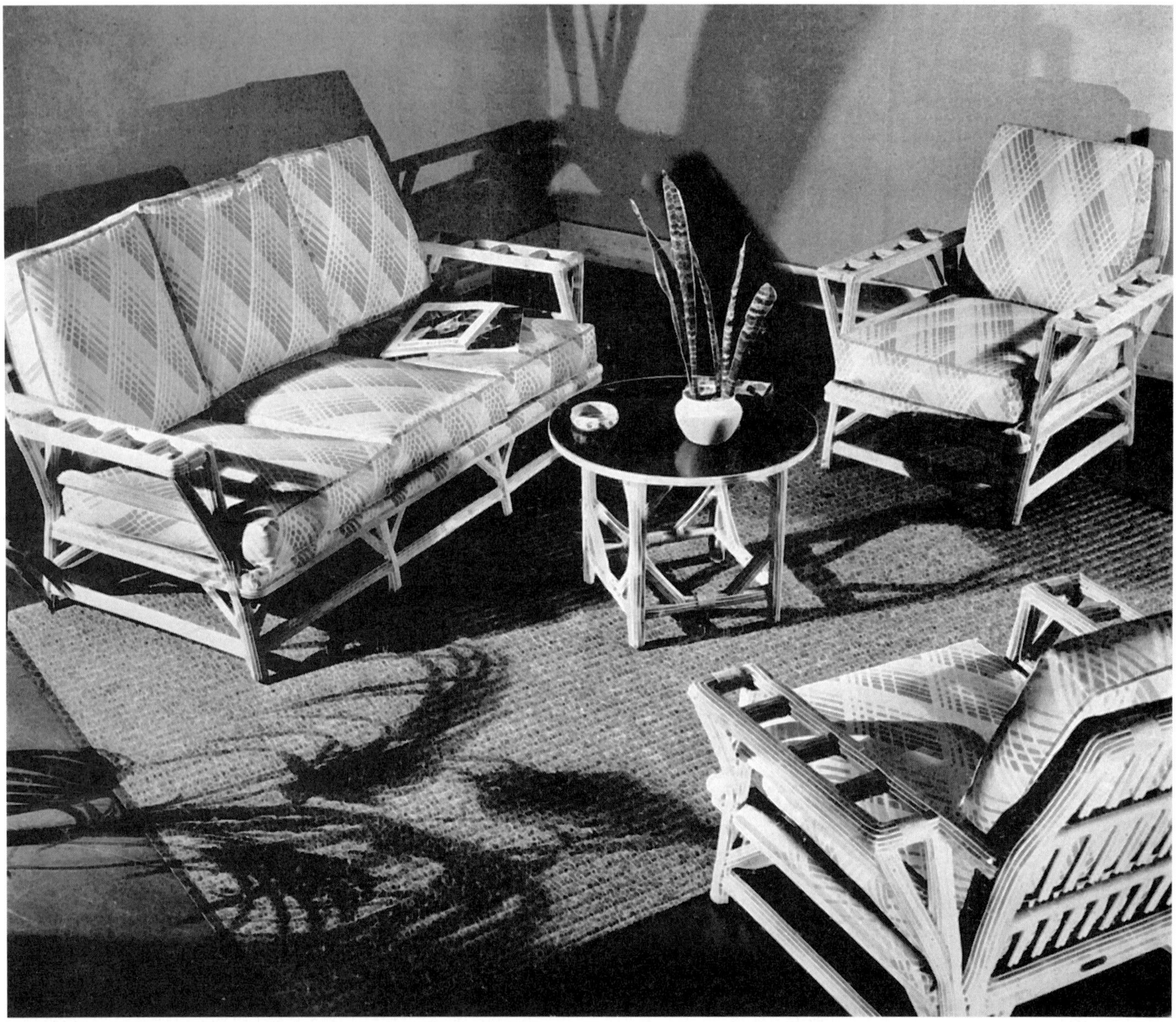

**Reed furniture for a sun room, lacquered bright yellow — upholstered in Orange Permatex Lustersheen — executed by the Ypsilanti Furniture Co.**

D O N A L D   D E S K E Y

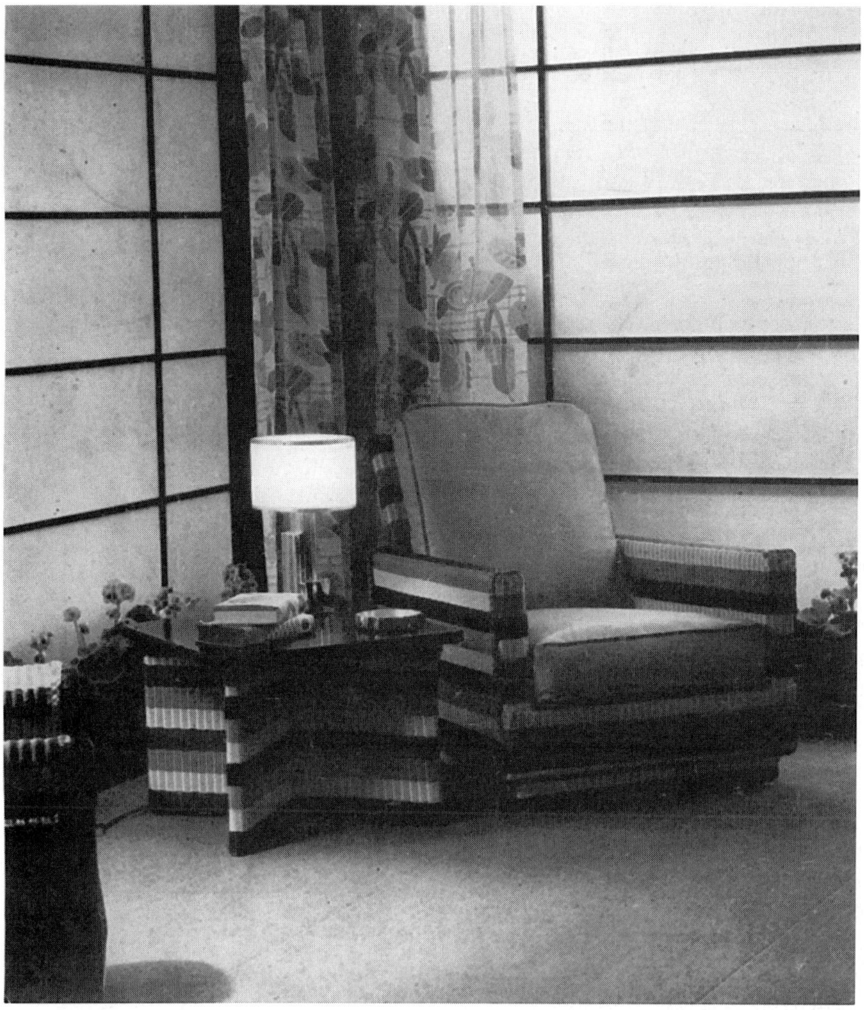

D O N A L D   D E S K E Y

Loom woven fibre furniture for sun room executed by Ypsilanti Reed Furniture Co. Du Pont Fabricoid Covering.

Home of Mrs. E. Seligman. Brushed chromium plated metal on vermilion wood.

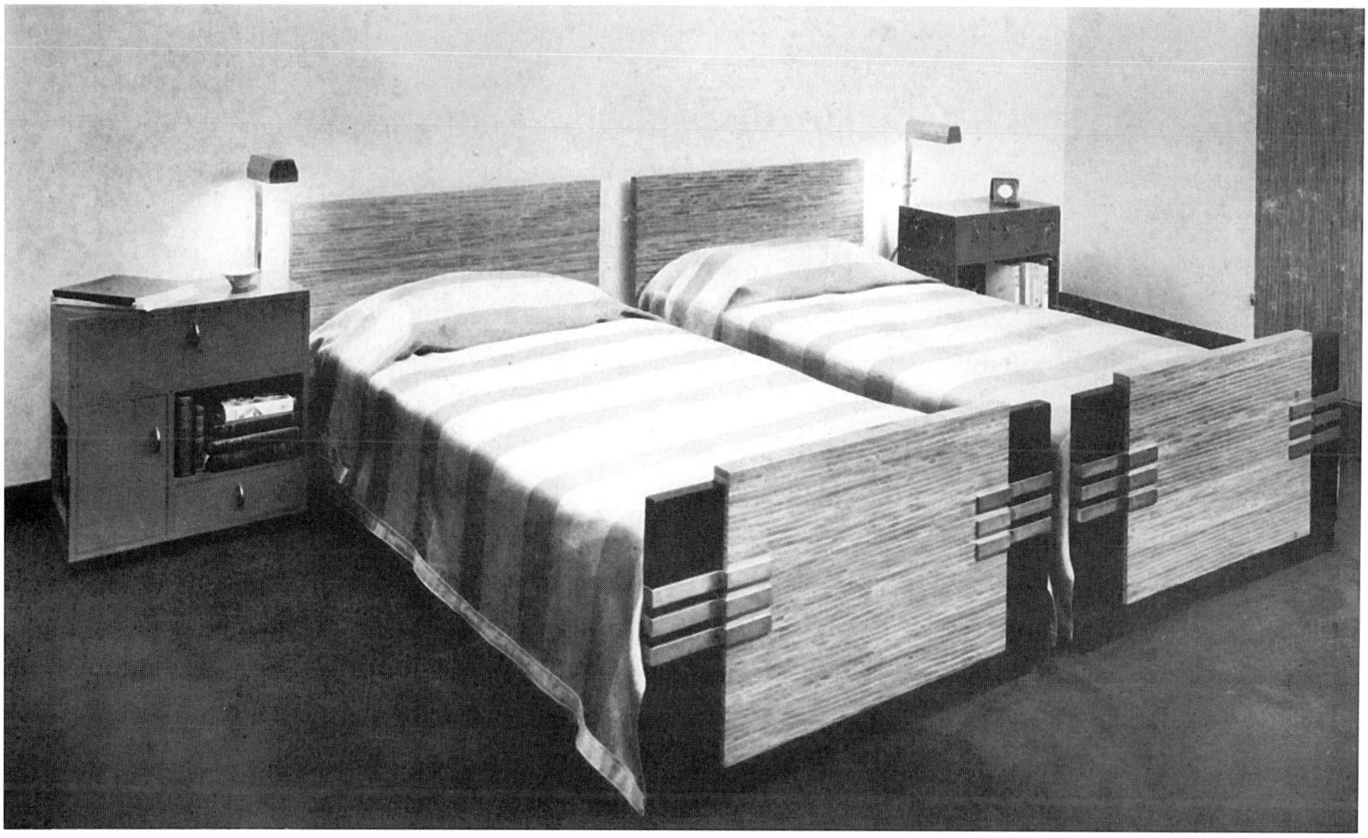

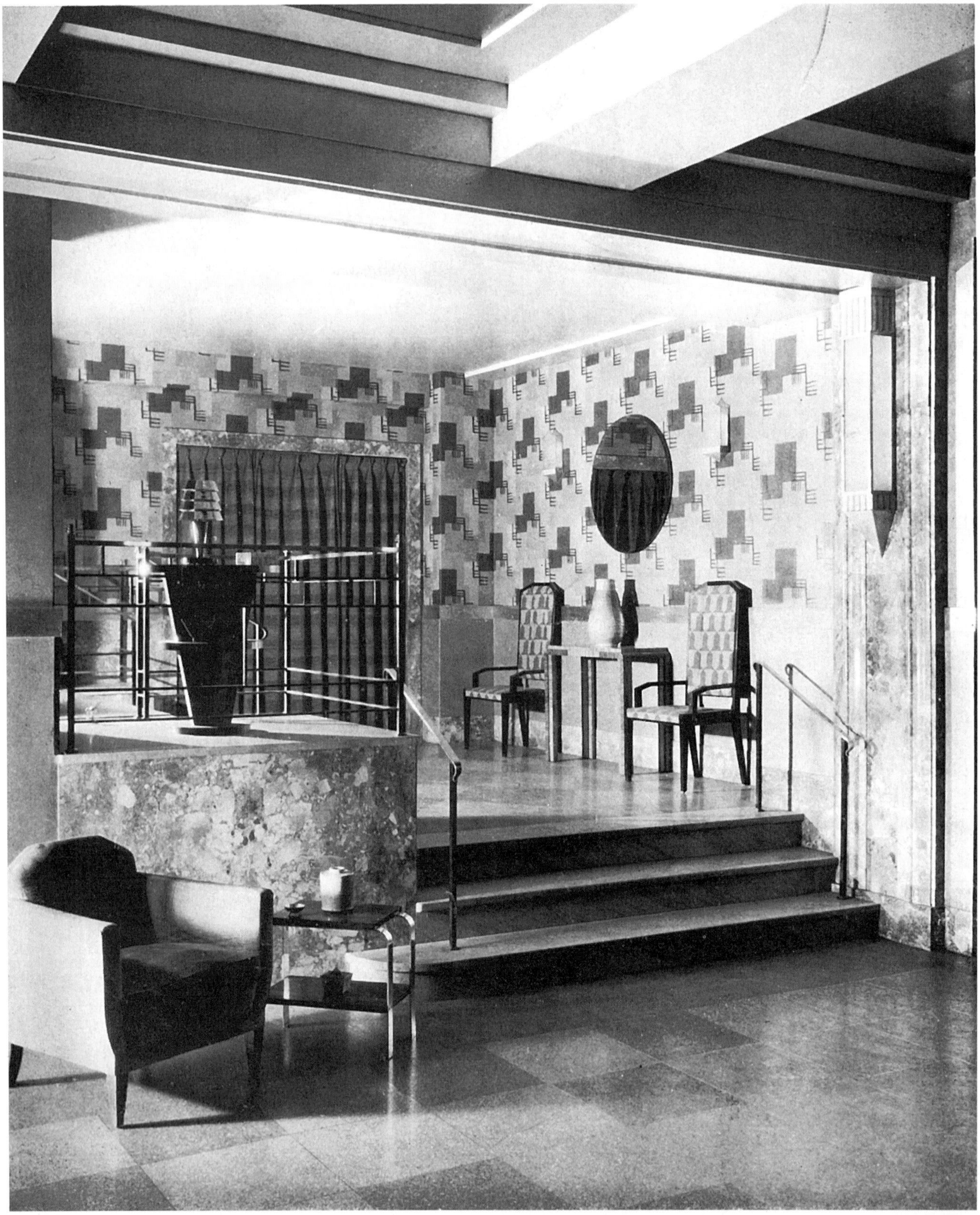

An arrangement of an apartment entrance hall in a building designed by Thompson & Churchill. Easy chair done in ombre rep from Schumacher and made by Moody, Dilg & Heald.

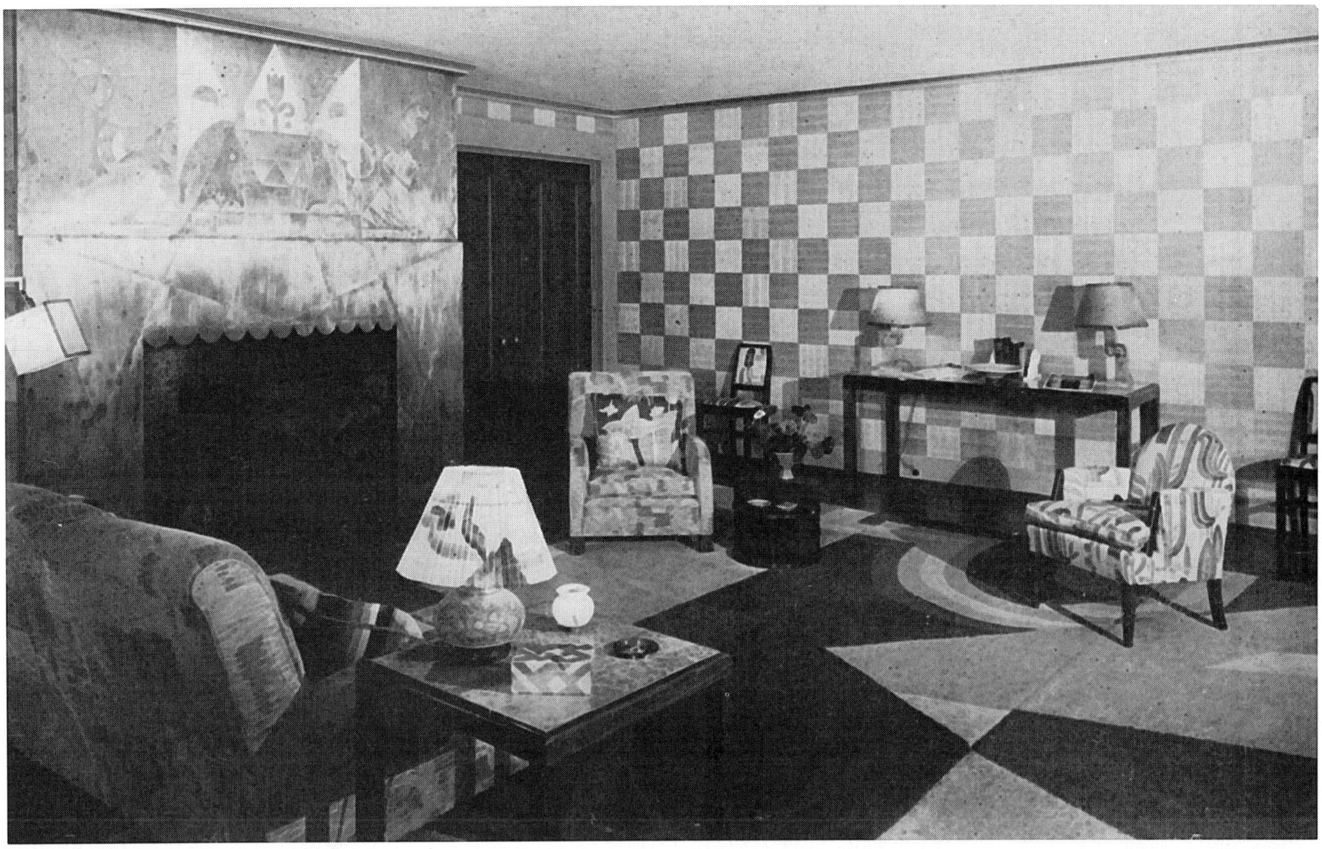

**Living room arrangement in the home of Chas. C. Merrill.**

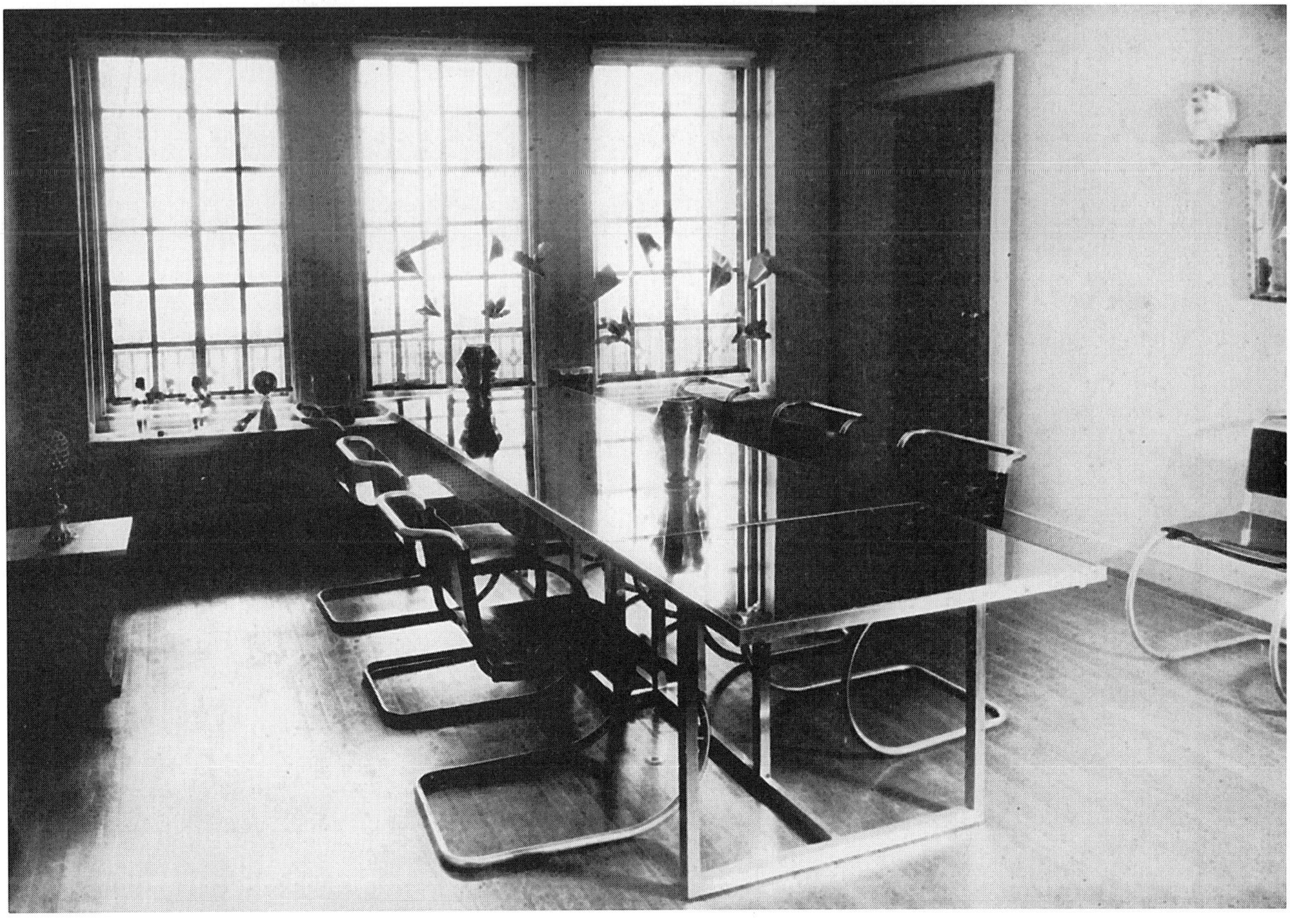

**Dining room arrangement in the home of Mrs. F. Abbott Ingalls.**
**Furniture designed by Donald Deskey.**

Hallway in the apartment of Mrs. T. S. Meyers. Gumwood used in furniture. Walls in chartreuse — seat upholstered in blue.

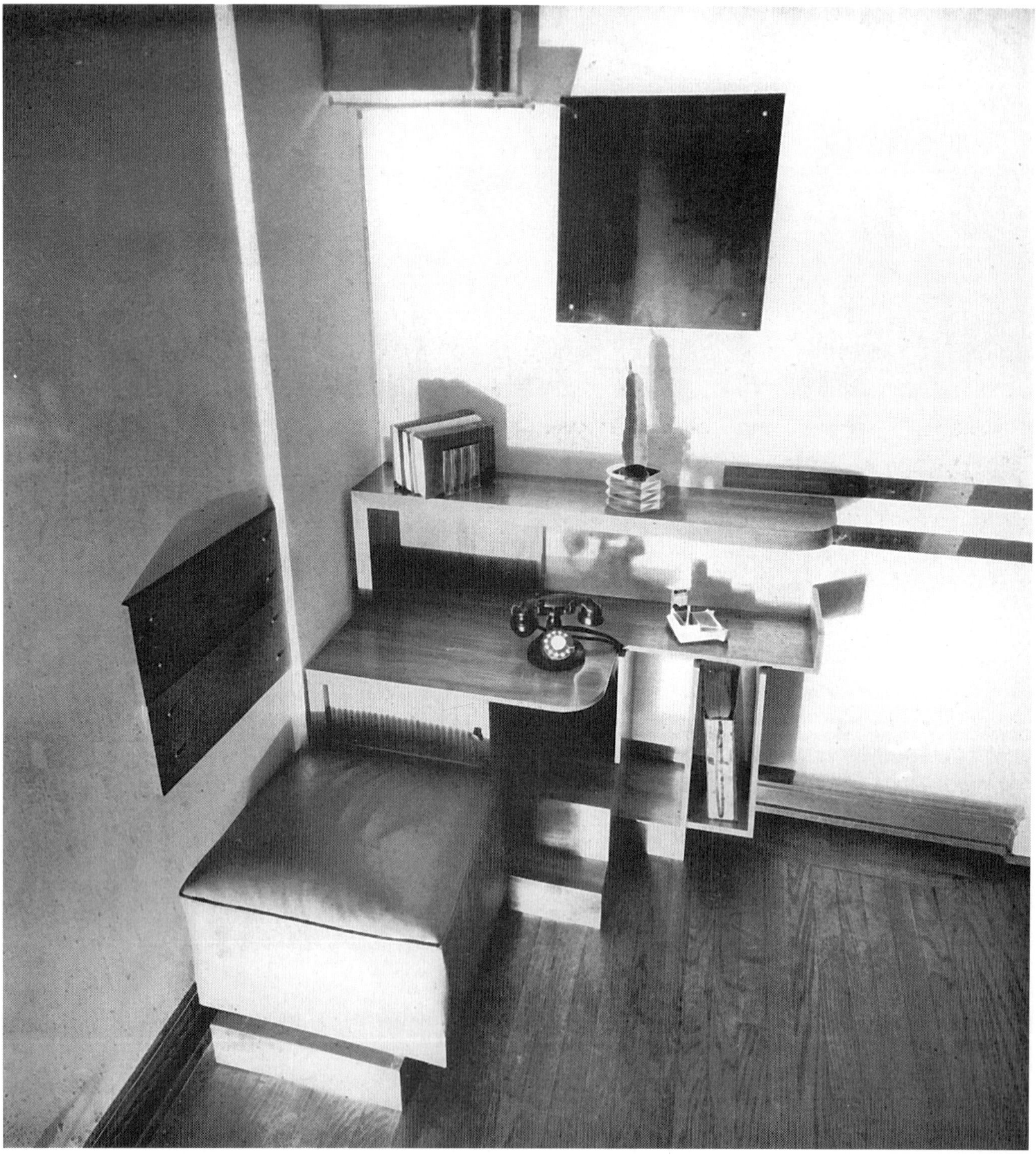

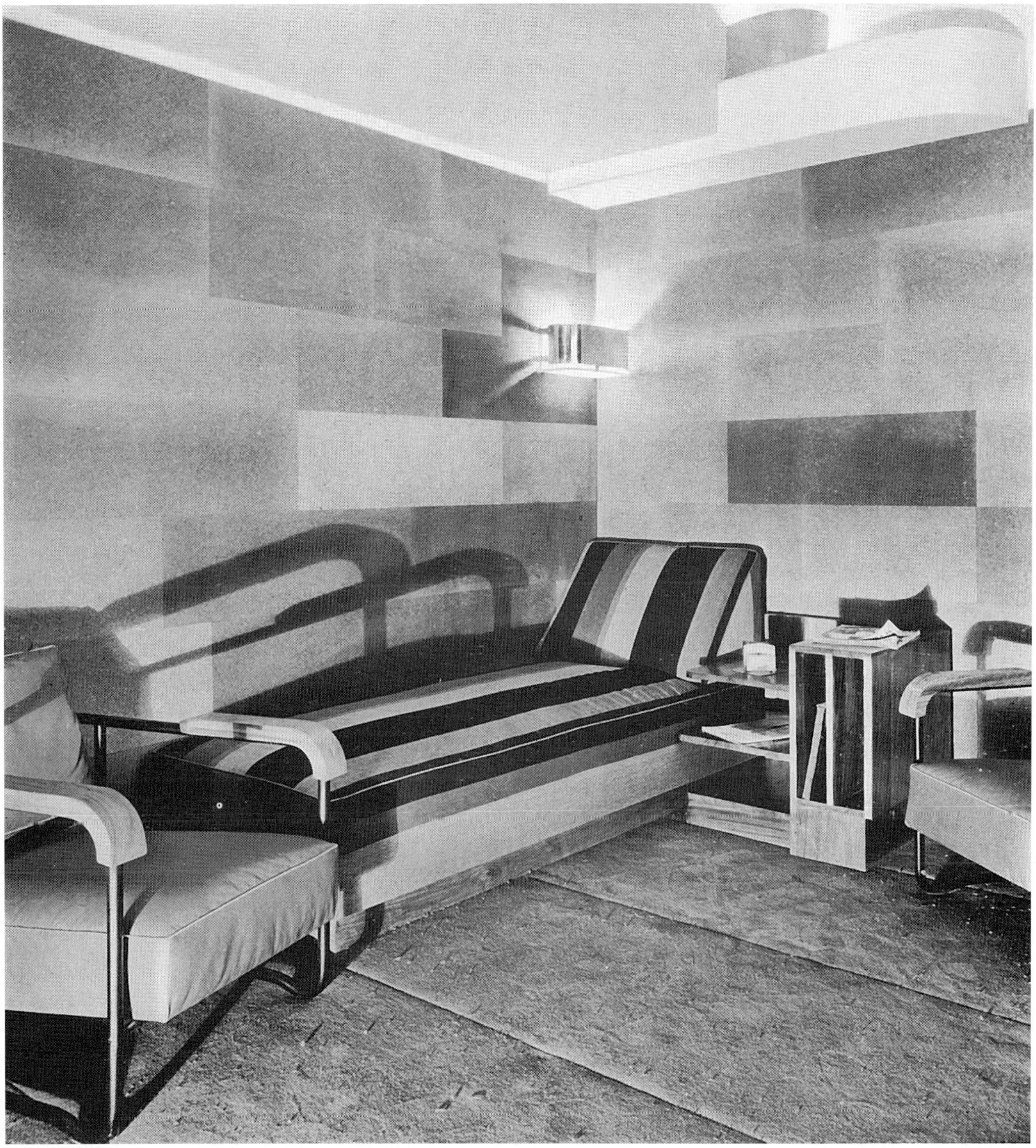

**The comfort and ease of the home brought into a private office of Andrew Geller. Cork used on walls to sound proof the room.**

**H O W E & L E S C A Z E**

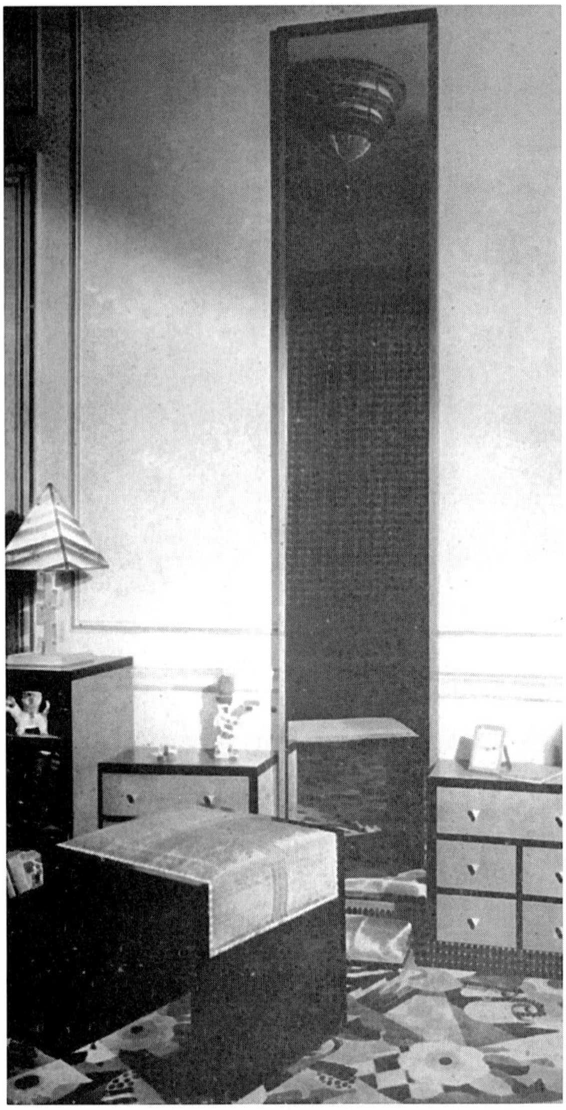

**H U G O  G N A M , J R .**
**Dressing table arrangement in blue stained maple.**

**Wall seat with decorative moulding matched to mirror frame in dance room of a private home.**

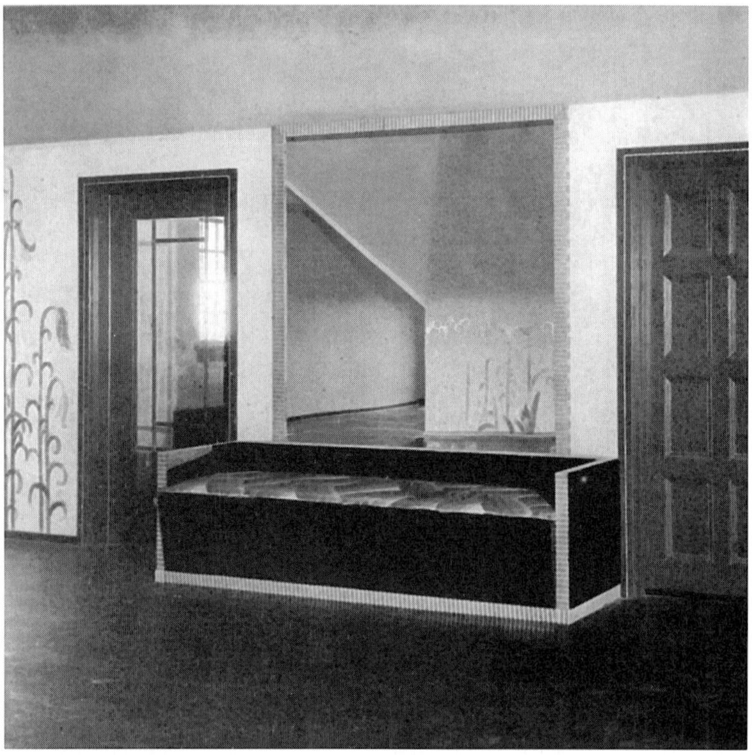

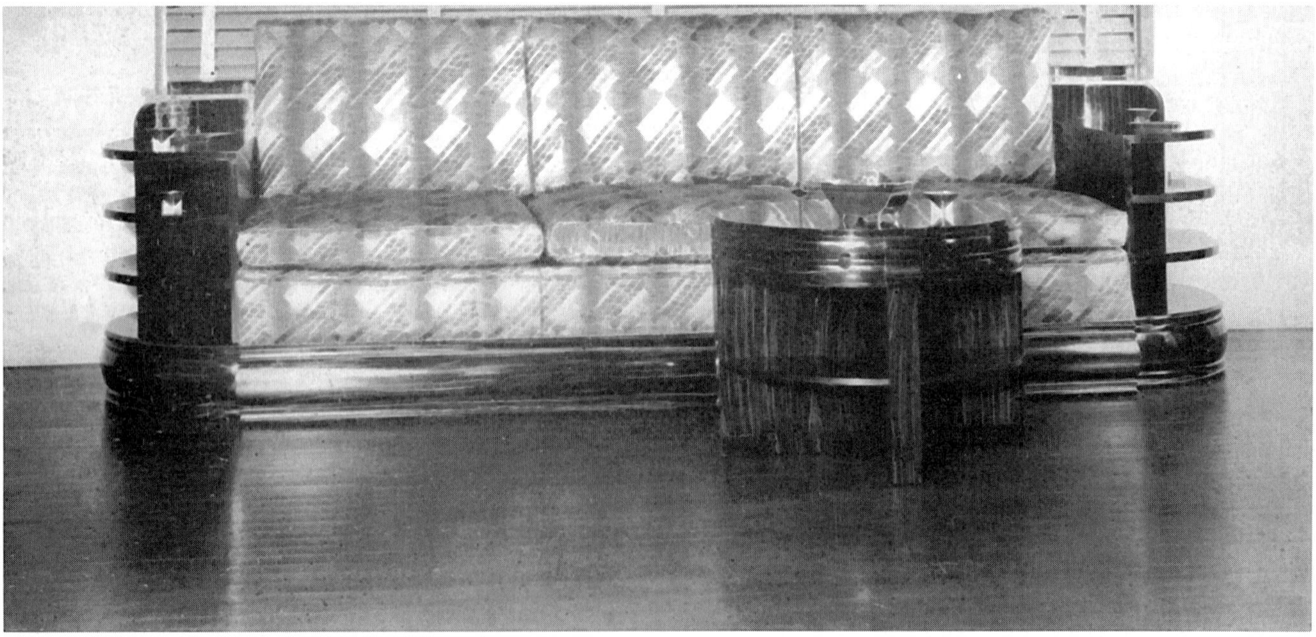

**A . D R E X L E R  J A C O B S O N** ***Macassar ebony couch and tea table.***

**PAUL M. ZIMMERMANN**

Bleached maple chest for I. Slack & Co.

**EUGENE SCHOEN**

Bedroom in apartment of Mrs. D — gray harewood and teak — peach walls and dark blue carpet.

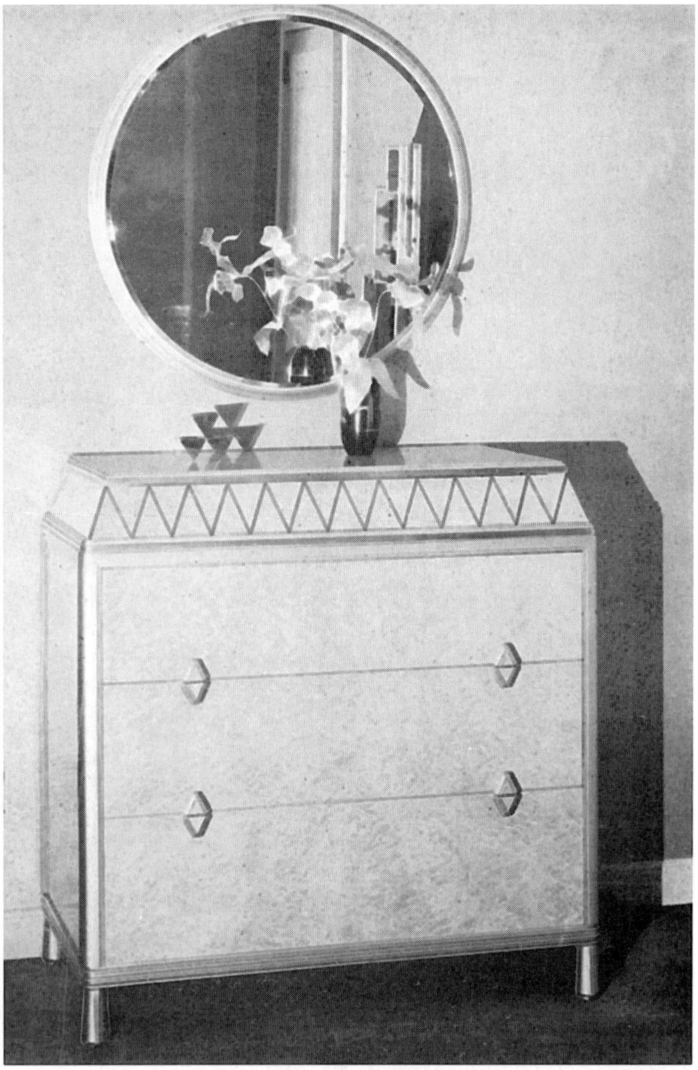

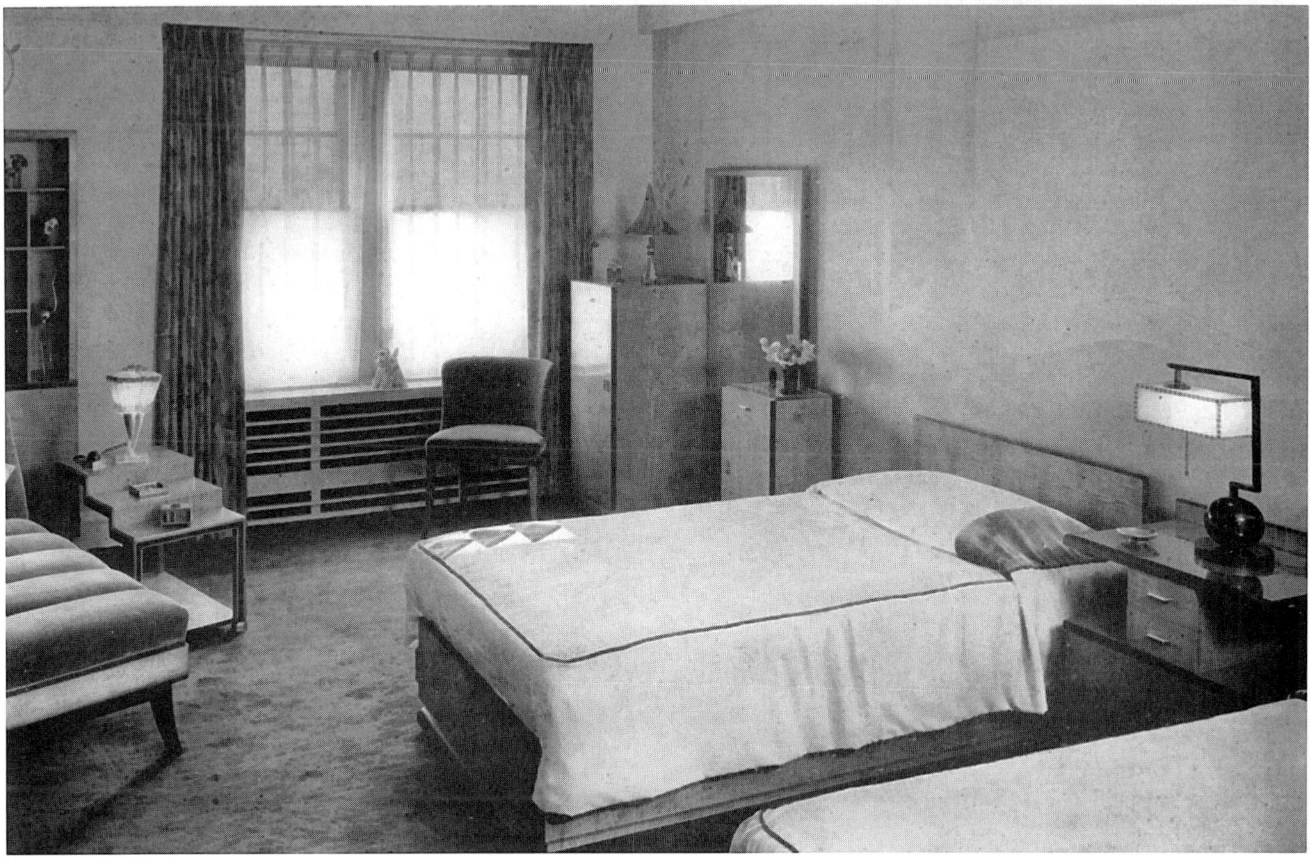

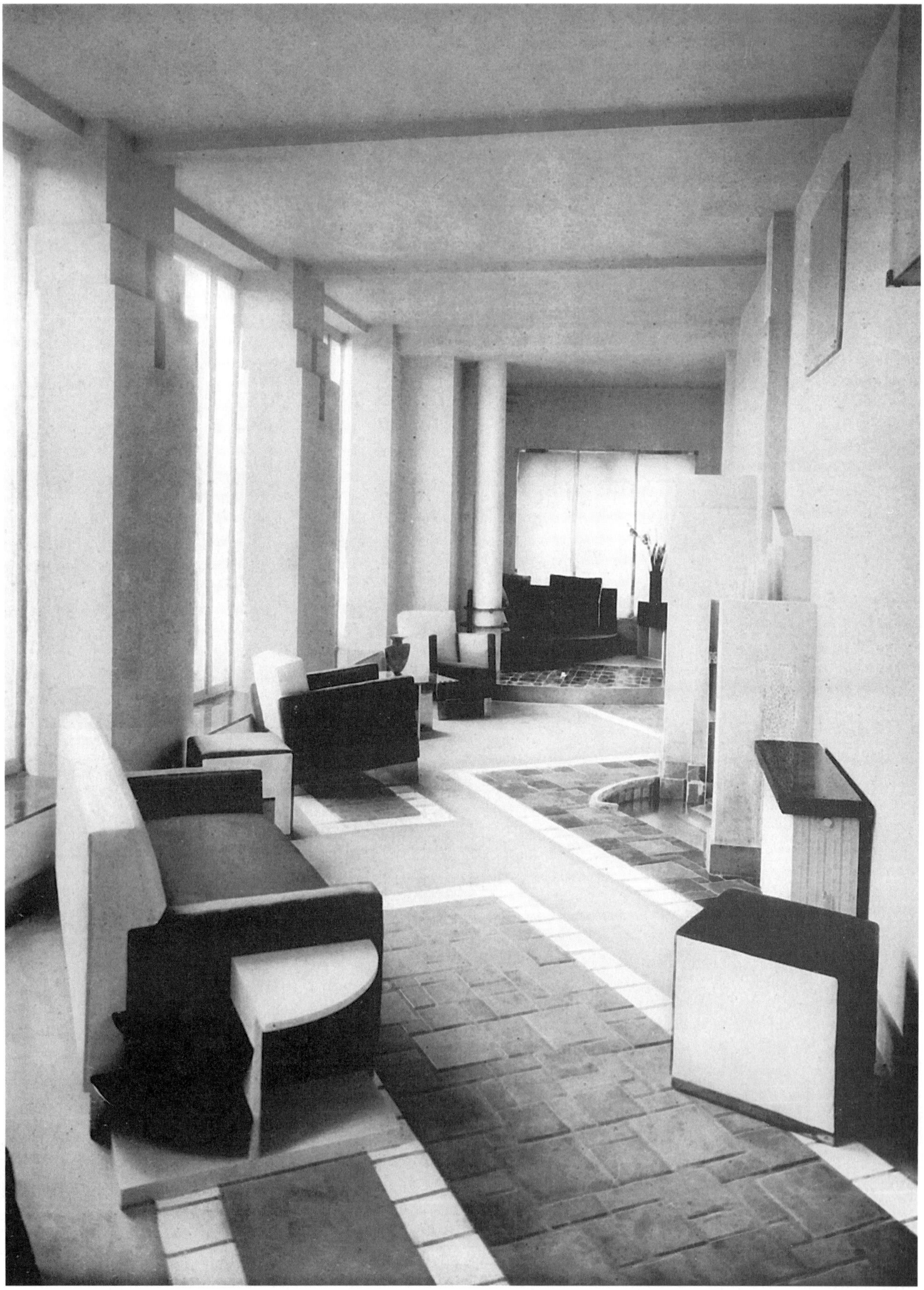

LEON CARROLL and JACQUES DARCY

Sun room in residence of J. T. H. Mitchell.
Furniture upholstered in Nemoursa.

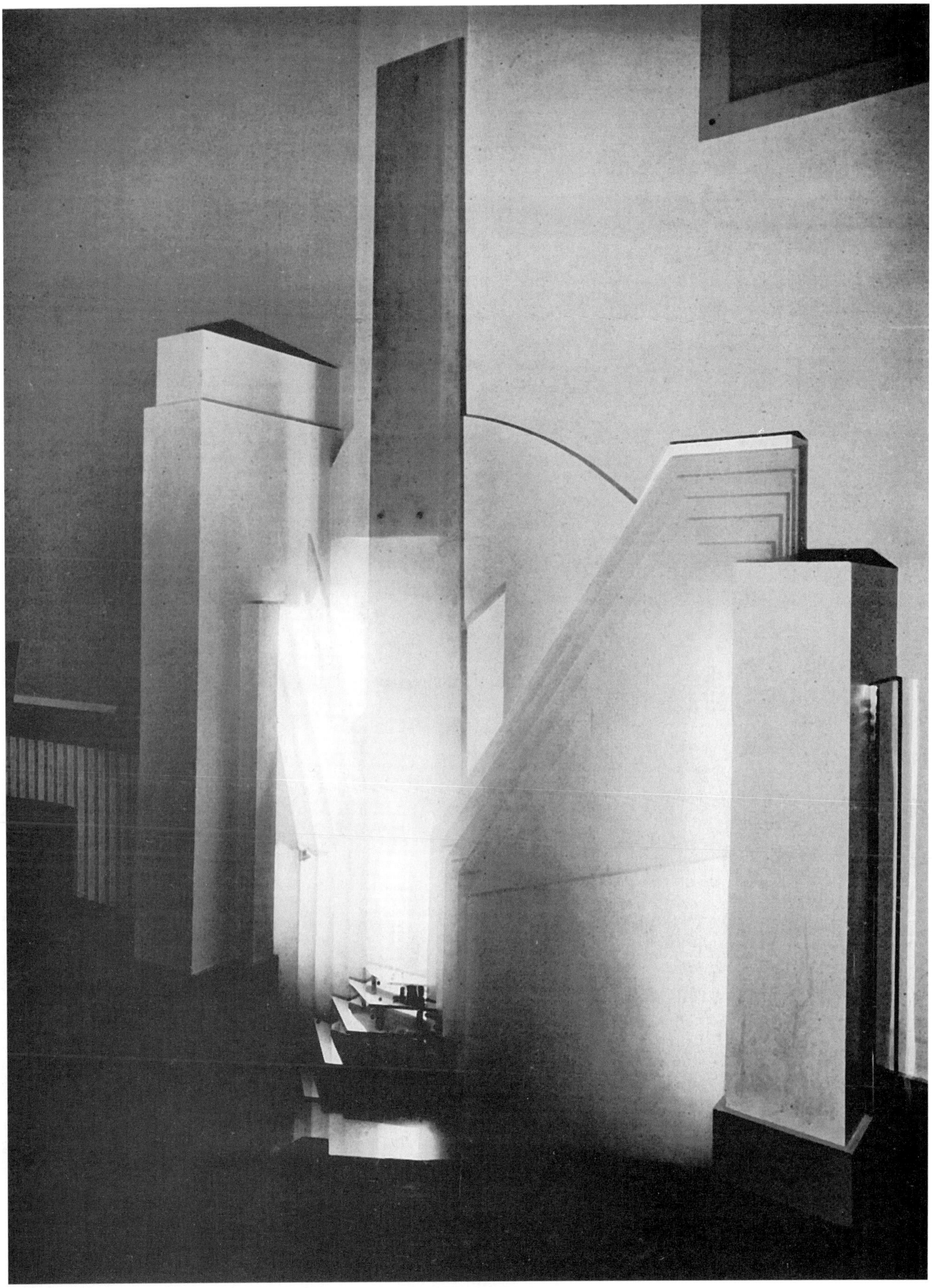

Illuminated fountain in Sun room.
Glass mirrors reflect concealed lights.

**WOLFGANG & POLA HOFFMANN**

Office of B. V. Becker, Chicago. Rubber back "Seamless Seamed" carpet from Collins & Aiken Co. Flexwood applied to Wall. Lamp executed by Luminator, Inc. Color scheme — brown and yellow.

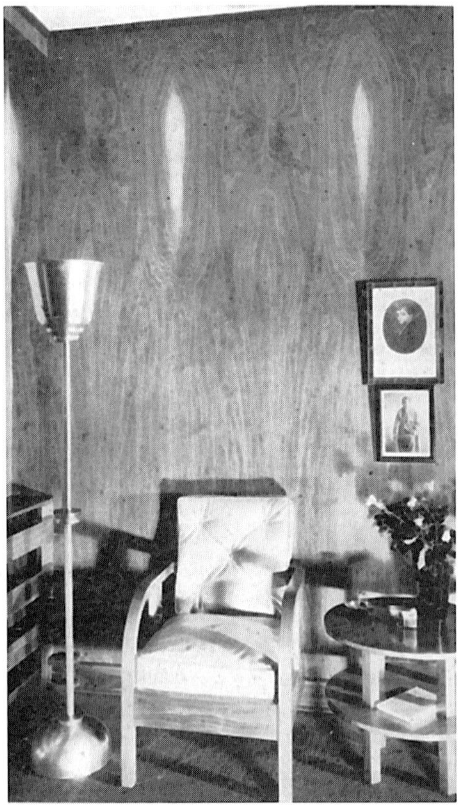

Waiting room in office of Dr. E. Kraus, New York City. Ombre wall paper, taupe carpet, green upholstered chair. Furniture made by Mallin Furniture Co.

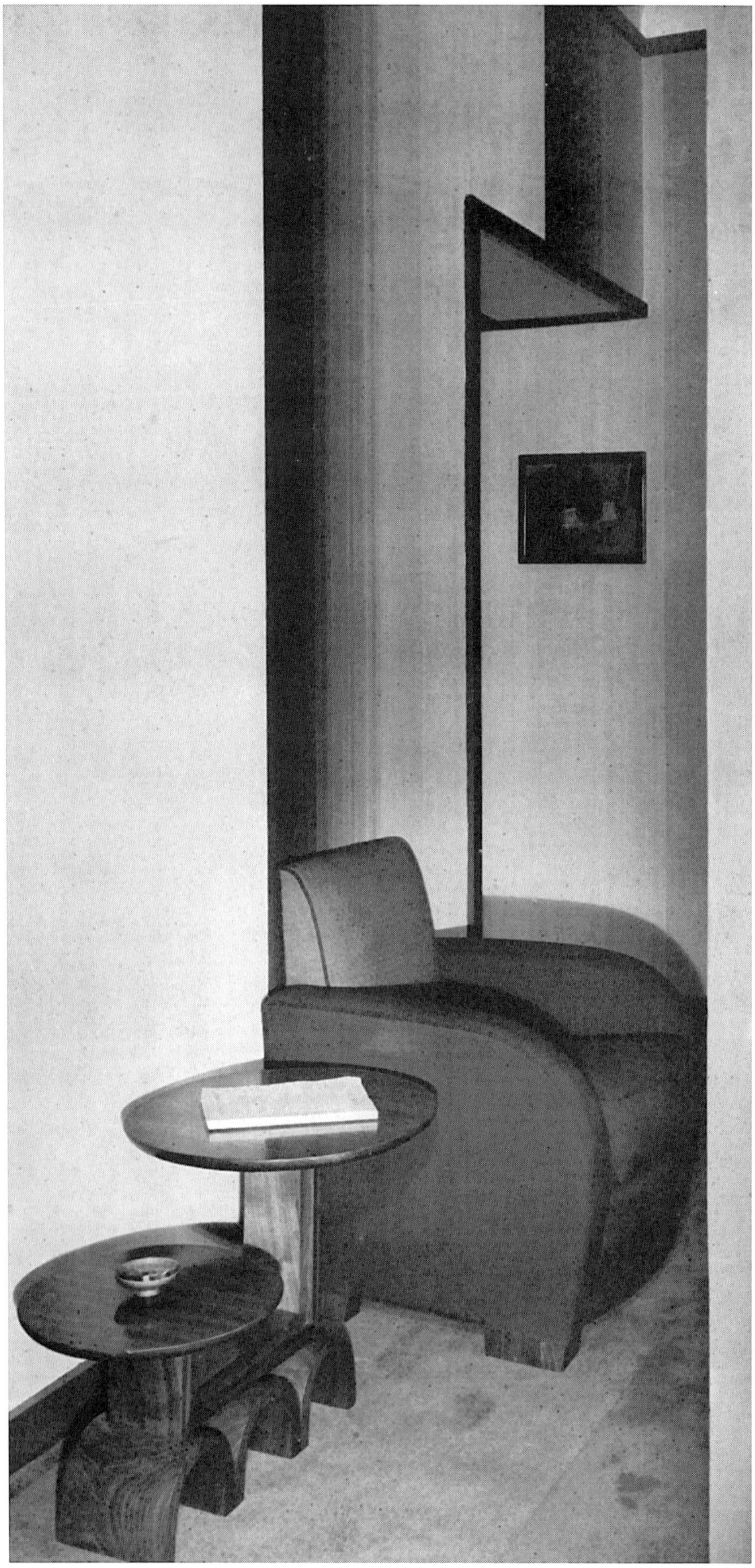

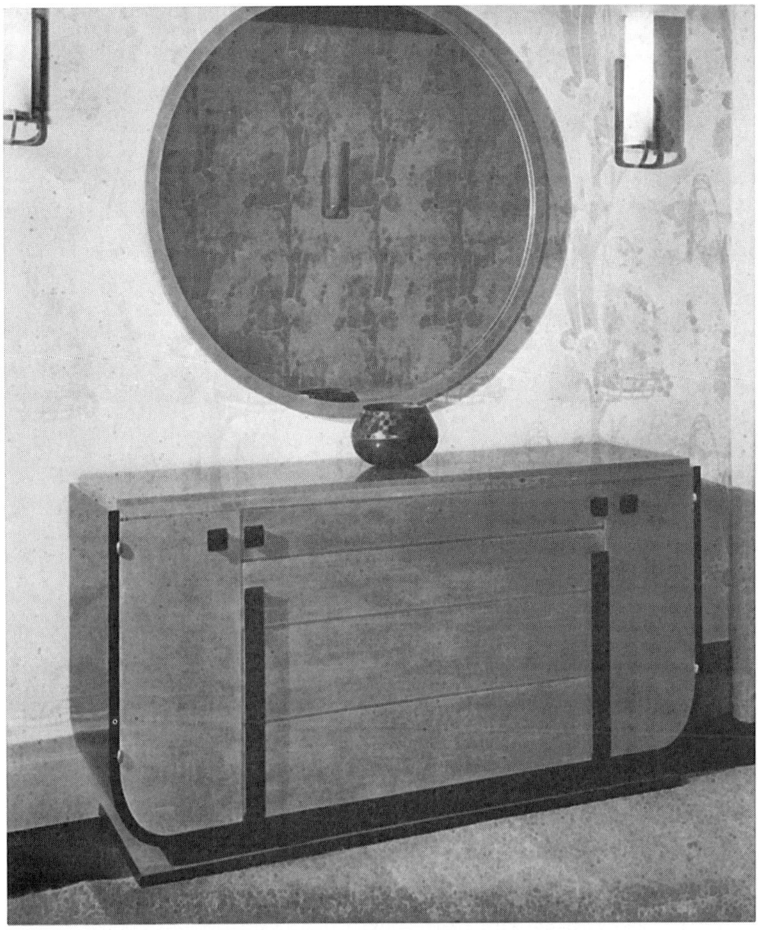

G I L B E R T R O H D E

Low chest of drawers in harewood and ebony.

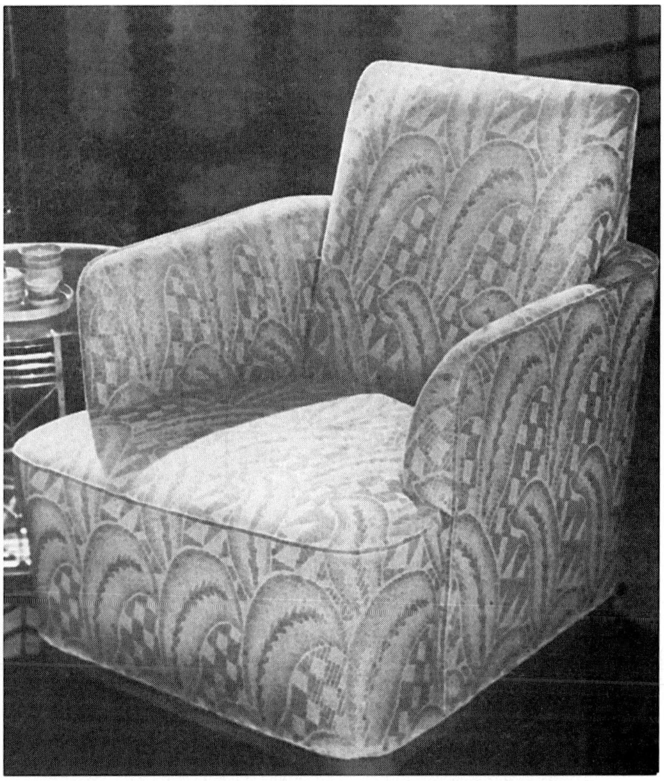

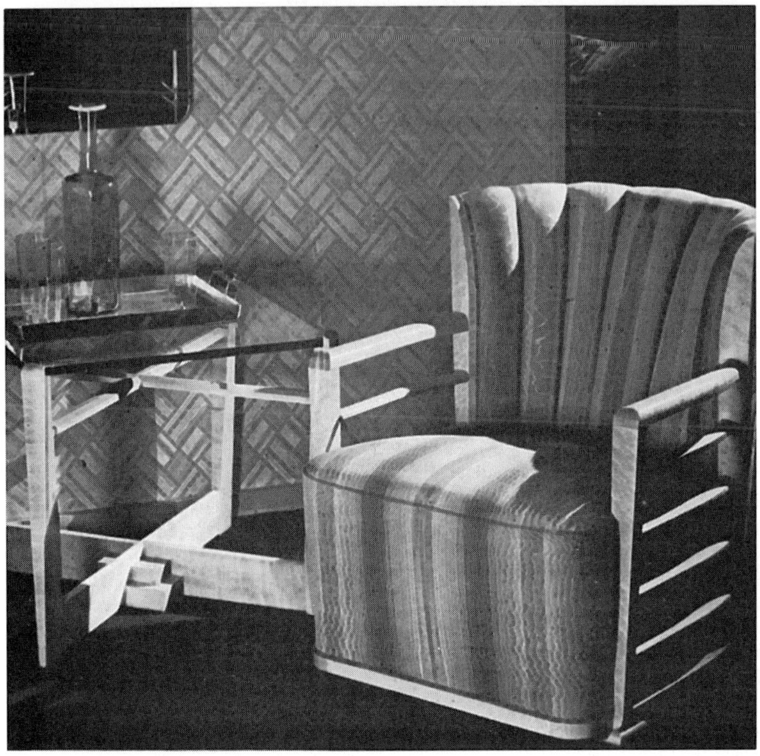

K E M W E B E R

Two soft upholstered chairs for the easy corner of the home.

SHEPARD VOGELGESANG

Serving buffet with secret drawers.

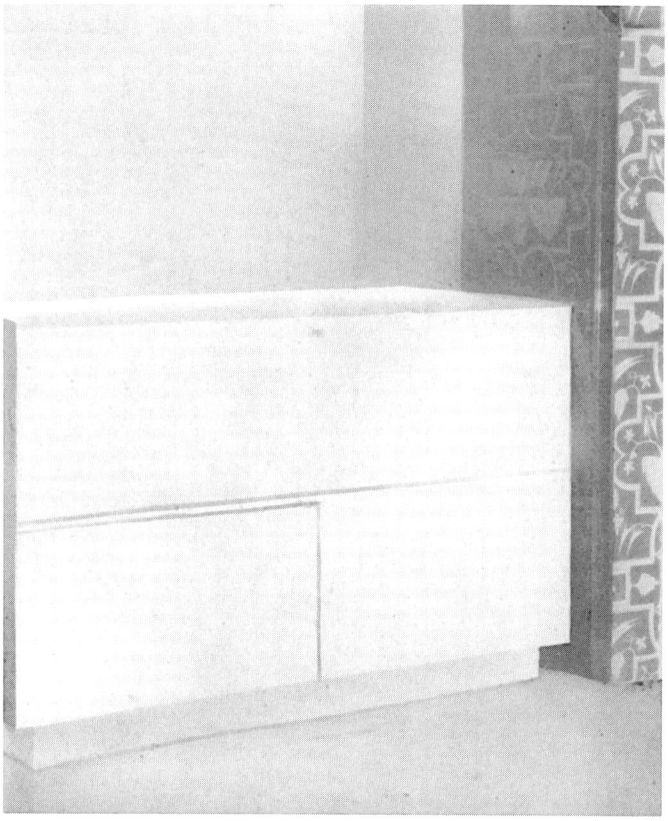

ALEXANDER KACHINSKY

Corner of a young girl's bedroom — furniture in white cherry. Tones of blue, gray and rose.

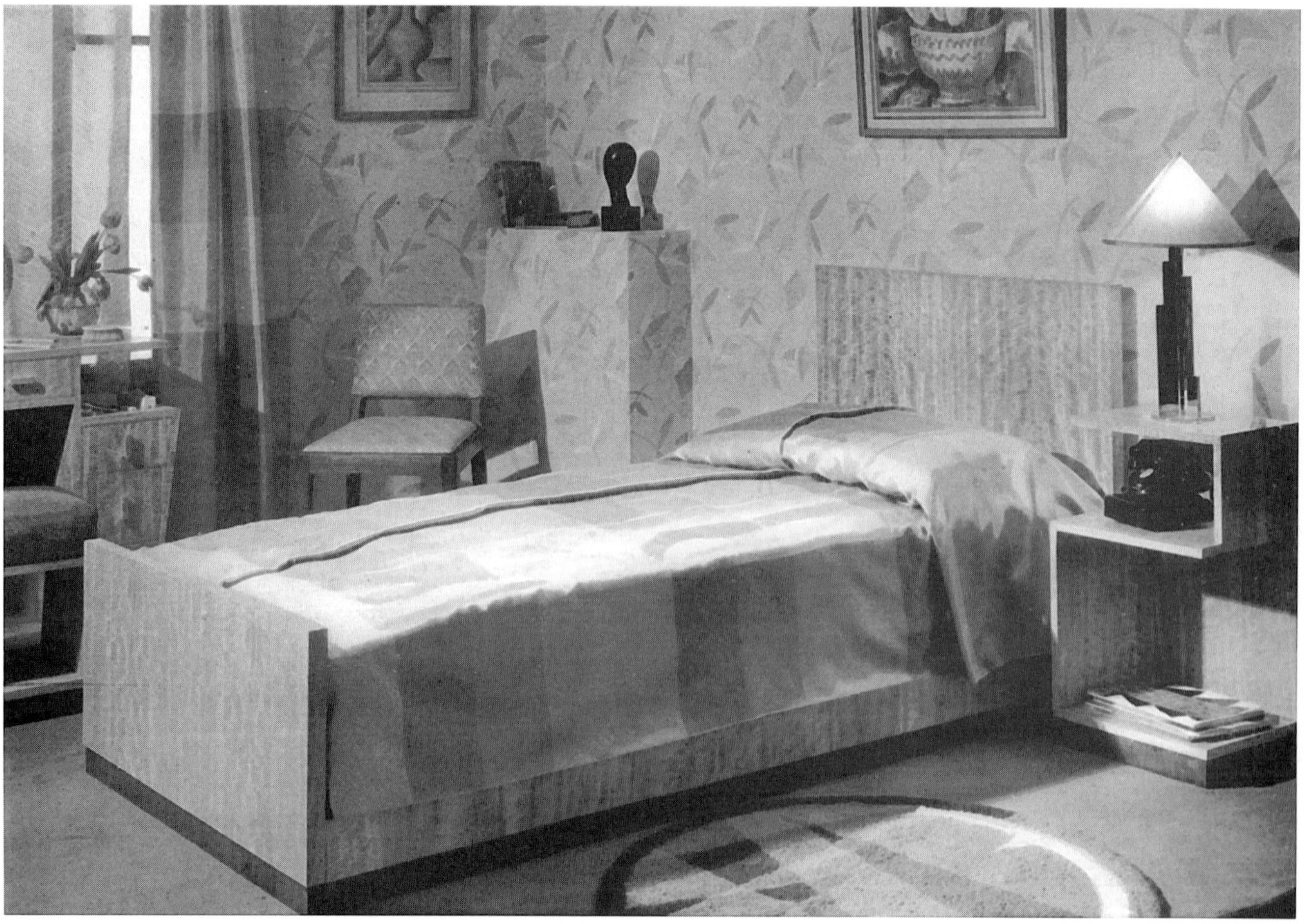

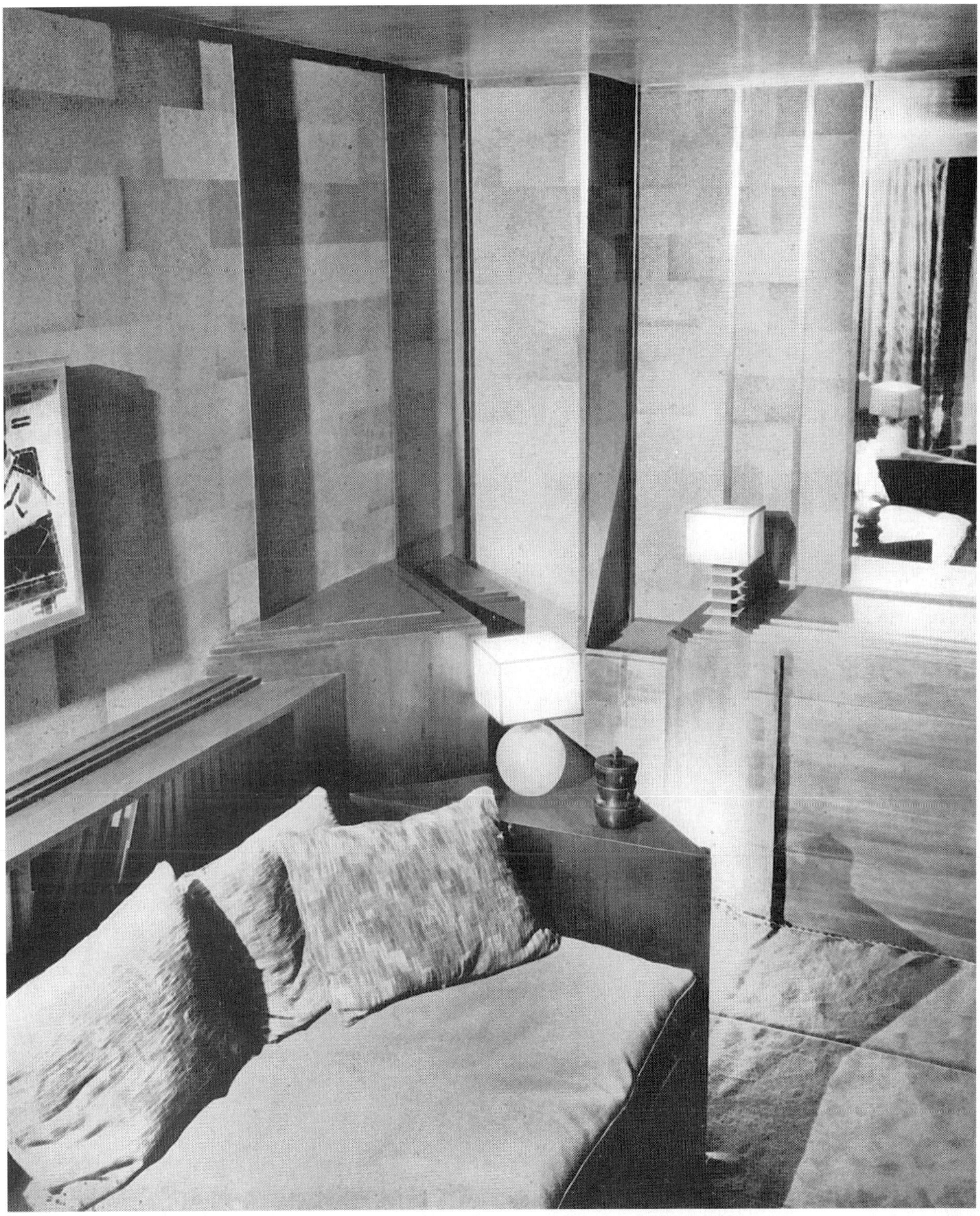

L E E S I M O N S O N

Apartment in the Hotel Delmonico. Corner of convertible bed room-study in California redwood. Dull blue upholstery, cork walls.

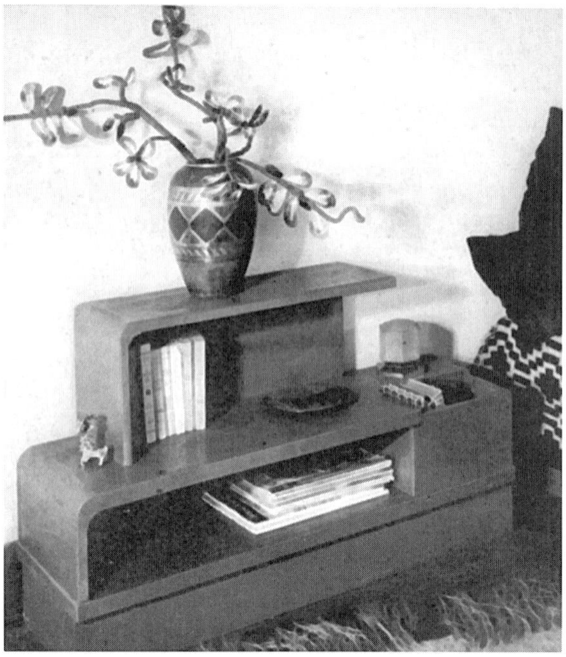

ELLEN M. KERN

Book shelf in red lacquered wood.

WINOLD REISS

Lounging room, Tavern Club, Chicago, in color scheme of gray, blue and green.

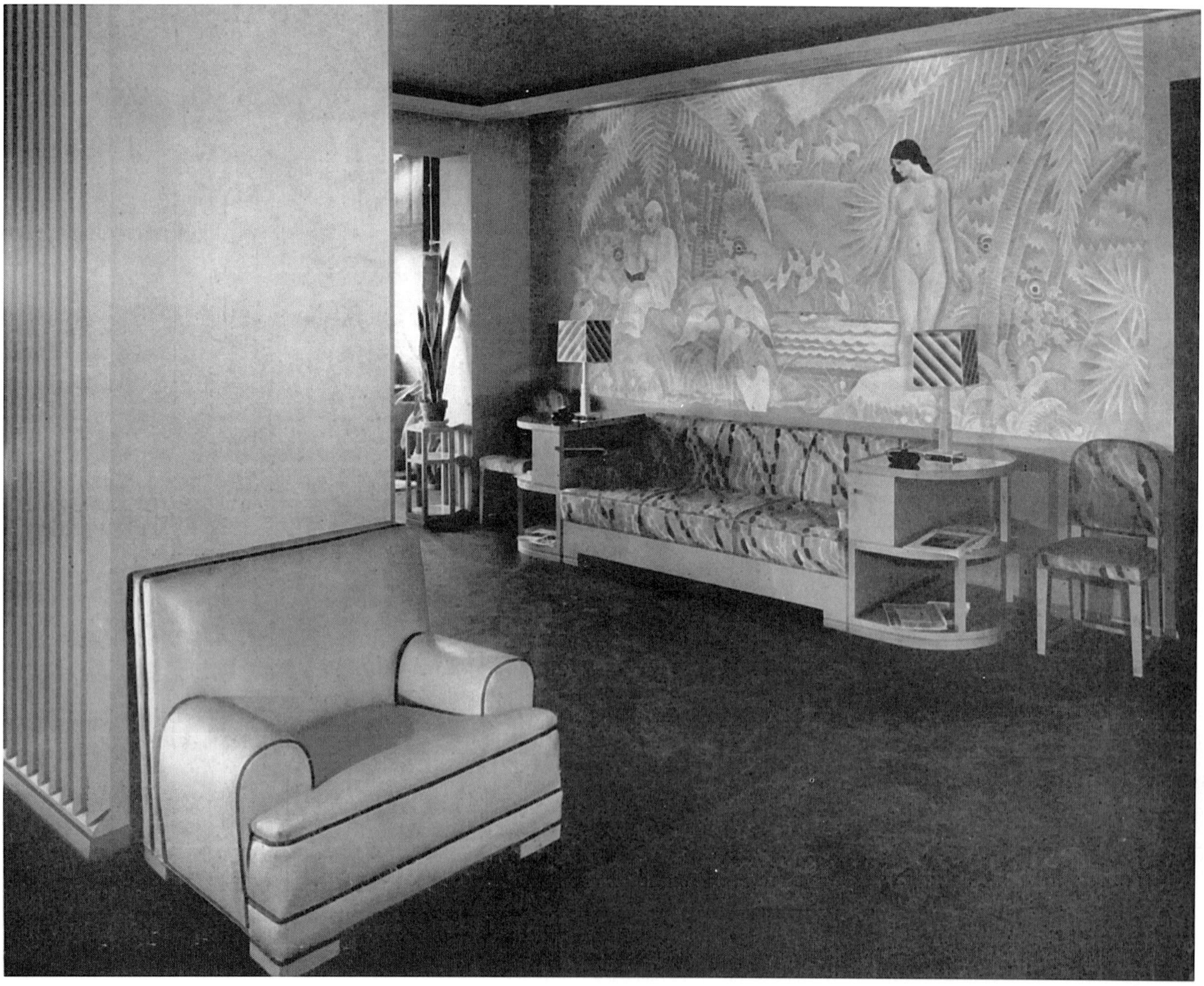

L U C I A N  B E R N H A R D

Breakfast room in a home in Westchester, N. Y. with concealed bar shown open and closed.

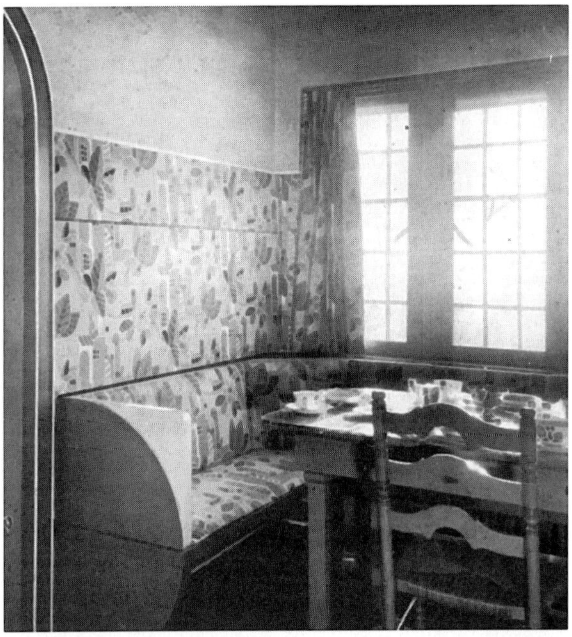

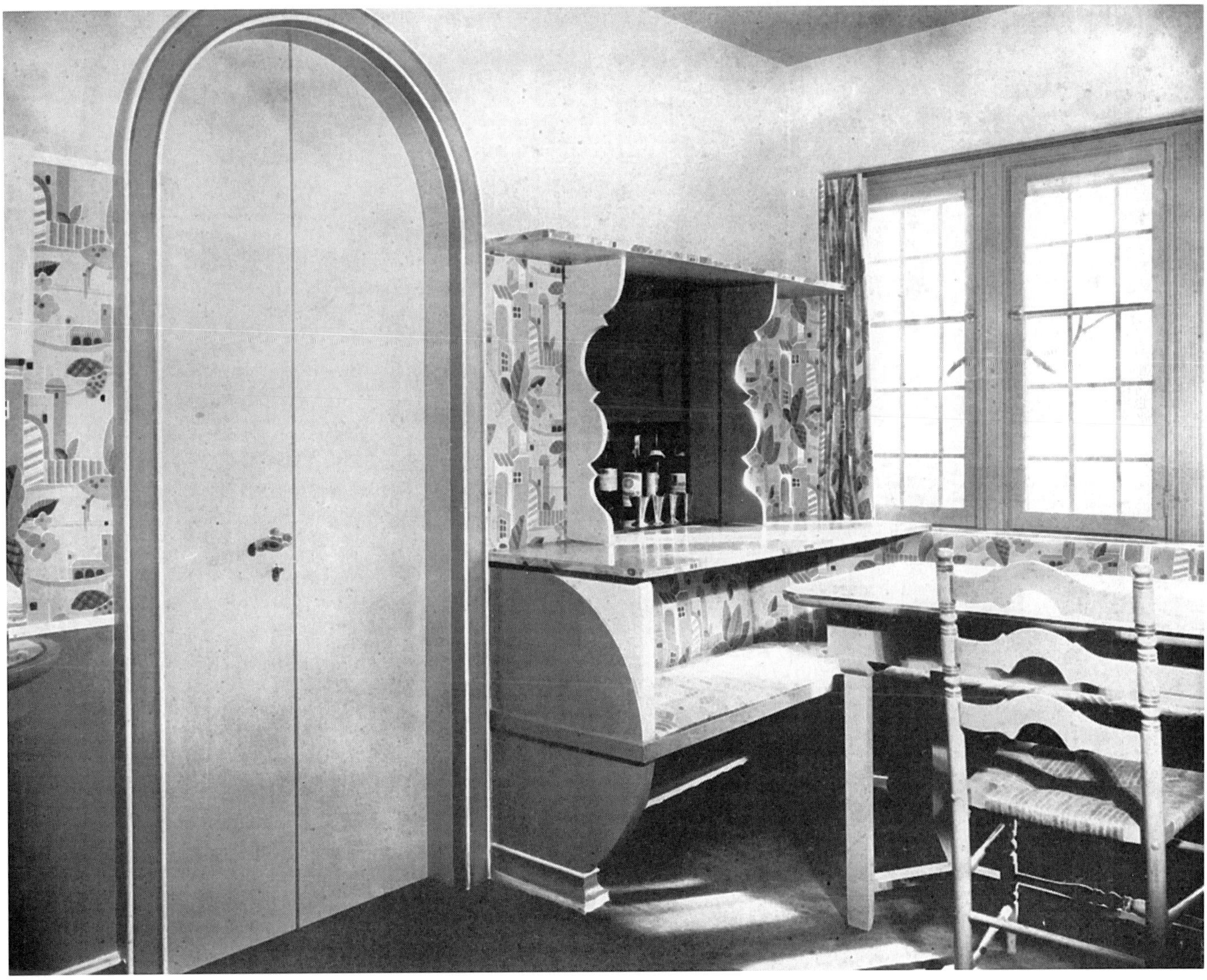

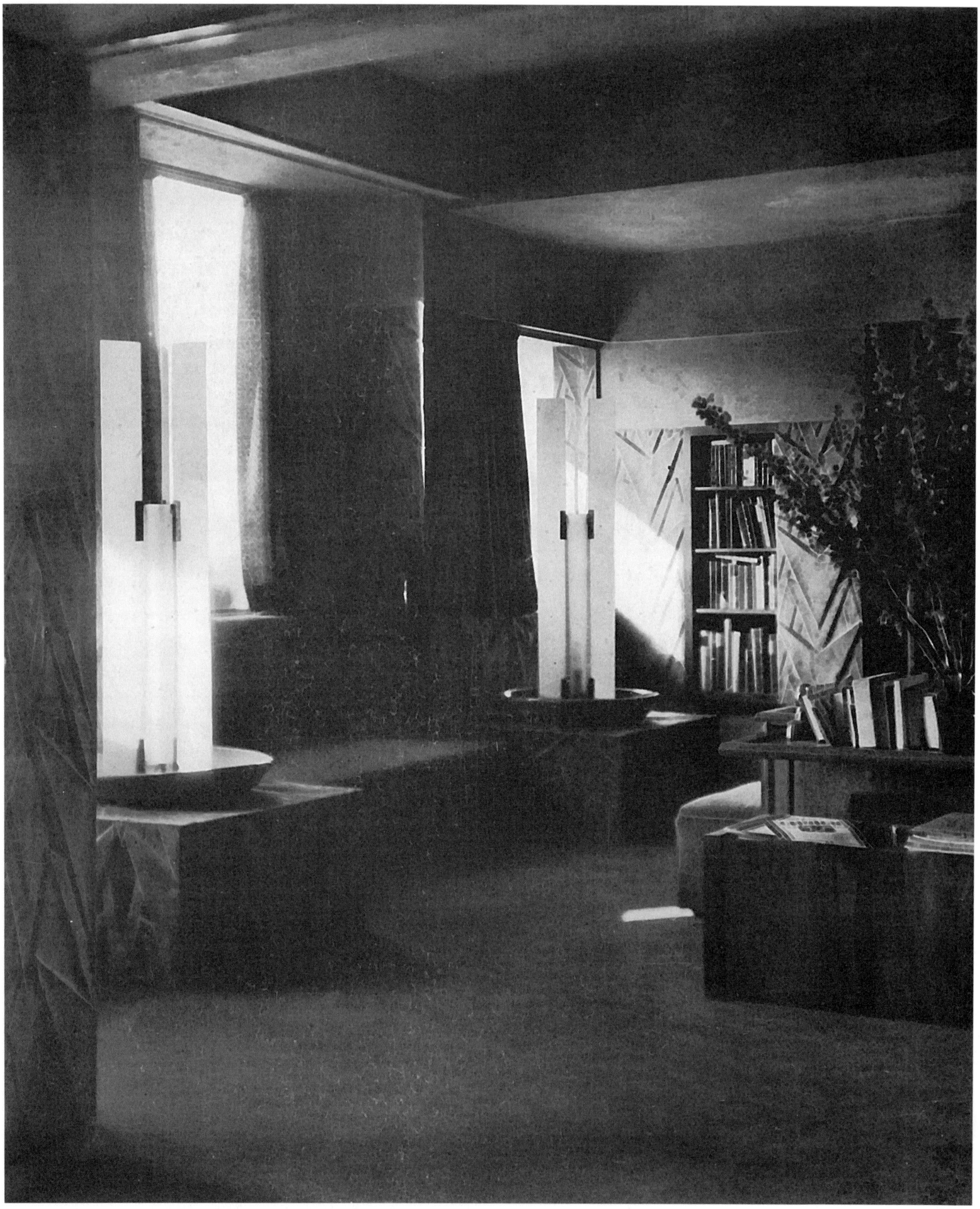

LLOYD WRIGHT Studio.

# M. D. C. CRAWFORD

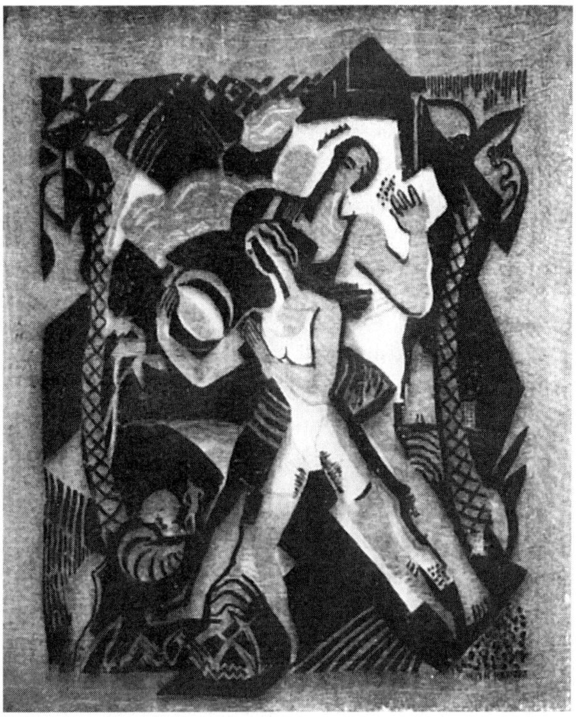

# textiles

There is no question that America needs a thoroughly individualized textile art of her own. We are big enough and old enough, rich enough and I trust smart enough to see the full advantages of such a need. This art, of course, must be in the current of the world's contemporaneous thought, but modified to suit our peculiar conditions. This need is not only in relation to our domestic but to our potential export markets and incidentally to our self respect. Such American products as have found a satisfactory foreign market have expressed our peculiar individuality. American machines and methods do not suffer in outside opinion. Our textile machines are slightly different but often better than their European competitors but our designs have been polyglot in motives, lacking in character and not our own, and seldom good if our own.

It is but fair to say, however, that our conquest of the machine in terms of quantity and quality and comparative low cost represents a very definite intellectual development. The added element of style is not so difficult to achieve as is generally supposed. It is obvious, however, that we cannot hope for any tangible results in this direction, from the ordinary run of meaningless designs executed on a commercial basis whether by so-called free lance artists, or by our highly commercialized studios. We will get designs on a par with those of France only as and when our textile art is recognized as a major phase of decorative expression. I, for one, do not question that we have adequate talent in America for this necessary achievement. In many fields of decorative expression we have shown complete independence of Europe, and in many industries the designer has become recognized as an essential element, and as such, is paid on the basis of American standards of profession renumeration. For some reason difficult to understand, the average textile mill looks upon design as a sort of necessary evil to be had as cheaply as possible and as nearly like what their foreign competitors have already sold in this country as the conscience of the average American manufacturer will permit.

I suppose this is a natural evolutionary stage. The history of decorative art shows how peoples borrowed from each other and modified their loans to fit their own circumstance. But perhaps never in the history of the world has plagiarism been carried to so high an art as in the last generation and particularly in the textile field in the United States. This is a matter of little national pride.

At some time or another in their history, all peoples produce art forms. From the earliest caves of Europe, the graves of prehistoric Peru, and our own South West, from the arrested cultures of the South Sea Island, from barren Alaska and from the pitiless frozen tundras of Siberia come arts showing how spiritual and esthetic necessities overcame the limitations of material and tools. In consequence, no ethnological philosopher should despair of awakening a creative instinct in decorative arts even in America.

The basis of this so much desired development in our latent textile art lies in an intelligent and sympathetic relationship between the designer and the industry. This relationship is best illustrated by the comparison with the already established relationship between the architect and the builder. When the architect is good and strong and knows his business, the practical builder willingly yields to his advice. Where the architect has only the title and much theory, the builder's attitude is somewhat different—it should be.

Few of our artists and illustrators with sufficient talent to justify their being regarded as pathfinders for our textile industries have ever taken the trouble to learn the absolute physical limitations of our machines, or to study those curious currents of contemporaneous selection which we group under the general name of style. Most efforts of the best of illustrators in textile arts have been along the lines of self-expression with undue emphasis on individual idiosyncrasies. The woman who buys a fabric or dress, or decorates a home, or selects a piece of furniture seldom if ever is interested in an egotistical and theoretical dogma of something that someone else designates as art whether ancient, or modern. She is seeking that elusive quality known as charm and though she can be guided, and even at times warped when it comes to pictures, or statuary, in those fields of art where she judges herself as a supreme connoisseur, she is not guided by names no matter how impressive they may sound. She knows her own needs and needs no lecture on art phases.

I return to my first paragraph. An architect knows the history of man's building. He is not ashamed to resort to the classics for inspiration. He looks upon the Grecian, the Gothic, the Renaissance periods with respect at least, and while he realizes that new materials and new methods demand or at least imply new forms, this does not mean that these new forms may not have some reminiscence of the past. Just to be different is not the whole idea. In our language words more ancient than any living monument, phrases more enduring than nations are consistently unconsciously used. We do not build a new language every time we have another thought. Much that is called art is in reality a complete lack of taste, an absence of appropriateness, and even ugliness veiled by a meaningless phrase.

It is true that each artist has an individual message to deliver, but he also has a responsibility to those traditions which make it possible for him to express this individuality.

On the other hand, our manufacturing situation at the present time does not lend itself readily to creative art. Our mills, even the best of them, are built on the principle of mass production and while they have incorporated the doctrine of quality in many instances and have evolved elaborate systems to insure this quality they have not yet come to appreciate the necessity for laboratory experiments in design.

The artist who places egotistical originality before the sound canons of taste is in somewhat the same position as that of the dean of a southern college who believes the book of Genesis to be an accurate and scientific explanation of the great fact of life. The evolutionist on the other hand realizes that new forms and ideas are evolving according to the necessities of life through the "survival of the fittest" and through some indefinite and still undefined law of progress. But even the fundamentalist holds the belief that special creation happened only once and with ample authority. Many artists, however, believe that inspiration in form and colour happens every time they take up brush or pencil. Art does not start anew with each individual or age. Its growth is organic and through evolutionary processes.

It was not to be expected that the machine would adjust itself too rapidly to our social and economic ideas. The world is very slow in absorbing new mechanical facts, and it must be admitted that we have had plenty of other things to do in our few centuries in the new world. Other peoples who subsequently achieved great distinction in the arts were themselves somewhat slow in this same direction.

And I will say in happy conclusion that a few of the artists that I have known who have given some thought and attention to textile technique and style have produced designs easily on a par with the best from Europe and far, far above the general average of these designs which are usually accepted in this country as of artistic merit, simply because they have been imported. It is not necessary for us to dazzle the world with a new art in order to make our textile products acceptable in the markets of the world. All we need is a little common sense and a little co-operation between designers and mills and an honest and sane determination to treat the problem of textile arts with respect and sympathy.

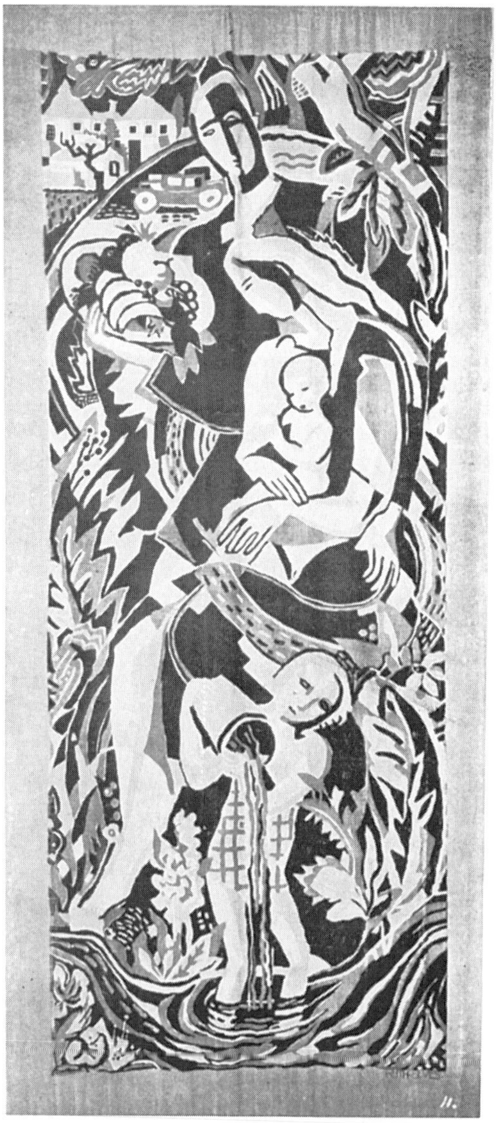

**RUTH REEVES**
**''The American Family''—**
**Printed wall panel. Shelton looms.**

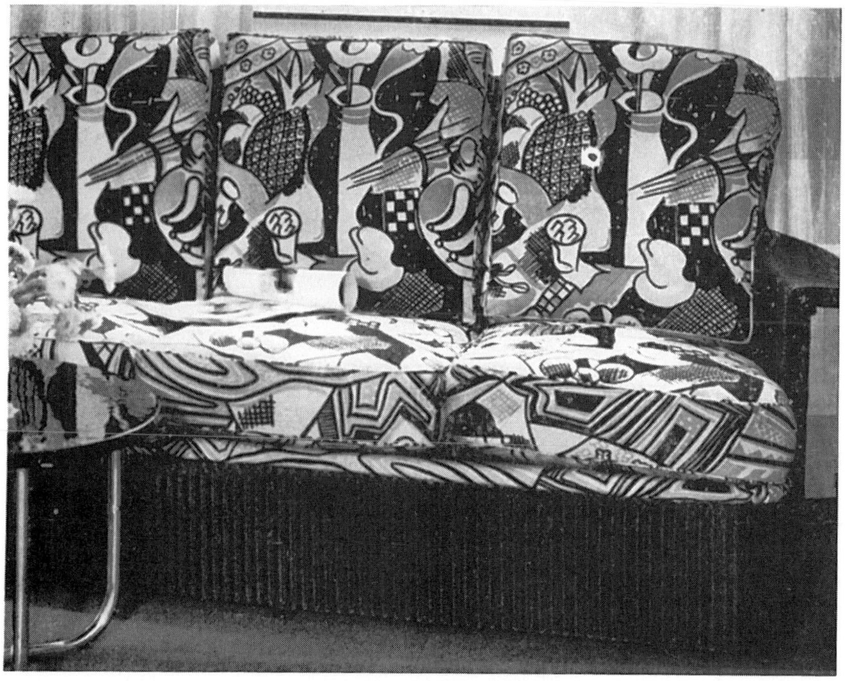

**Rayon Print—''Matisse'' used on Ypsilanti Reed Furniture.**

**Preceding Page—''The Bathers''**
**Printed wall panel on Du Pont rayon.**

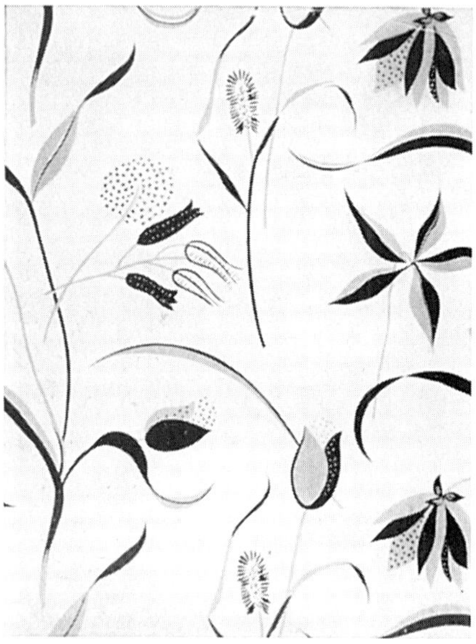

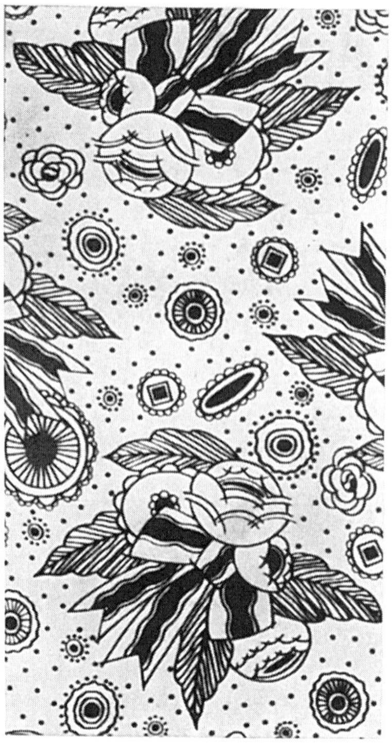

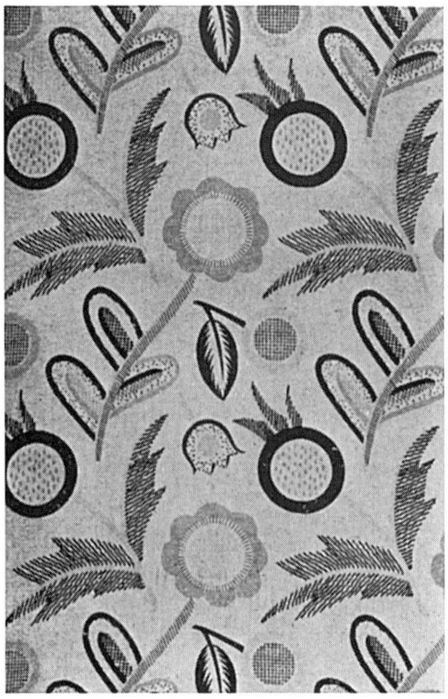

T E R E S A   K I L H A M
Permatex Lustersheen.

H E L E N   D R Y D E N
Design for Stehli Silks Co.

I L O N K A   K A R A S Z
Mohair fabric for Lesher-Whitman & Co.

W I N O L D   R E I S S
Two renderings of same design in different fabrics for the Shelton Looms.

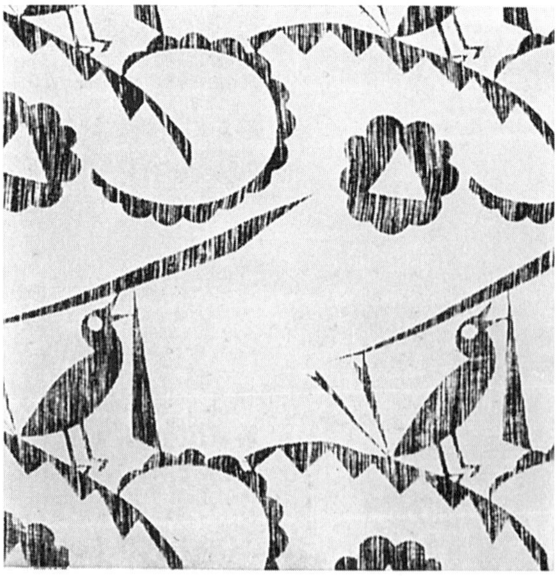

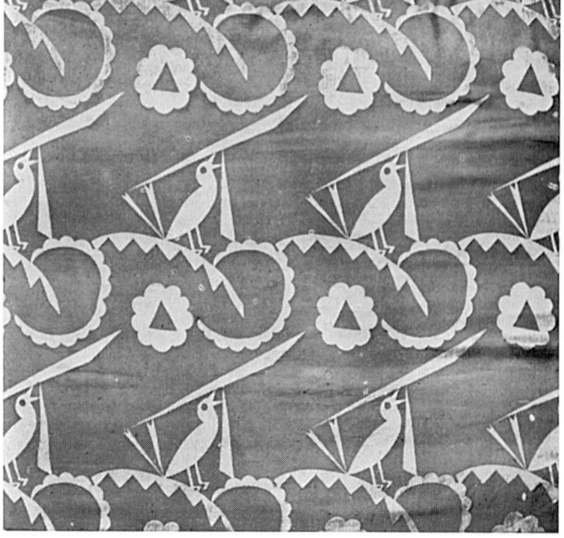

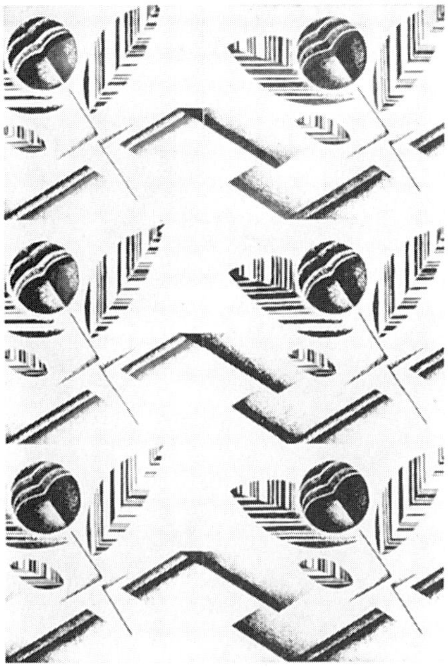

**ROBERT L. LEONARD**
Design for Shott Mfg. Co.

**JENNIE GREENE**
Cretonne for Cyrus Clark Co.

**DONALD DESKEY**
Hand blocked linen. Lehman-Connor Co.

**DONALD DESKEY**
Mohair monoprint. Lesher Whitman & Co.

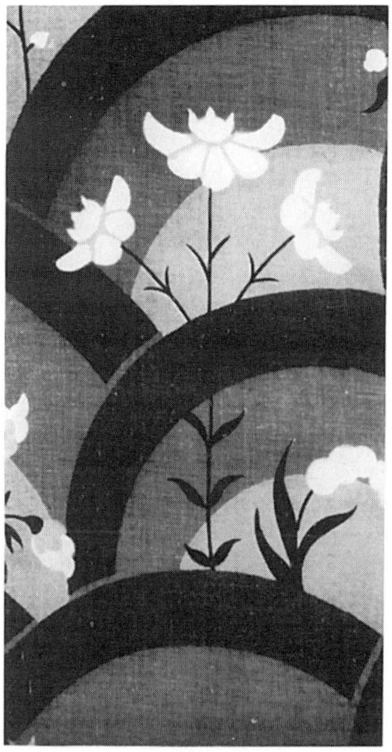

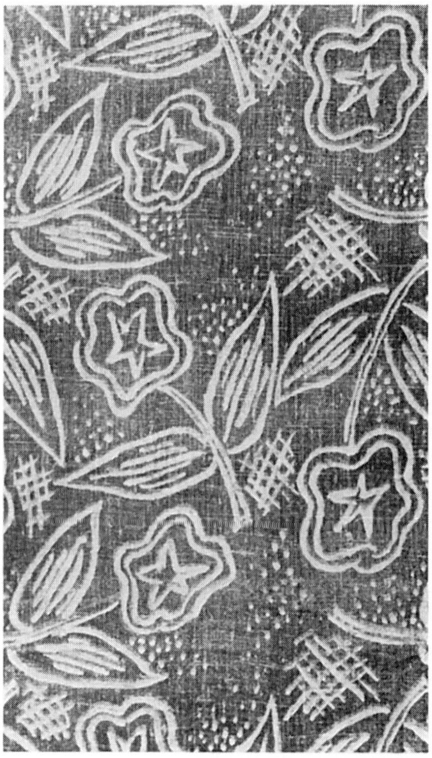

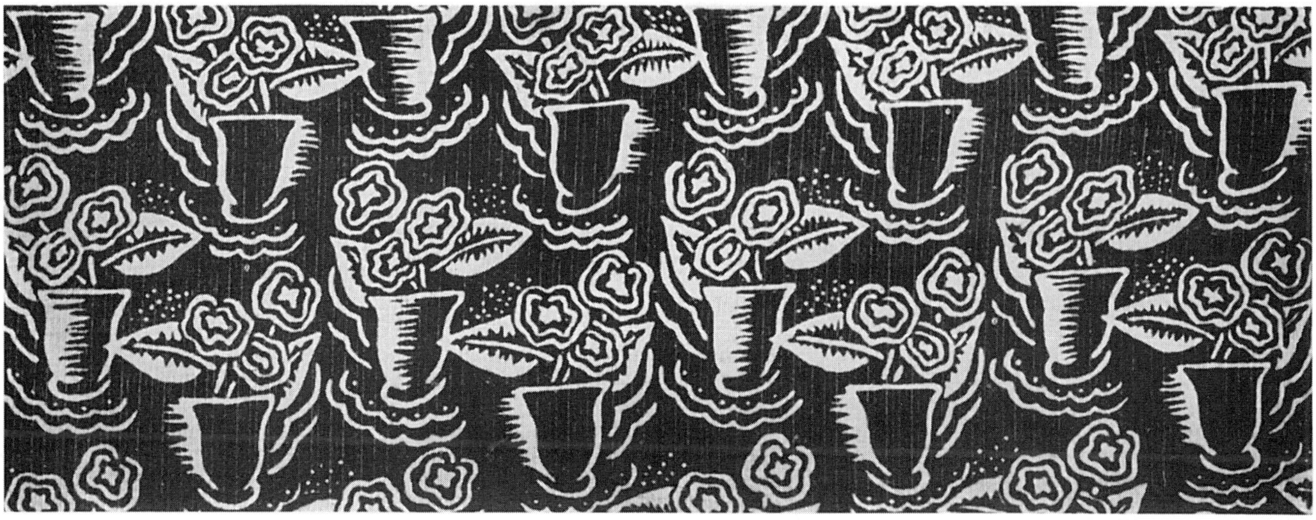

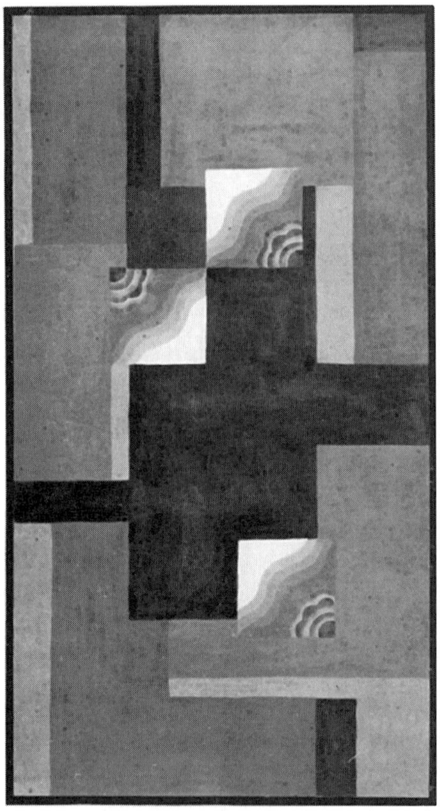

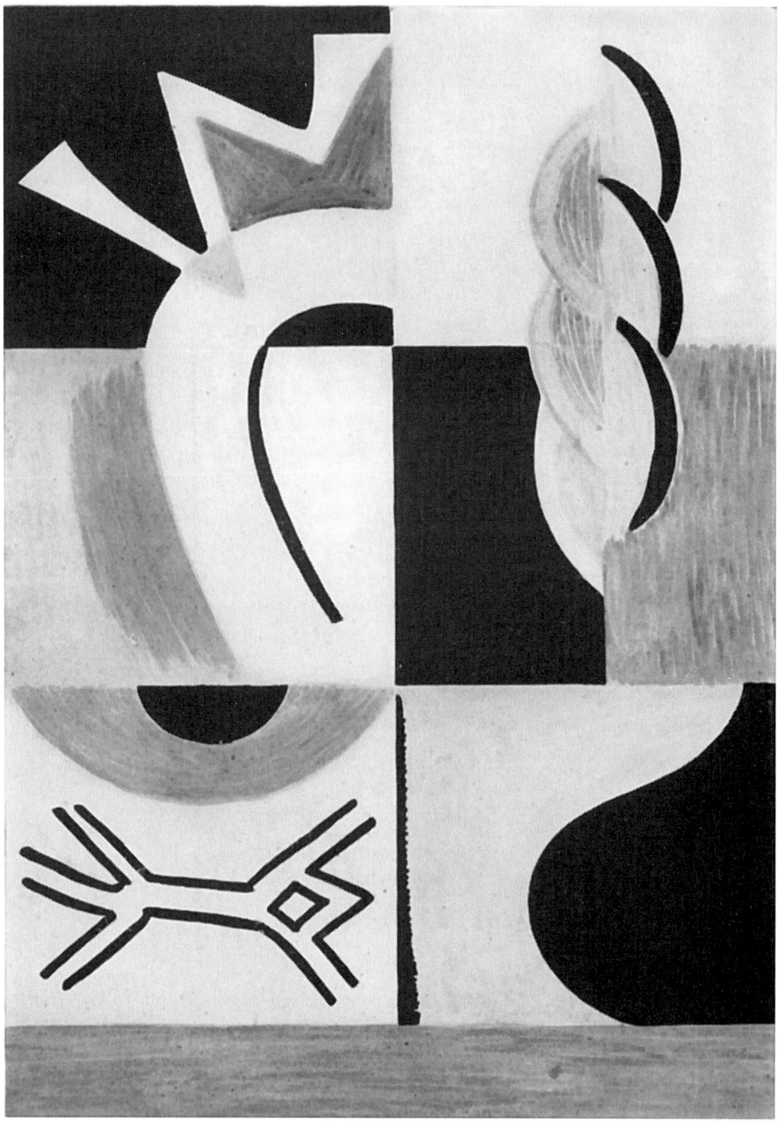

L Y D I A R A H L S O N
Woolen rug. Grays, blues, rose.
Executed by Hill, Gerhard Company.

E D U A R D B U K U L R E I C H
Two woolen rugs, the lower one hooked.
Executed by Ralph M. Pearson Studios.

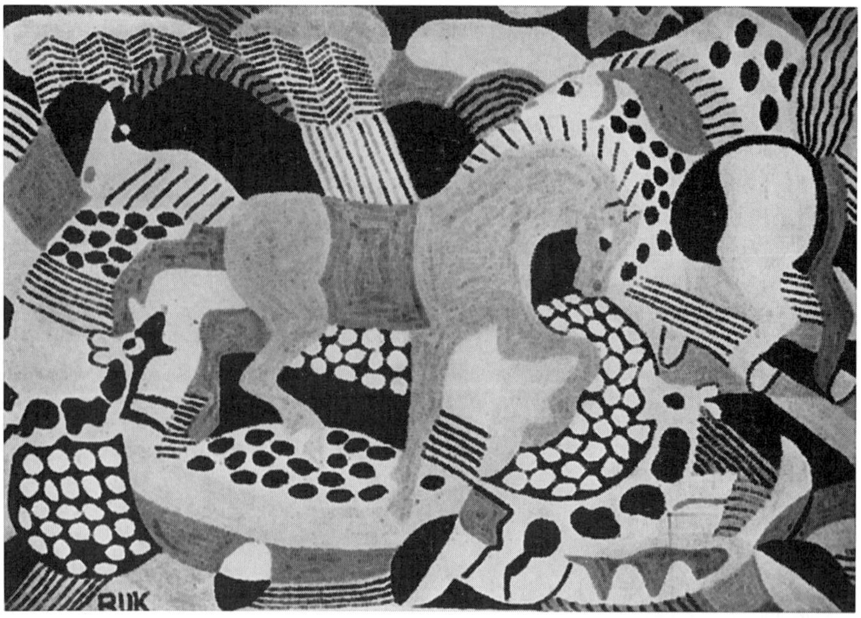

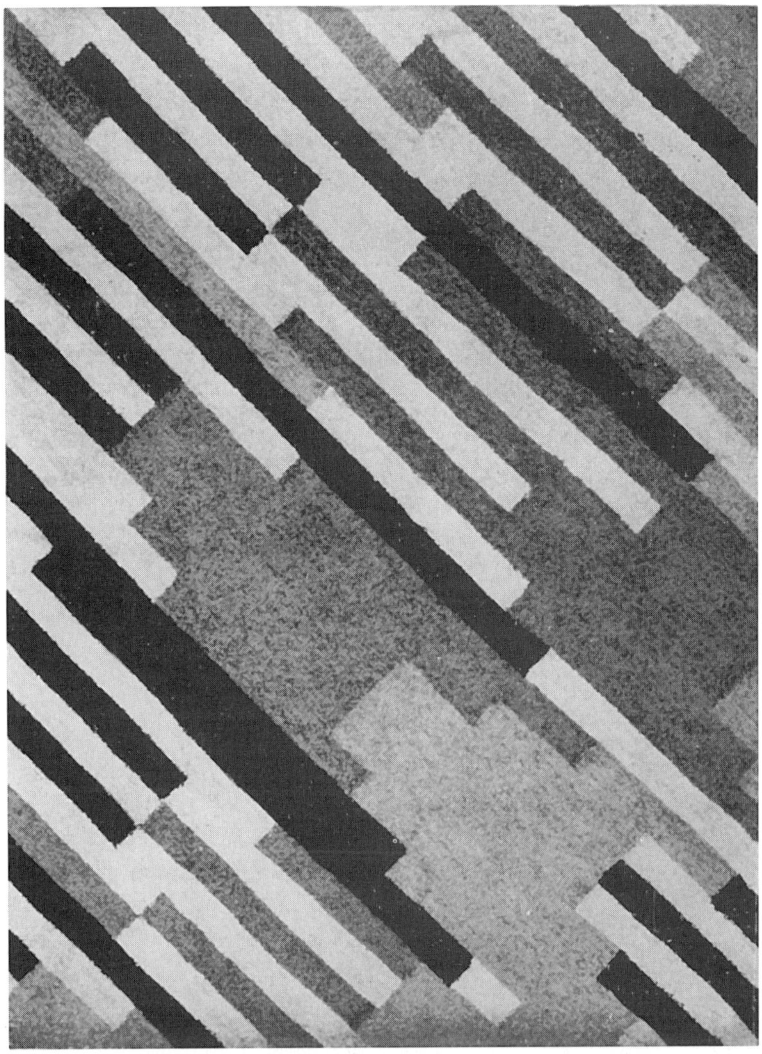

H E N R I E T T E R E I S S
Hand woven woolen rug — Ralph M. Pearson Studios.

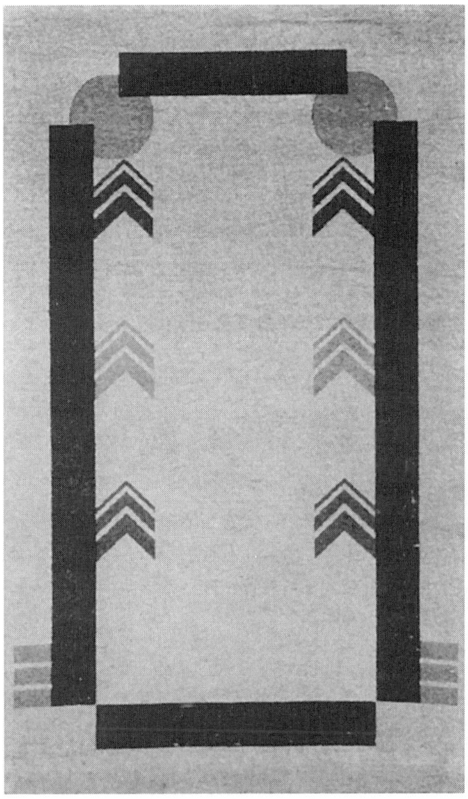

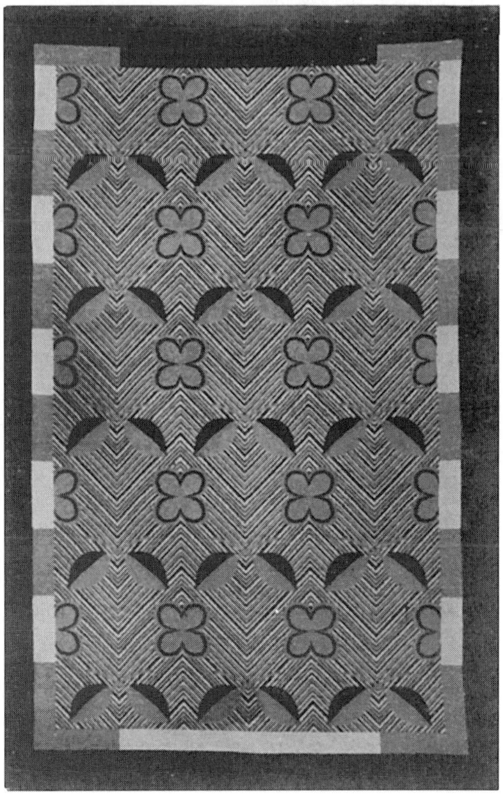

T E R E S A K I L H A M
Machine woven woolen rugs.
Executed by Kilmarnock Corp.
For R. H. Macy & Company.

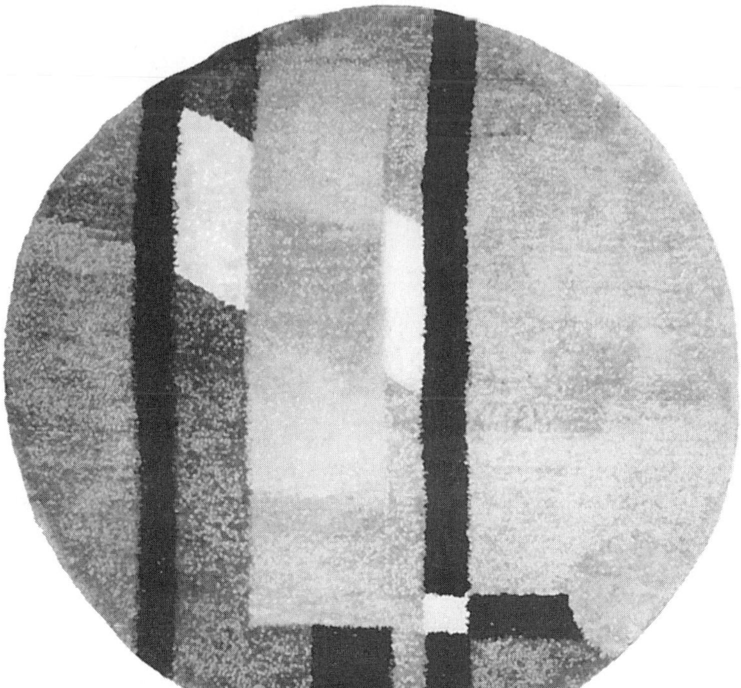

G I L B E R T R O H D E
Hooked rug with initials "N. L."

V A L L Y   W I E S E L T H I E R

Stitched and printed children's design on rough linen. Four bright colors in six different combinations. Distr. by Schumacher & Co.

The castle and houses in this design are printed on a stitched background. Also four colors — all bright — are used, in six different combinations. Distributed by Schumacher & Co.

Decorative islands in multicolored effect printed on a ground of rough linen. In six color combinations. Distr. by Thibaut & Co.

Toy figures, in many vivid colors, printed against a rough linen ground. In six color combinations. Distr. by Schumacher & Co.

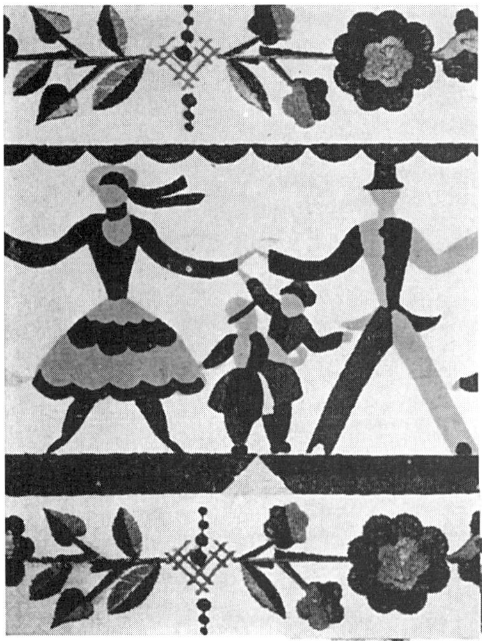

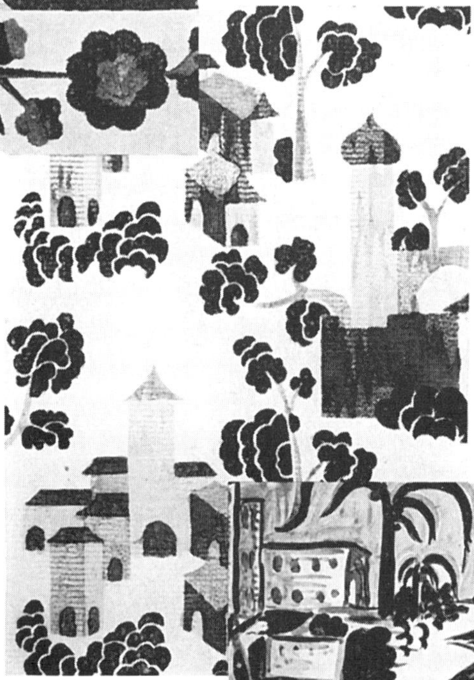

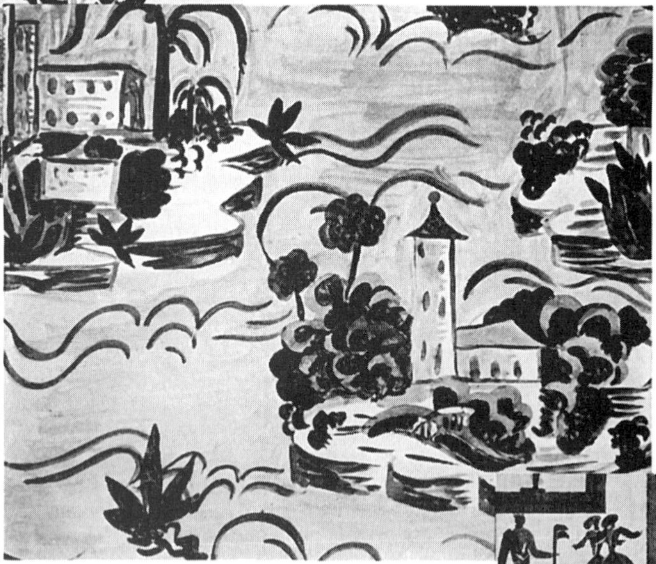

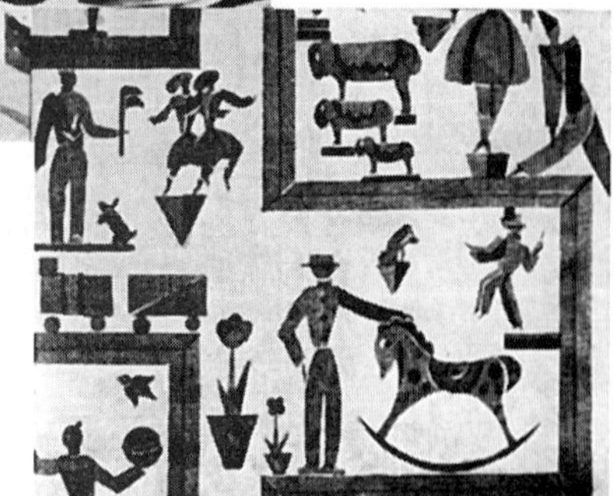

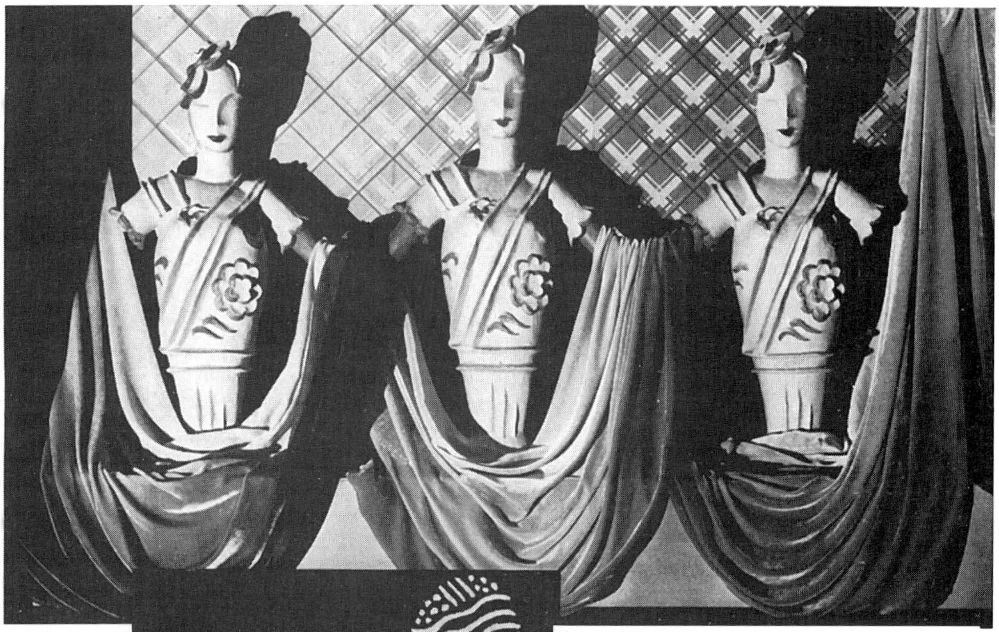

A trio of papier-mache figures, designed for use in displaying silks in shop windows or cases. The figures may be used individually, or as a pair. In white and terra cotta colors.

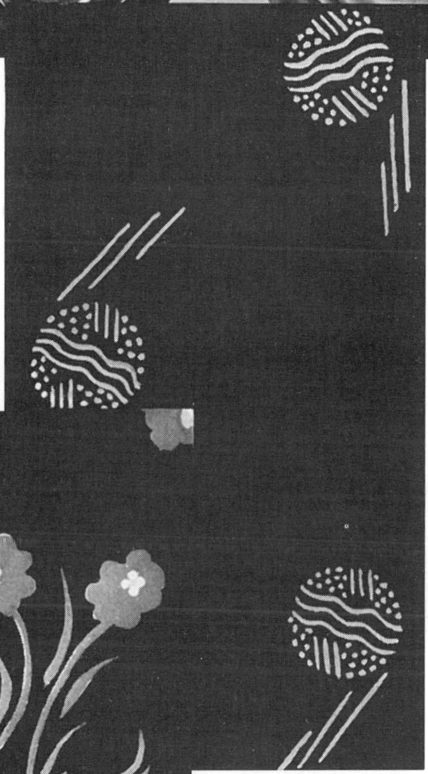

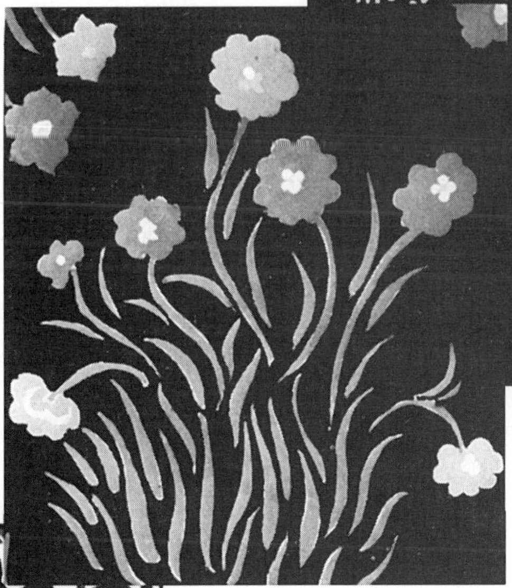

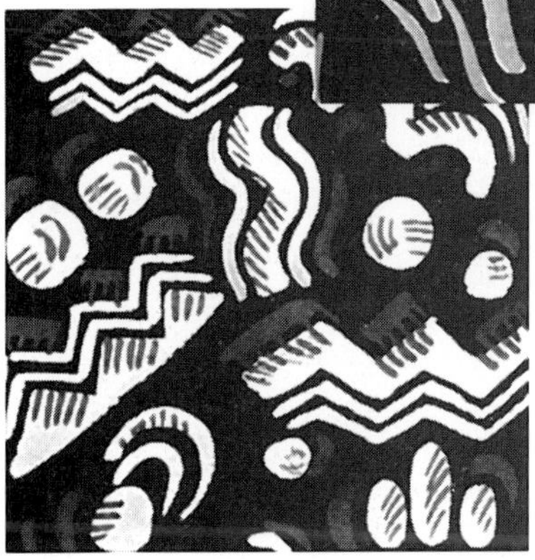

Designs for dress silks. The first utilizes white on black, the second employs a rose and beige design on dark green ground, and the last expresses geometric motifs in white and grey on a black ground.

These designs all made for Contempora, Inc.

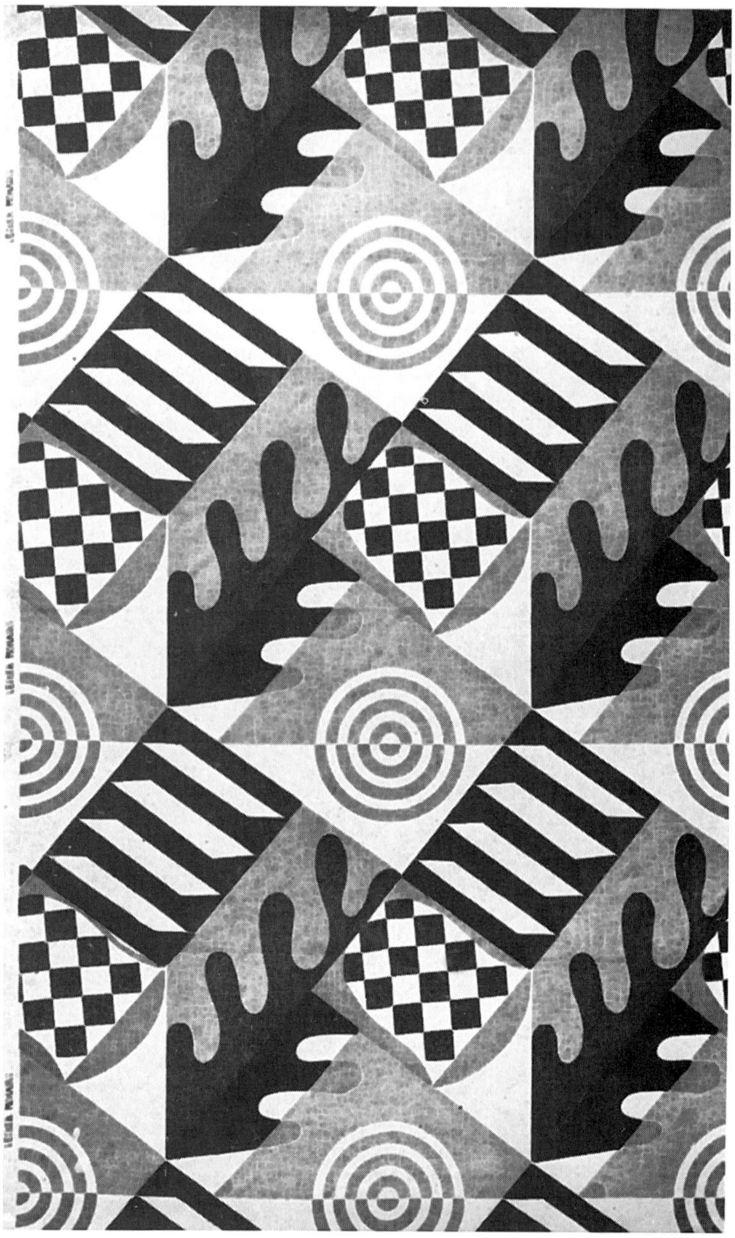

**I L O N K A K A R A S Z — "Oak Leaves"**
Mohair fabric for Lesher-Whitman Co.

**D O N A L D D E S K E Y**
Permatex Lustersheen. Pattern in yellow, green and orange.

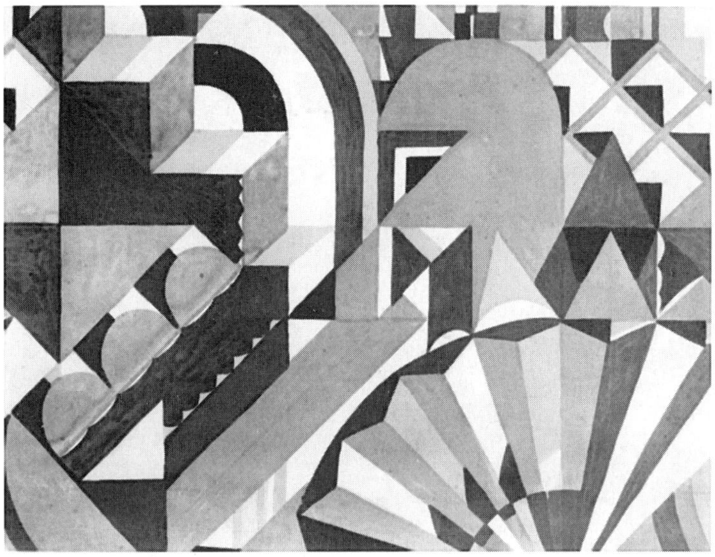

E L L E N M . K E R N
Original design for painted linen.

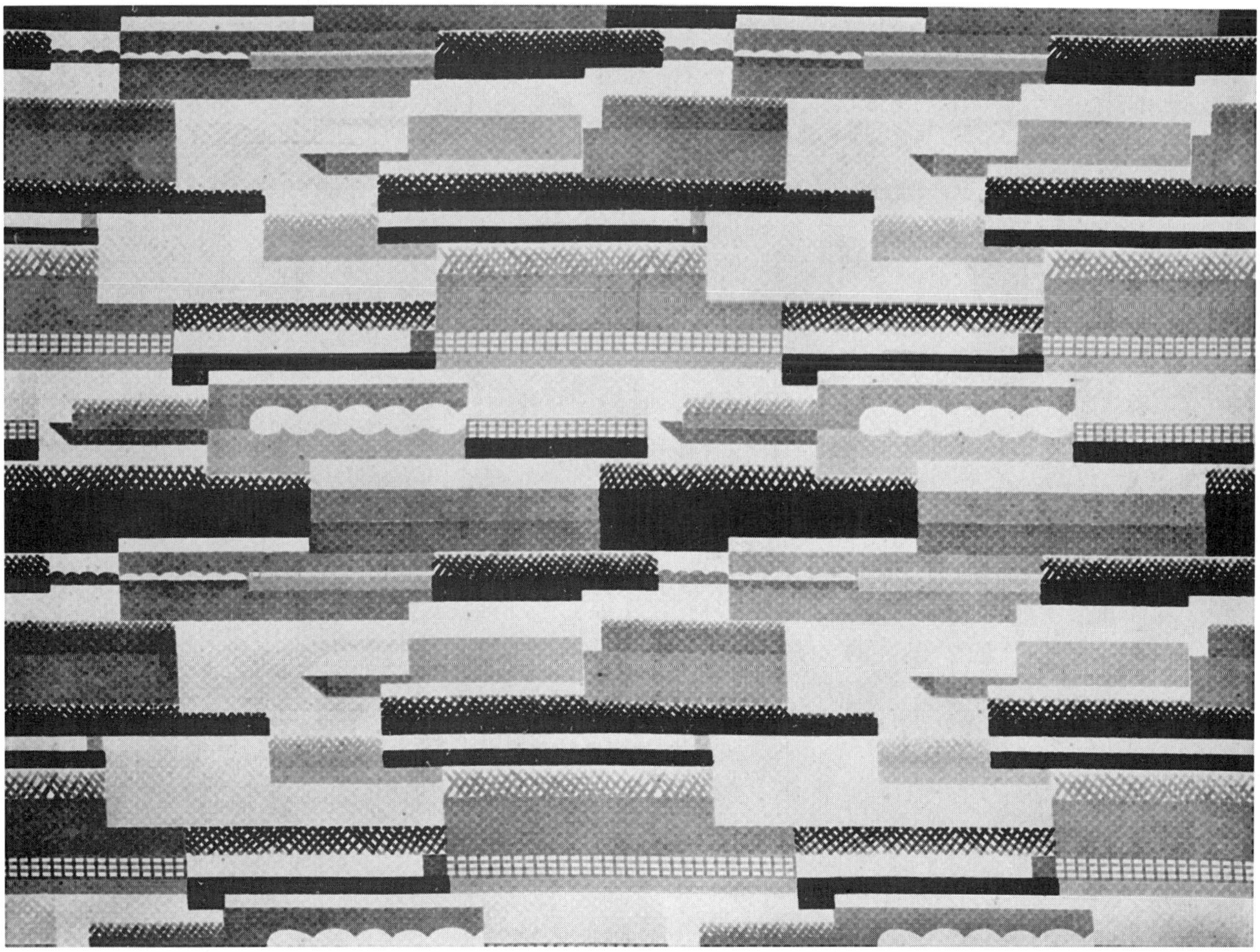

I L O N K A K A R A S Z
Mohair fabric for Lesher-Whitman Co.

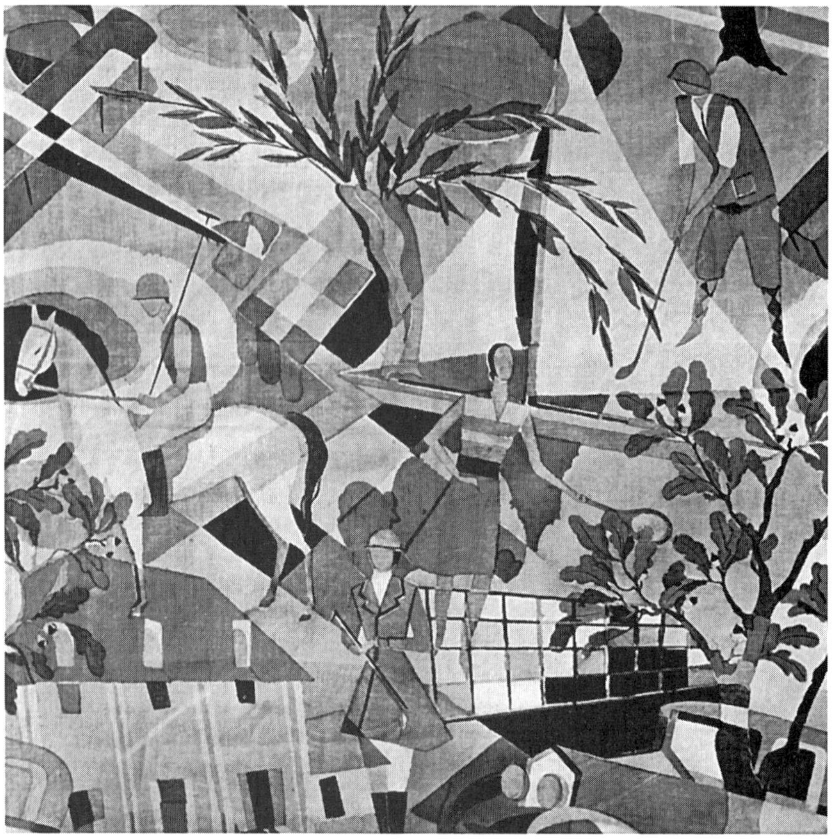

**A L I C E   D O N A L D S O N**

**Hand-blocked linen printed in twelve colors for Derivale Linen Co.**

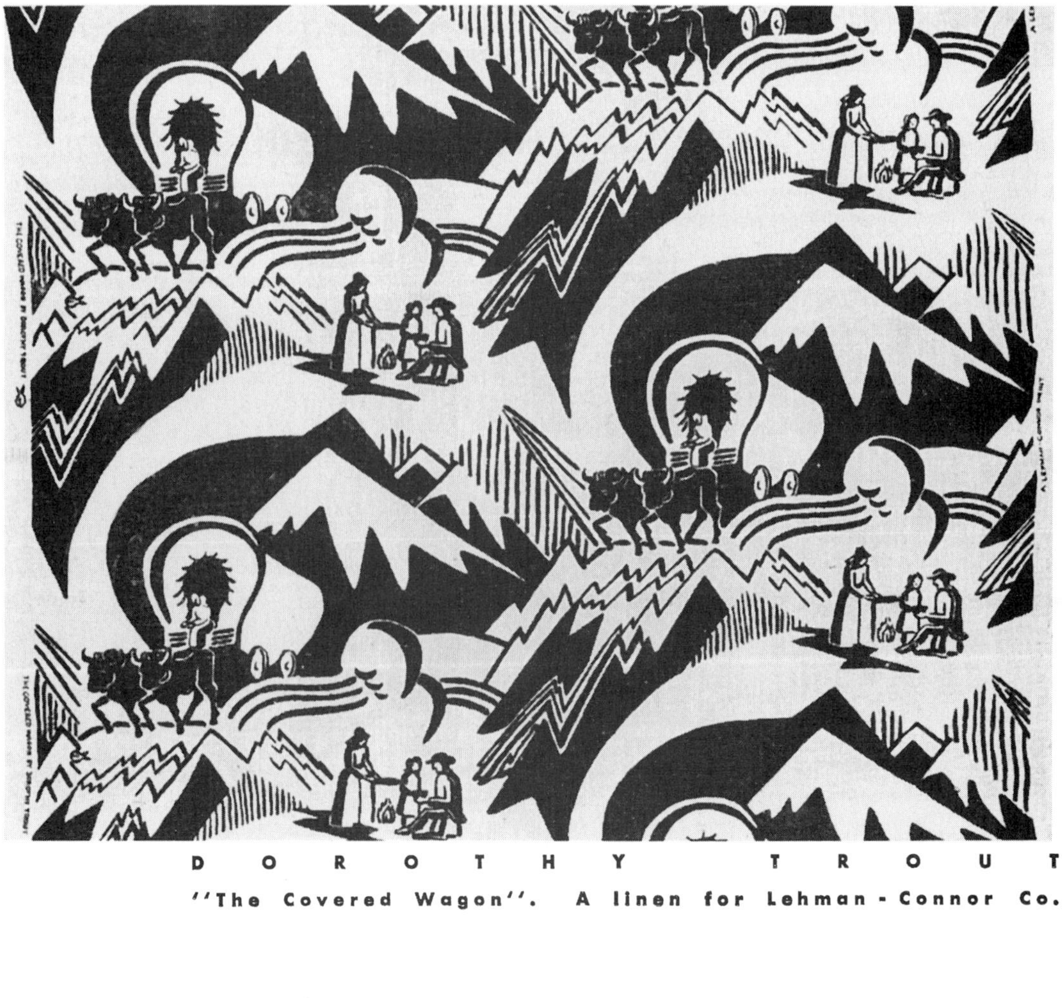

**D O R O T H Y   T R O U T**

**''The Covered Wagon''. A linen for Lehman - Connor Co.**

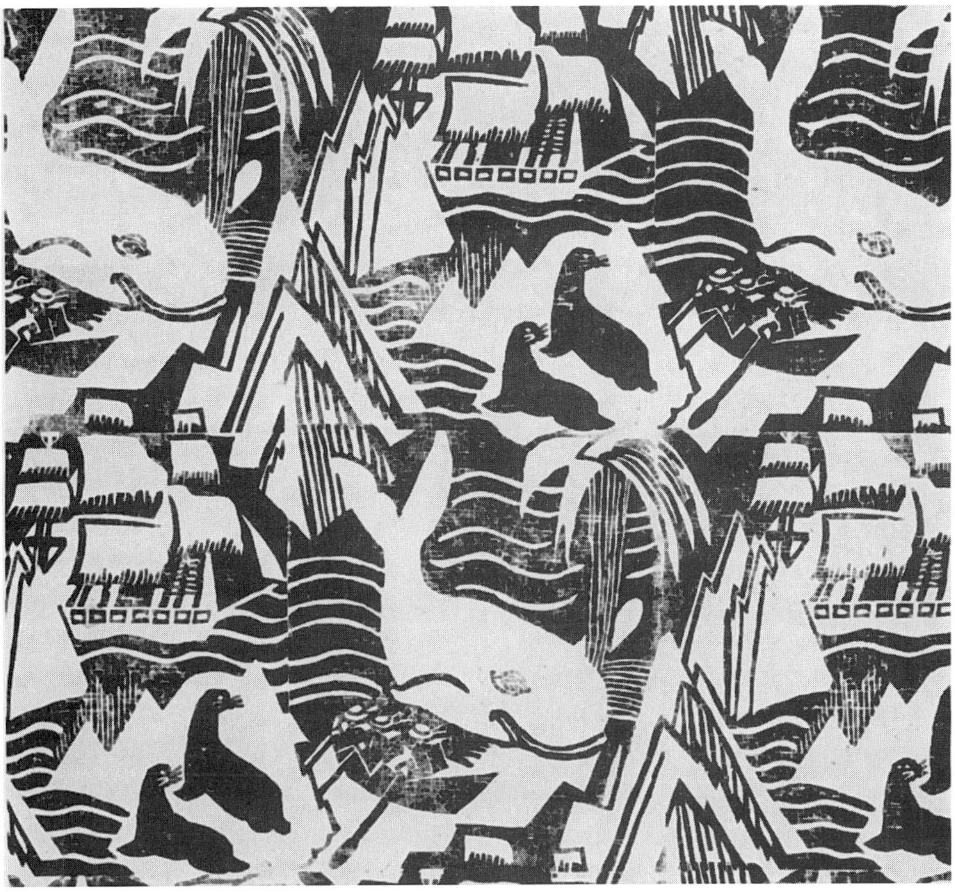

DOROTHY TROUT

''Moby Dick''. A print in blue, green or black on natural linen. Made by Robert McBratney Co.

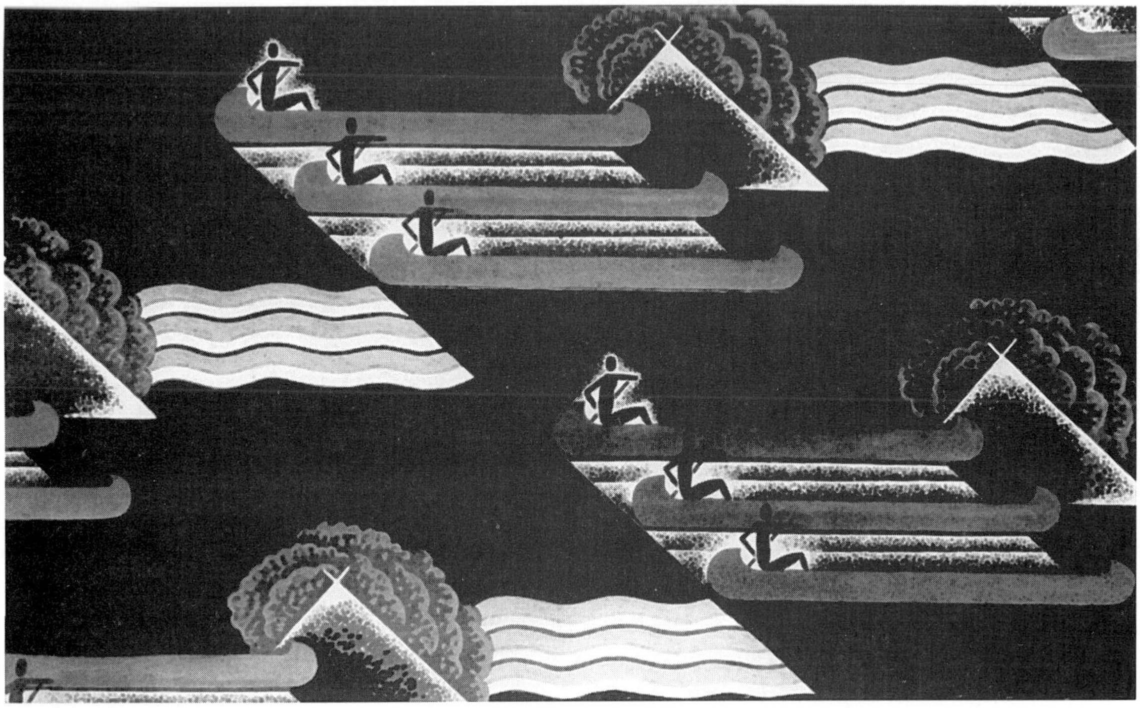

ROBERT L. LEONARD

Printed textile for outdoor furniture made for Shott Mfg. Co.

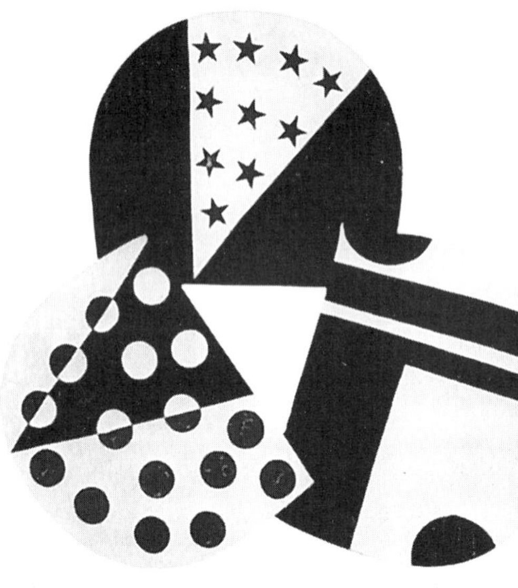

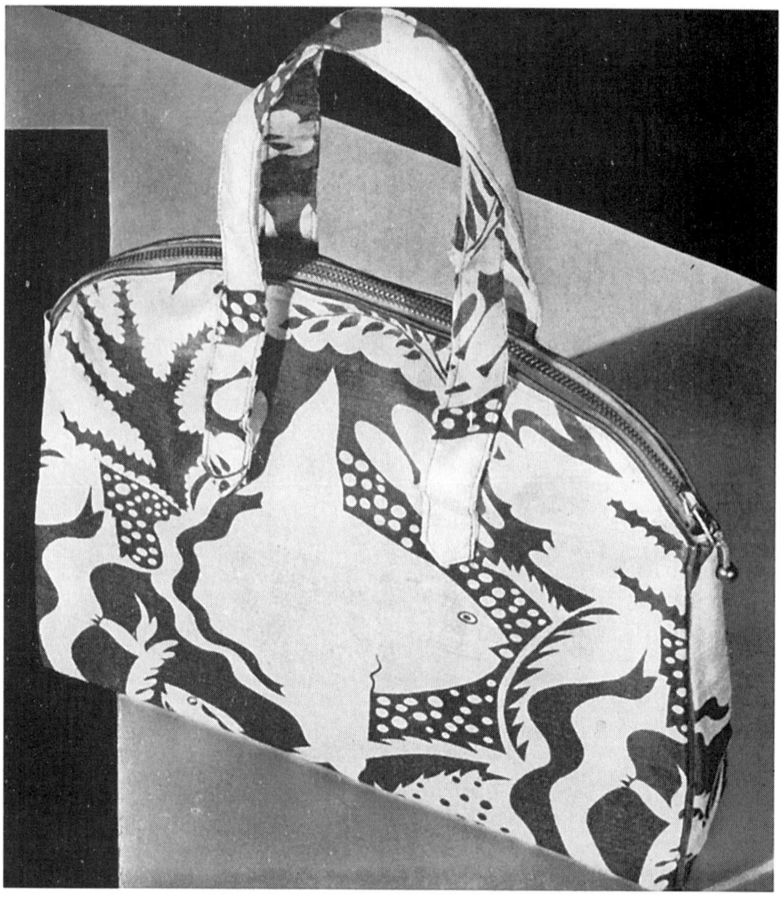

MARGUERITA MERGENTIME

A group of three bathing caps and a beach bag designed for I. B. Kleinert Rubber Co.

Green and white Shantung pattern made for Cohn—Hall—Marx & Co.

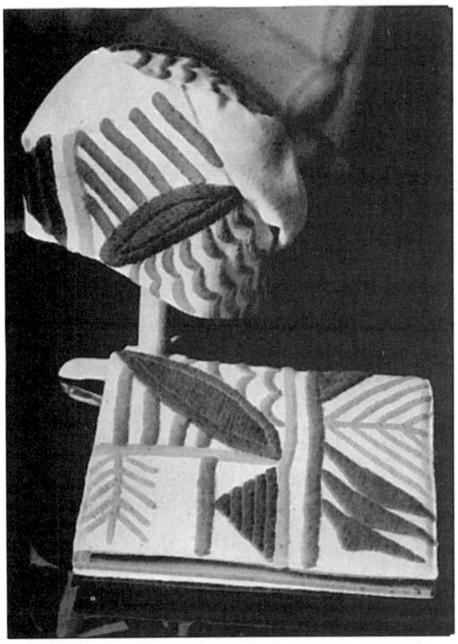

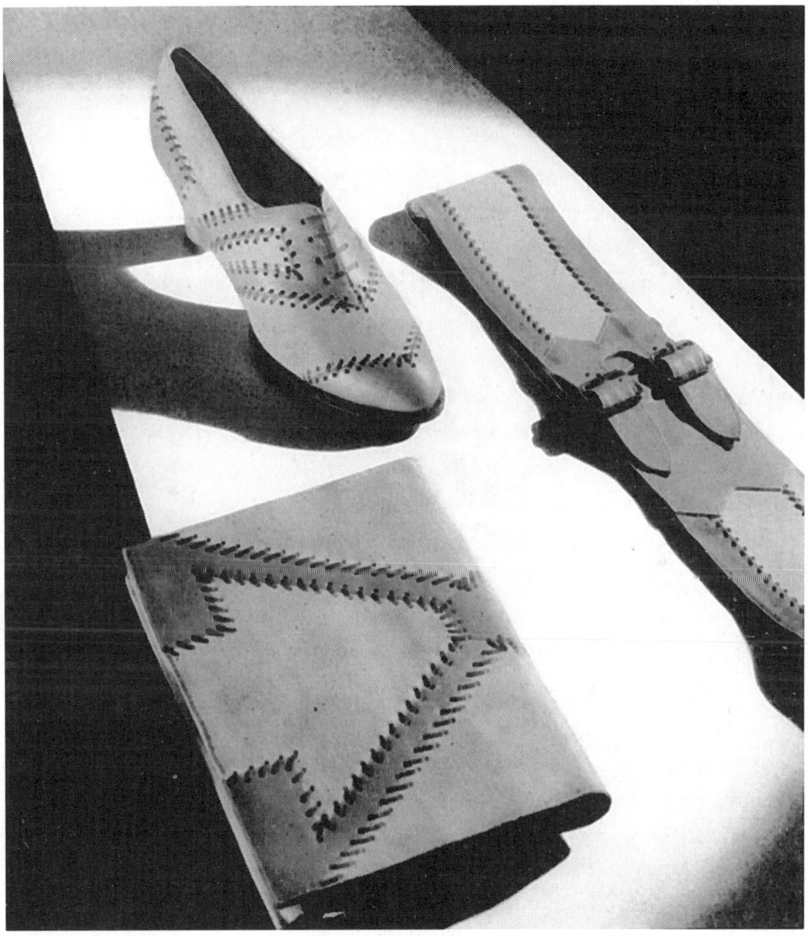

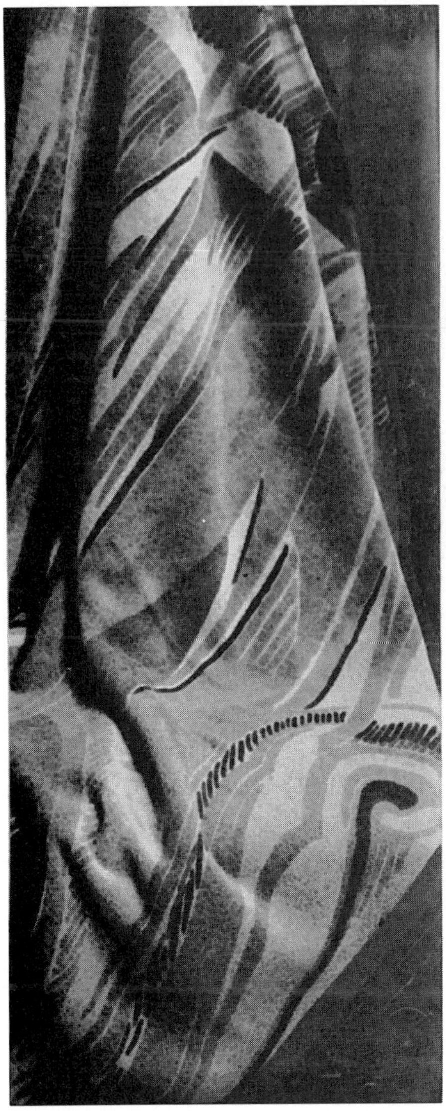

M A R I S K A K A R A S Z
Ensemble in wool embroidered flannel — Color scheme, blue, white and red.

M A R Y B E N D E L A R I
Ensemble in suede trimmed with calfskin.

E L L E N M . K E R N
Deep-pile plush motor robe made by L. C. Chase & Co.

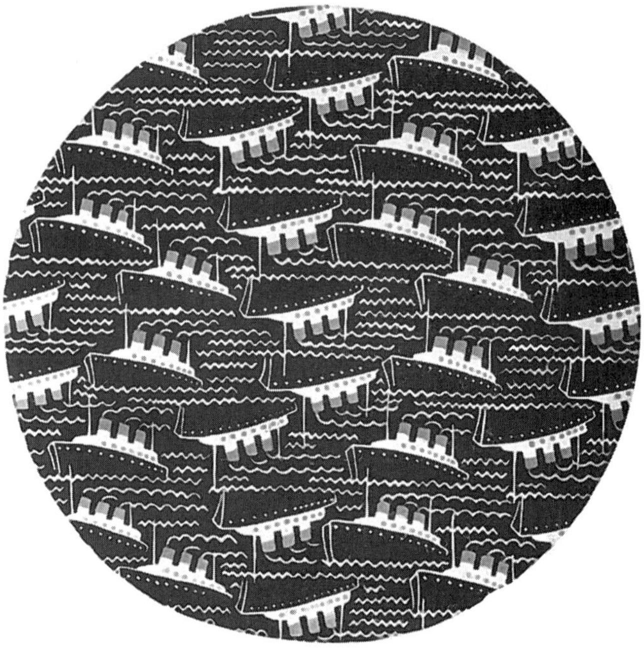

R O B E R T  S C H E Y
Textile Print "Boats".

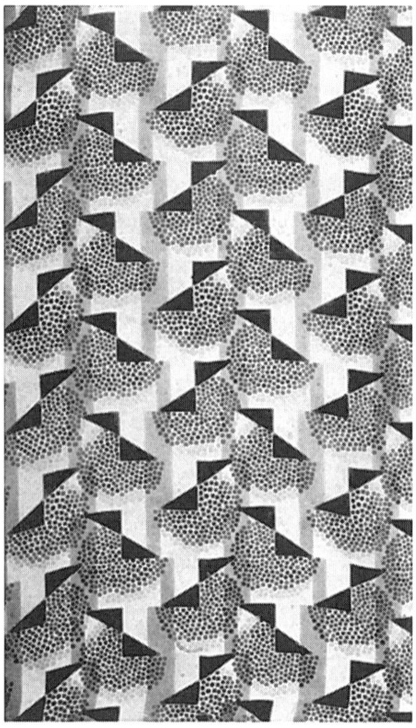

T E R E S A  K I L H A M
Dress material for Galey, Lord, Inc.

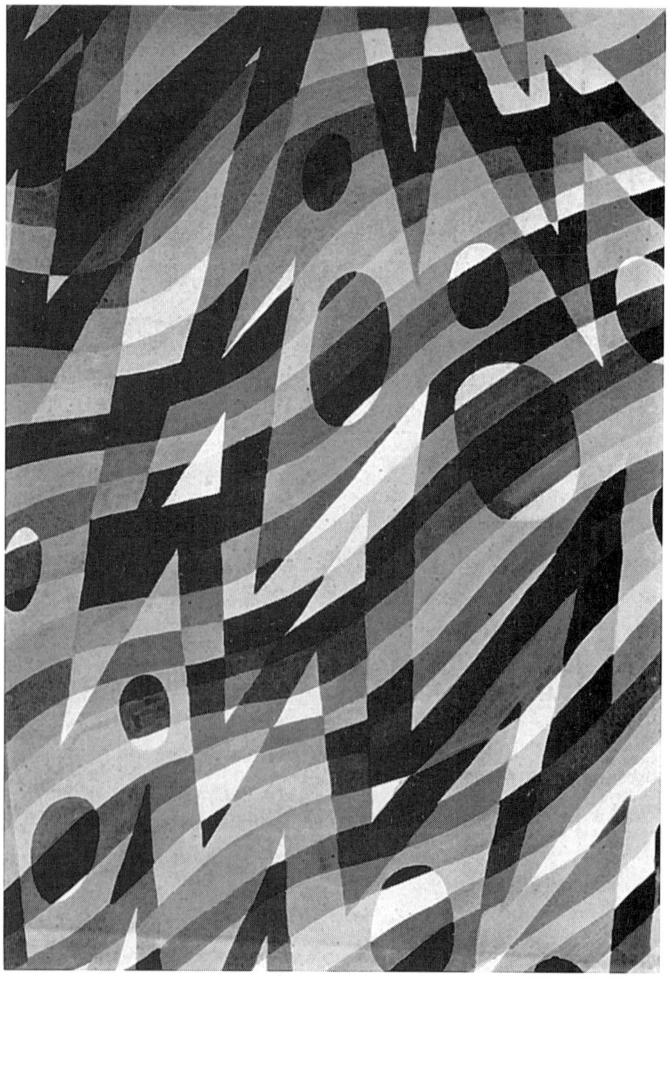

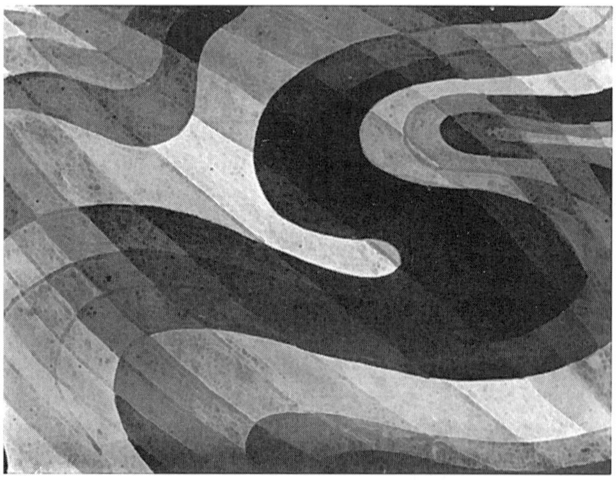

H E N R I E T T E  R E I S S
"The Wave"—Design for silk print.
Chiffon design for Haas Bros.

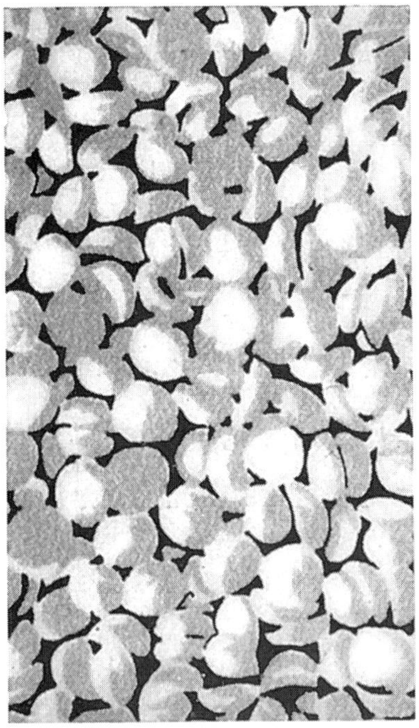

KNEELAND L. GREEN
''Asperin'' silk print.

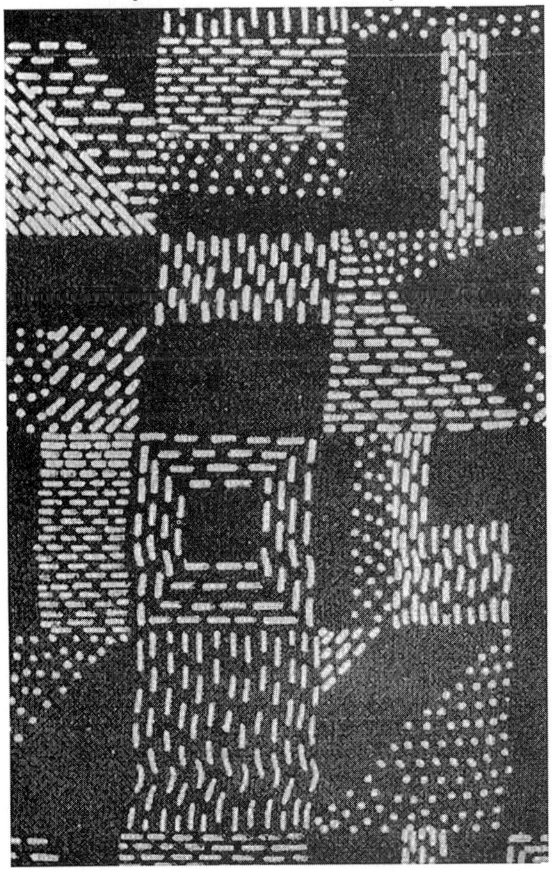

JENNIE GREENE
Wool fabric for J. A. Migel.

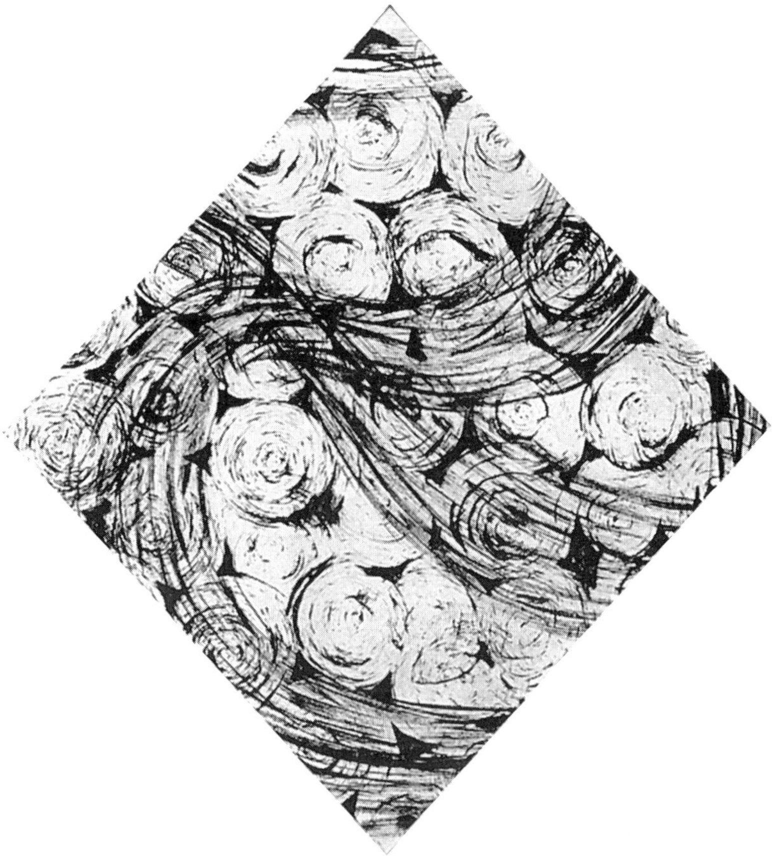

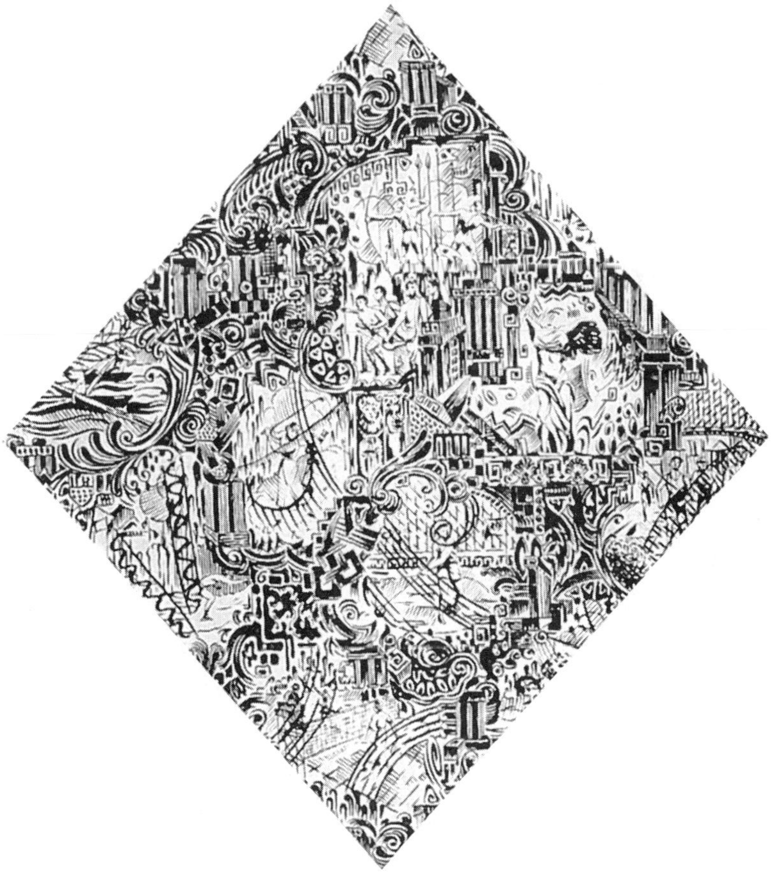

ROBERT SCHEY
Original designs for printed fabrics.

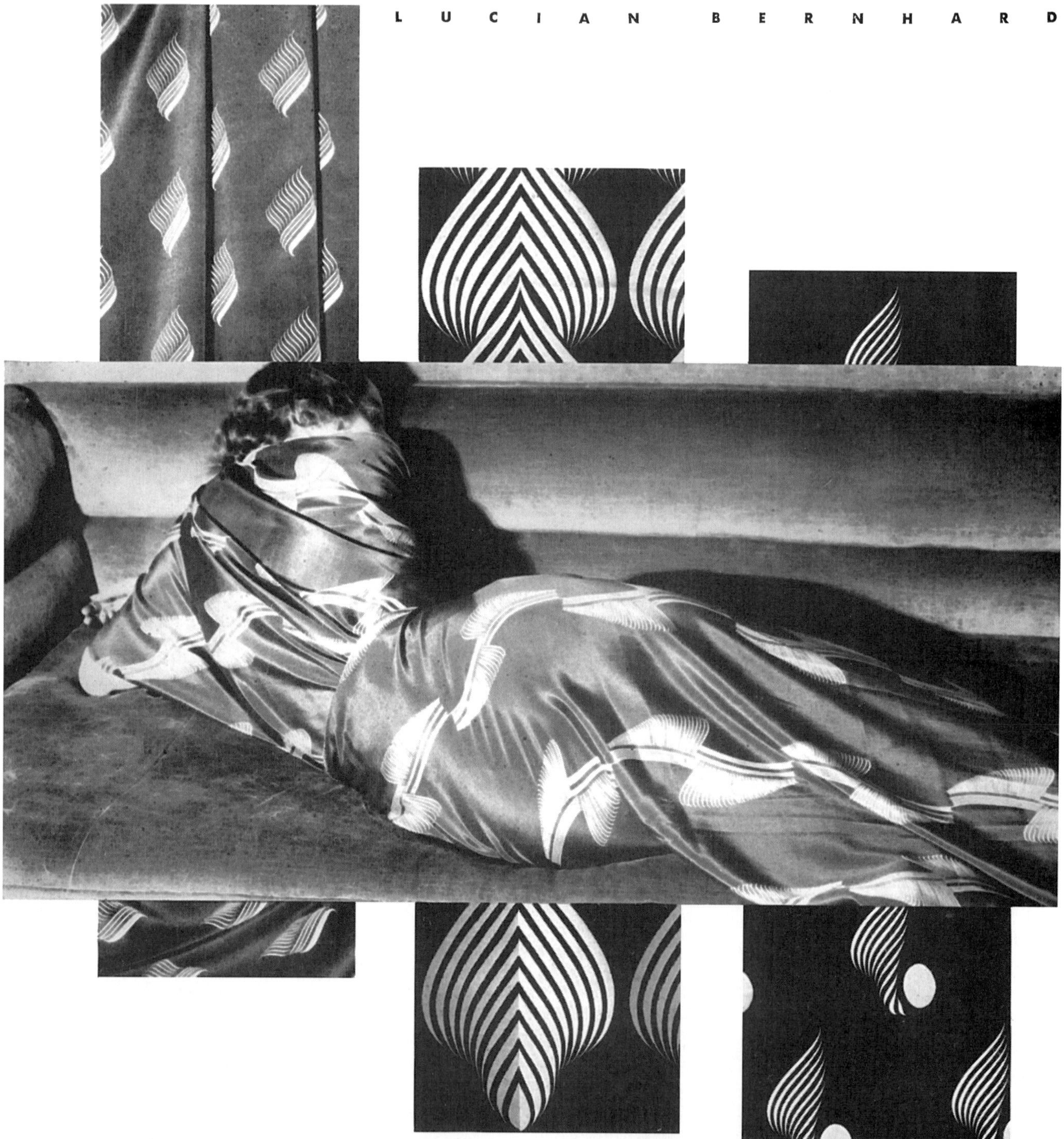

**"Penstroke Silk Design"—A printed crepe showing the effect when made into a costume. The pattern is white on navy, red, or black. Designed for Contempora, Inc.**

# N E W M A T E R I A L S

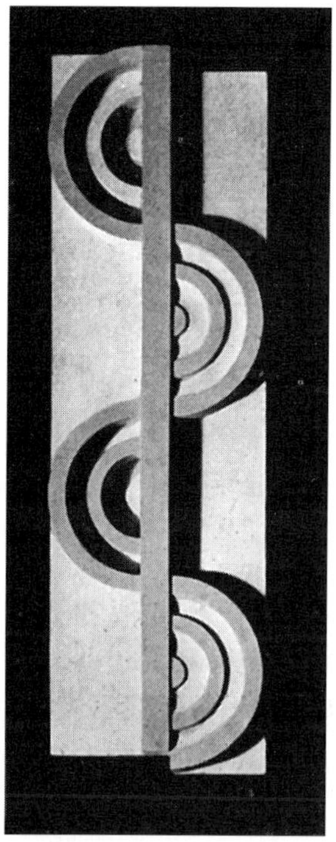

n e w m e t h o d s

n e w m a t e r i a l s

L E E S I M O N S O N

Modern design as applied to the decoration of interiors—particularly the refurnishing and refurbishing of homes—faces a perennial crisis. Its ideas are modern. The processes of fabrication on which it relies are not in the least modern but a survival of the handicraft processes of the centuries which ante-date modernity—i. e. the machine age. Much modern architecture suffers from the same disability. Any skyscraper during its construction presents a graphic and ironic contrast between modern and medieval technique: the steel core shoots skyward with speed and precision. Then for months progress is retarded while armies of workmen paste layers of brick or stone on its surface and manicure its interior with successive coats of plaster stroked with trowels which are finally slicked off with successive layers of paint. But because architects use in quantity materials that can be standardized this dis-unity is not permanent. It is already being done away with; the first experiments have been made. The surfaces of our buildings, of assembled units of glass, steel and concrete, will presently be fundamentally related to their structure. But unlike architects, interior designers in attempting to create new forms, cannot evolve their patterns to any such extent by the process of repeating standardized units on a large scale. Their ideas remain tentative and experimental, suited to individual tastes and personal needs. The fewest offer any present prospect of distribution wide enough to warrant a manufacturer installing $50,000 worth of new machines or dies necessary to reduce the unit price of a new design.

In consequence this so-called new movement in the applied arts is deprived of any possibility of vital and widespread growth. It remains an occasional luxury for the upper classes. As a movement it resolutely and successfully refuses to echo or copy the traditional forms and ornaments of the 15th, 16th, 17th and 18th centuries. But it refuses just as resolutely to find any other method of having most of its designs executed except by the handicraft methods of plasterers, cabinet-makers and metal workers of the 15th, 16th, 17th and 18th centuries. These workmen are daily becoming rarer in an era of mass production. Their wages remain persistently high. In consequence, the cost of a house or apartment furnished in the "modern manner" remains prohibitive for all but the very rich.

The simplicity of modern design defeats its own purpose. Mouldings, cornices, turnings, carving and any amount of applied filigree ornament have been eliminated in vain. A room panelled in flat veneer requires such an amount of skilled hand-labor, in fitting, gluing, shellacking, rubbing and polishing before it is ready to be fitted into place, that the cost is staggering. The cost of the wood itself, even the rarest, is an almost negligible fraction of the total expense involved. And when the fitting and installation on the job are added, the total cost is apalling to any designer who looks forward to a wide acceptance of modern design during his lifetime. The addition of a few flat metal mouldings is often just as costly, if not more so, than elaborately carved Renaissance or Georgian ornament. An unornamented metal lighting fixture can be more expensive than an antique Chinese bowl wired to hold a lamp shade.

My feeling that modern design will be stultified if it is limited to the upper classes is not based on sociological grounds. I have no inherent prejudice against plutocrats and millionaires. They are, as masters of our raw materials, fuel, water-power, credit and communication, undoubtedly predatory and exact tribute more successfully than any previous working alliance among the bandits, robber barons, pirates and war lords of history. But our democracy has proved to be so congenitally incapable of initiative and intelligent planning in almost every activity affecting the ultimate welfare of a community, that disinterested and successful attempts to foster the progress of the arts and sciences are usually the result of the individual benefactions of a merchant prince or a captain of industry. Had we expropriated every millionaire a generation ago we would probably have destroyed in embryo the few independent journals of opinion, important collections of modern painting, our best experimental schools and the most effective agencies for social research which we now possess, and probably half the progress of medical research as well. Nevertheless, the plutocrats who make so much modern experiment possible tend to demand historic patterns in their personal surroundings. Because their position as a ruling class is not an acknowledged and official one, they derive satisfaction and re-assurance from the feudal magnificence to be achieved by copying the domestic backgrounds of the acknowledged ruling classes of previous centuries. They live in reconstructions of baronial halls, manor houses, castles, chateaux and villas of Tudor and Georgian landed nobility, Spanish grandees and Italian princes of the Renaissance, Norman barons of mediavel France or the court of Le Roi Soleil. They sustain the market for antiques and stimulate the reproduction of antiques. They will remain, I think, effective patrons of almost everything but modern interior design except as an occasional diversion.

Meanwhile, there are thousands of potential patrons who crave and need the simplicity of modern design, but who cannot afford it: lawyers, doctors, authors, professors, journalists, engineers, scientists, artists, the successful professional classes and the huge non-professional, successful and educated middle classes, who are being forced to live and work in smaller and smaller rooms whether in apartments, suburban houses, or garden cities. A millionaire can afford to have three or four tabourets, originally meant to hold tankards of beer or an unbuckled rapier, as end tables in his drawing room and as many servants, if necessary, to keep them in order. The apartment dweller appreciates the adroit compactness of a modern table which will hold his pipes, cigarettes, ash receivers, magazines, and cocktail glasses. At Lord & Taylor's exhibition a few years ago, I remember seeing a desk by a well-known French designer which consisted of two long shelves in the form of an L. It was not a desk for a high-powered exectuive and his secretary either at home, or in an office. It was, however, an almost perfect arrangement for an author or journalist, who could keep within easy reach at his left elbow reference books, clippings and successive revisions of manuscript and still have ample working space in front of him for pen or typewriter. But the price, between four and five hundred dollars as I recall it, limited the desk to precisely the persons who would find no real use for it. The inventory, if space permitted, could be continued to include any object in daily use.

The first step out of this impasse, is, I believe, the exploitation of new methods and new materials. It is absurd that we must mess around interiors with wet plaster and wet paint waiting for this to set and that to dry. It is equally absurd to construct furniture by the process of gluing together veneers used by the ebenistes of the court of Louis the XIV. Considering the present state of technical research, there is no reason why we cannot evolve a composition wall material supplied in standard sheets of various sizes, in itself fireproof and an adequate insulation against sound, heat and moisture, that can be quickly and easily applied to the bare brick or lathe walls of a room, manufactured in a wide variety of textures and an equally wide and subtle range of color infused in the process of manufacture itself according to an accurate and standardized color chart such as Ridgeways now used by horticulturalists. The only additional work on the job of rapidly fitting the material which should be made to cut almost as easily as cheese, would be sealing the joints by a plastic form of the same composition colored to match with chemical accuracy at the factory. Similar composition materials are needed for furniture, incapable of warping, as easy to cut as white pine, not subject to scaling or splitting so as to give accurate joints, again with a wide variety of color and texture made part of the material itself by the process of manufacture, with nothing to be done by way of finish but wiping with a damp rag. Lighting fixtures should be capable of being assembled of units of glass and colored metals, the metals again to be colored, as glass is now, in the process of manufacture. Floor materials should be developed as easy to cut to any size and lay as linoleum, more beautiful and varied in texture and as easy to keep clean. Only a few uses of composition materials are here suggested but an extensive list can be easily compiled. The trowel, the plane, the paint brush and even the scrubbing brush are obsolete. The modern interior should be more than half complete with the process of manufacture, the labor of assembling and fitting reduced to a minimum.

The idea is not fantastic or Utopian. In 1928 at Frankfort a. M. I visited the factory where 'Bimsplatten' were being turned out for municipal housing projects — sheets of fabricated stone about four inches thick and six by ten feet in size. The base was disintegrated pumice-stone from nearby deposits mixed with a certain proportion of concrete and other binders, cast like concrete in wooden forms by a few unskilled workmen, and baked for twenty-four hours in ovens of different temperatures. At the end of that period they could be stacked and erected forty-eight hours later for the walls of workingmen's houses.

Experiments of this sort are as important for the future of modern design as the evolution of modern design itself. Europe is constantly making them. Until we as a professional class co-operating with engineers and technicians can compete and imitate similar efforts, our "modern movement" will prove abortive. The fact is obscured by our lavish methods of merchandizing and the extravagance of our real-estate speculations, so that the future of modern design seems assured because it is occasionally used to give novelty to the lobby of a hotel or an office building, the sales room of a department store or a beauty shop, part of its excessive cost being written off to advertising and publicity. Possibly modern applied design will have a spectacular career as a well paid vassal to our present extravagant technique of advertising and retail selling. But until it curbs its own extravagance by radical experiments in the use of new materials and new methods of manufacture, its career will not be an important one. It will fail to have any widespread effect in re-forming American taste nor will it become a vital influence in recreating the background of American life.

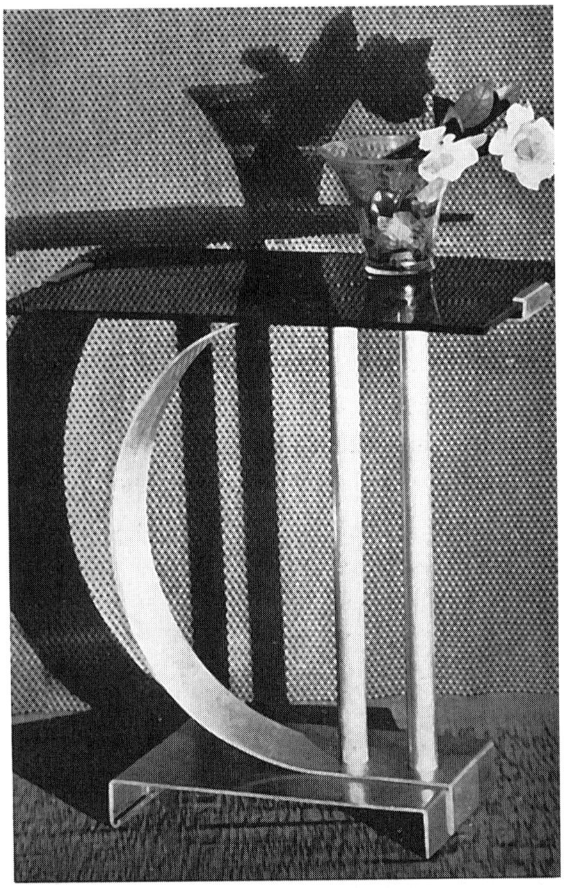

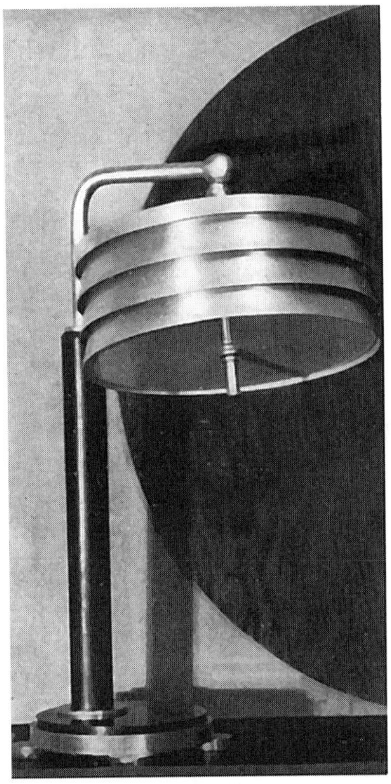

**W A L T E R   V O N   N E S S E N**

**A desk lamp and two occasional tables employing aluminum, formica, plated brass and hard rubber in various combinations.**

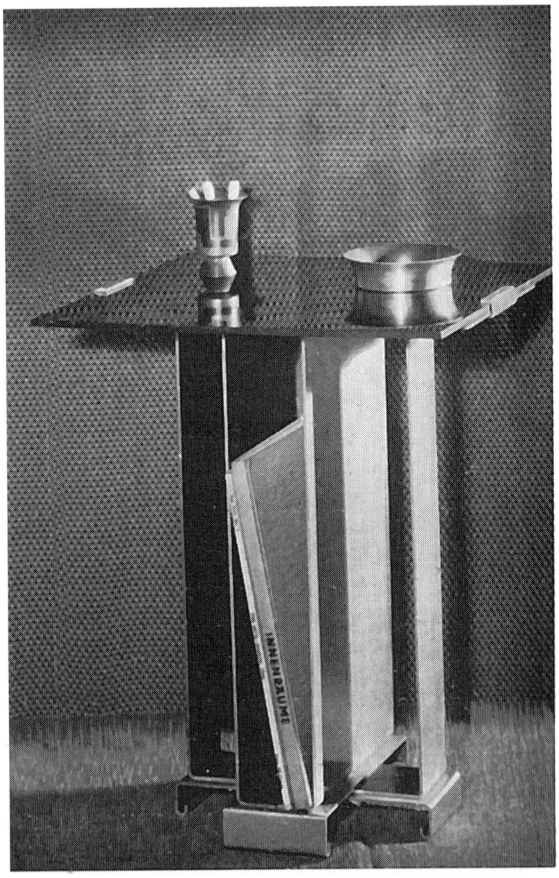

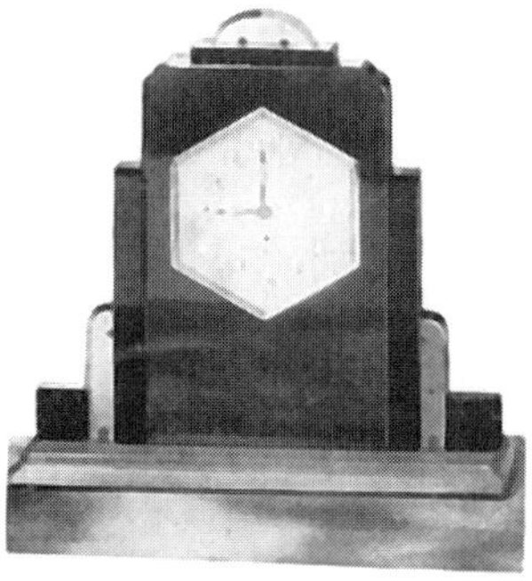

E R I K M A G N U S S E N
Two clocks in rare stone, marble and metal. The lower one made of gray agate.

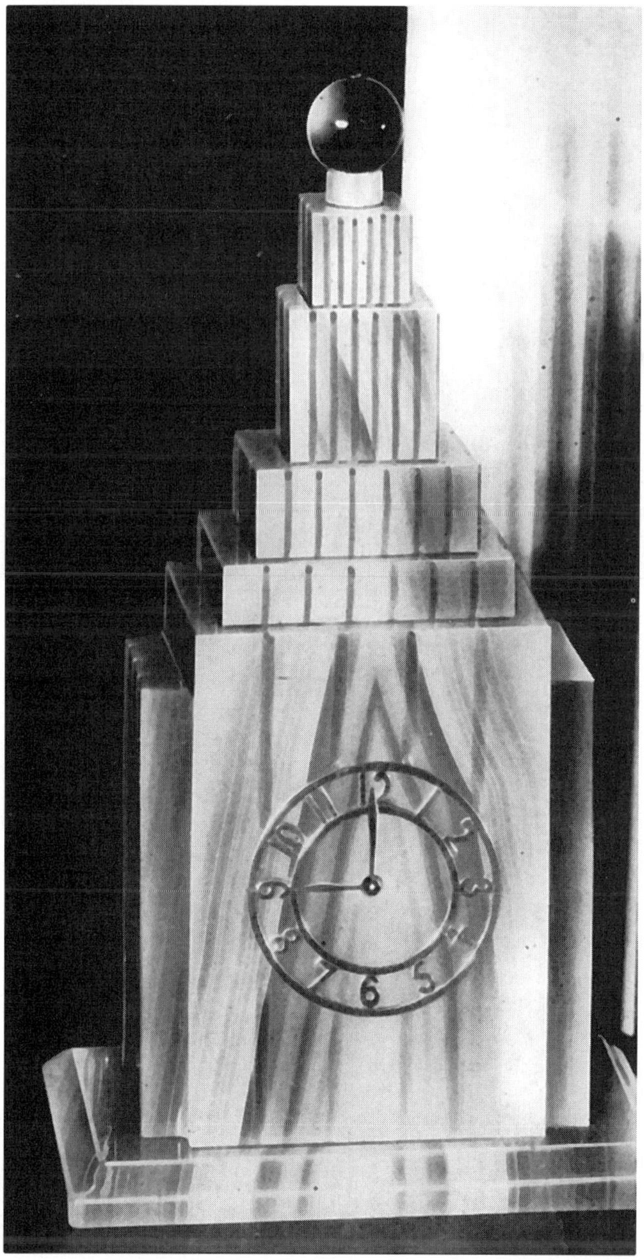

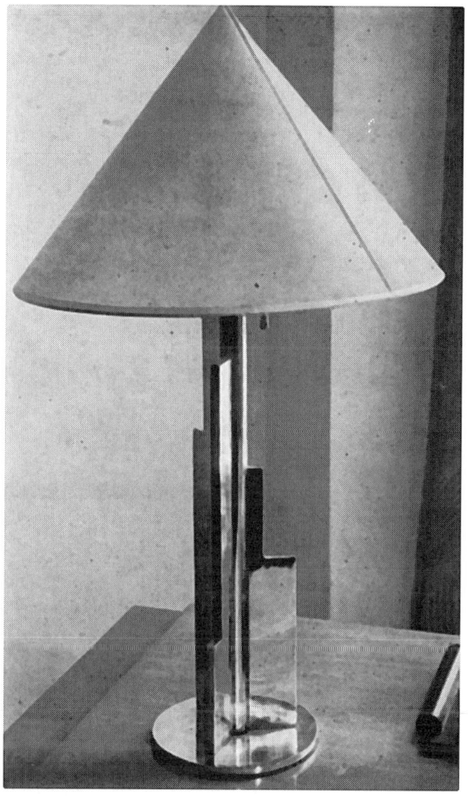

A L E X A N D E R K A C H I N S K Y
A chromium plated desk lamp with parchment shade.

H E R M A N N   R O S S E

Entrance hall of a New York Apartment House. The metal work is cadmium plated. The walls, divided in panels are in four shades of gray as are the marble base boards and terazzo floors.

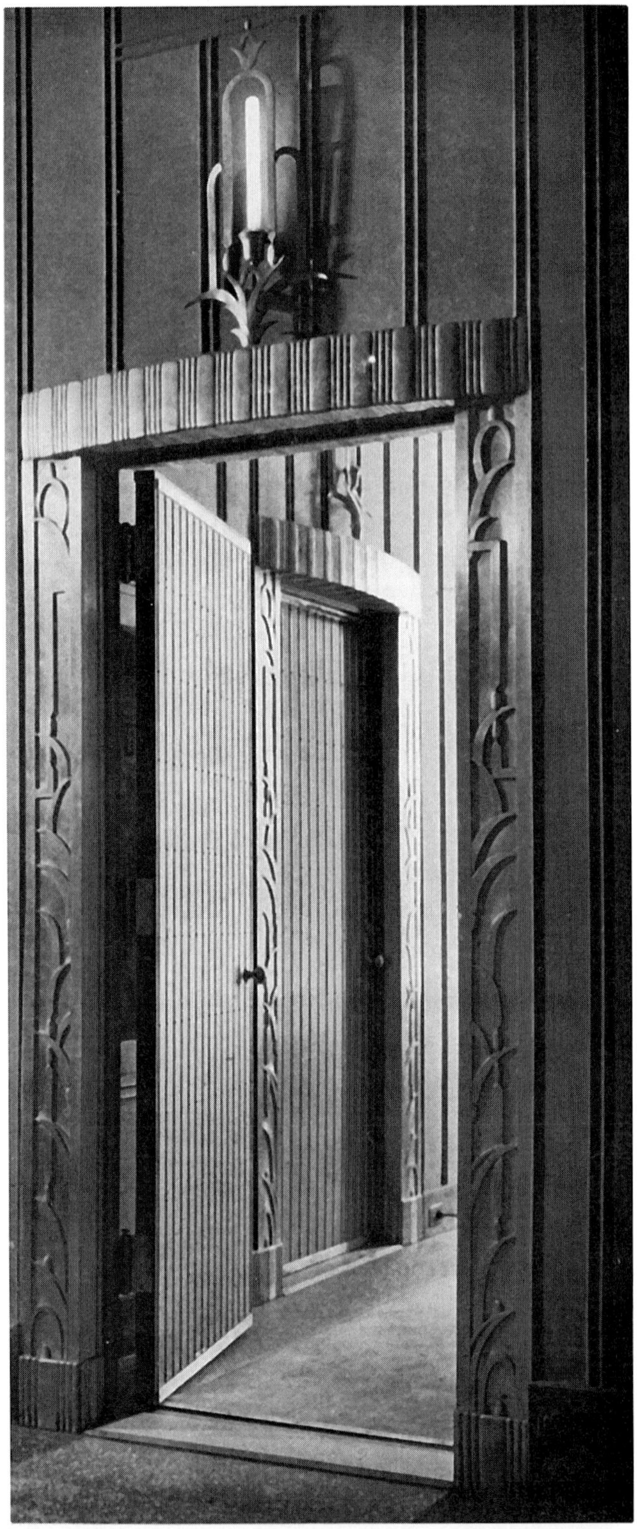

A U S T I N   P U R V E S

Portion of a mosaic garden seat. Executed by Ravenna Mosaics, Inc.

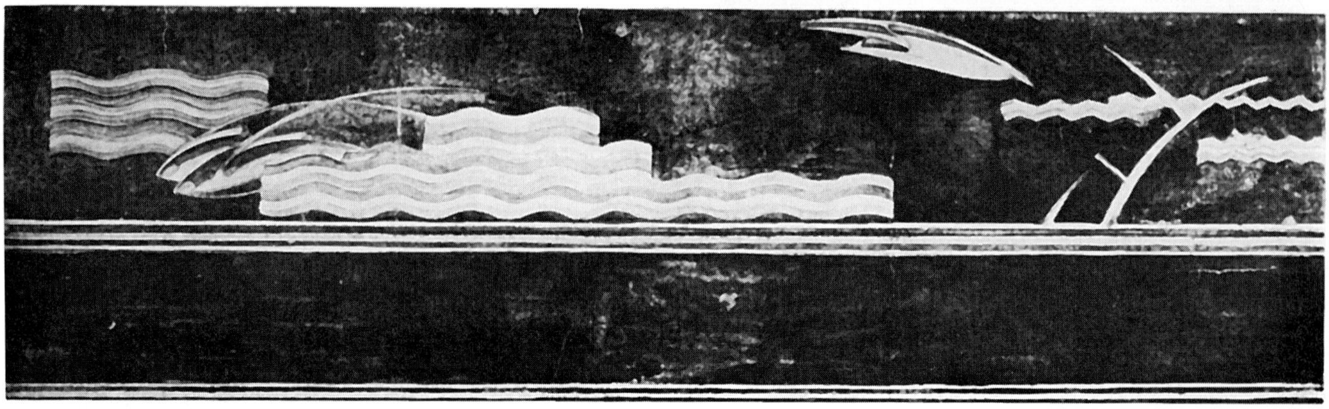

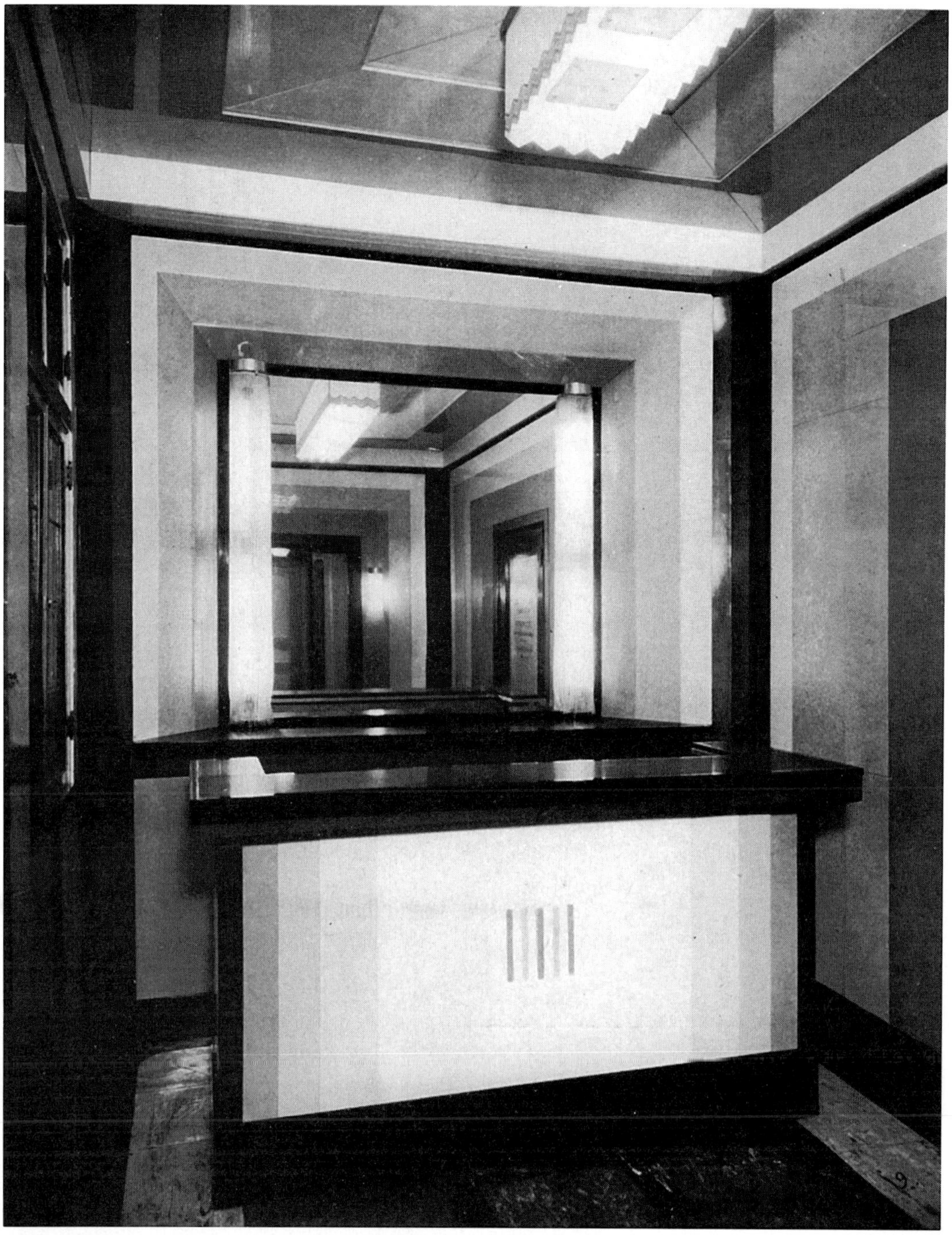

Vestibule for a display room and a grille in vitriolite; a structural opaque glass. Vestibule done in two shades of green, black and ivory. Executed by the Vitriolite Company, Chicago.

F R A N K   S O H N

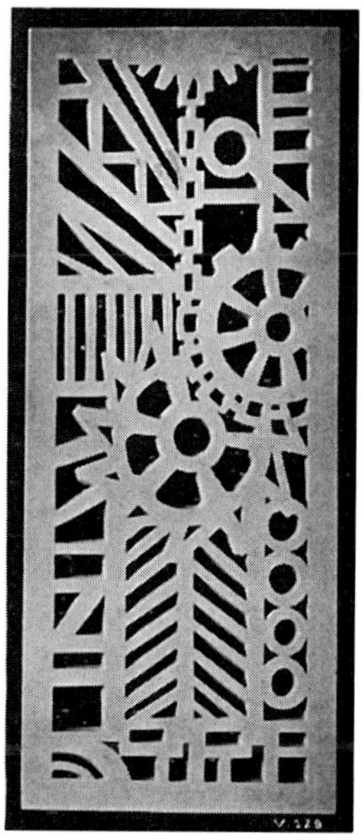

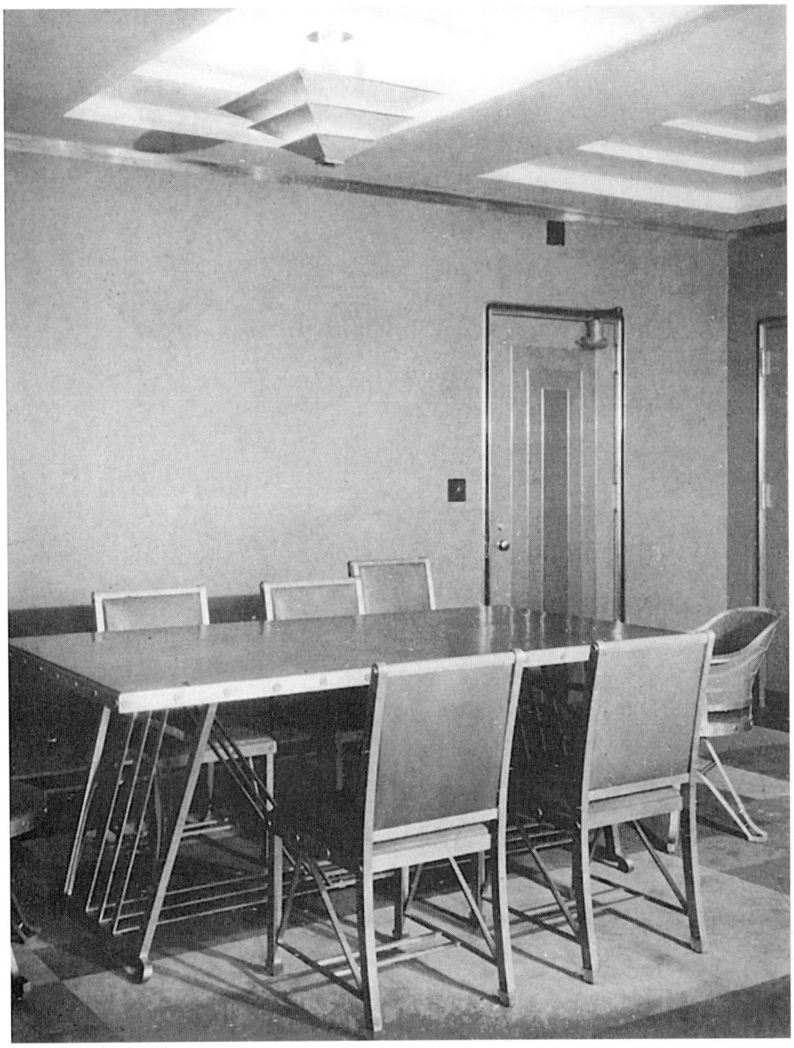

A director's conference room and private office for a firm located in the News building, New York. The furniture is aluminum upholstered in leather. All interior trim done in aluminum. Cork used on floor.

R A Y M O N D   M .   H O O D

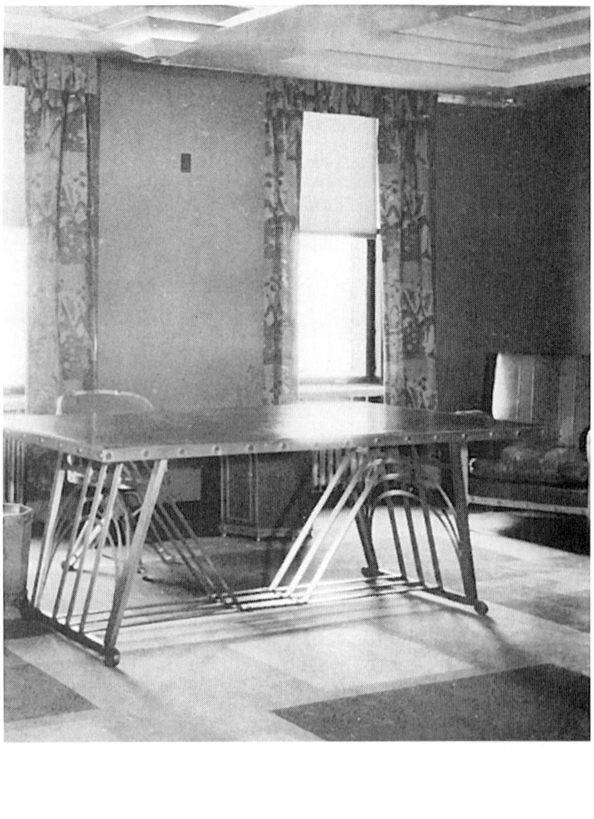

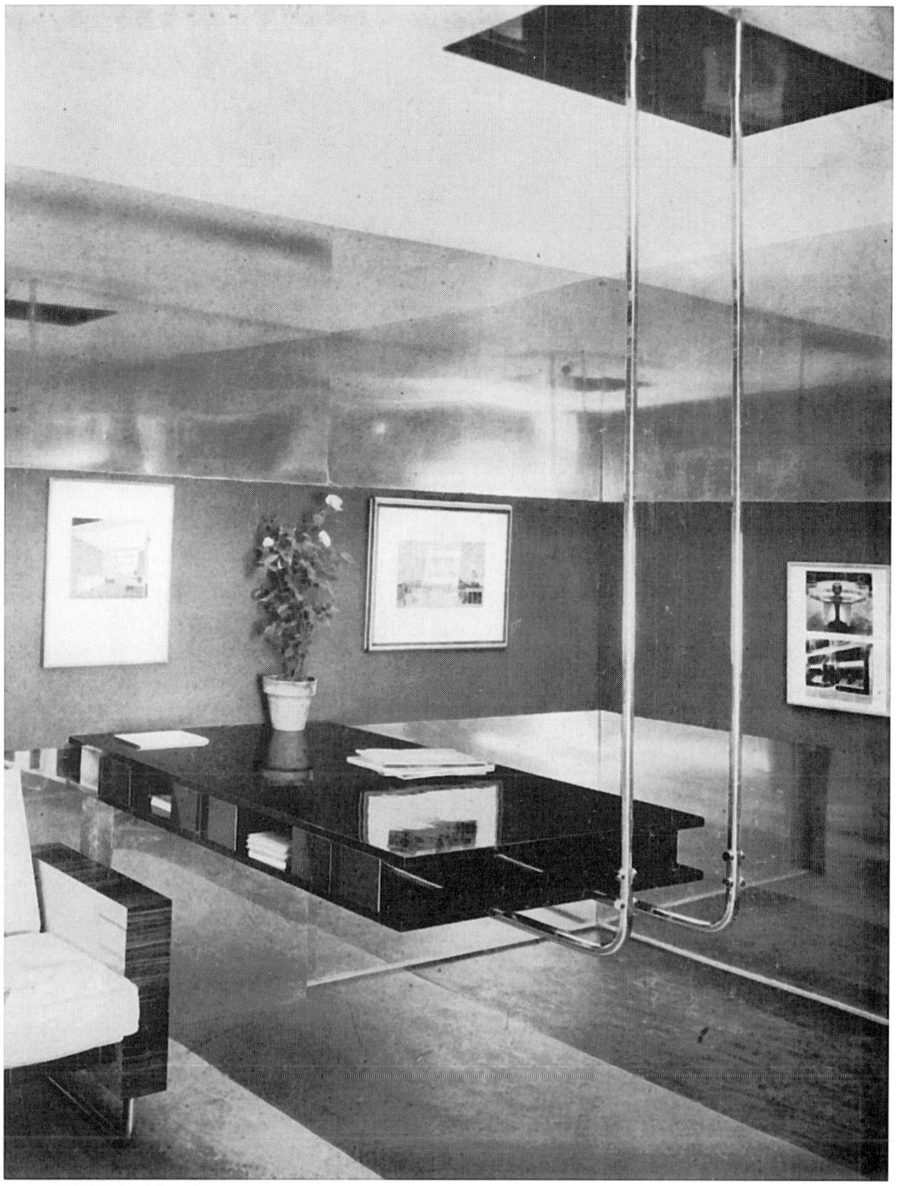

"Flying Desk" made of formica suspended on metal tubing from ceiling. Lighting concealed above metal plate near ceiling. "The Secretary" desk with swivel seat for a stenographer, and stand for telephone.

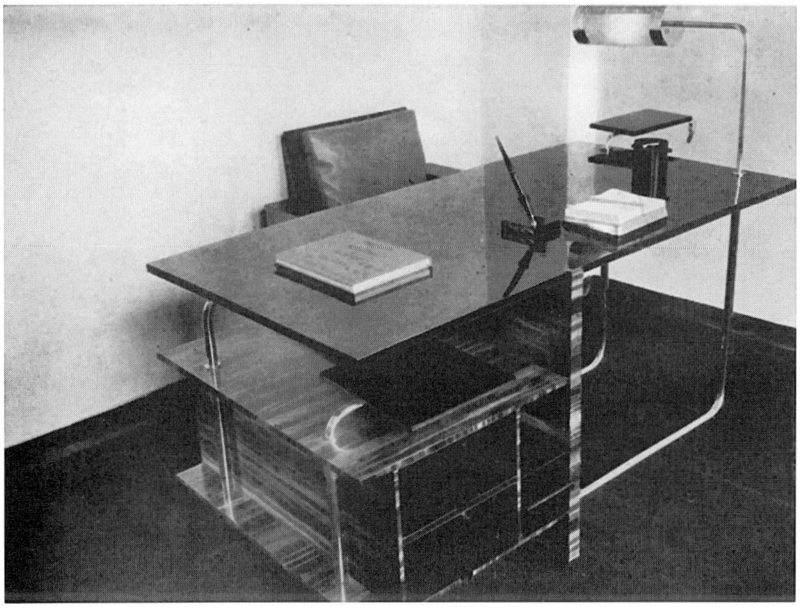

F R E D E R I C K J . K I E S L E R

WALTER VON NESSEN

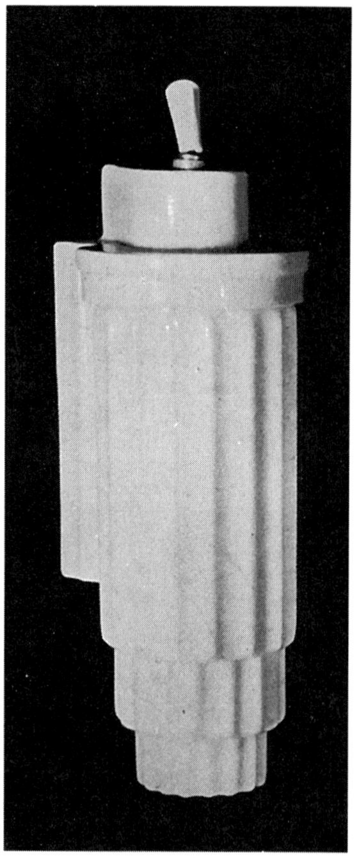

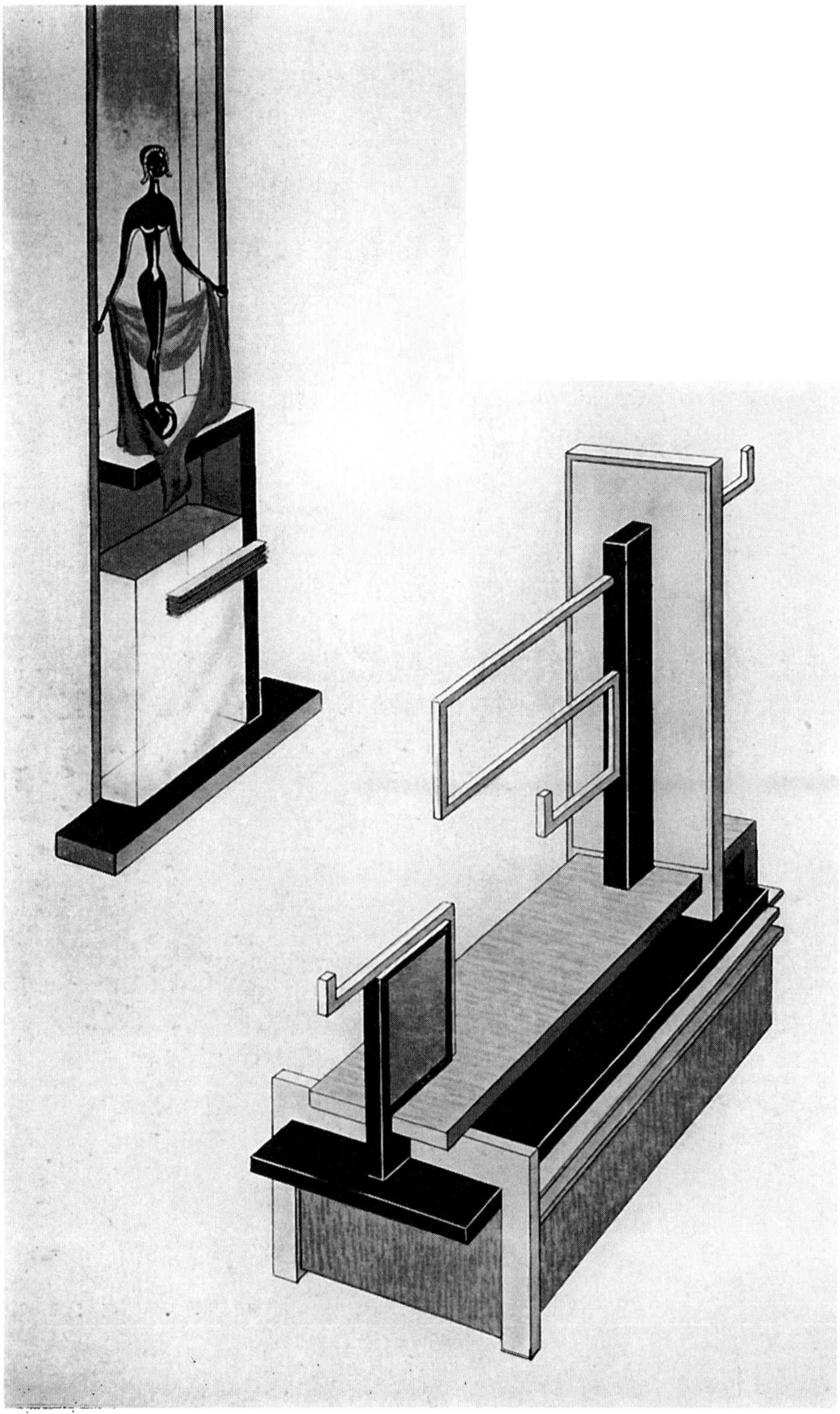

EGMONT H. ARENS

**A combination show case and pedestal supporting a lay figure and a display rack for silks designed for Cheney Bros. The show case is made of ebony, chromium plate and glass. The mannikin is of beaten oxidized copper. Beneath it is the glass case lighted from behind the metal cross members. Behind the frosted glass in the upright member of the rack are lights to illuminate the silks displayed.**

**Courtesy Fashion Coordination Bureau, Inc.**

**Porcelain ceiling and wall bracket lights of Durock vitreous china in white, metal or colored finish made by the Efcolite Co.**

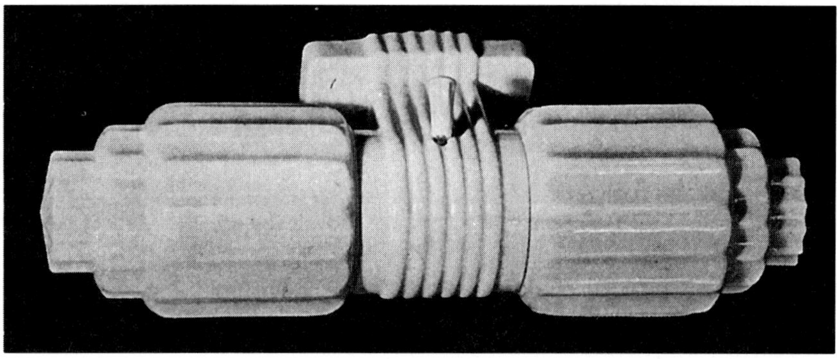

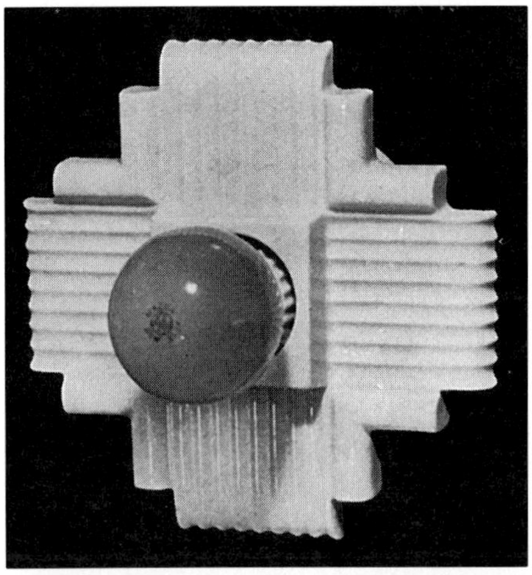

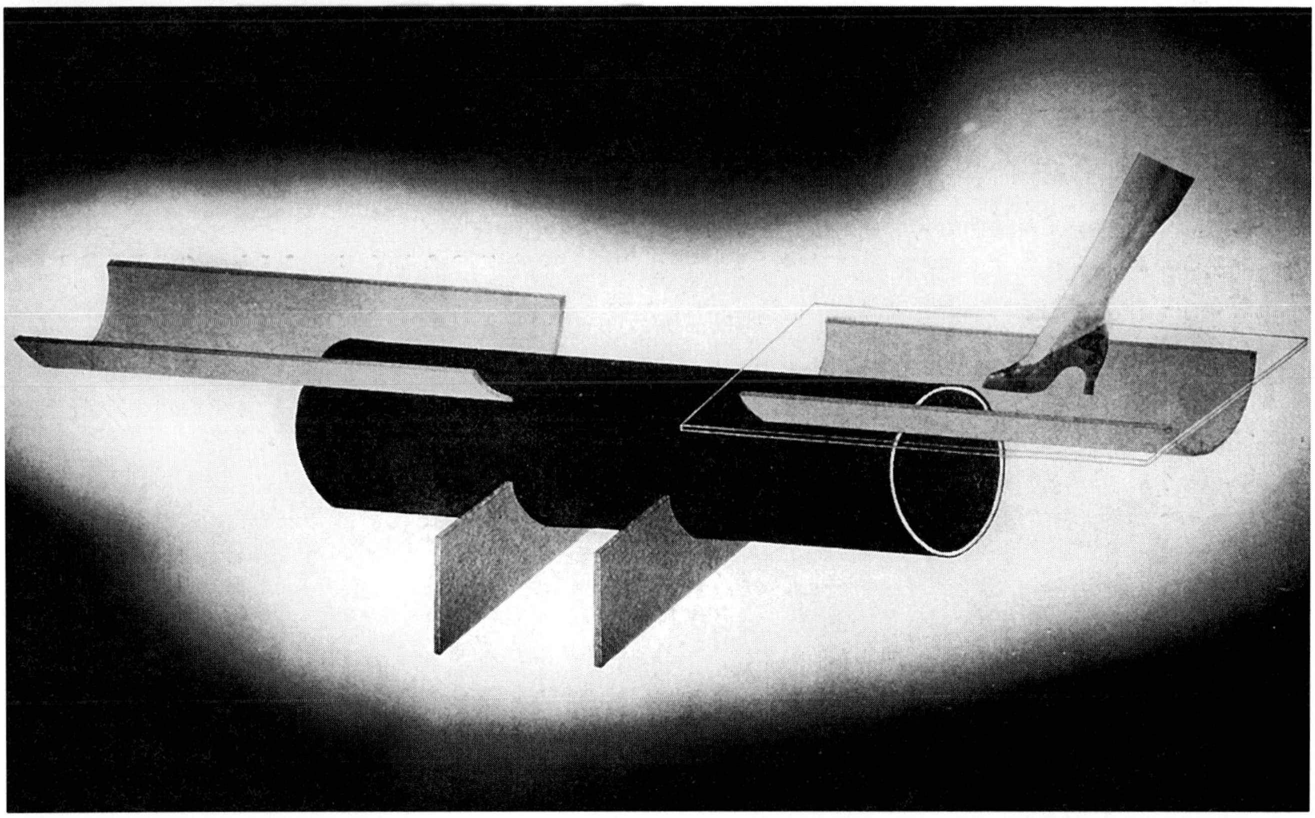

F R E D E R I C K J . K I E S L E R

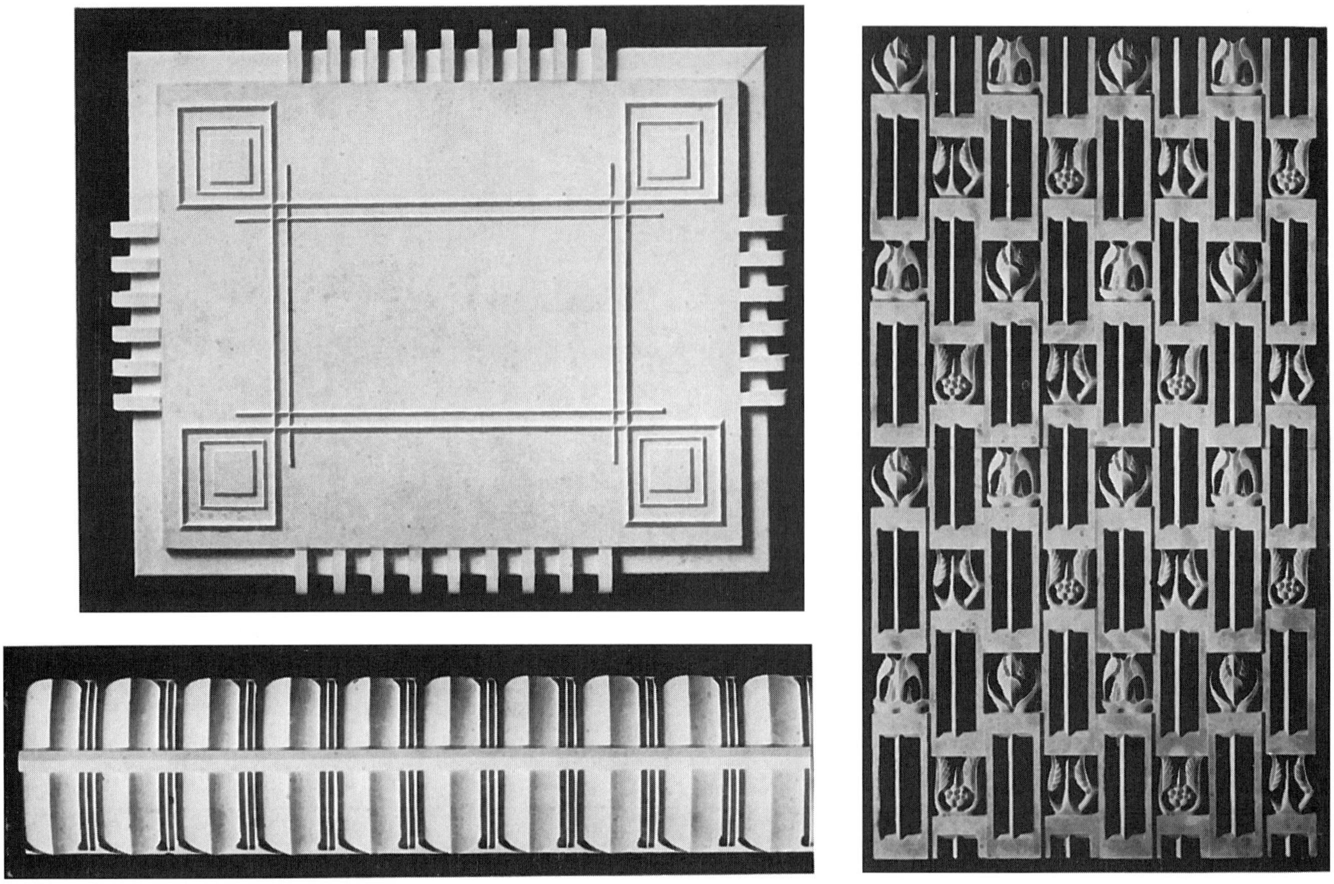

A. DREXLER JACOBSON Plaster grille, ceiling ornament and moulding des. for Jacobson & Co.

Bed and night table designed for the Simmons Co. made of black lacquered steel with chromium trim. NORMAN BEL GEDDES

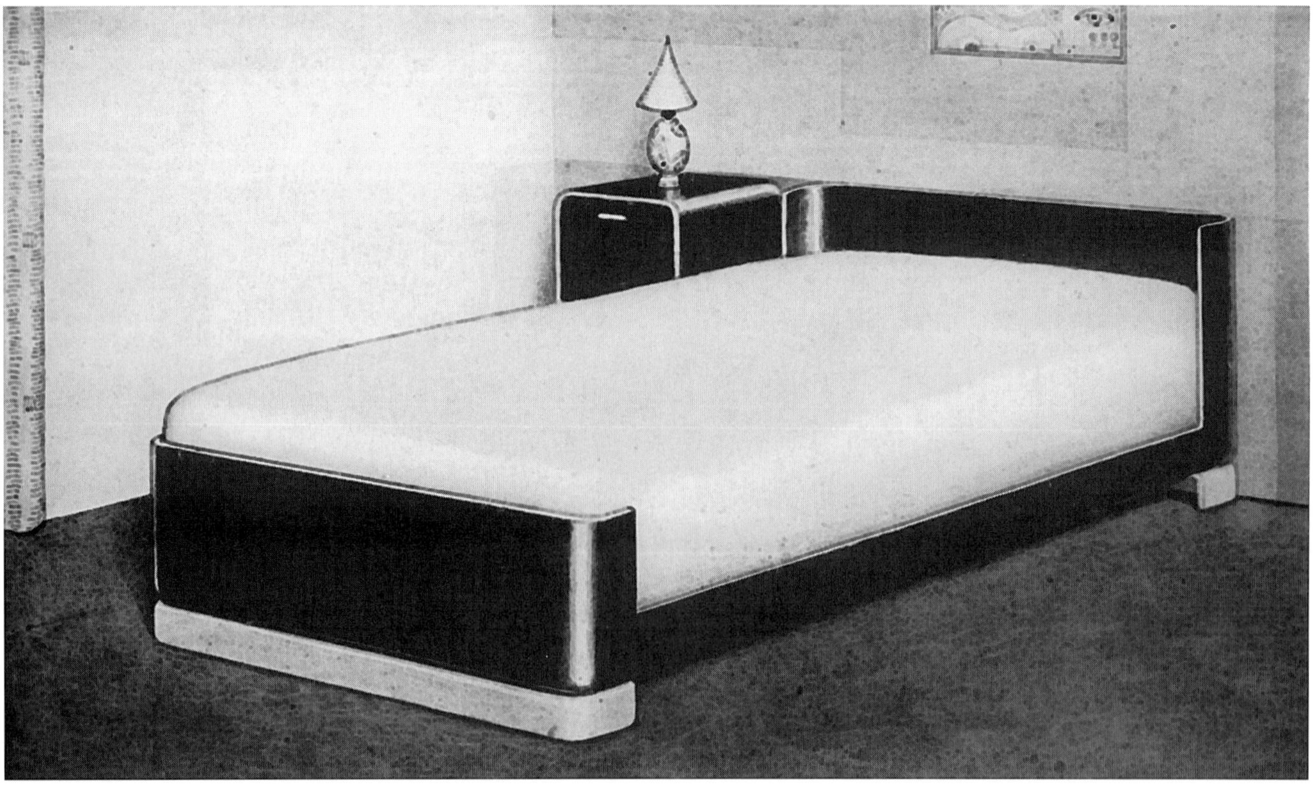

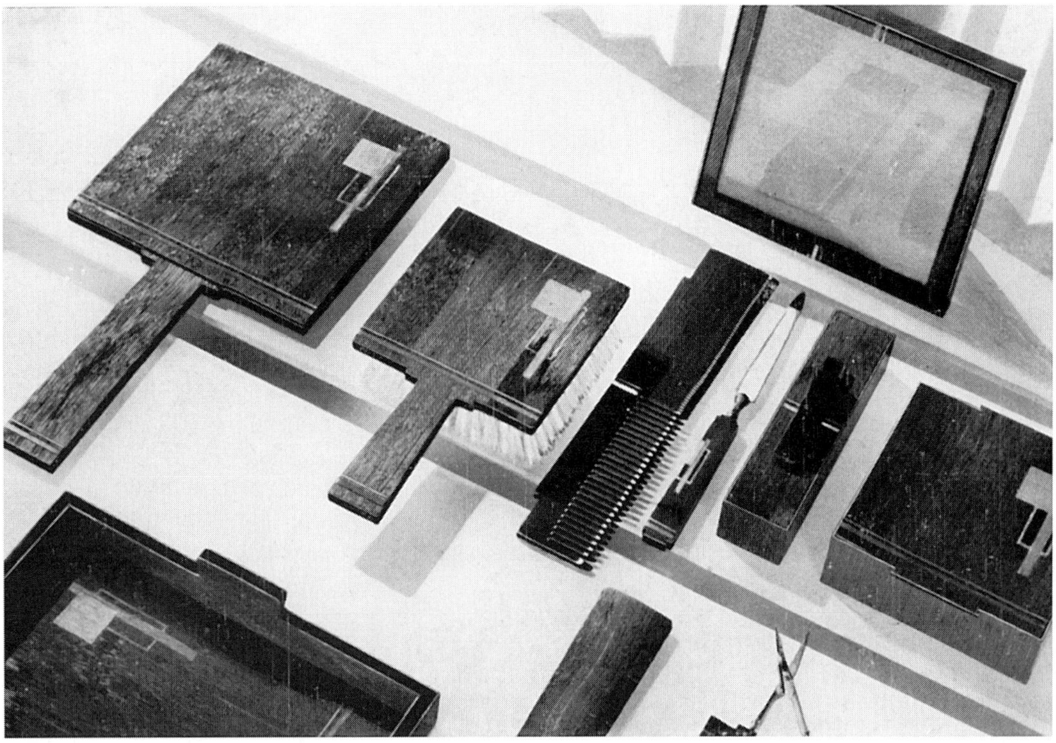

P A U L   T .   F R A N K L

**Two toilet sets designed for the Celluloid Corporation of America.**

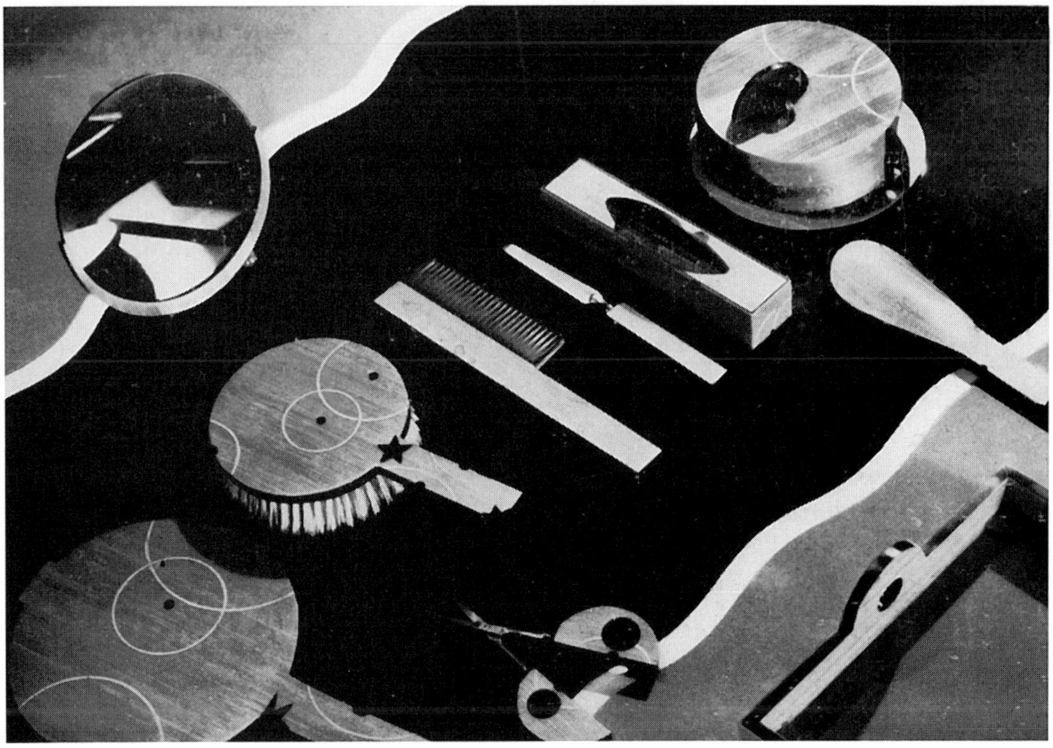

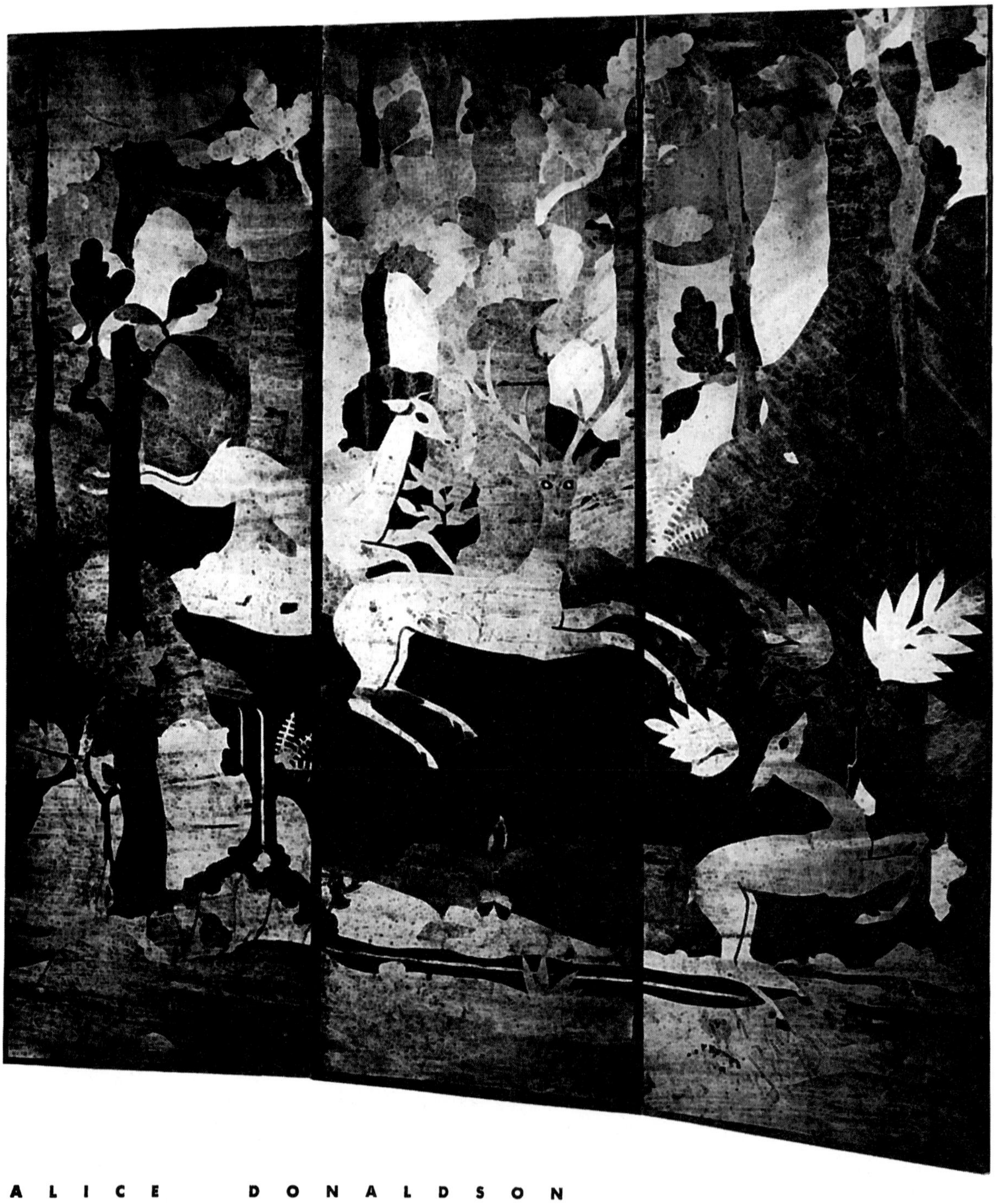

A L I C E   D O N A L D S O N

**A screen whose pattern is made entirely of gold paper so applied that the contrasting surfaces form the design.**

# INDUSTRIAL DESIGN

## RICHARD F. BACH

## THE RESURGENCE OF QUALITY

It is a simple truism today that the maintenance of art-in-industry and of art-in-trade is an economic necessity. This statement has nothing to do with the development of a great art, but rather with the fostering of quality in ordinary art, of the kind or kinds that daily serve the "cross section of the people," contributing to its comfort, convenience, or pleasure. This element of quality, however vital, is bound up with many cruder ones of insistent routine, variously described as market, supply and demand, fashion or vogue, merchandising, advertising, all of which are active agents of prodigious power. In the complicated enterprise of making-selling-using, in which all of these are factors, the quality element has often gone astray, or been lost out of the mixture, not infrequently has been wilfully ignored, due to a mistaken notion rescued from the backwash of sales psychology and called "trading down."

Critics and moralists have blamed all this on the machine and on factory organization. They must have a monster to point to. Whatever the concepts machine, machine age, mechanistic, may stand for in most minds, we can be certain of only one thing: that they imply nothing that is not also present in fact or in principle in an ordinary hammer, a hand-thrown bobbin, a foot-power potter's wheel, or the simplest bellows forge. These are all tools. So also is every egregious complexity of wheels, cogs, shuttles, gigs, spindles and tappets that may be called a Jacquard loom, a moulder or shaper, a tunnel kiln, a trip hammer, a die-casting machine. As each grows more complex, it may get larger, work faster, produce more, but it does not of itself make either better or inferior goods unless geared that way. To use a machine, itself a fine thing, with skill and understanding is a matter of character. To produce a poor design with such a tool means stultification of the entire process, from creation to sale, and damns use before it is begun. Emerson's dictum applies to hand and machine work alike, for neither "can execute anything higher than the character can inspire."

Tradition, hard work, willingness or desire to be an artisan, pride in workmanship, creative endeavor, studied use of the best implements of the trade, nay, even capacity for organization so that the result shall crown a group activity—these are not trade secrets. They have to do with character and so with quality. But quality includes something more: effort is not enough, principles in themselves are not salable. The only guarantee is the attractiveness (call it design and try to define it!) of the finished product, and for the well-advertised average man this can be supplied only by machine. The craftsman cannot improve either taste or production by ukase, but he can by example. It is for this that we need him, for we must visualize his function now as twofold: to produce as a craftsman, for individual production will always be an essential of culture; also, and much more important, to make the initial model for quantity production, thus aiding and abetting, in some degree even supplanting, the factory designer. Only by this last step can we be assured that the machine will make and not unmake. The resurgence of quality in quantity means the resurgence of craftsmanship in the sense of "designing in the material."

But this does not eliminate the designer himself as a visualizer; it does not remove from the industrial picture either the draftsman, the model maker, or the pattern maker; it simply restores to industrial art production an old, well-tested resource. Again, every industry will not promptly lend itself to this addition; nor yet, save the mark, shall we see waiting legions of craftsmen who will and can make themselves useful in terms of quantity production. They must be trained to work together: the factory and the craftsman. For in the factory as in the studio, design must remain a composite of struggle and compromise in which material, process and ultimate usefulness are the garments by virtue of which the ideal takes on the semblance of reality, the guise in which it participates in daily living.

And the training for this new kind of co-operative job? Some schools that we now have can do this, but only a few; it is a task for the near future to develop the type of institution which will train designer-craftsmen to lead industry and thus serve the community, to produce the model and so guide the factory, to know process and market sufficiently well so that material and investment will not go glimmering down the byways of profit and loss.

This is not a complicated job; it is the practical daily routine of the business of production. Indeed, has not industry sought to help itself, having all too keenly felt the pinch of the new-old competition characteristic of today, the competition in design-quality? Industry has sought the designer and the craftsman and has blessed its fate whenever it has found them in one person. Industry has often in recent years been led by inferior talents in design, not because there is a dearth of designers, but because they have not revealed a grasp of the economics of production.

Meanwhile, something else has been happening, one might say, as a process of nature. Quite apart from either designer or craftsman, but as the reasonable outgrowth of invention and the intelligent use of materials and tools, the concept of craftsmanship has again taken hold. After all, craftsmanship is not a fact but a quality, which locomotives and lighting fixtures possess alike, as do teaspoons and theatre settings. If we begin with an inherited mantle of craftsman feeling, we may be right—or we may suffer from either arrogance or inbreeding. If we begin with material and process, produce with these something that can conquer the market, meet the buying demand of the intelligent consumer, and withal hold to our standards, we shall foster the growth of the modern craftsmanship which industry now everywhere reveals. A sober growth is cultivated by invention and labor. It will provide the stalk on which design may flower.

We have been too impatient, wishing at night for the perfect designer and a new-made contemporary style; expecting by morning to see all factories and shops made over according to the revised pattern, store counters loaded with merchandise with never a counterfeit of any historic motive, and the designer as dictator. In the fevered vision of a new style many things may happen, but time proceeds more or less at the same speed. Only time can make styles visible. Our style is growing—of that there can be no doubt—but we, the living, have no perspective of it. Meanwhile, we lunge in this direction and in that, sometimes scoring a touch; and industry seeks, so to speak, to make the best of our lunges while hoping for the touch. For industry cannot stop; if the good design of character and quality is not available, the next best thing must be used. The next best thing, however good, is a bid for mediocrity.

Industry has been guilty of many misdemeanors against the good name of design. It has played down to the mass; it has foisted endless historic near-duplicates upon design-hungry consumers, who have had to buy below their level of taste; it has often stultified excellent creative effort in behalf of the advertising page; what is more, we need have no great expectations that industry will suddenly "get religion." Industry caters to the whole people; there is a kind of gravity of intelligence as there is of mass, and the lower levels must be supplied, in some measure, at least, in terms of what they can be persuaded to buy. That, let us say, is business; thoroughly "depersonalized" as to design, and the picture gives ample occasion for inane vaporings about the ugliness spewed by machinery over our forming culture. It is that phase that Spengler has in mind when he speaks of "this Devil's technique."

Morale is needed and morale comes from character, which for us is expressed in quality. That quality is not to be sought in the dregs; nor does the existence of dregs explain or excuse any lack of quality at higher levels; high purchasing power is no index of taste. Morale in the mass comes from the inspiration of its leaders. The qualified designer, better said, the designer-craftsman, is a leader. In no other way can his calibre be made to count, but such leadership demands its own qualities. We have fallen down before the idol of Technology the Liberator and called its works holy; but in the light of the new day the designer - craftsman again emerges as an invigorating force, making of technology a skilled laborer in the cause of design and of industry the well-managed servant of industrial art. Ford says: "We think of the machine as something in itself instead of as a method of making power effective."

The perpetual challenge of the machine (if challenge it be) cannot be met by railing at mechanism, weeping over the lot of handicraftsmen, or setting up direction signs at the city gates to divert the evil god of mediocrity. In our regimentation of non-human energy we now once more take account of quality. Wells need no longer speak of the "race between education and catastrophe"; education will win, and no small part of it will come through the honest cultural value of quality in design produced by industry and borne on the winds of trade.

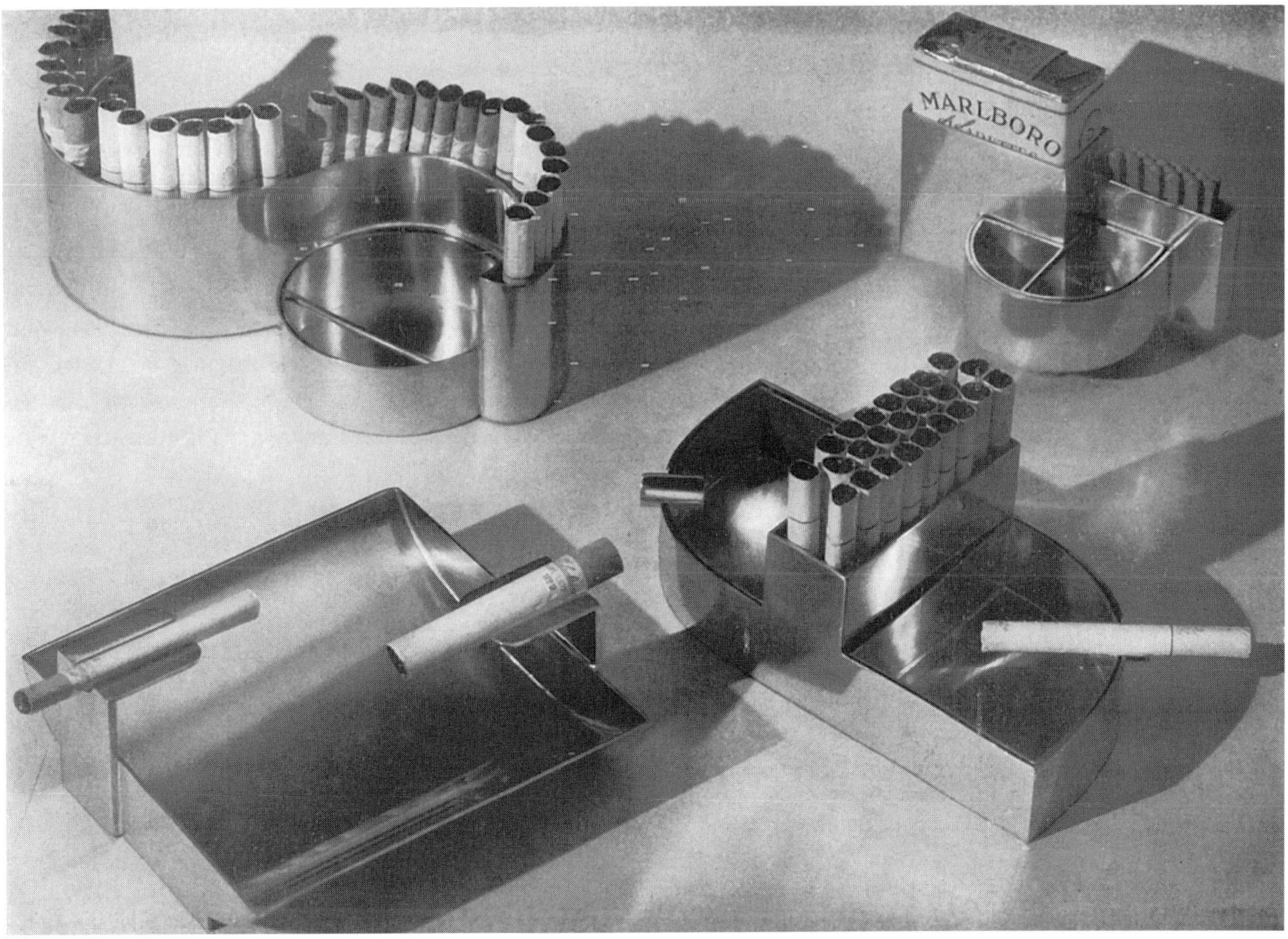


WOLFGANG & POLA HOFFMANN

Light pewter cigarette and ash trays. Executed by the Early American Pewter Company.

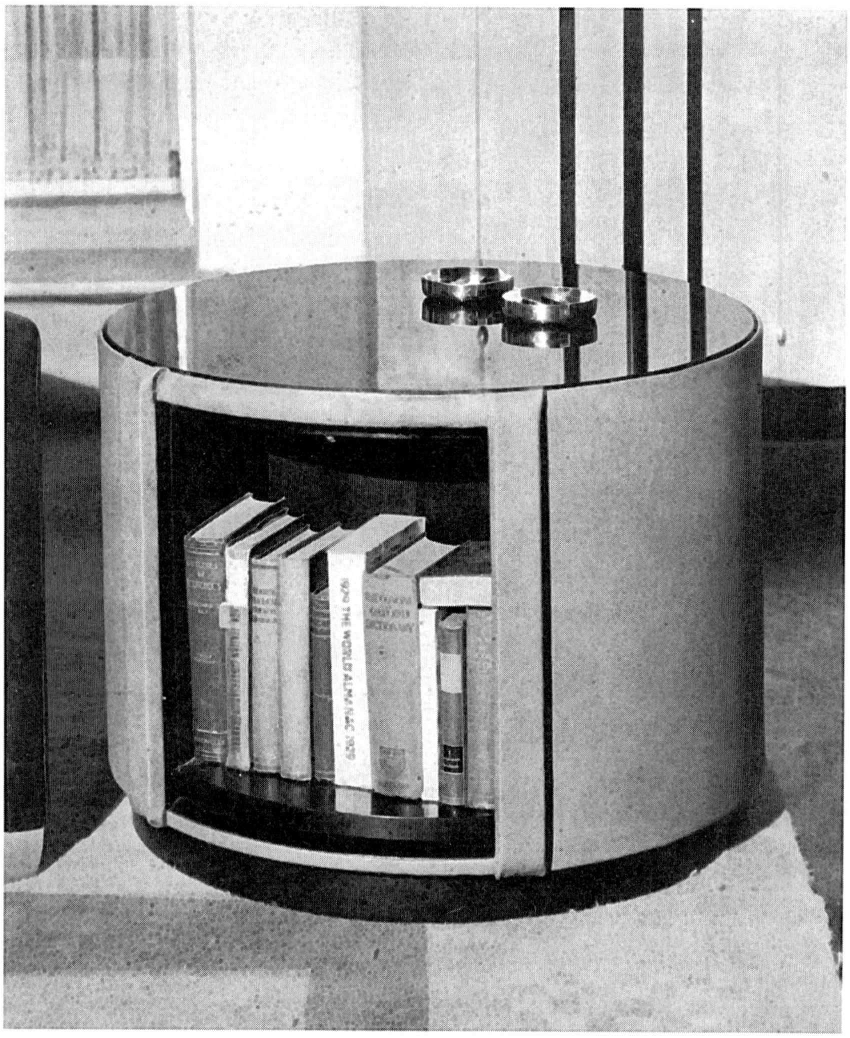

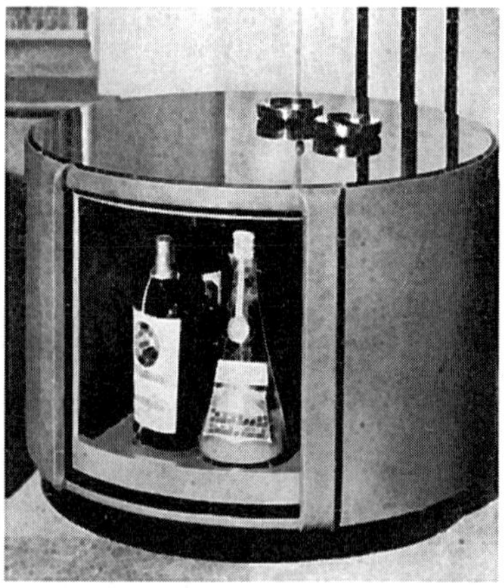

G I L B E R T   R O H D E

Three views of the "Rotorette," a revolving cellarette. This is a revolving unit with four divisions; one for books, two for glassware and one for bottles. In the locked position, only the book compartment is visible. Unlocked, the interior may be revolved. Sides of leather; top of black glass; base and interior lacquered black.

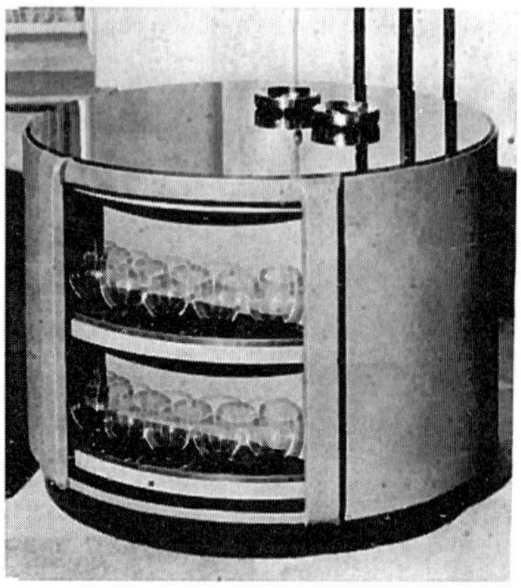

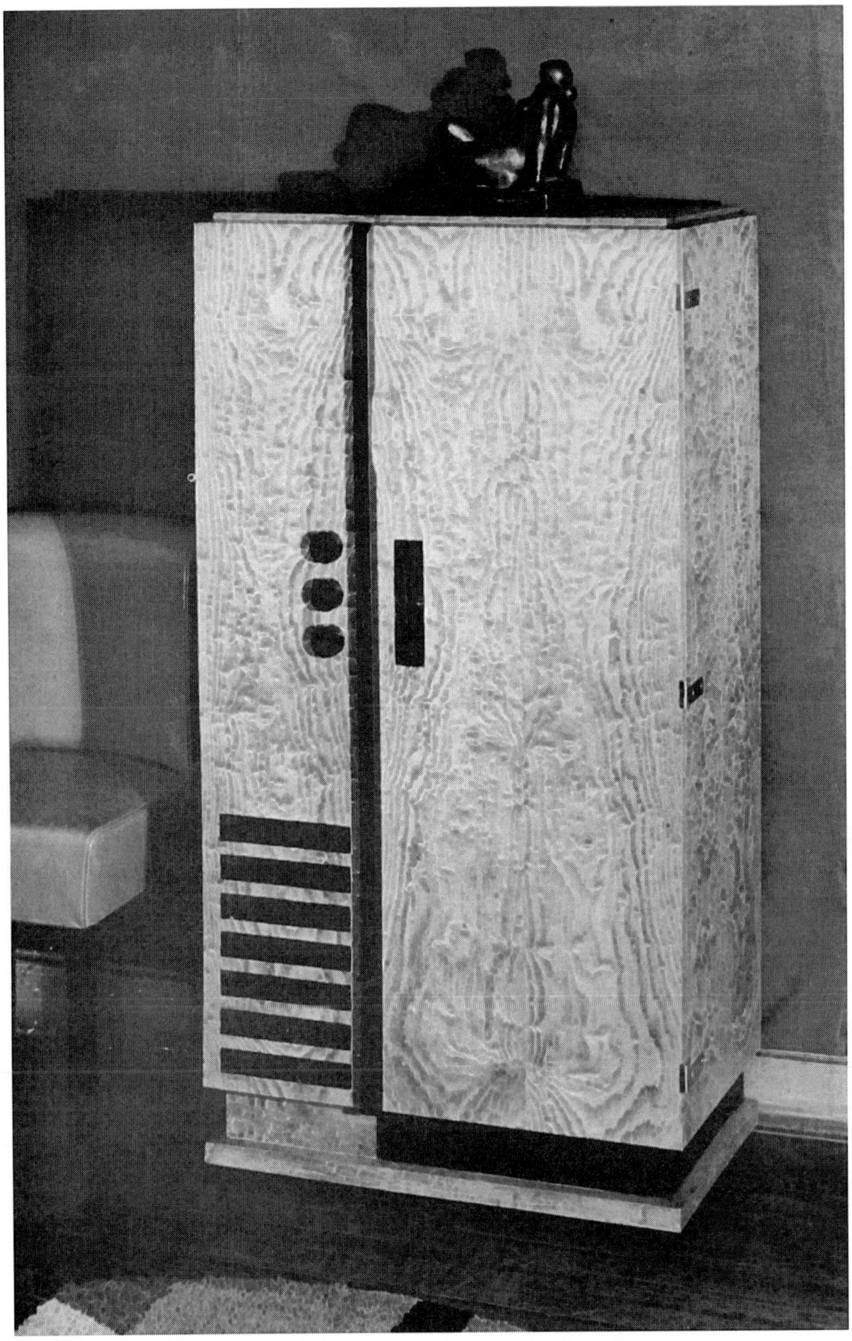

Radio and phonograph cabinet showing the door swung open to reveal the phonograph with shelf for records. Radio dials are on the face of the cabinet.

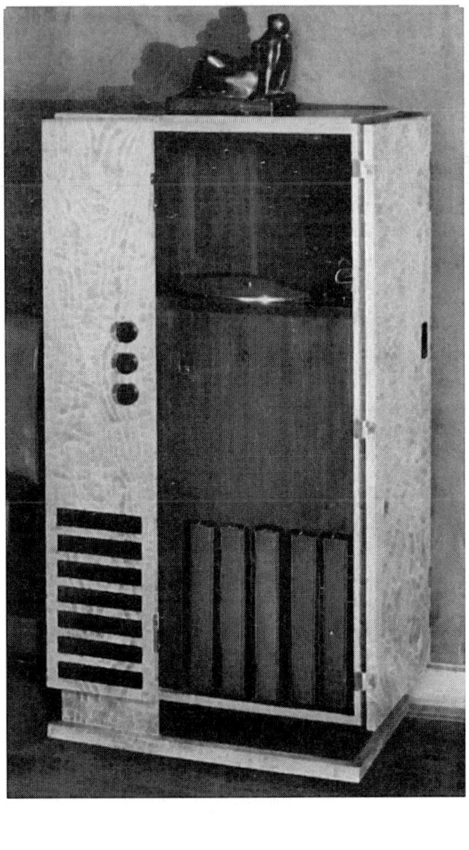

**N O R M A N   B E L   G E D D E S**

**Two "Island" weighing scales made for the Toledo Scale Co., Toledo, Ohio. The scales in white porcelain, support black glass counters. Monel metal rods, or bands used to avoid rusting.**

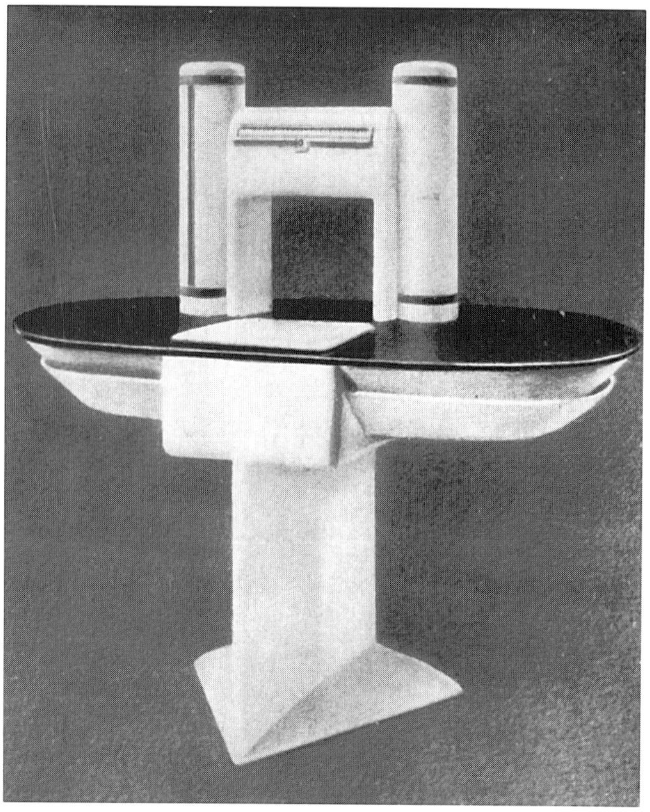

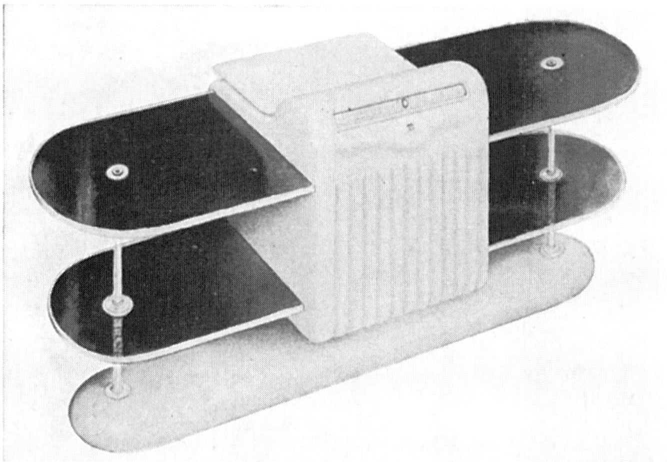

**T H O M P S O N   &   C H U R C H I L L**

**Mail box of bronze in the State Tower Building, Syracuse, N. Y.**

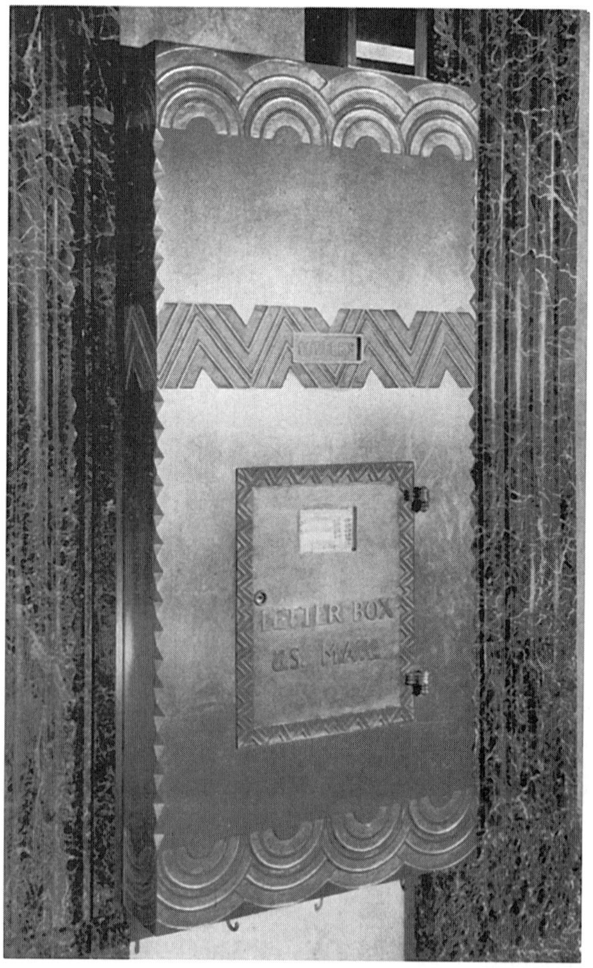

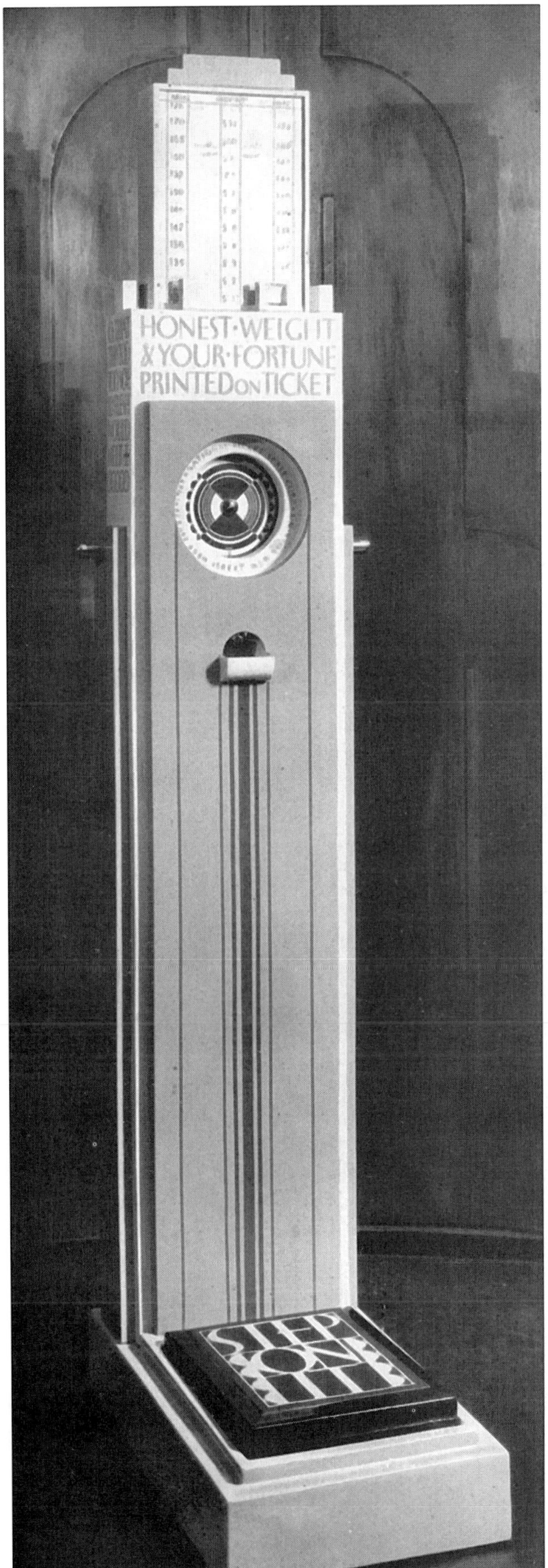


J O S E P H  S I N E L
Ticket printing weighing scale designed for the International Ticket Scale Corporation.

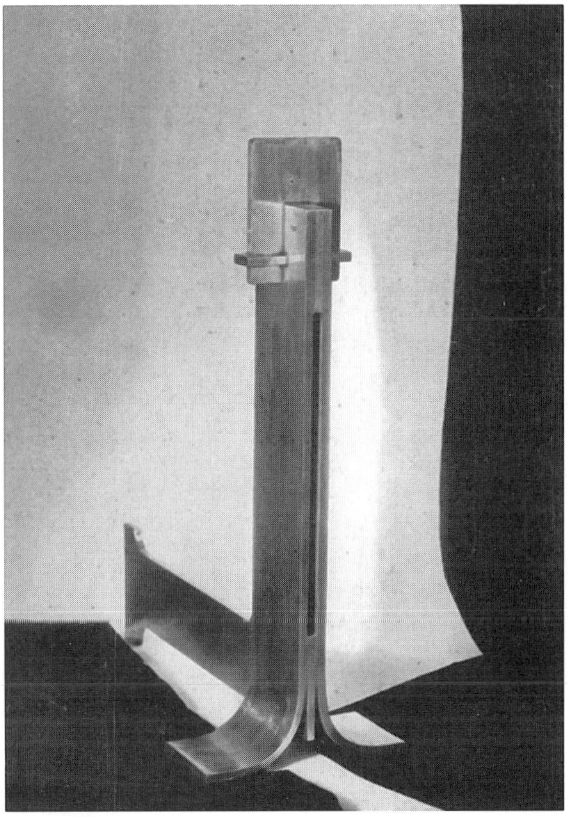

P A U L  A .  L O B E L
Andiron of steel and bronze made for Elsie Cobb Wilson, Inc.

WALTER KANTACK
Lighting pendant made for Aluminum Co. of America. Executed by Kantack & Co.

PAUL A. LOBEL
Ceiling fixture in brass. Executed by Lobel-Uris, Inc.

WALTER VON NESSEN
Indirect lighting floor lamp. Nessen Studios, Inc.

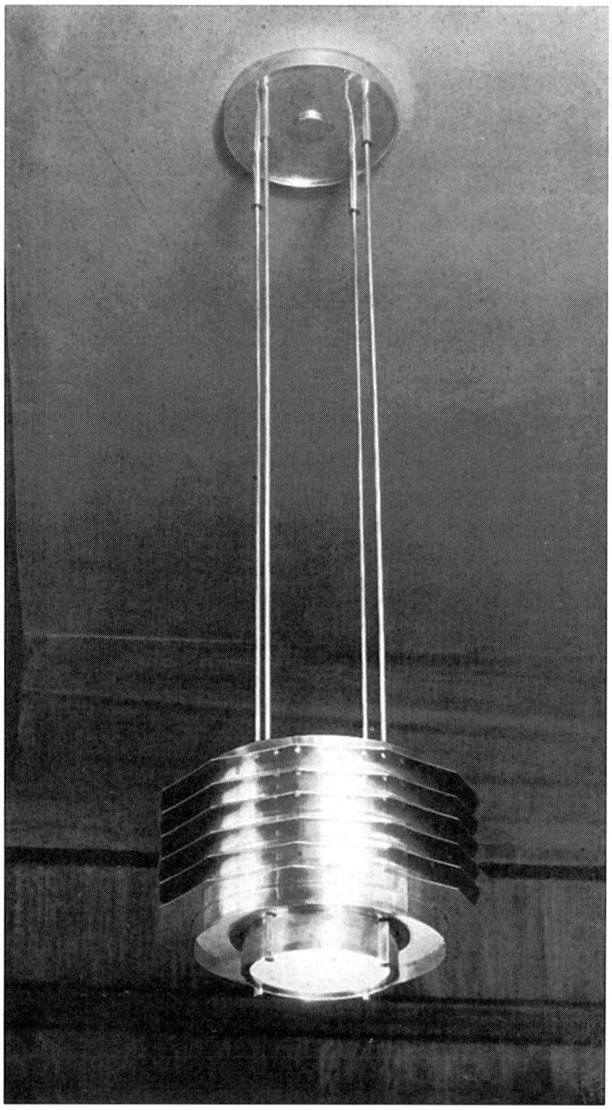

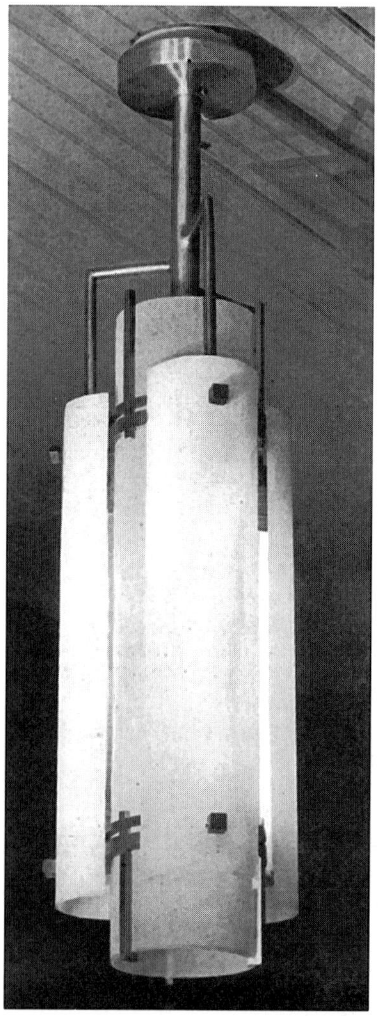

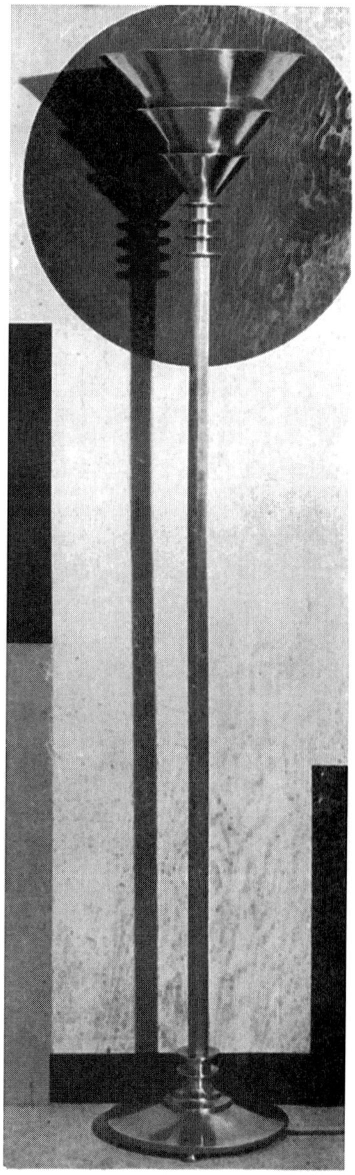

D O N A L D   D E S K E Y

**Adjustable reading lamp in polished nickel.**

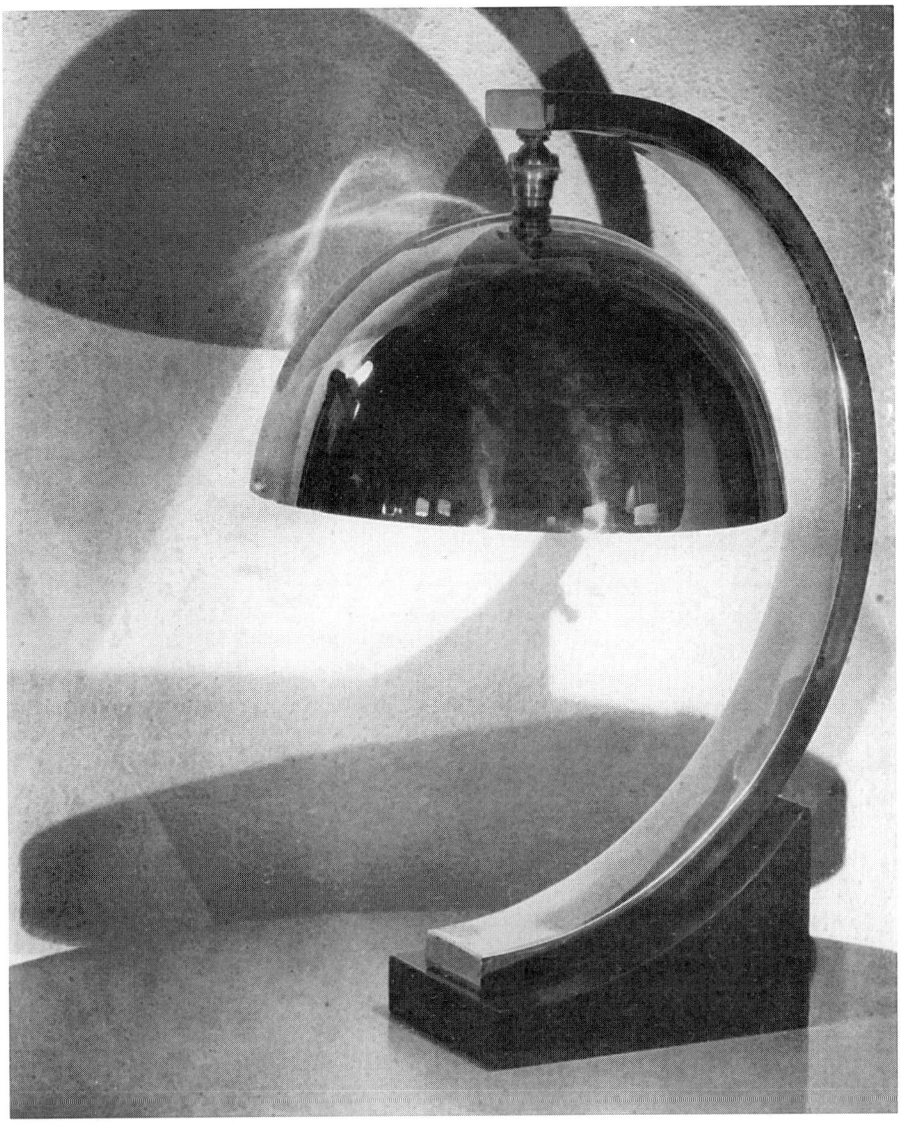

**Combination bridge lamp.
Indirect or direct light.
Polished chromium plate.
Executed by Deskey-Vollmer, Inc.**

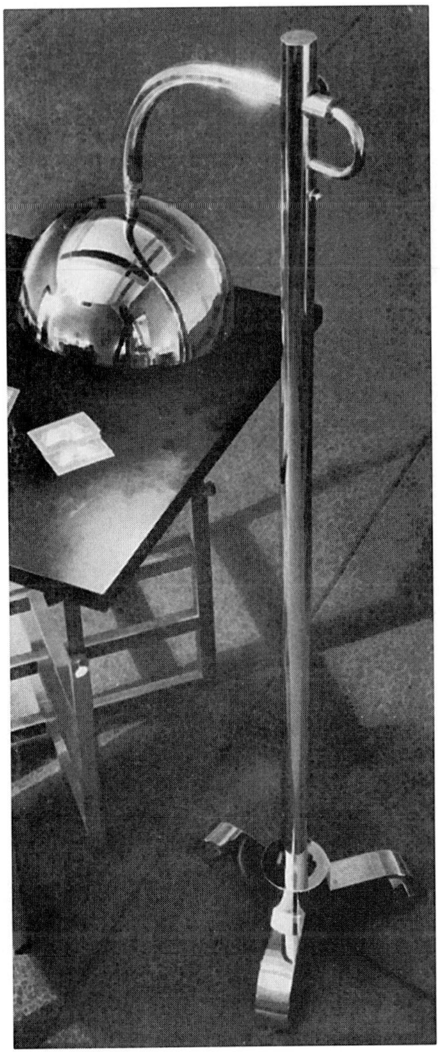

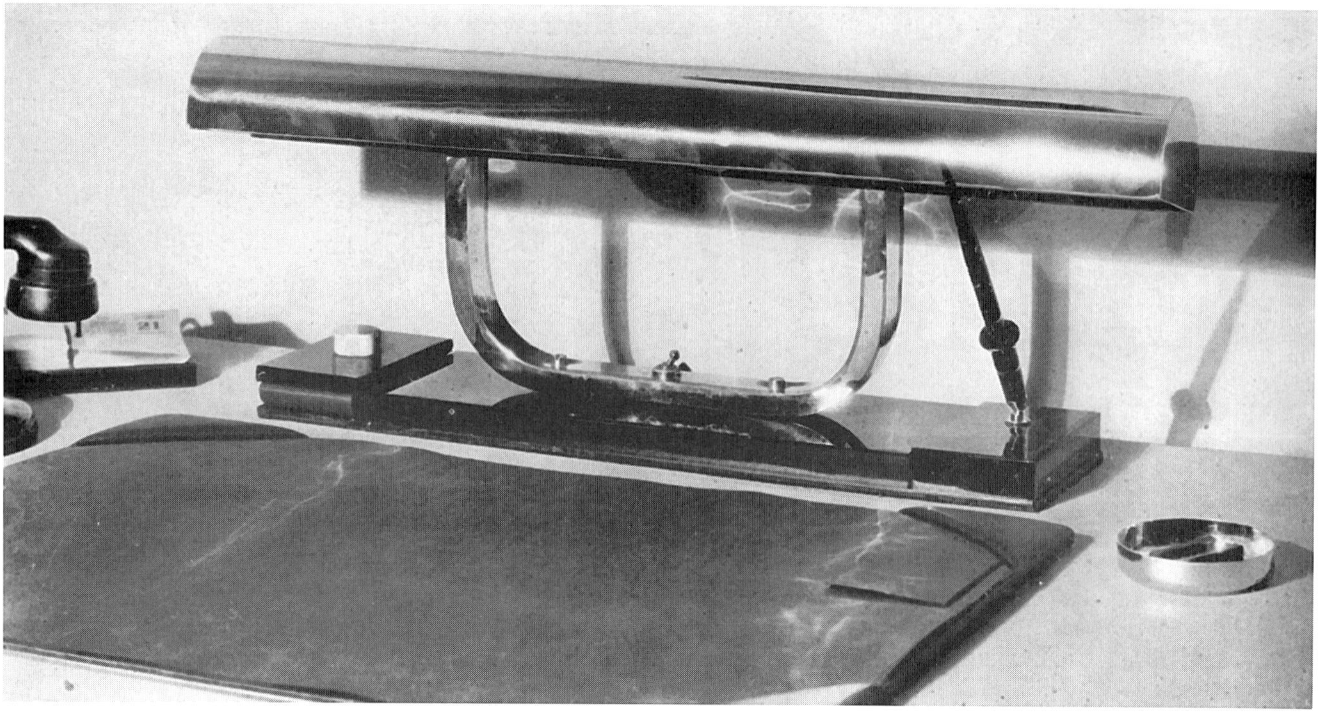

G I L B E R T   R O H D E

Desk lamp set with fountain pen and leather block, composed of polished chromium plated metal and black glass.

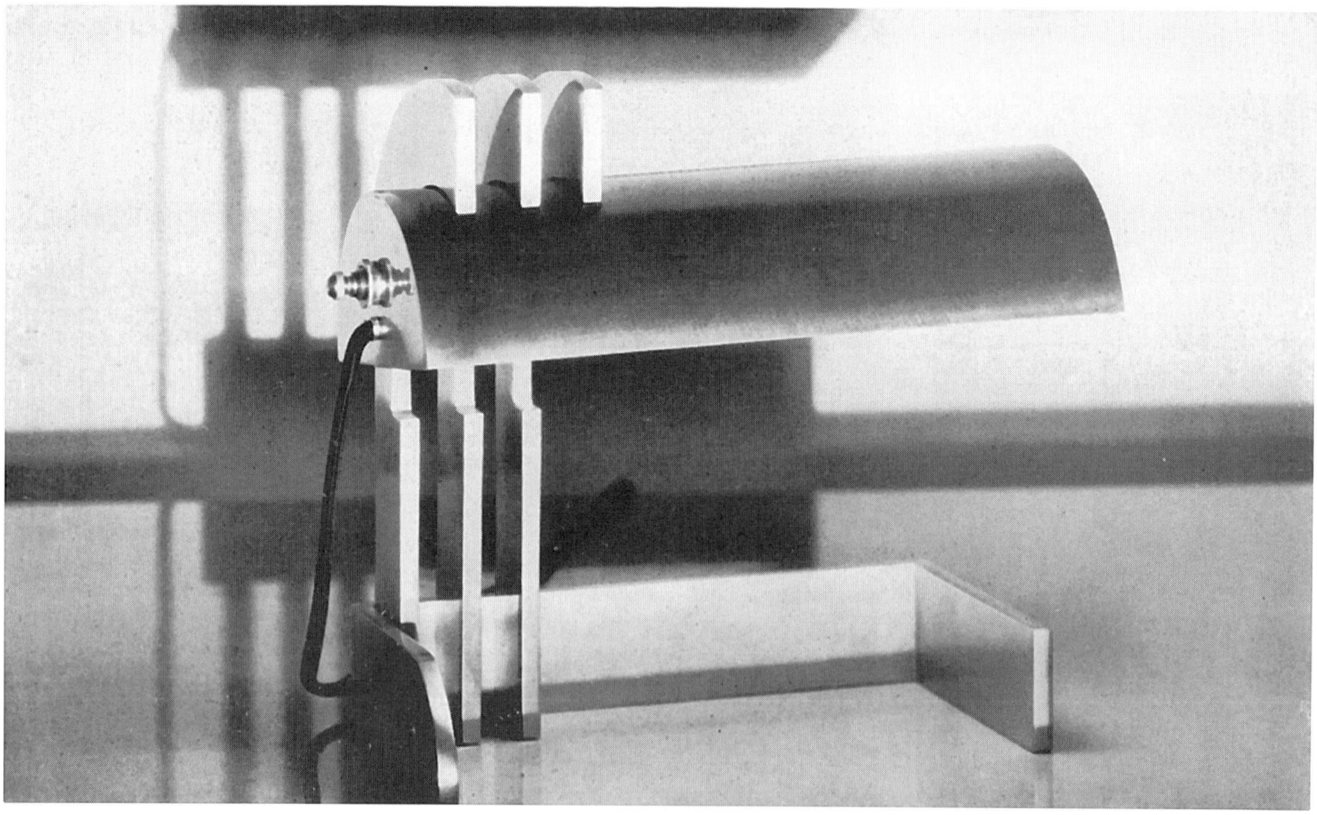

D O N A L D   D E S K E Y

Adjustable reading lamp of brushed chromium plate. The shade revolves within the three uprights. Executed by Deskey-Vollmer, Inc.

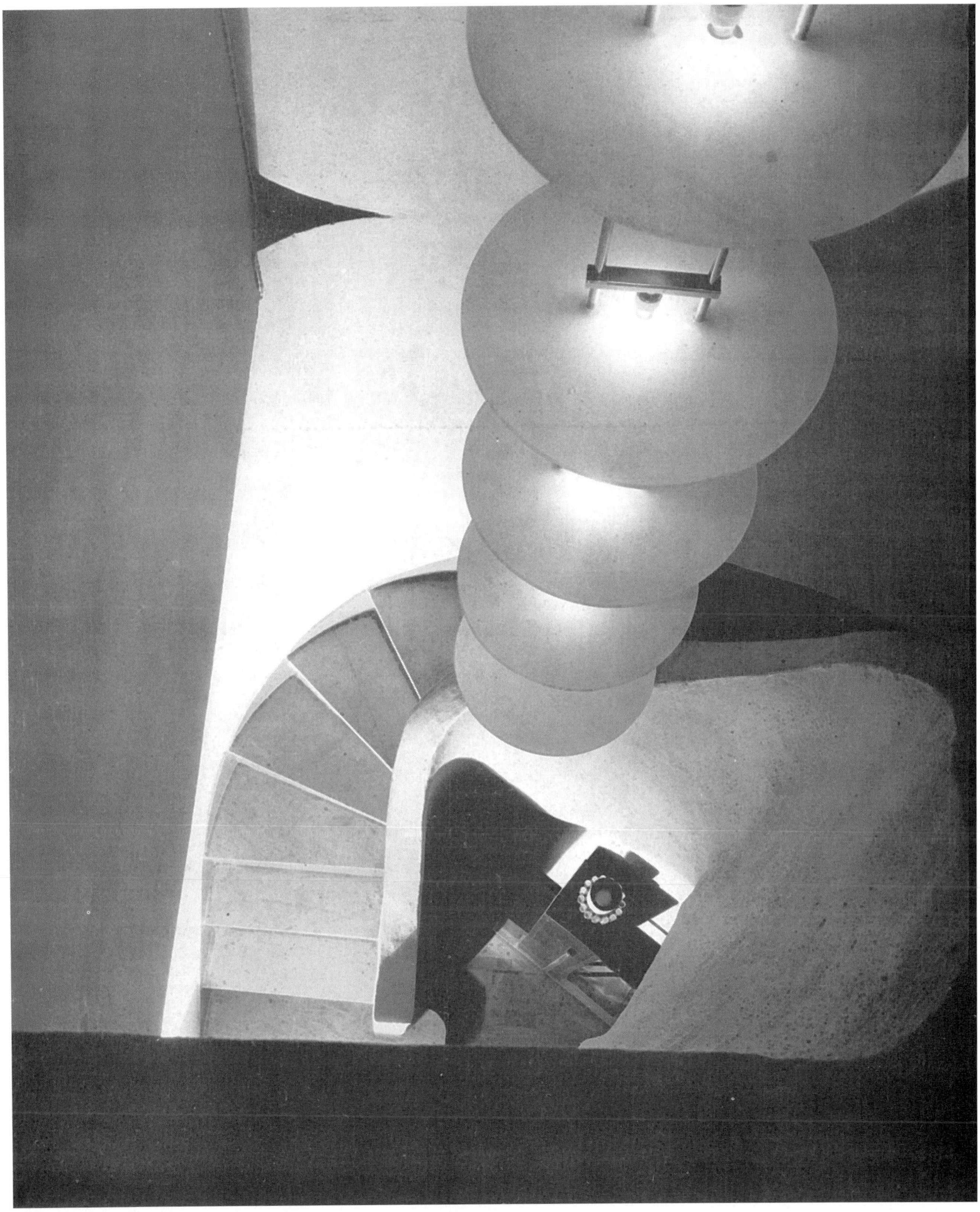

G I L B E R T   R O H D E

**Light in the stair well in the apartment of Mr. Norman Lee, N. Y. C.**

**Constructed of sand-blasted glass and chromium plated metal.**

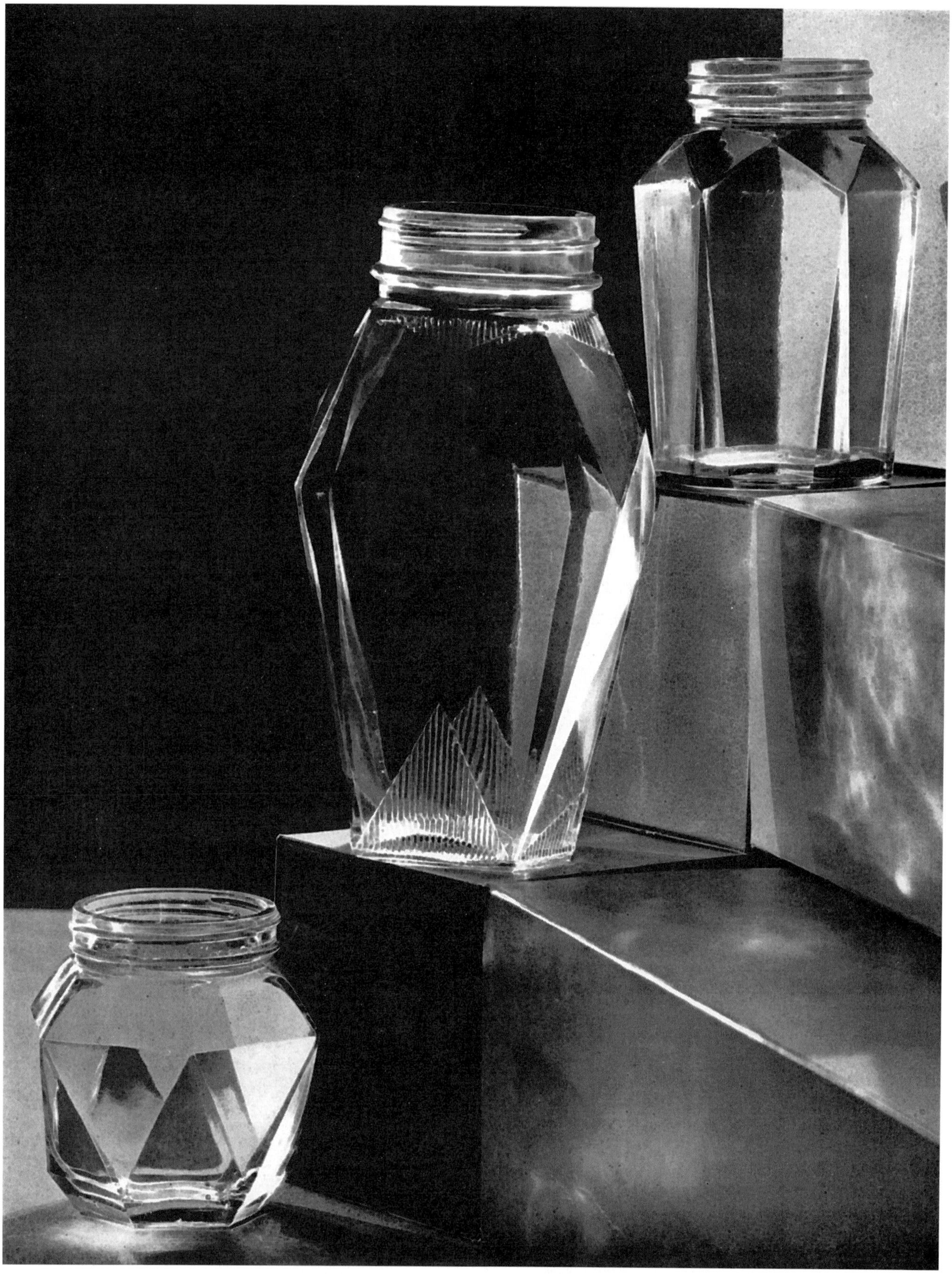

W A L T E R  D O R W I N  T E A G U E

**Three glass jars designed for Turner Glass Company, Indiana.**

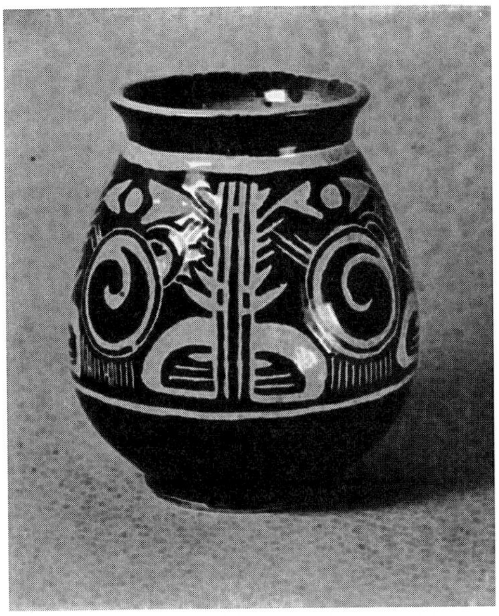

JULIUS C. MIHALIK

Slipware vase in red and cream. Bowl in two tones of green underglaze.

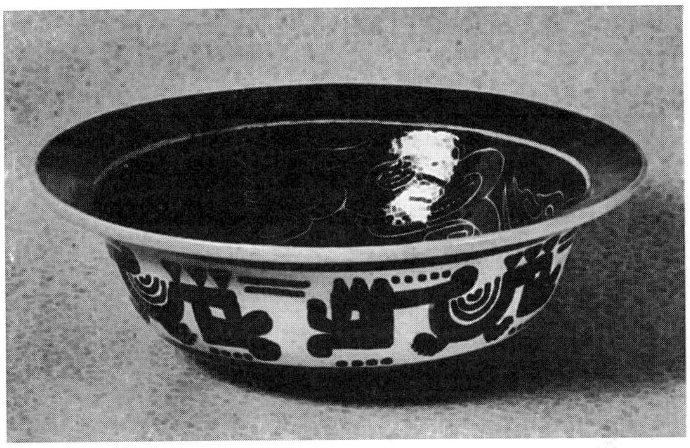

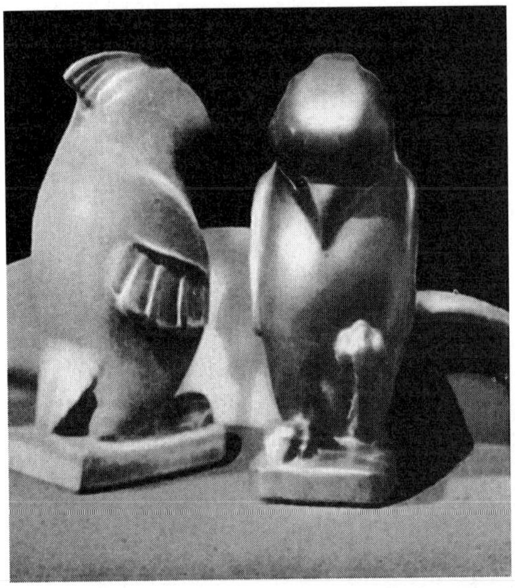

A. DREXLER JACOBSON

Three sets of ceramic book-ends in black, silver and copper glaze. Executed by Cowan Potteries, Inc.

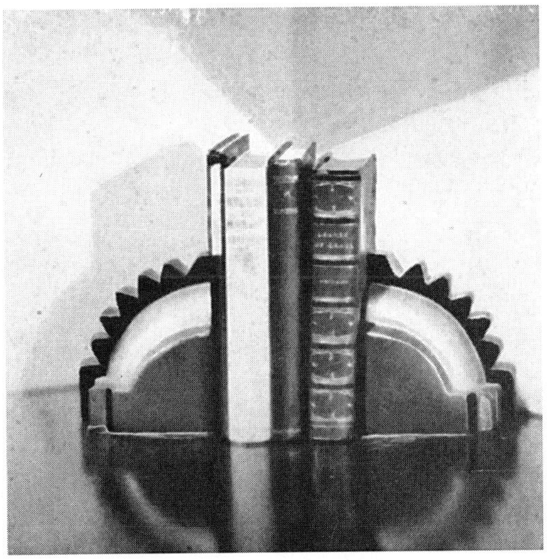

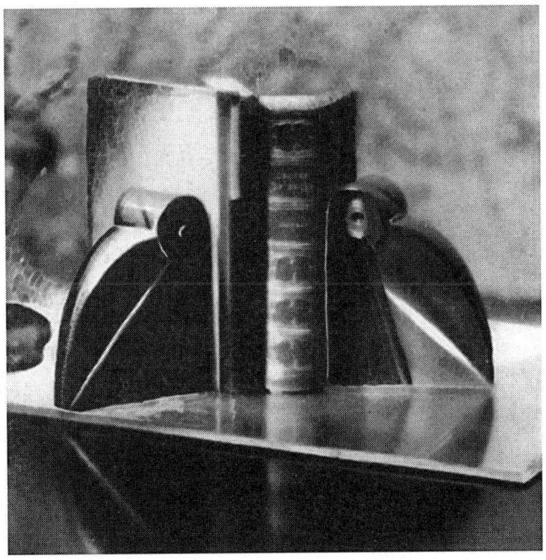

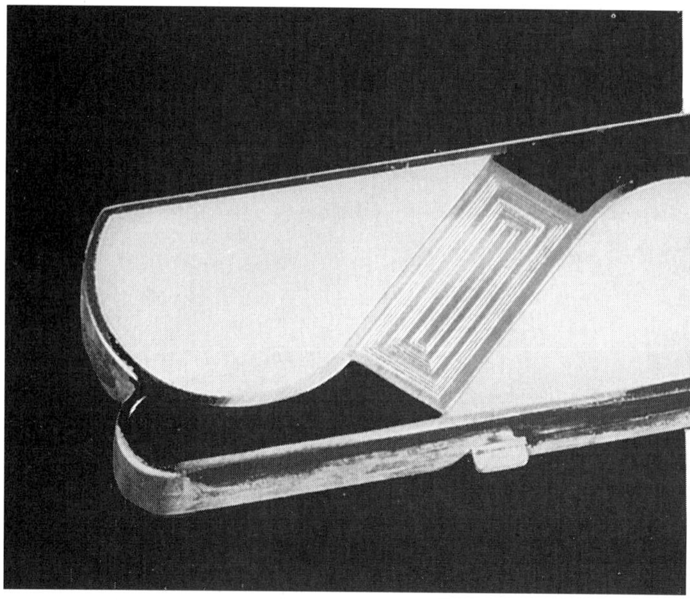

**ROBERT L. LEONARD**
**Design of compact for Vantine.**

**JOSEPH SINEL**
**Desk set, book ends and waste paper box in black calf and gold tooling. Made by Star Case Co., New York.**

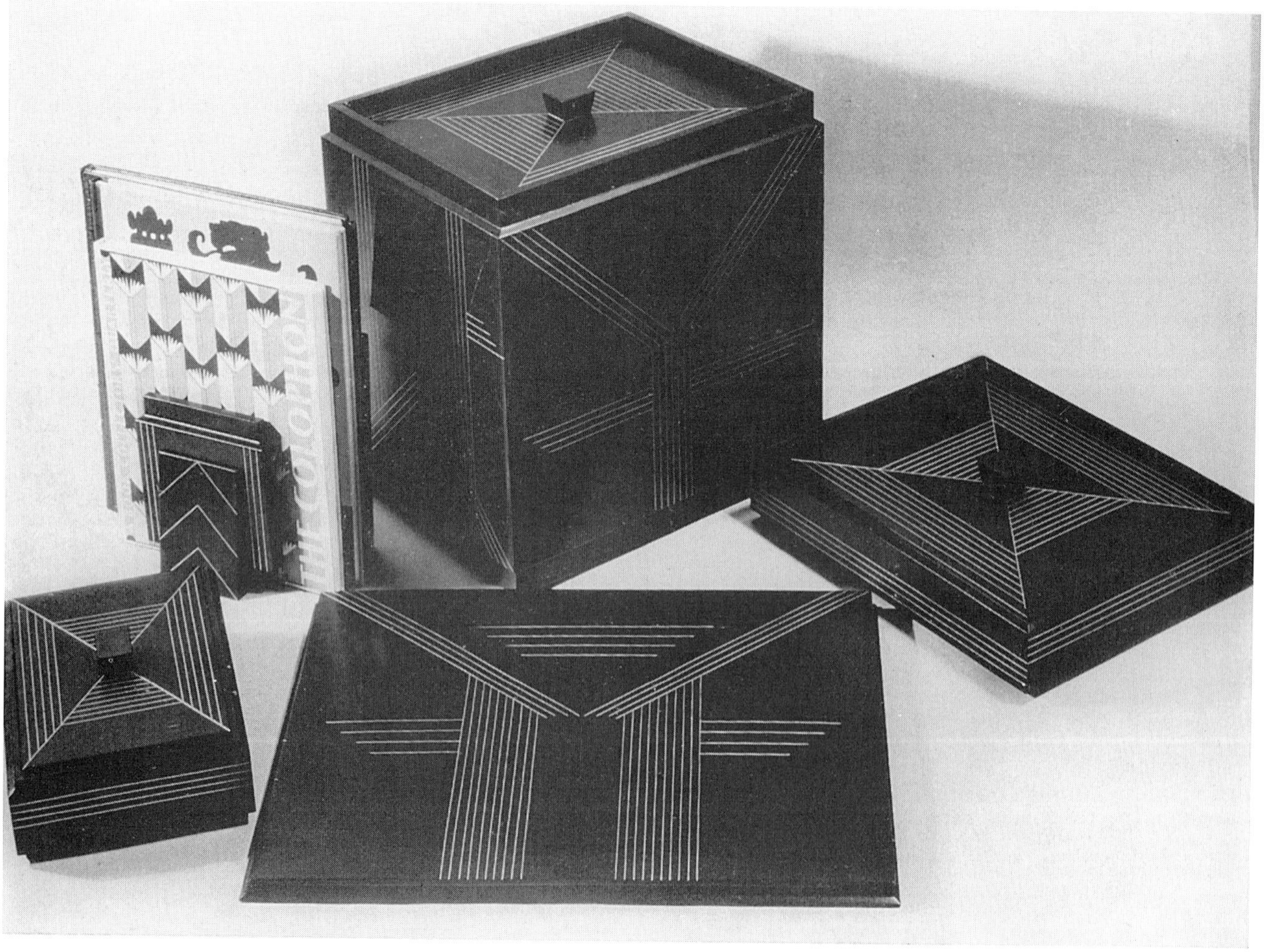

**R O B E R T   L .   L E O N A R D**

**Package design for Richard Hudnut.**

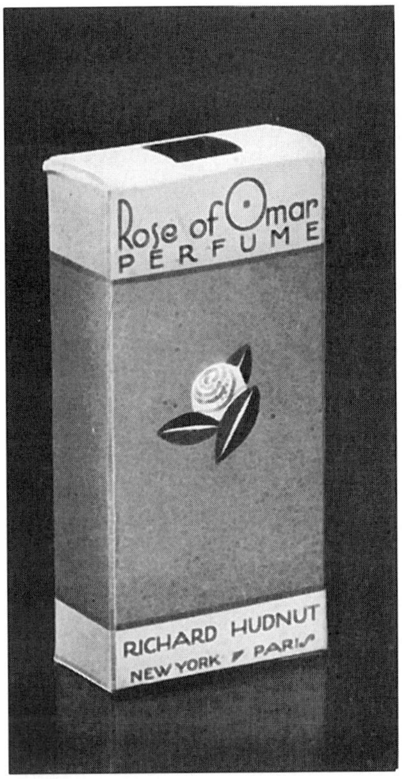


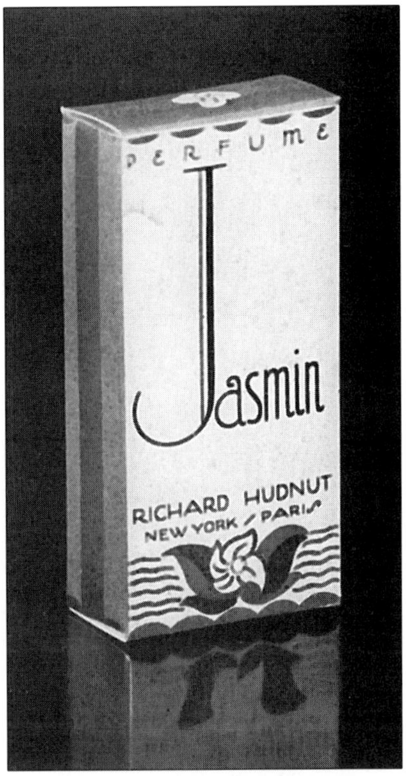


**J O S E P H   S I N E L**

**Product containers in fabricoid and paper. Fabricoid cases made by Star Case Co., N. Y.**

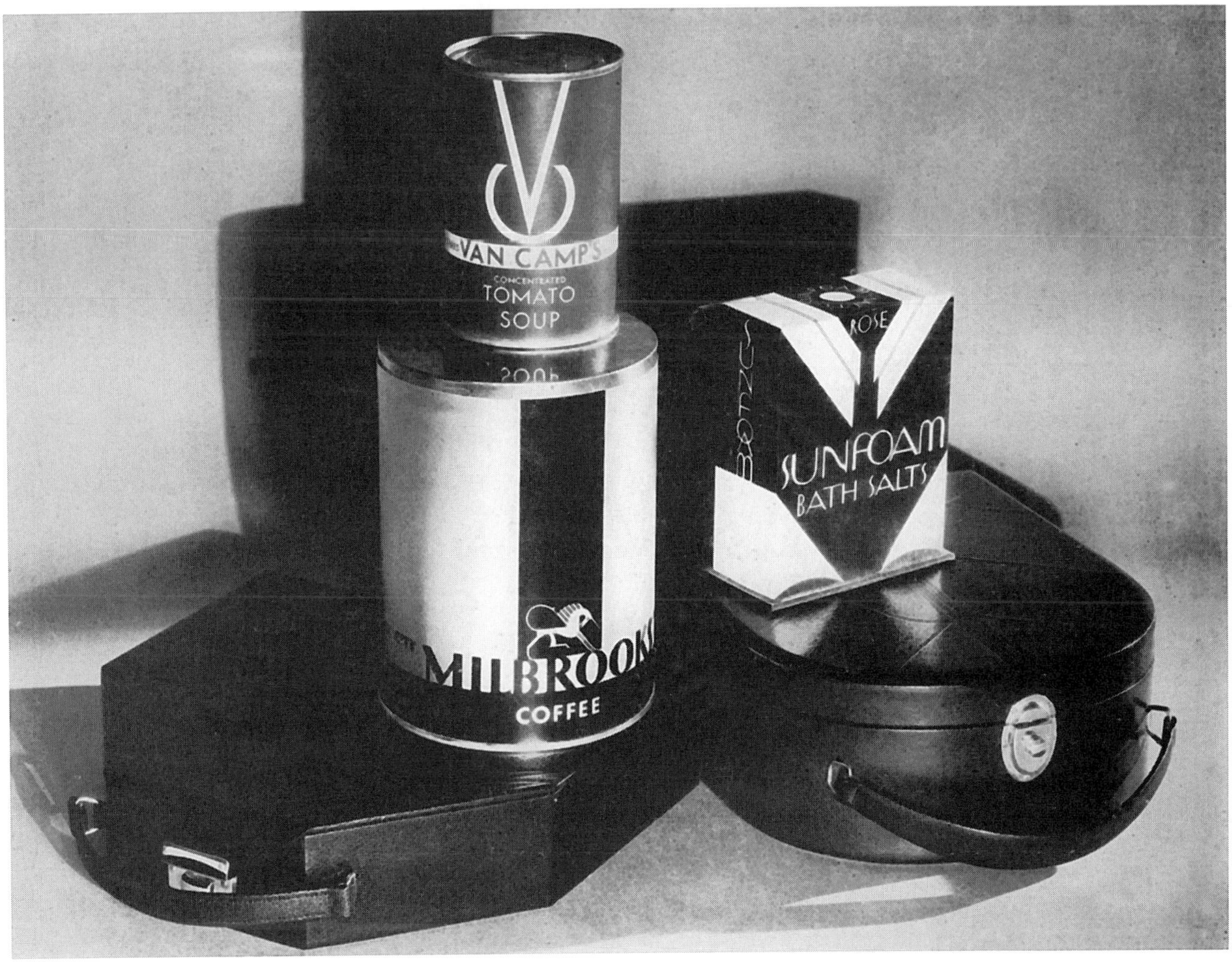

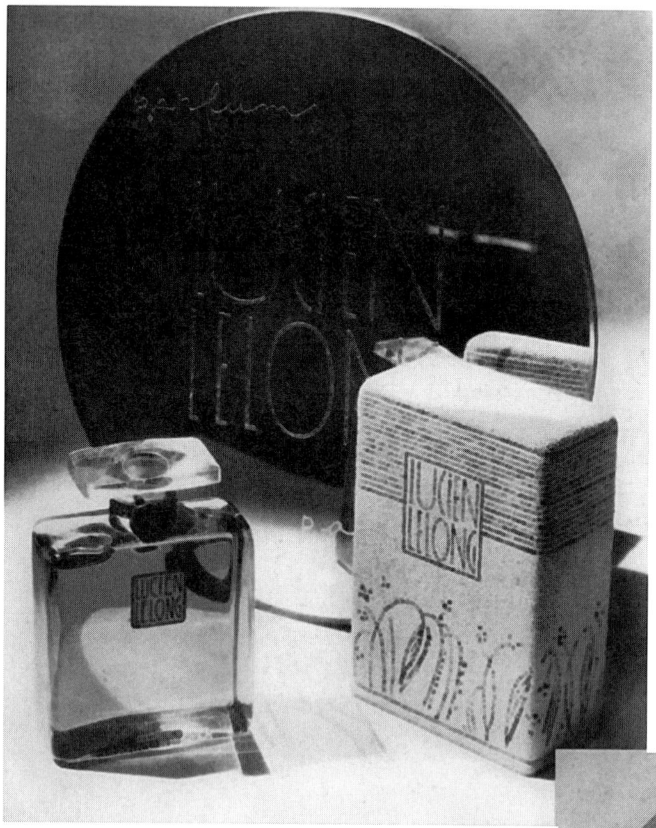


Counter mirror and package designed for Lucien Lelong

Container in blue, black and white designed for Gilbert Products Corporation.

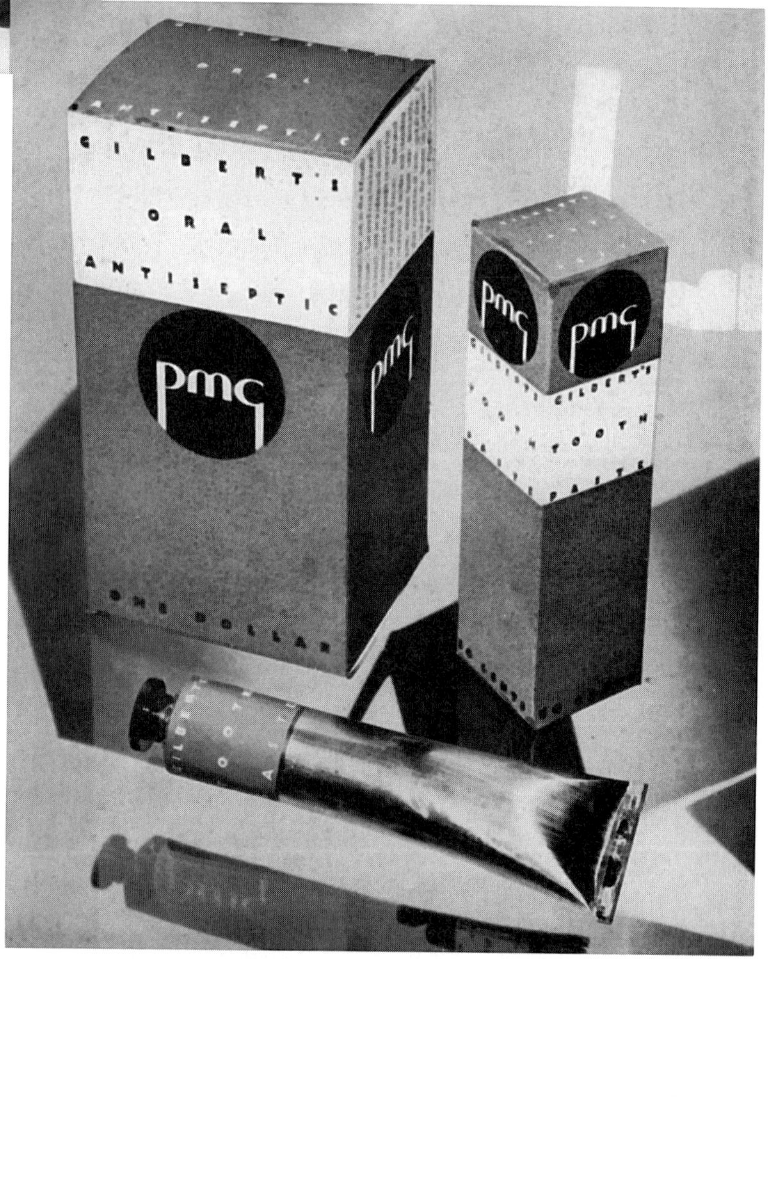

# J E N S E N

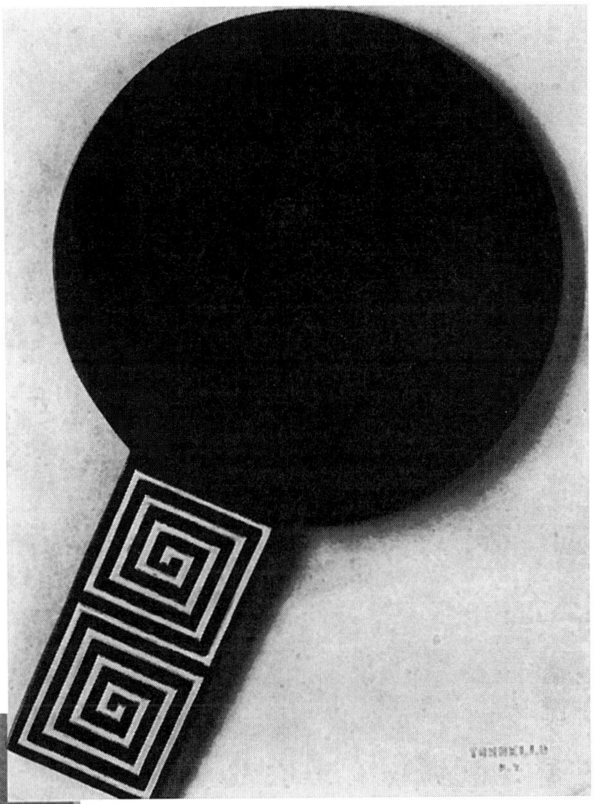

Black and silver hand mirrors of Viscoloid designed for the Du Pont Company.

Model of a percolator in bright metal designed for The Edison Electric Company.

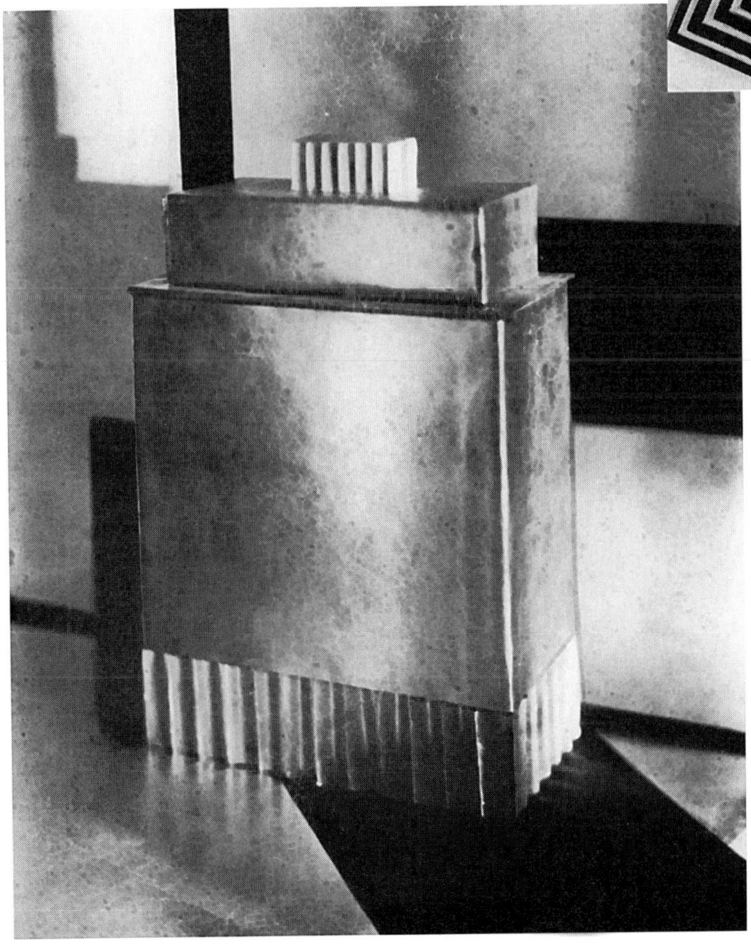

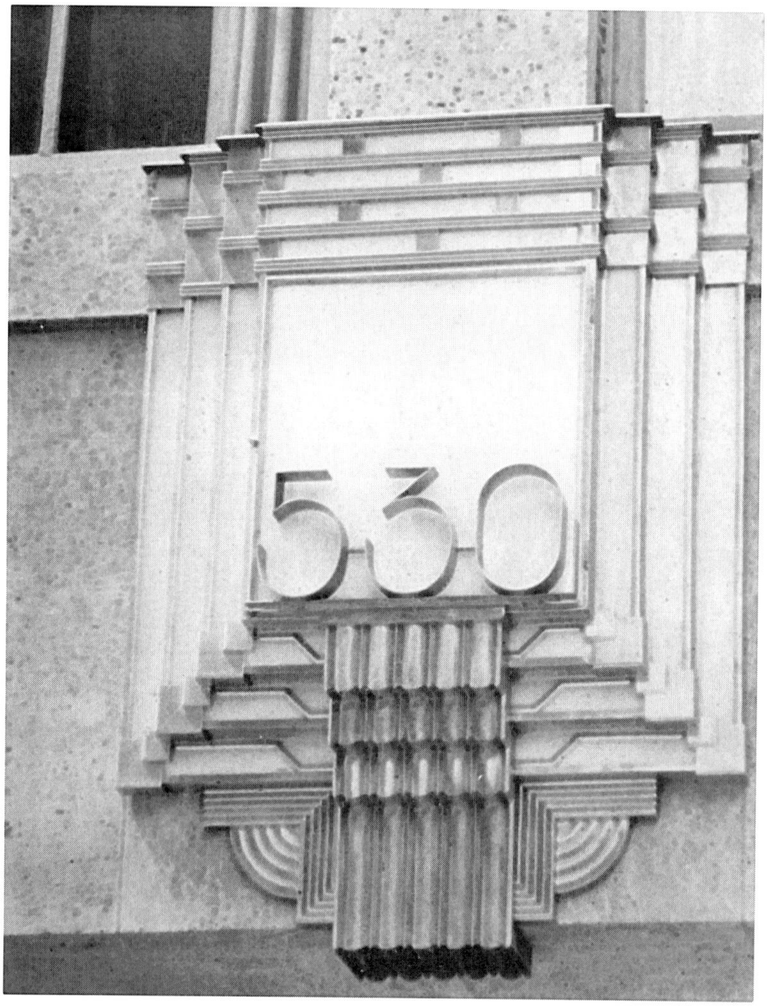


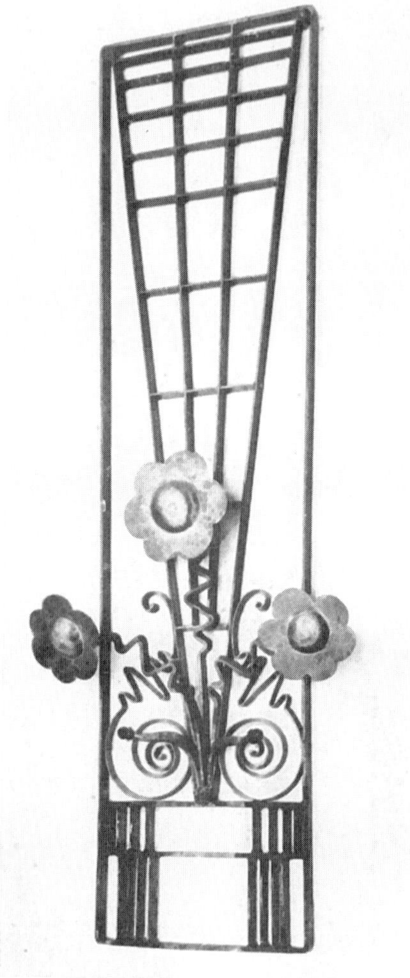

W A L T E R   V O N   N E S S E N
**Street lantern and house number in bronze.**

P E T E R   L A R S E N
**Hat and coat wall hanger in iron.**

E R I K   M A G N U S S E N
**Hand wrought silver bowl.**

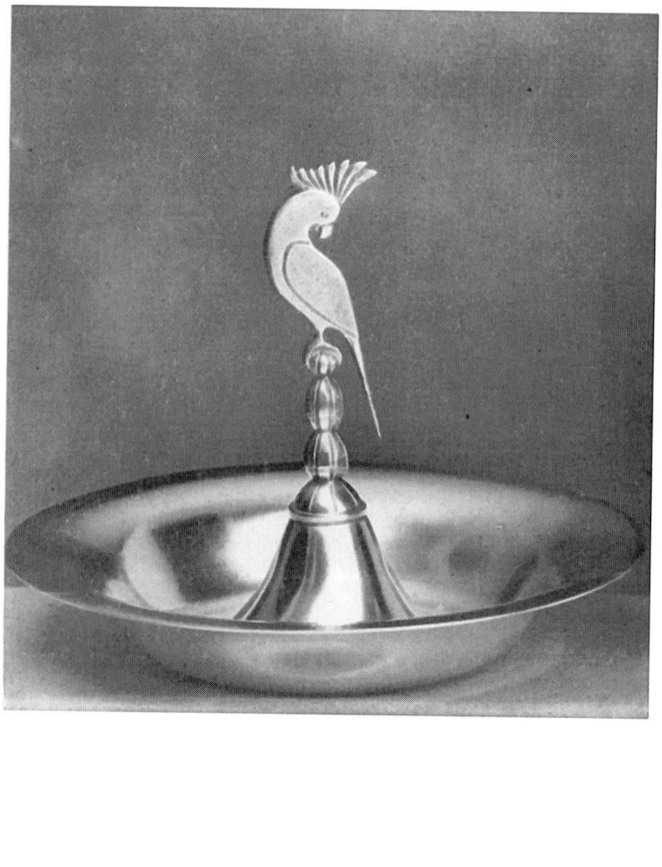

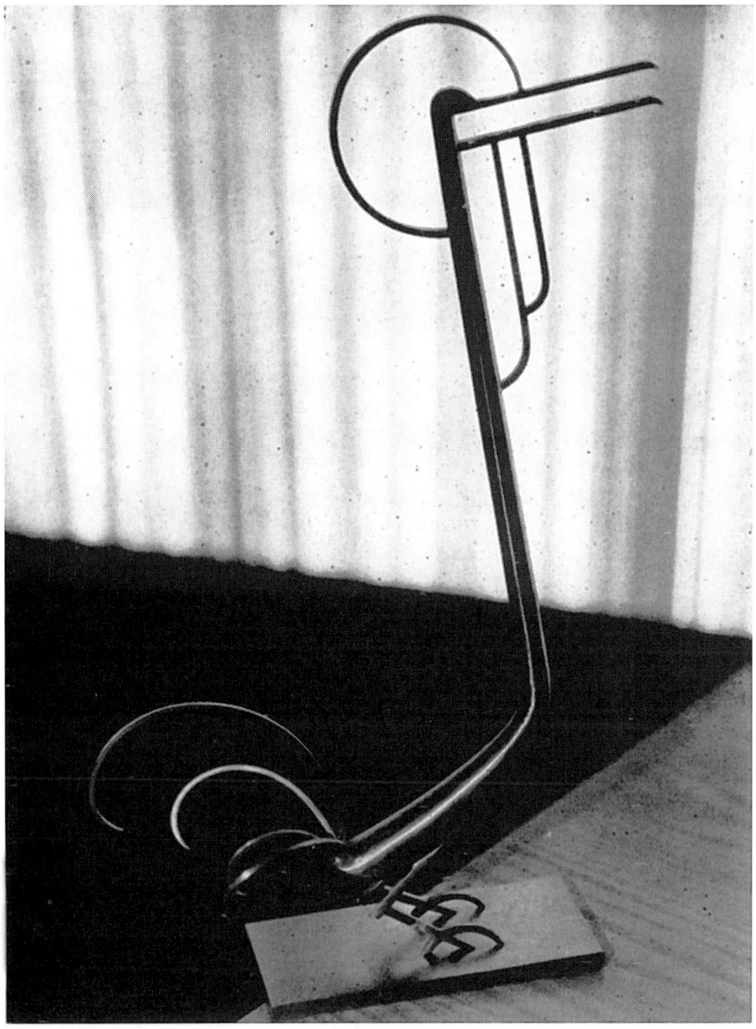

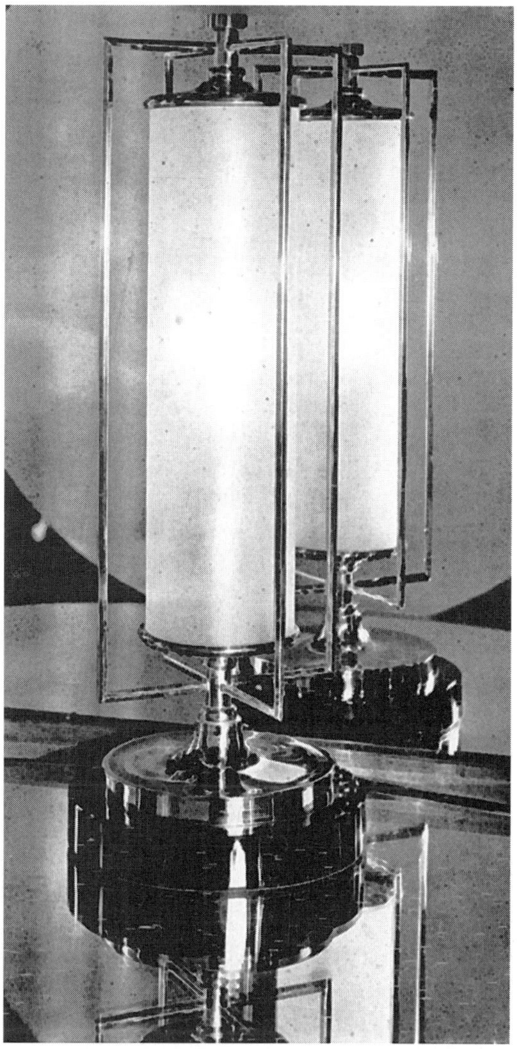

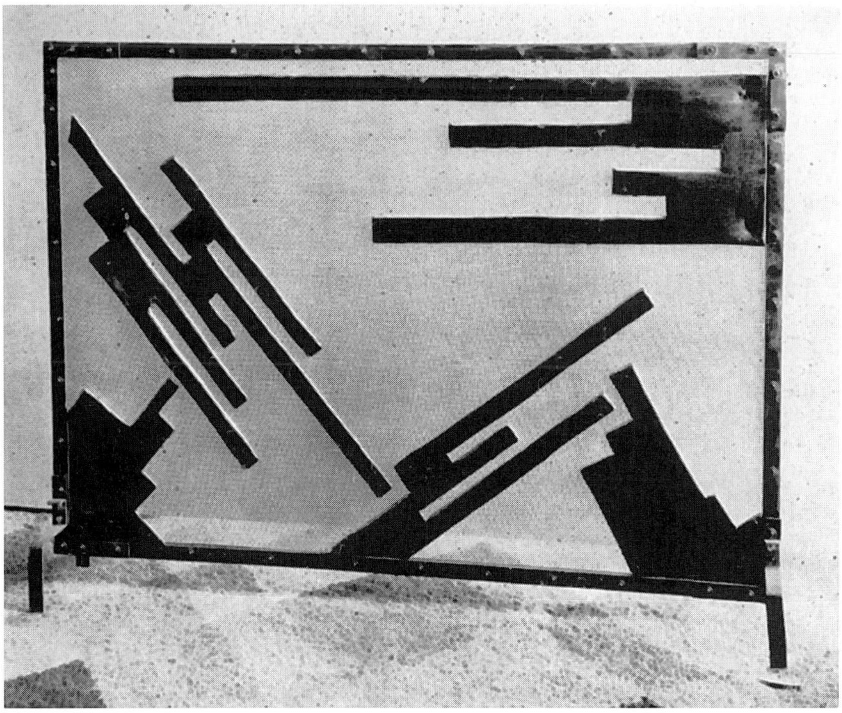

**ROBERT E. LOCHER**
**A dressing table lamp in chromium.**

**PAUL A. LOBEL**
**Door stop in cold rolled steel.**

**GUS BUNDY**
**Fire screen of hammered metal on mesh.**

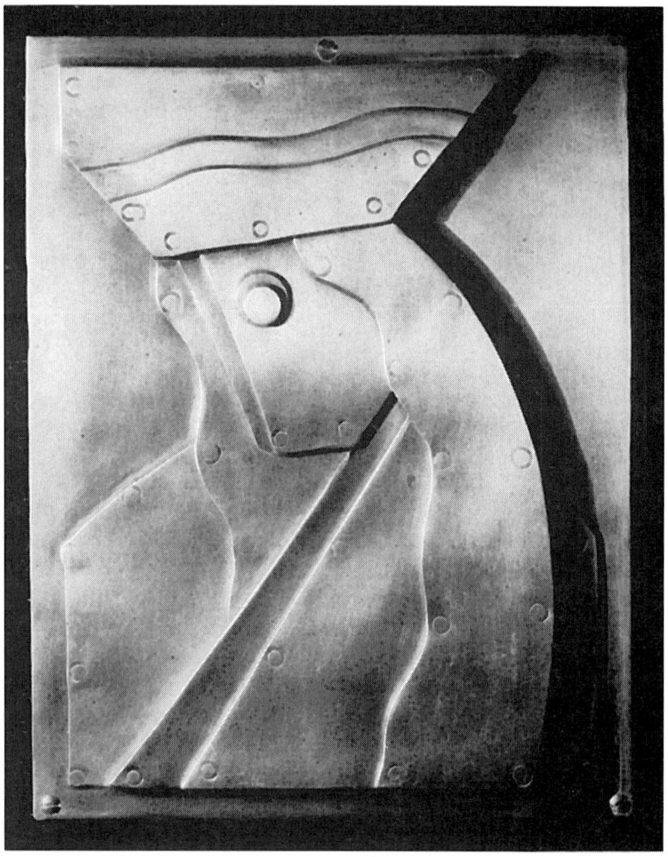

B E R N A R D   W .   F I S C H E R
Decorative plaque in copper, brass and Monel metal.

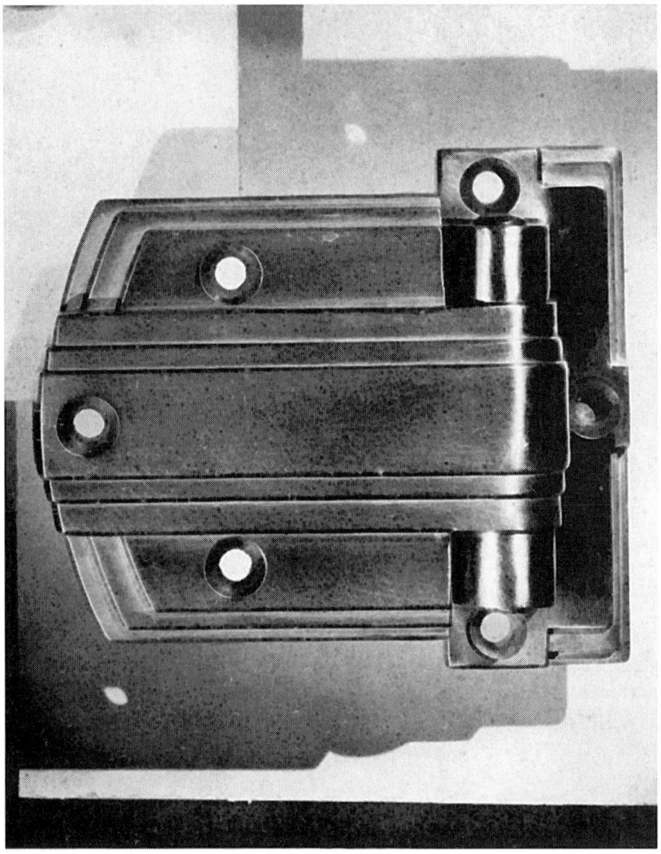

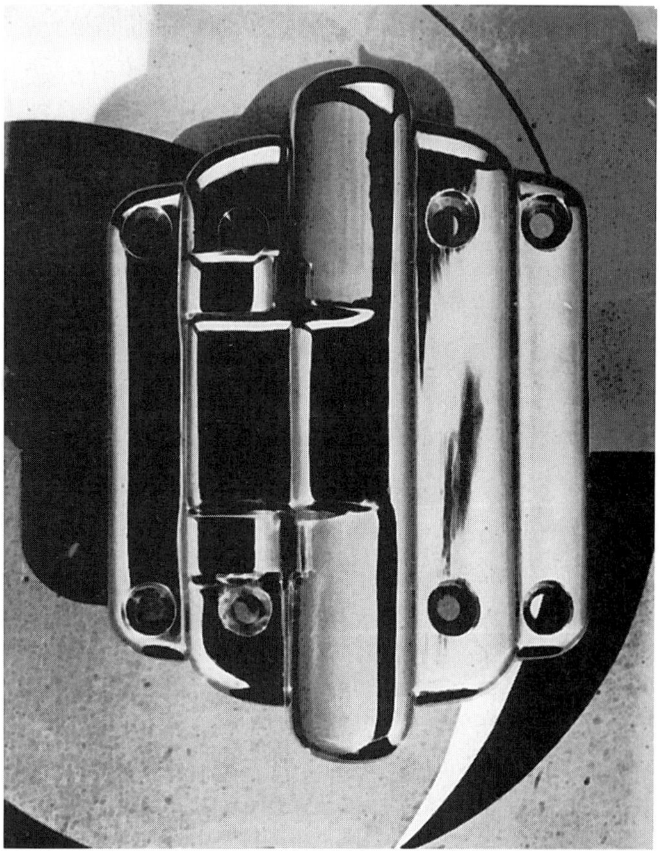

H E L E N   D R Y D E N
Two metal hinges designed for the Dura Company.

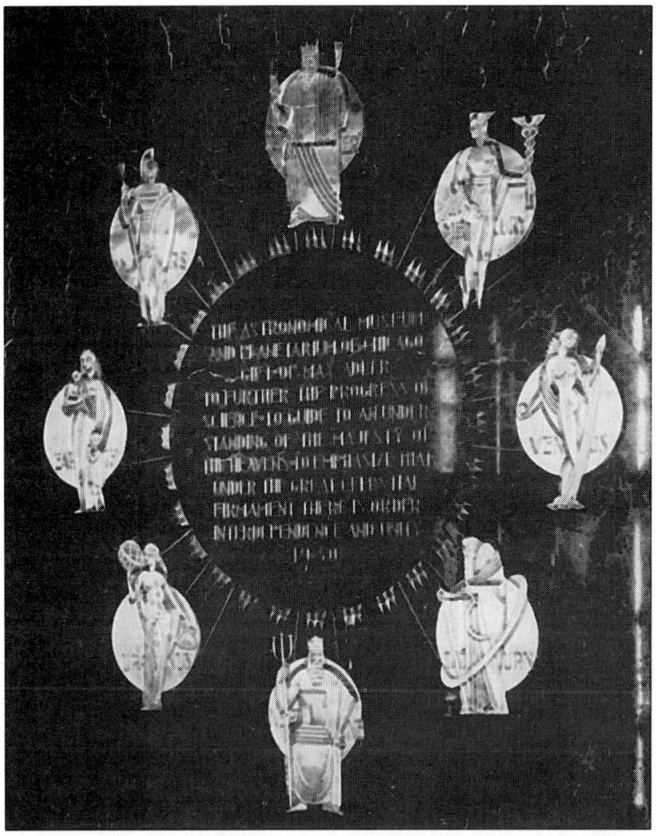


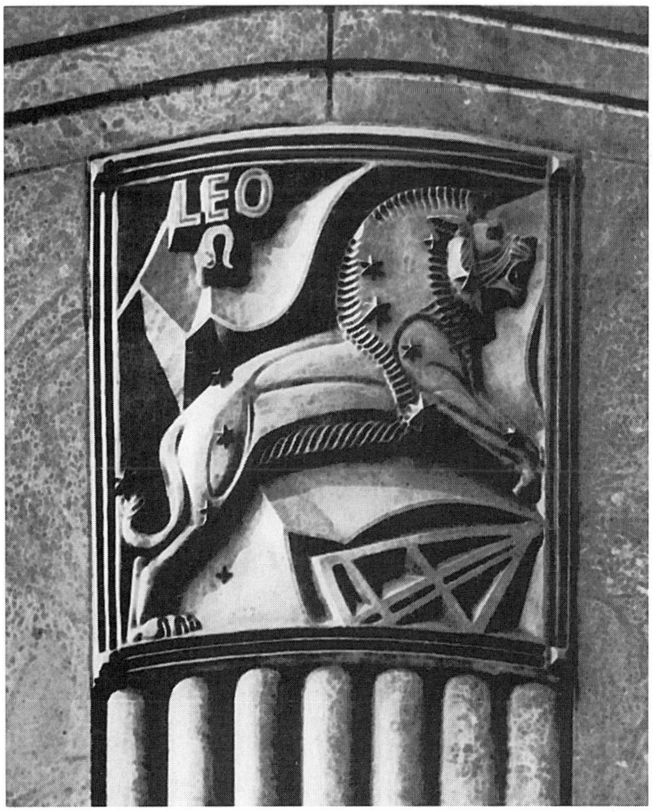


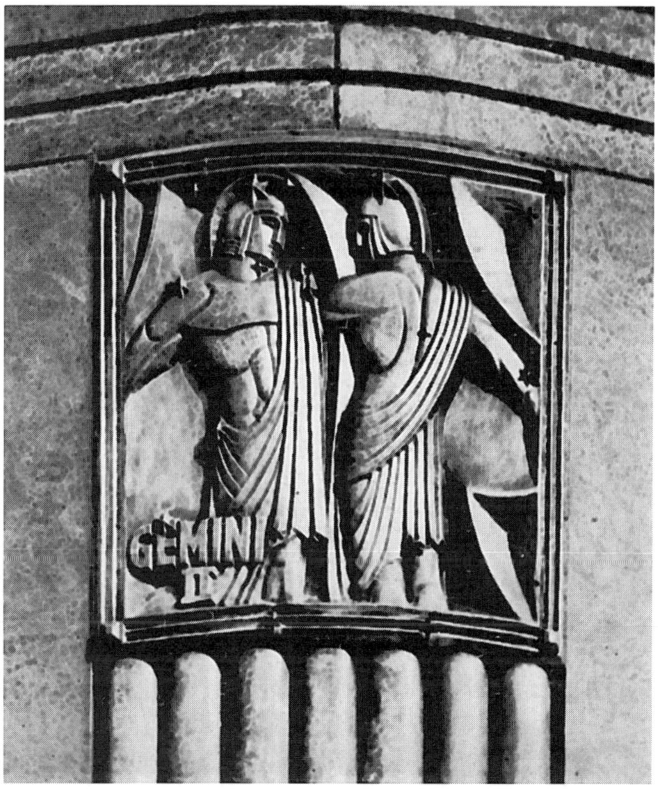


**A L F O N S O   I A N N E L L I**

**Sculptures from the Adler Planetarium, Chicago. The interior dedicatory plaque in nickel-silver on red marble. Two exterior plaques in bronze.**

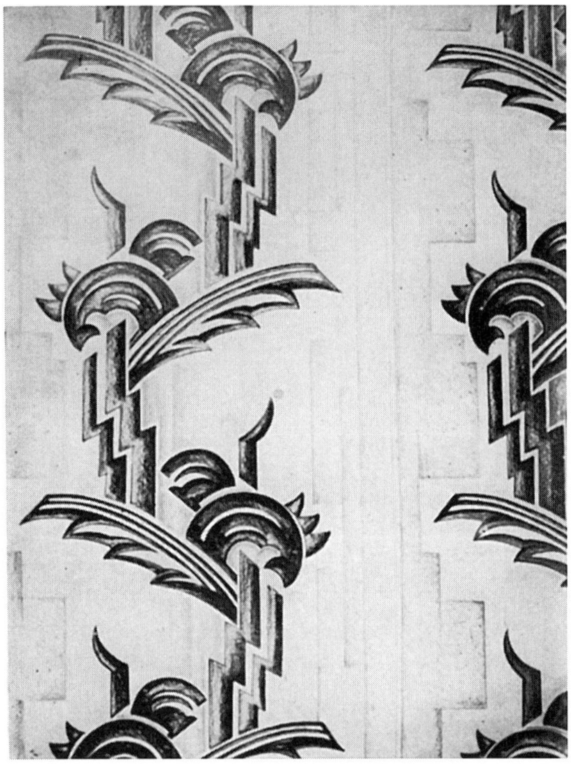

E L L E N M . K E R N
Wallpaper design in vermilion, dark blue, green, yellow chrome and ochre on cream background.

T E R E S A K I L H A M
Varnished washable wallpaper for bathrooms. Designed for Richard E. Thibaut, Inc.

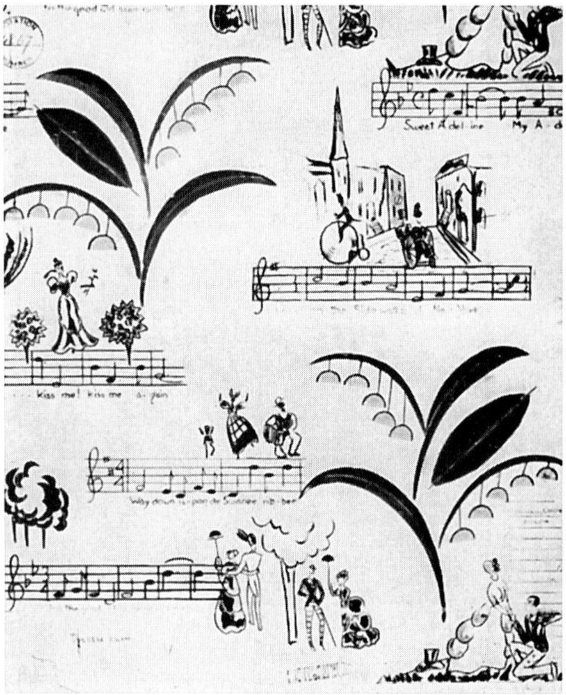


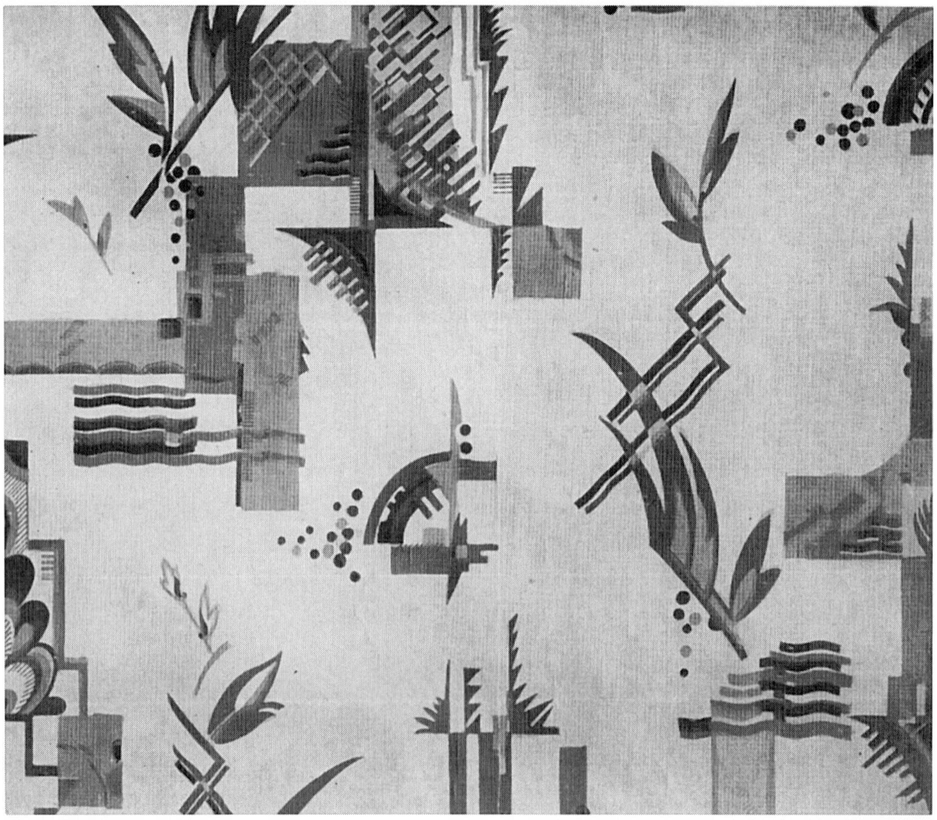

Wallpaper design in salmon, gold, green, yellow, and gray on tan background. Made for the Baeck Wall Paper Co., N. Y.

# FRANK LLOYD WRIGHT

# PRINCIPLES OF DESIGN

■ Pale paint and metallic patine do very well for certain artificial effects. There may be enough in them for a slender school of Art and Decoration. There is not enough in them for more than a very slender phaze of Architecture. Use them for what they are worth.

■ The insensate, characterless flat-surface, cut sheer, has geometric possibilties—but it has, also, the limitations of bare Geometry. Such negation in itself is sometimes restful and continually useful—as a foil.

■ Reflections and refractions should be used with moderation. A rare artist he who can manage them in exuberance.

■ The natural materials are richly gifted and lend a depth of their own to intelligent use that no artificialities or manipulation can hope to rival nor ever need to equal. Glass is a natural material. Metals are natural materials.

■ Geometry is to Architecture only what mathematics is to Music.

■ Human-sensibilities are interwoven with organic-growths of every kind, emotionally susceptible to their living rhythms and opulent textures.

■ Abstraction of these nature-elements in purely geometric terms is what we ought to call pure-design.

■ But nature-pattern and nature-texture in materials often approach conventionilization, or the abstract, to such a degree as to be superlative means ready to the designer's hand to qualify, stimulate and enrich his own effort.

■ Realism—sub-geometric,—however, is the abuse of this fine thing.

■ The "fine thing" is Reality.

■ Reality is spirit, the Essence brooding just behind the Aspect.

■ Reality is super-geometric, casting a spell or "charm" over the obvious geometric or any geometry, as such, in itself, we may imagine . . . . if we are artists.

■ Obvious symmetry wearies the eye, stultifies the imagination, closes the episode before it begins.

■ A sound constitution is pregnant with graceful reflexes.

■ That form is most imaginative or "happy" that is most radiant with this "aura" or overtone of super-form.

■ Geometric shapes through human-sensibility, have thus acquired to some extent, human-significances as, say, the Cube or Square—integrity: the Circle or Sphere, — infinity: the Straight-line,—rectitude; if long-drawn-out,—repose. The Triangle, aspiration; etc., etc.

■ Human-sensibilities are the strings of the instrument upon which the true artist plays—"abstract"—but why not avoid the "symbol," as such? It is too literal.

■ Let us abolish Art and Craft as literature in any form whatsoever.

Floor plans of the St. Marks Tower showing roof-garden floor, living room floor and studio.

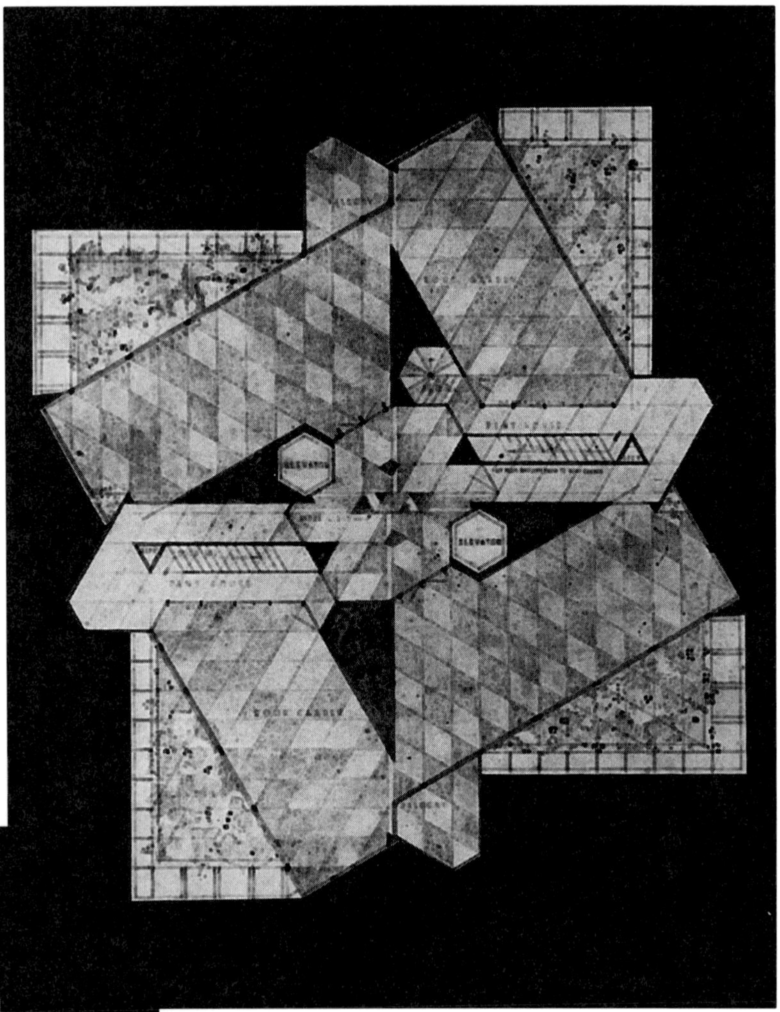

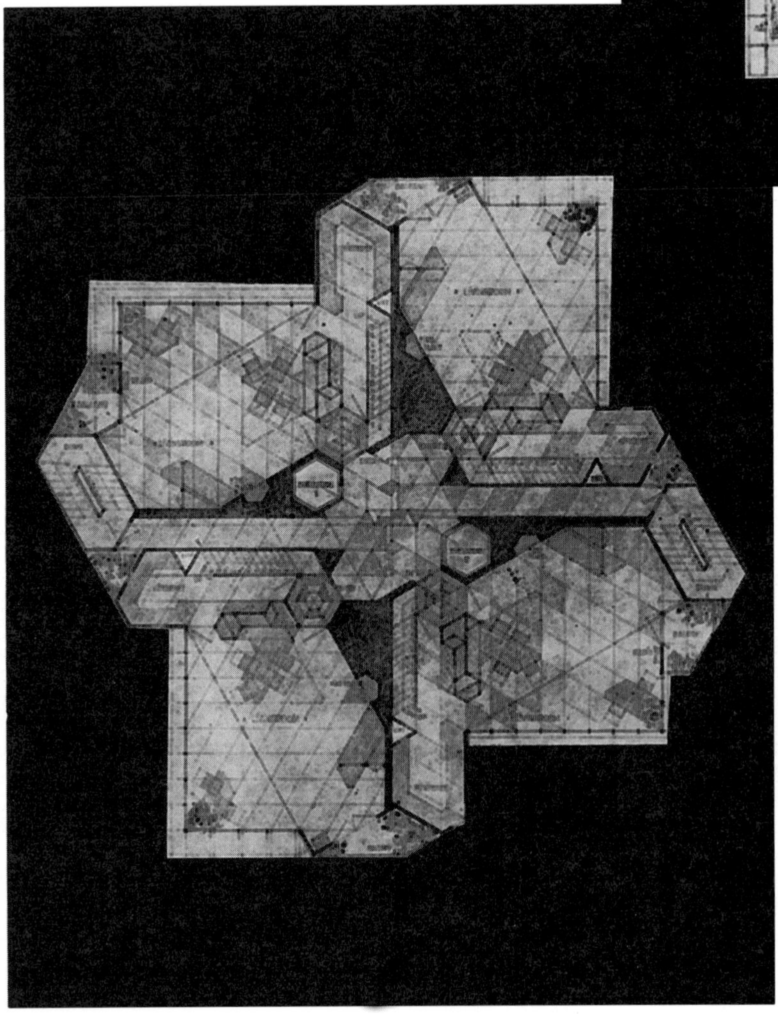

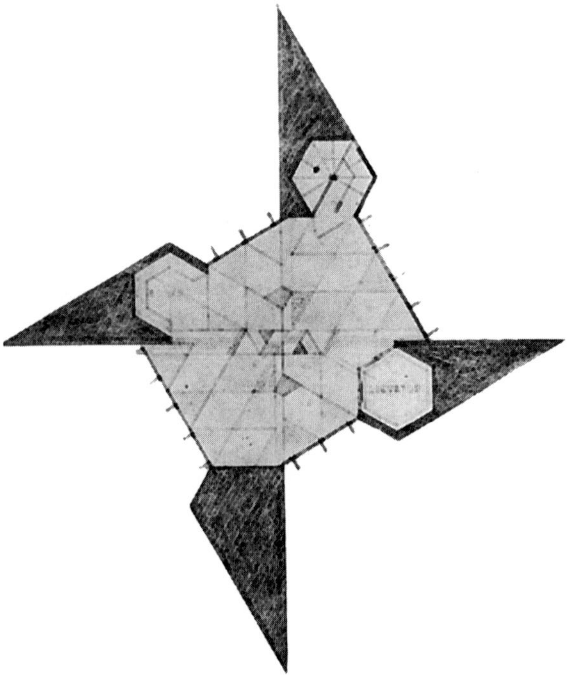

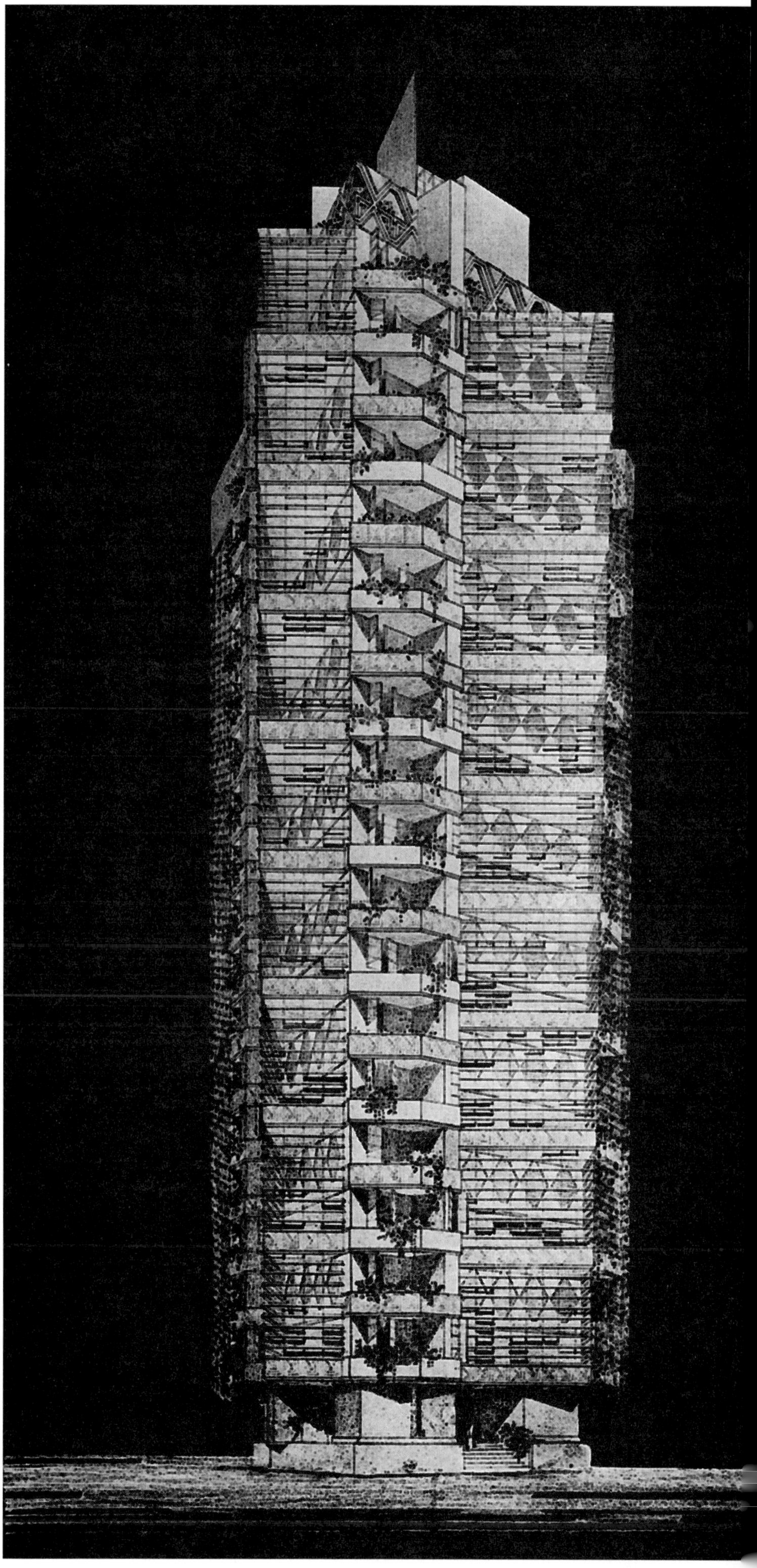

St. Marks Tower — an apartment house planned for erection on St. Marks Place, in the Bowery, New York City, to be entirely of glass and steel.

■ The sense of rhythm—how deep it is planted in human-sensibility. How far above other consideration in Art!

■ Boxes are all very well in themselves to put something into—I like beautiful boxes. Buildings may be boxes too.

■ Boxes may be set up on posts also.

■ But the box idea of a building is childish (not childlike)—because when holes are cut in the box the beauty of the box is gone. It is no longer simple.

■ Box-buildings are at the present time only the Expedient again as ever before. A mode.

■ Emulation shows itself as a Mode.

■ The box is divorced by nature from Nature.

■ The box must be attached-to, fixed-upon, set-in, stuck-up or put-over-on—environment.

■ The contrast, well managed, may be entertaining, but soon becomes an offense to the more developed sense of the whole.

■ An artist's work should "click" with environment or nothing has happened except more effigies of the mutilated-box, in the offing.

■ Artificiality is no virtue in itself, rather, as such, a defect.

■ Artificiality or artifice, is only a means to an end—in Art. The End?—more human joy —more humane living. More of our innermost life in all the things of our life. In other words, more of what imagination perceives as Reality.

■ "ART is ART precisely in that it is not NATURE?" That was all that was the matter with Art as we have known it for the past five centuries. Do not bring it back to "Art and Decoration" again to frustrate humanity for another epoch.

■ Let us now seek Art as much Nature as Nature herself. We are developed enough to desire it as "human-nature?"

■ We must ourselves make it—Yes Artificers—all: but artificial only as humble means to a greater integrity with Nature, this . . . . the great atonement . . . . possible to the human race. Without this atonement the race will die—and should die, and American will never have been born.

■ Novelty; charms: Freshness; beguiles: Justice of relation and proportion sustains,—the human spirit.

■ Human use and comfort should not be taxed to pay dividends on a "designer's" idiosyncracy.

■ Human use and comfort should have intimate possession of every interior—should be felt in every exterior.

■ Human use and comfort are the soul of "furnishing."

■ Decoration is intended to make Use more charming and Comfort more appropriate, or a privilege has been abused.

■ Decoration asserts the whole to be greater than any part and succeeds to the degree that it helps make this good.

■ The "Protestant" is useful but seldom beautiful. The world soon wearies of Negation. But when the protestant becomes constructive he loses his value as a protestant. The new protestant arises to take his place.

■ The business of the protestant-minded is disorder.

■ The business of the catholic-minded is order.

■ To render the negative service of the protestant and keep the positive values of the catholic—that, is the business of Greatest Art.

■ To the great Artist negation is impatience.

# ARCHITECTURE

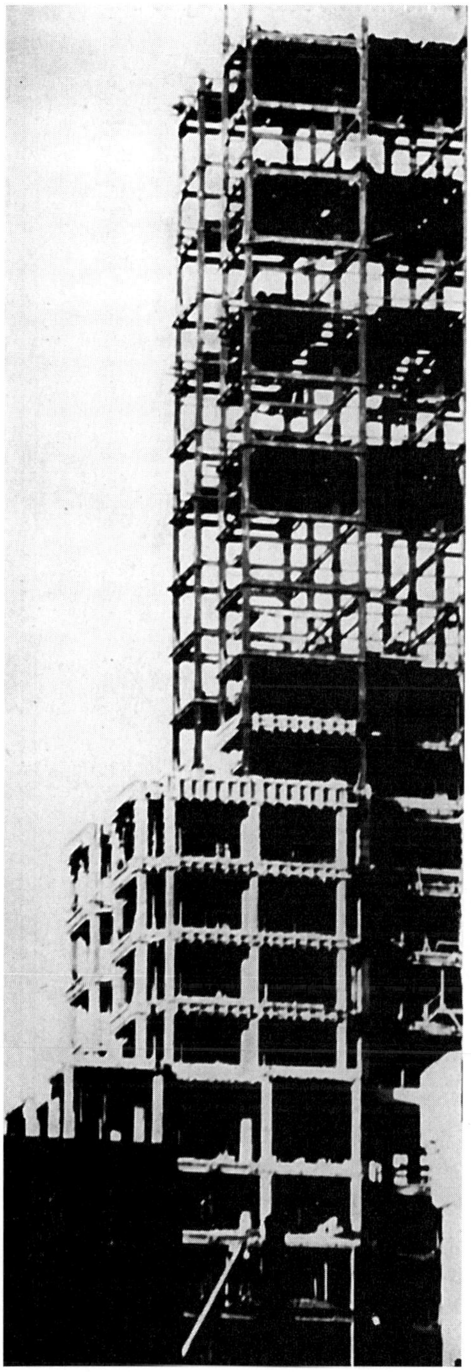

## HUGH FERRISS

## the real traditions of architecture

It is generally agreed that the great conflict which is stimulating architectural thought today lies between the Traditionalists on the one hand and the Modernists on the other. Designers who select for their facades an architectural style of the past are spoken of as Traditionalists: designers who have abandoned the familiar styles and are engaged in inventing a new style are understood to be Modernists.

If we are really interested in the nature of the current movement in architecture, let us abandon at once this general but ridiculous misunderstanding.

It arose no doubt from the fact that to many people architecture is what can be seen by the eye—just that and nothing more. In short, architecture is a matter of appearances. The architecture of a building is synonymous with the facade of the building. Thus, if the facade is a copy of a classic facade, the building is "a classic building": if the facade is Gothic in appearance, it is "a Gothic building". To such a type of mind, the "traditions of architecture" are necessarily traditions of appearances. And those architects whose concern (after the engineer has put up for them the substance of the structure) is whether to adapt "Classic" or "Gothic" for the facade are necessarily the true students and upholders of the Tradition.

From the same diverting point of view, a building whose external appearances is altogether novel is necessarily regarded as being untrue to the traditions: if a number of contemporary facades are found to be thus unfaithful to past styles and also somewhat to resemble each other, they come to be spoken of as constituting a "modern style." And anything that looks like this "modern style" is naively called "modern architecture."

To the serious student it is necessary to say that there is more in architecture than meets the eye. From his point of view, a work of architecture is not a visual appearance only, but also, discerned by the mind, an internal organization as well. He sees and discerns simultaneously; and his criterion is that what is seen by the eye and what is discerned by the mind must be found to be indissoluble. Thus illumined, the term "architectural tradition" signifies something quite different from its popular connotation.

For architectural traditions apply to buildings as wholes. Whatever may be the traditions of appearances, and however fascinating to historians of style and fashion, they are not traditions of architecture. The latter are not of such order as "A Corinthian entablature is composed of just such and such parts" or "St. Peter's dome is proportioned just so and so".

True architectural traditions are of this order: A building, to be a work of architecture, must fully but precisely reveal the material whereof it is built, the method whereby it is built, and the purpose wherefor it is built.

Now with this conception of the real tradition of architecture in mind it will not take long to see which brand of contemporary architects are the real traditionalists.

Of what materials are the typical buildings of today composed? It is no exaggeration to say, of unique materials. While it is true that wood, brick, stone continue of use—although now of secondary use only— we have, for primary use, steel, reinforced concrete, various metal alloys, innumerable special compositions—all products of the machine and all simply unheard of in past architectural epochs. And by what methods do we build? Briefly, modern structural engineering is unique in the history of building. Similarly, the purposes for which we build,—our industrial and commercial requirements—were undreamed of by Greek or Goth: even our residential requirements would seem most strange. Quite aside from the subjective impulse which leads every generation to regard its characteristics as novel, we may here, speaking objectively, state the fact which can be scarcely be denied: the Machine Age has produced materials and methods and motives for building which, in the history of man, are literally and absolutely new.

This is the novel but actual environment which contemporary designers are called upon to mould architecturally. But how are the designers of the two categories under discussion responding to the environment?

The first category—the so-called "traditionalists"—comprise those who seem but partly conscious, and often quite unconscious, of the fact that machine production, proceeding in complete disregard of the wishes of architectural scholars, has completely revolutionized the material factor of architectural design. They seem oblivious to the fact that the very ground under their feet has changed. Unmoved by th stark actualities of new material, new methods and new purposes— unmoved in short, by environment, their interest continues to be mainly or solely in heredity. In designing, their first thought is of an historic, a familiar appearance. Eclectics, they decide upon a style. They produce, let us say, an exquisite copy or a clever modification of Classic or Gothic; meanwhile, for the sake of an appearance, they deny their steel with stone, deny with a pointed arch the girder, and deny the industrial or commercial mode of life with, say, deeply revealed windows. To what kind of tradition are they being faithful? Clearly to traditions of appearances, externals, styles, fashions. Indeed, do they merit the title Architect or do they merit the title Stylist?

In the second category—the mis-named "modernists" (the reference is not of course to the copyists of modernistic appearances, who are again merely stylists) we find those designers who, unconcerned with revivalism or romanticism, address themselves at once, and realistically, to the basic problems of material and method and motive—the architectural What and How and Why. If their first experiments seem unfamiliar and strange, it can only be said that they are unconcerned with the factors of either familiarity or novelty of appearance; their concern is to hew from a unique material, with a unique tool, a perfectly rational form. When Sullivan, decades ago, uttered his famous axiom, "Form follows Function" it seemed at the time so strange a saying that the majority did not comprehend its import and the minority made of it the basis of a movement. But it was not, in fact, the announcement of a novel principle: it but seemed so to minds which could not or did not realize that in the masterpiece of the past it had always been a principle. It was true in Greece. It was true in Egypt. It had become obscured thru the recent centuries of architectural eclecticism: indeed, with that whole long period unmarked by any vital work of the first order and marked only by innumerable "revivals" of the past, the principle was eventually forgotton. But of old, and now, and always, a veritable work of architecture is a complete and precise statement of what, of how and of why it is built.

Let the chips fall where they may. Just here is their resemblance to the master-builders of old; it is the direct and unsentimental approach that justifies the title Architect.

To sum up, the so-called "traditionalists" rather than being engaged in a serious effort to preserve architectural traditions, are engaged in simply a solemn effort to preserve architectural appearances. They are thoroughly false to the true tradition. And the so-called "moderns" rather than being engaged in breaking down traditions are engaged simply in breaking down false fronts. It is precisely the "moderns" who are faithful to the real traditions of Architecture.

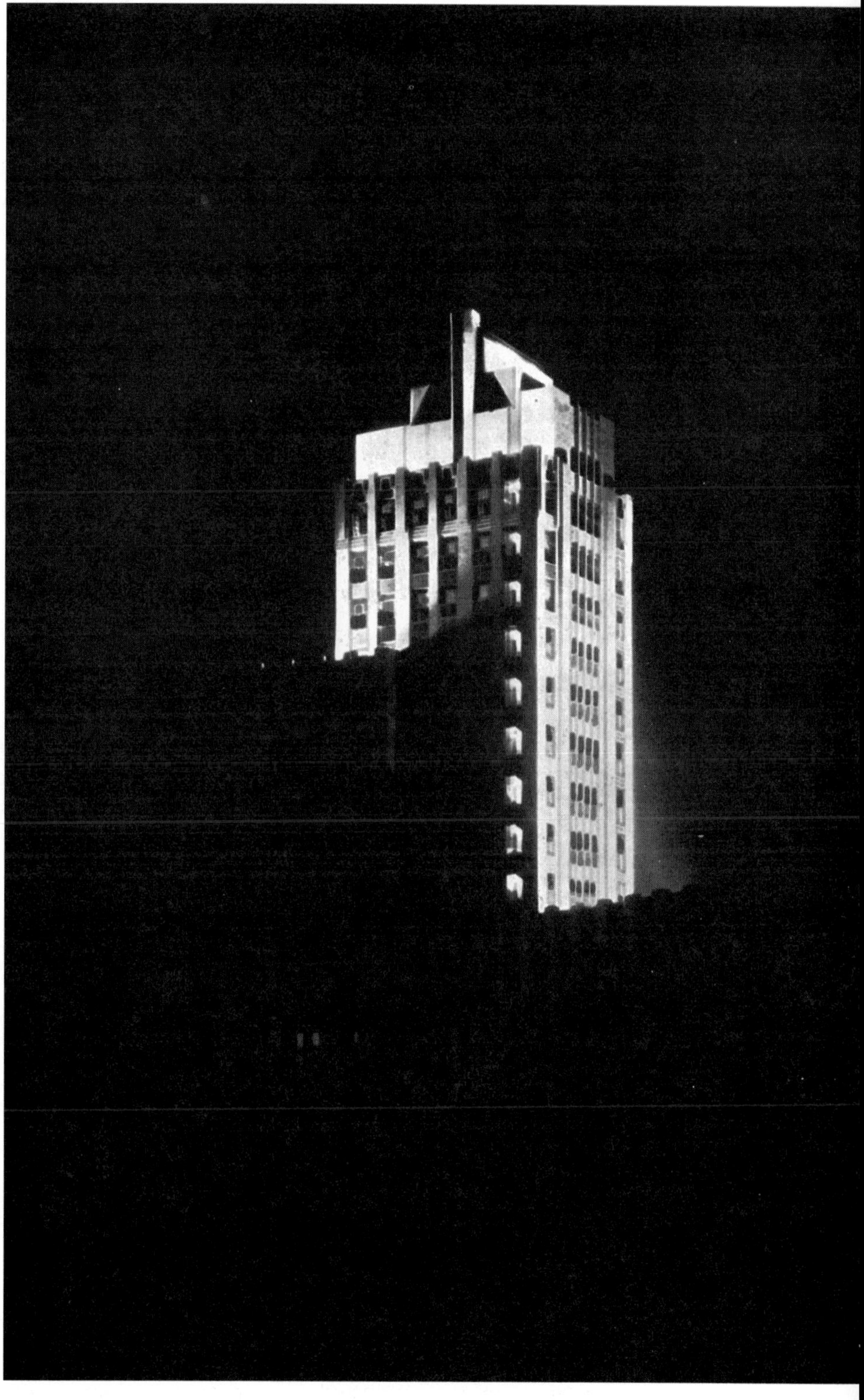

THOMPSON & CHURCHILL

**Flood-Lighting State Tower Bldg., Syracuse.**

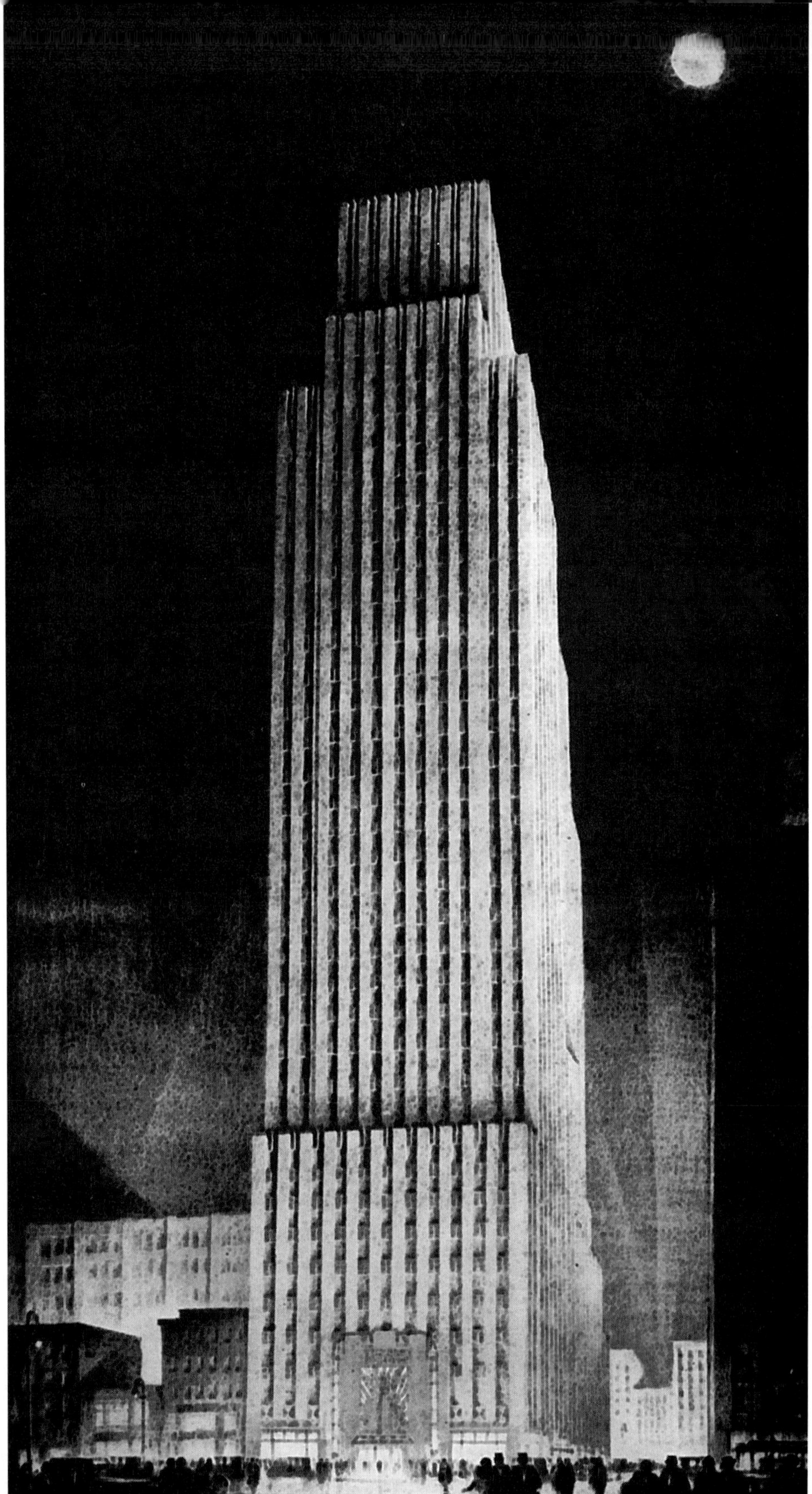

The News Building, New York City. The absence of superfluous ornament is especially to be noted.

R A Y M O N D   M .   H O O D

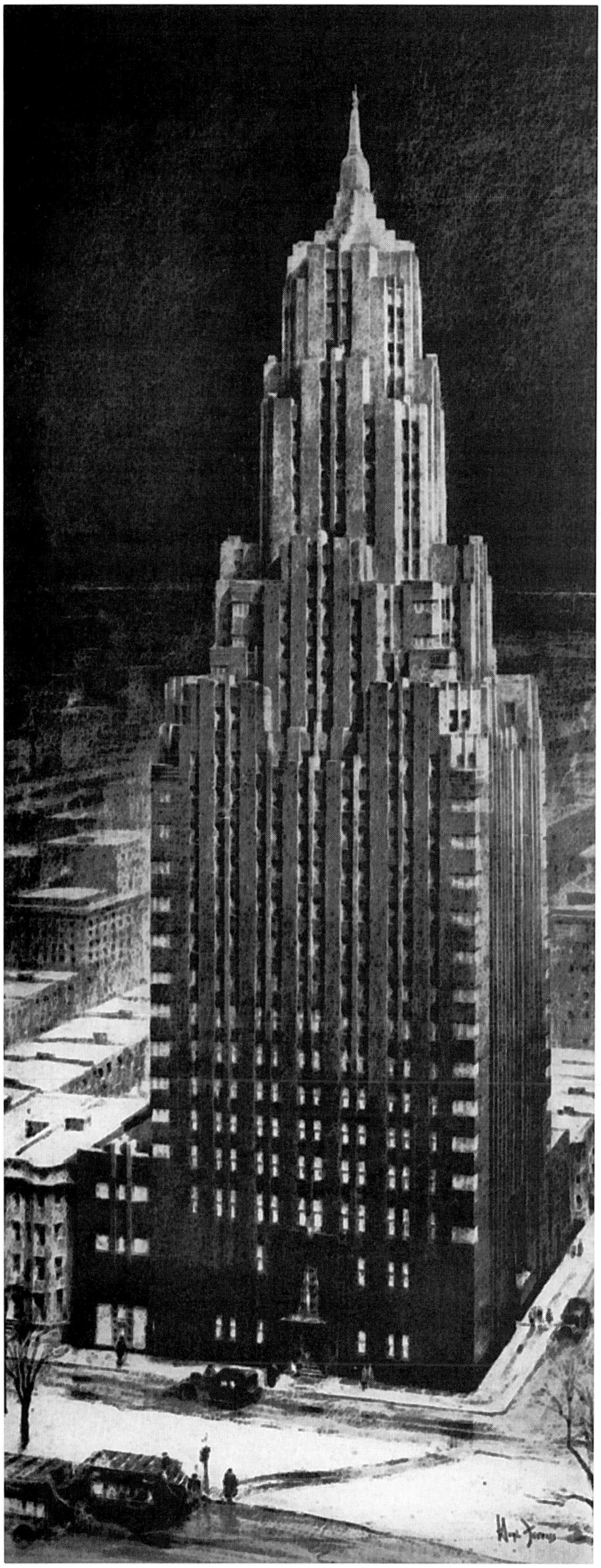

**The Roerich Museum, Master Institute and Apartments — Riverside Drive, New York City — Drawing by Hugh Ferriss.**

**The Pennsylvania Power & Light Company Office Building, Allentown, Pa.**

**CORBETT, HARRISON & MACMURRAY**

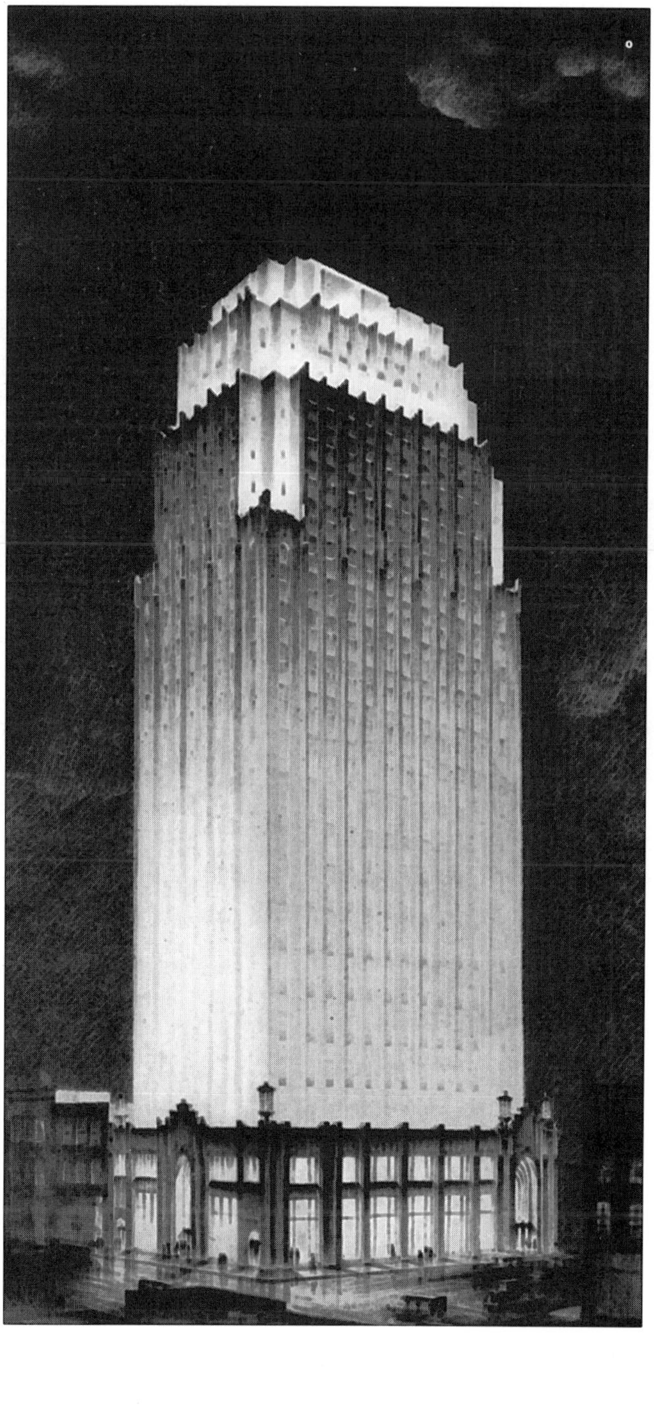

## NORMAN BEL GEDDES

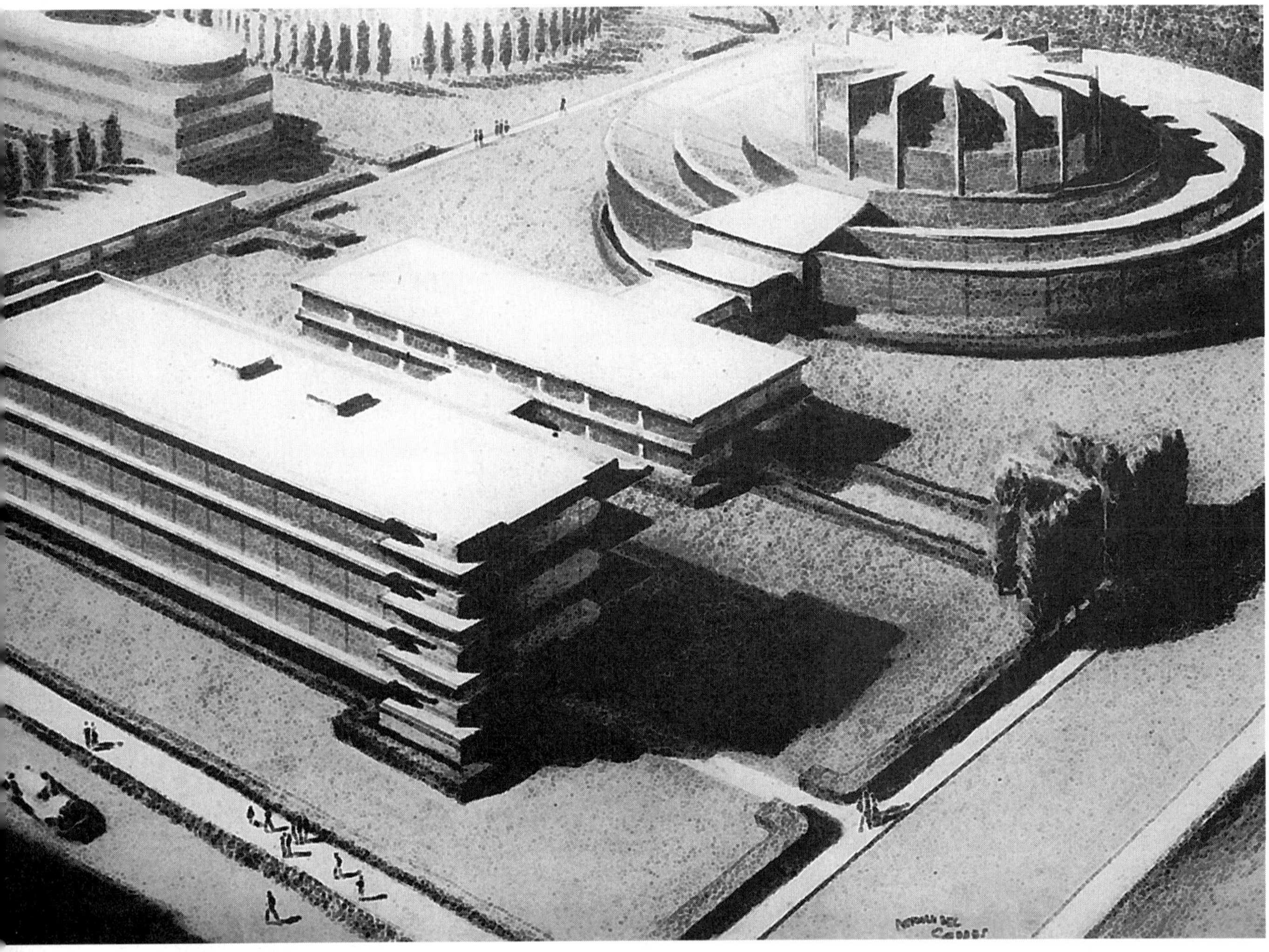

Factory and laboratory buildings for Toledo Precision Devices, Inc. The Scale Factory is a Monitor type building with walls entirely of glass. It is roofed with alternate high and low bays affording clerestory light. The building covers more than five acres. The Precision Devices group of buildings shows the Experimental Shop, Machine Shop, Connecting Corridor, Shipping Building and Laboratory. Walls in monolithic rubbed concrete.

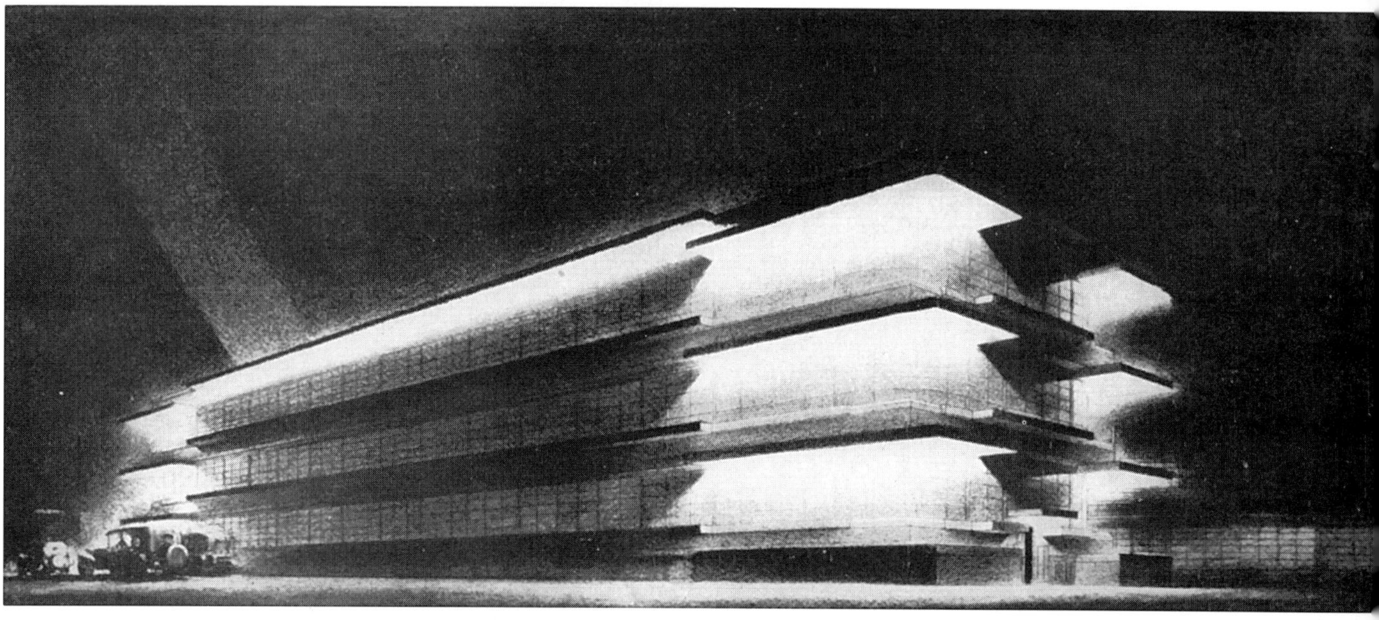

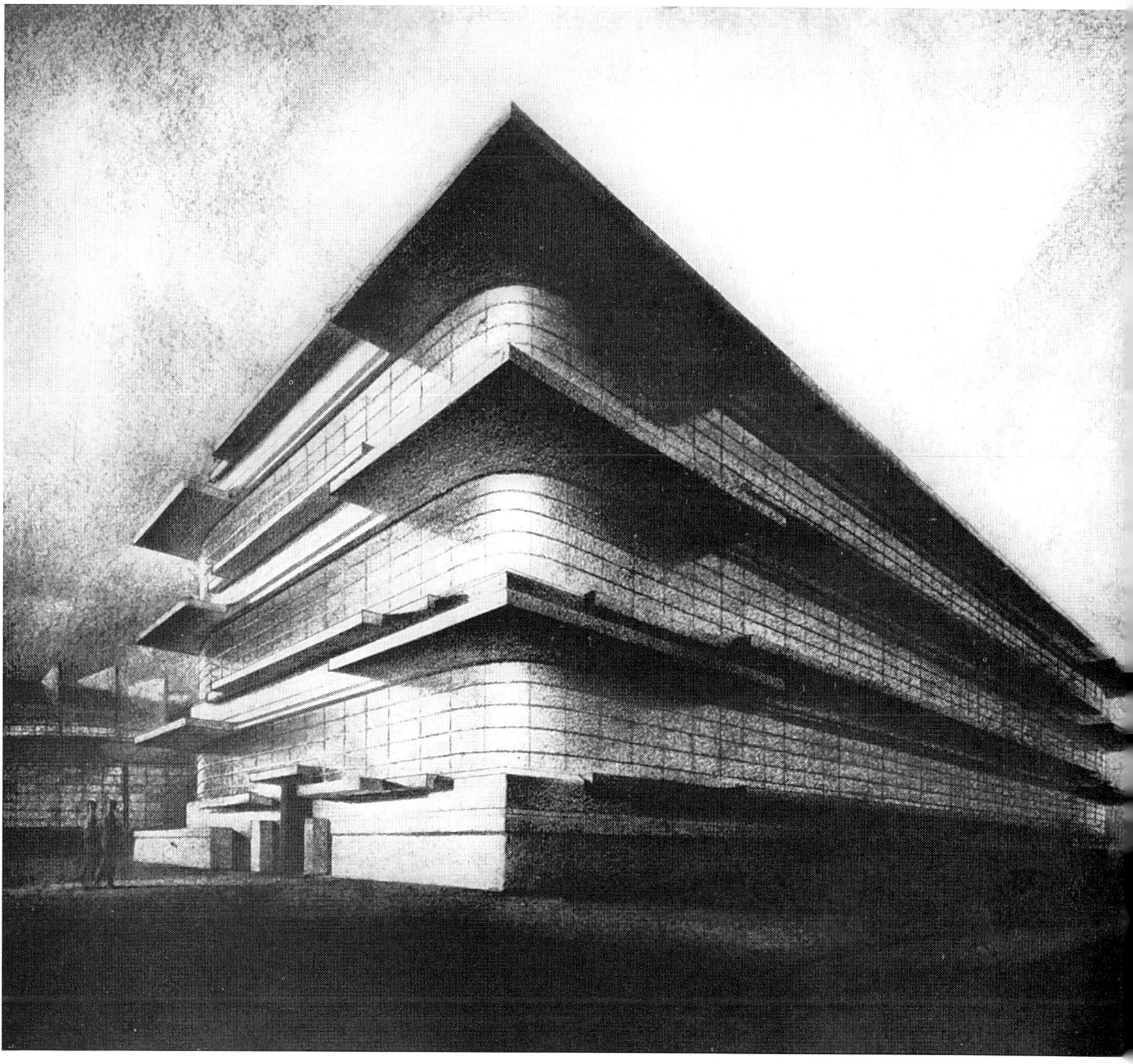

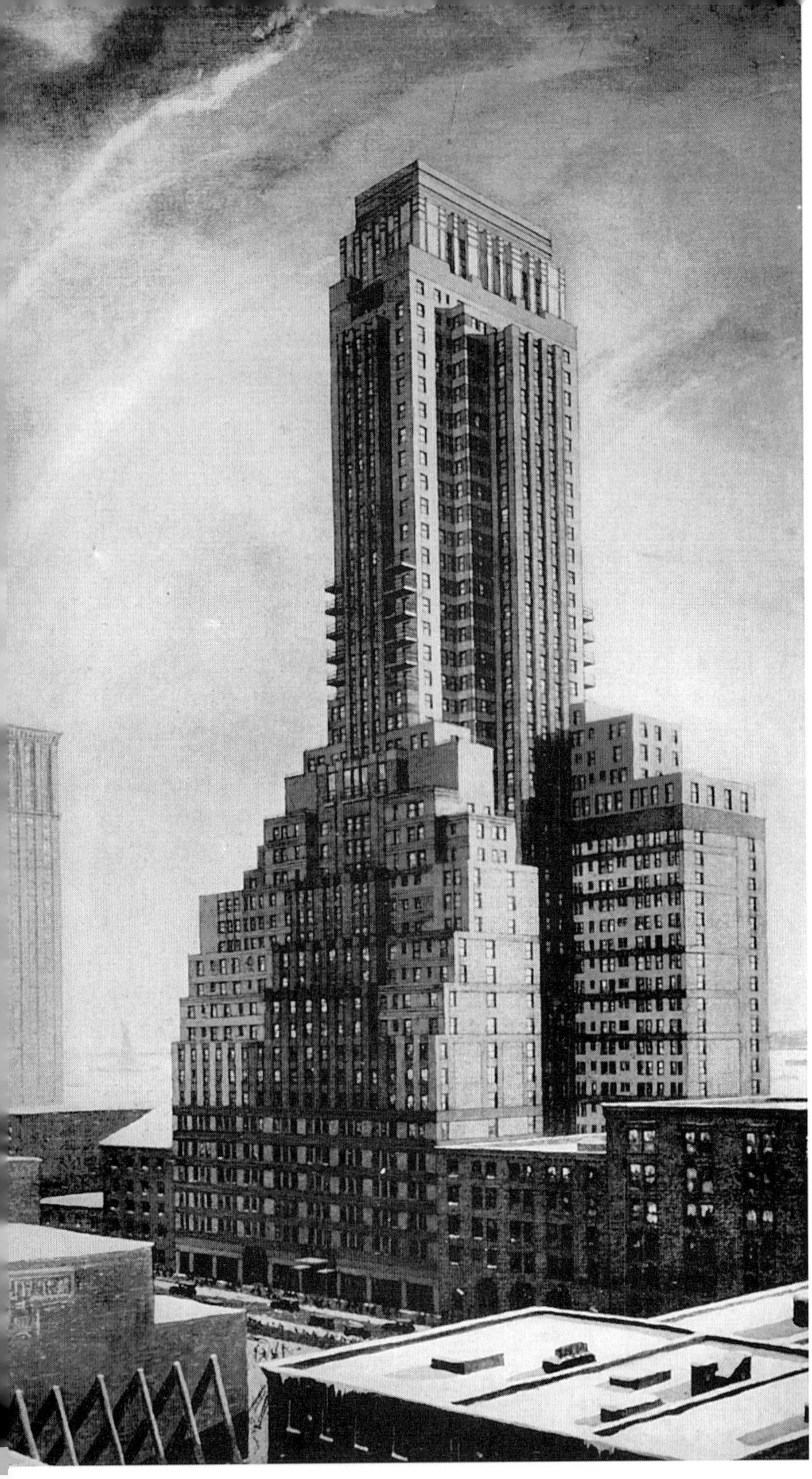

THOMPSON & CHURCHILL

Battery Tower, New York City.

Sketch for the architecture of a skyscraper emphasizing window space.

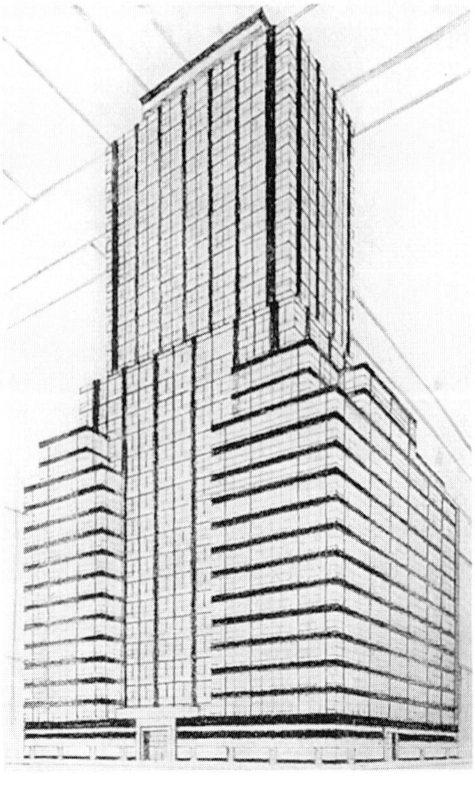

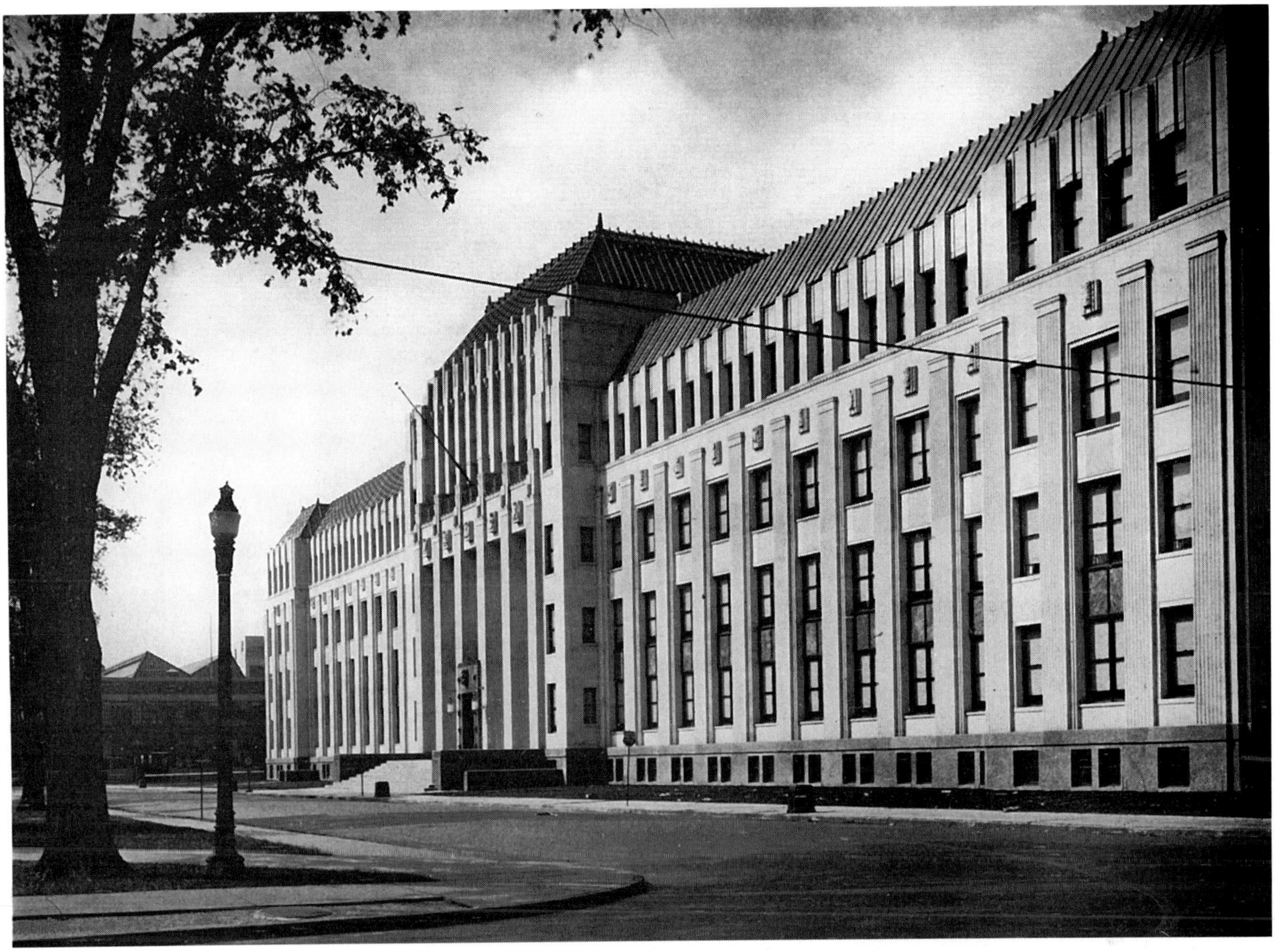

ALBERT KAHN

Administration building for S. S. Kresge Co., Detroit, Mich.

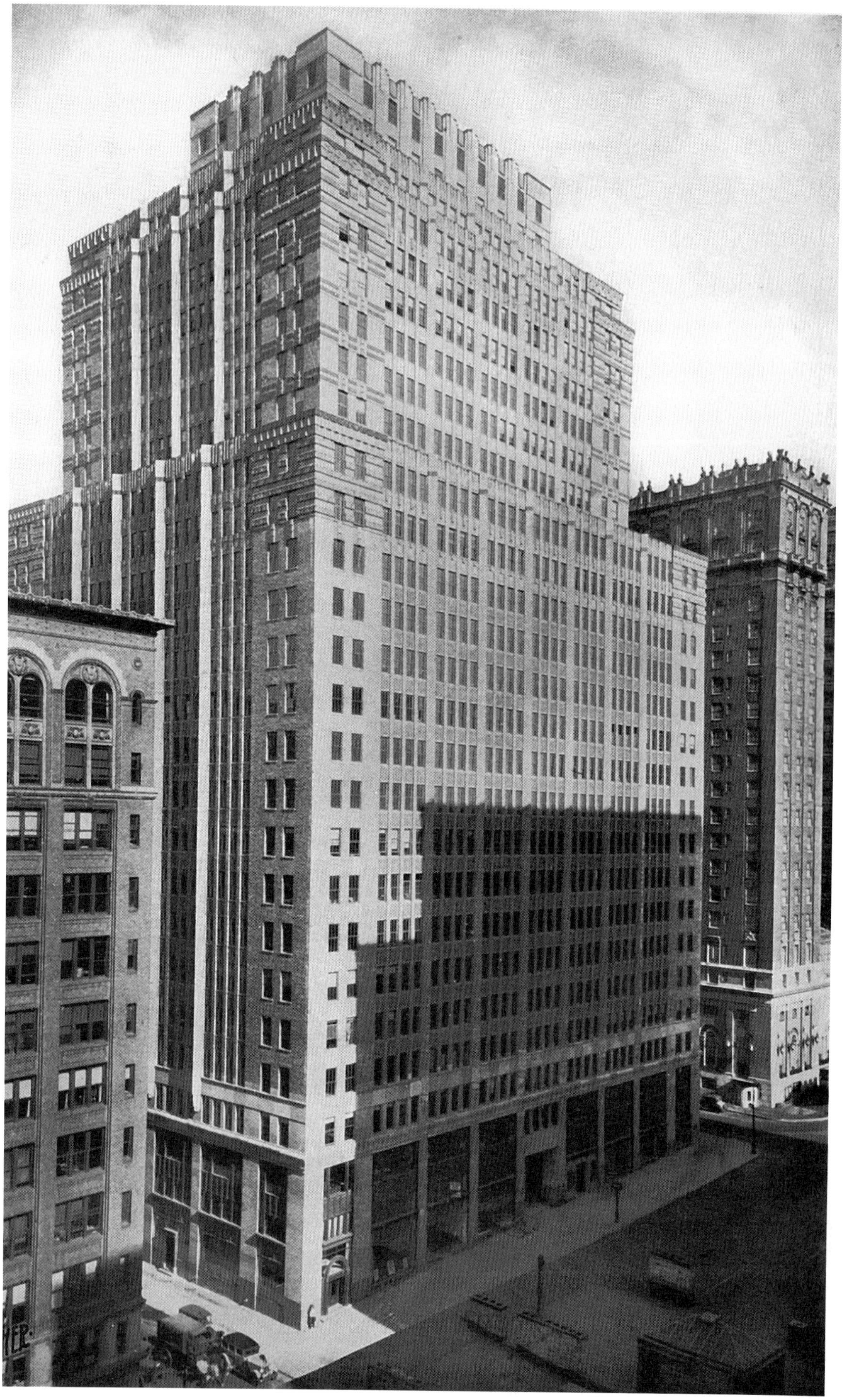

E L Y J A C Q U E S K A H N
2 Park Avenue, Office Building, New York City.

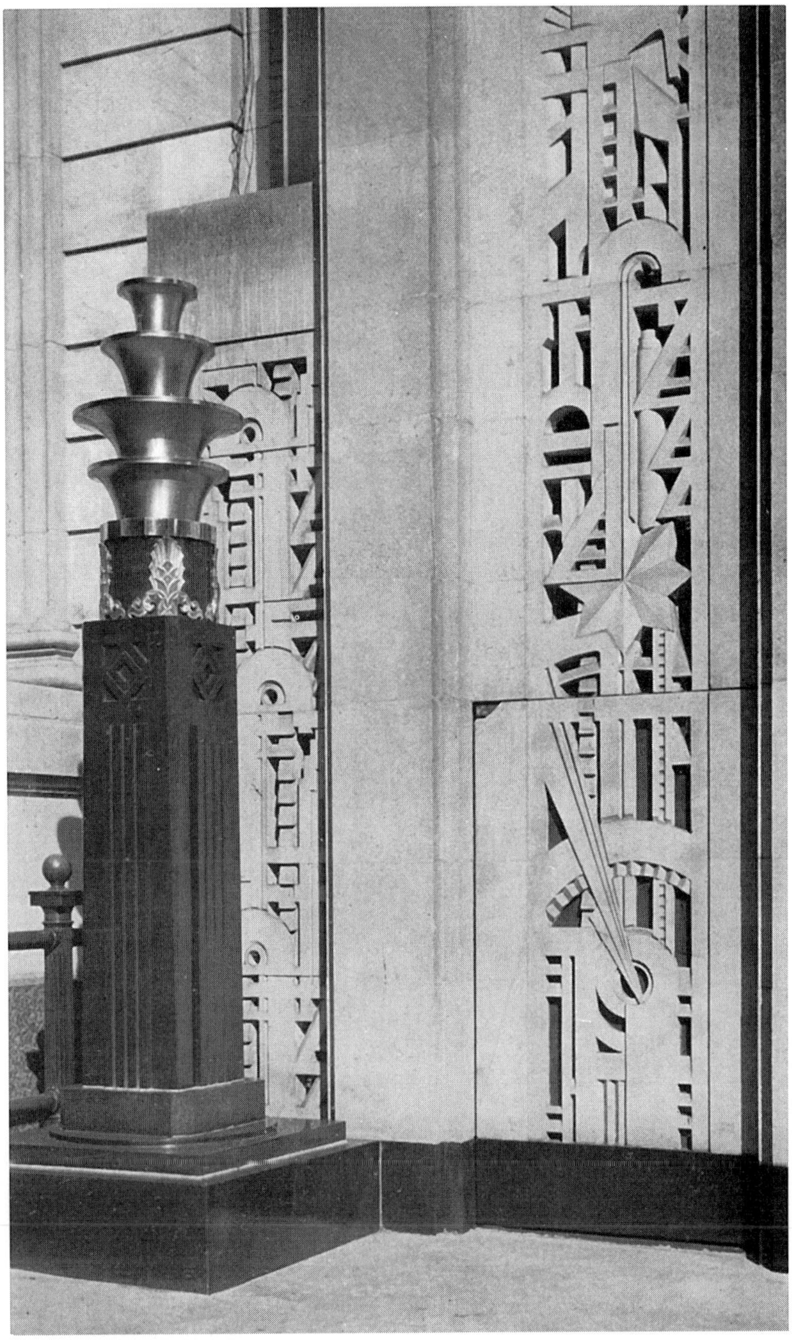

ELY JACQUES KAHN

Architectural detail of doorway in bronze in 2 Park Avenue Bldg.

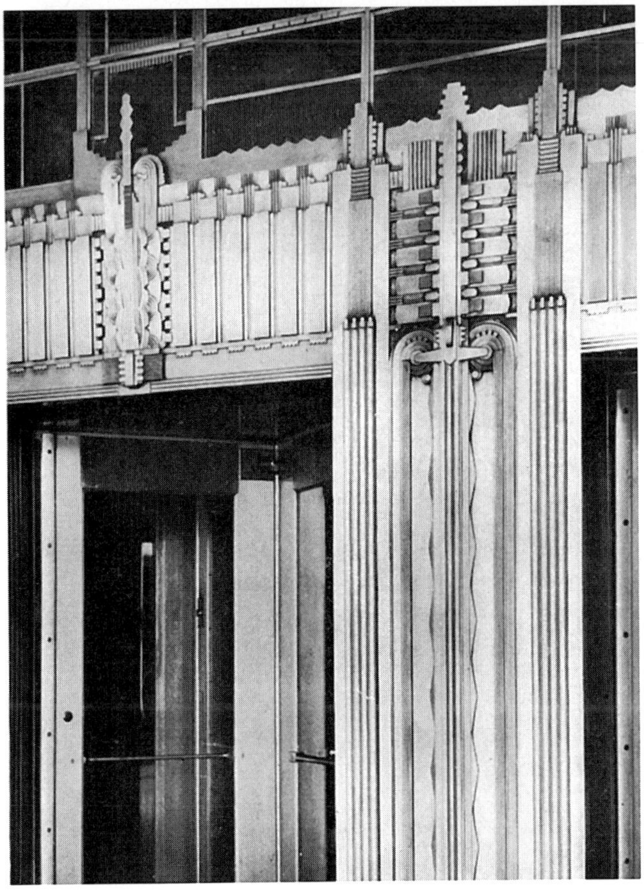

CORBETT, HARRISON & MACMURRAY

National Title Guaranty Co., B'klyn—Architectural detail of facade.

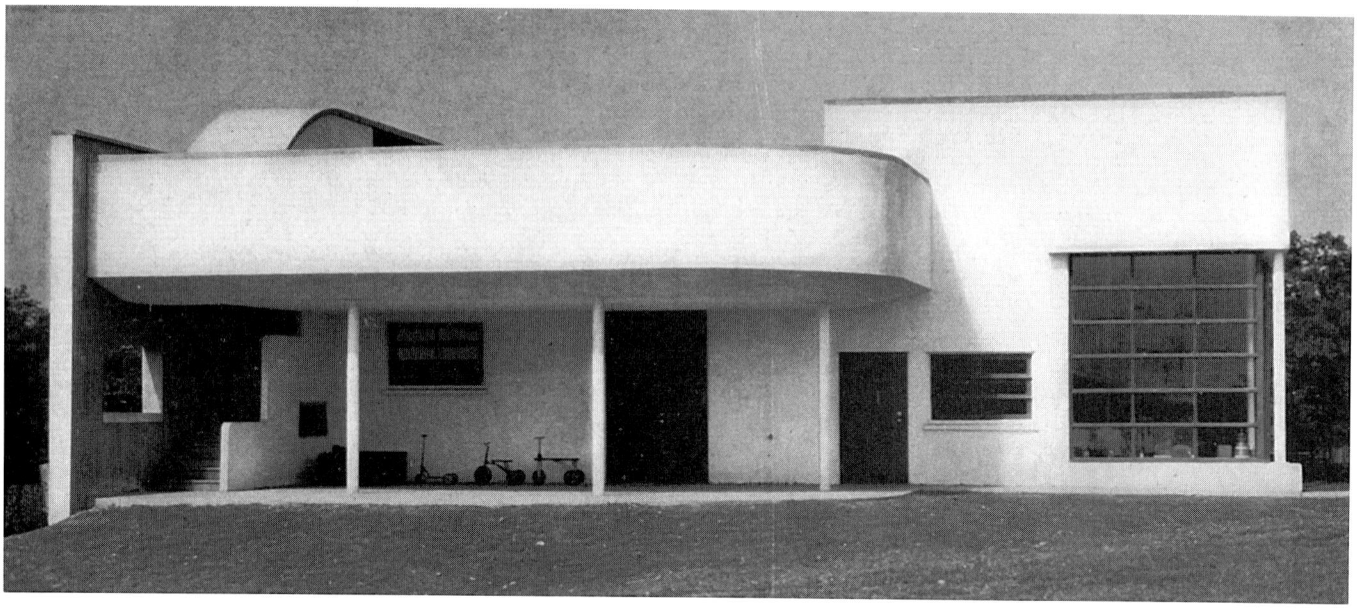

H O W E & L E S C A Z E

Oak Lane Country Day School, Philadelphia, Pa.

Residence of Wm. S. Wasserman at Whitemarsh, Pennsylvania.

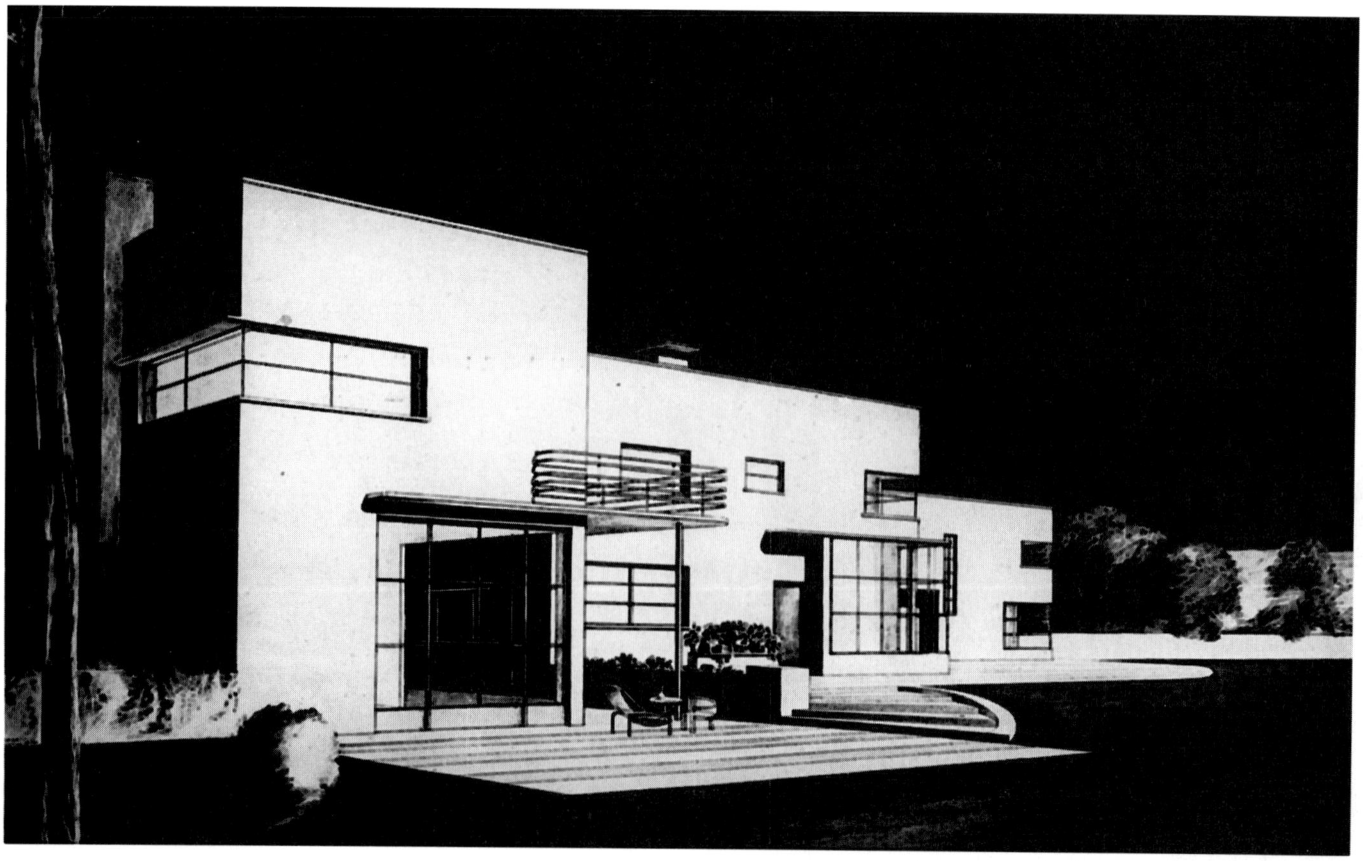

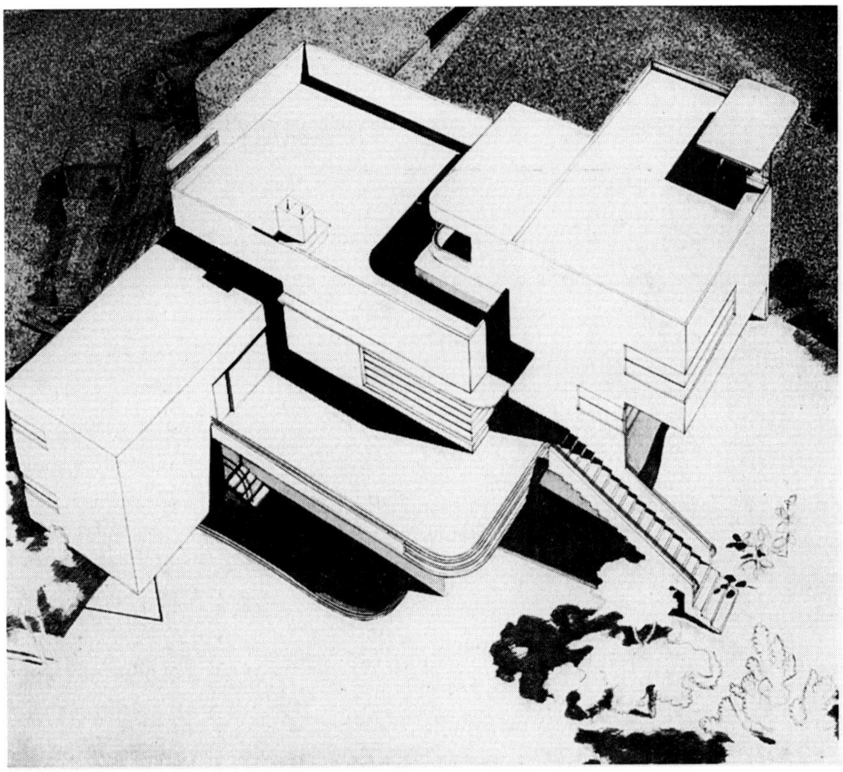

H O W E & L E S C A Z E

Mrs. George F. Porter's winter country retreat in California.

F R E D E R I C K J. K I E S L E R

Project for a modern museum. Constructed of stainless steel, opaque and transparent glass. Lower section hermetically sealed with white opaque glass; lighted and aired artificially.

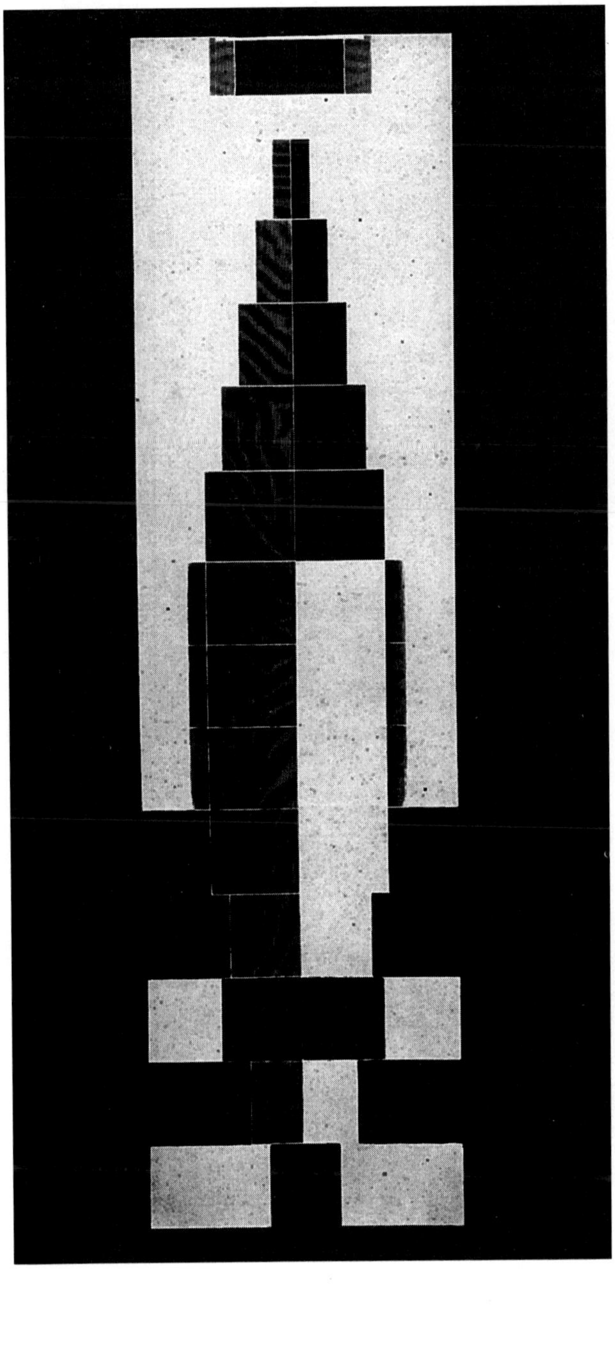

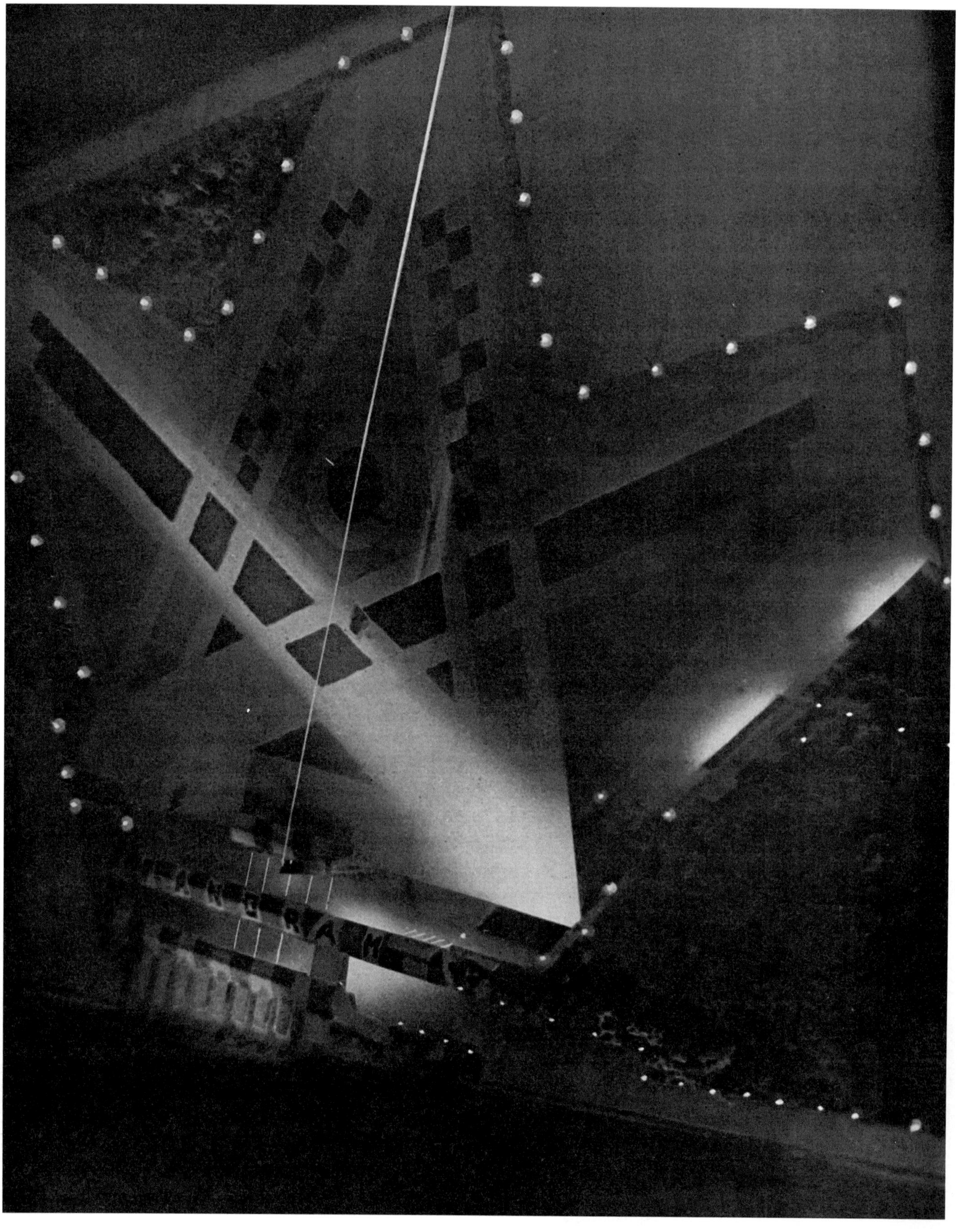

## LLOYD WRIGHT

Airport in California.

Louis Samuel residence in Los Angeles
Exterior in verte-green copper and plaster.

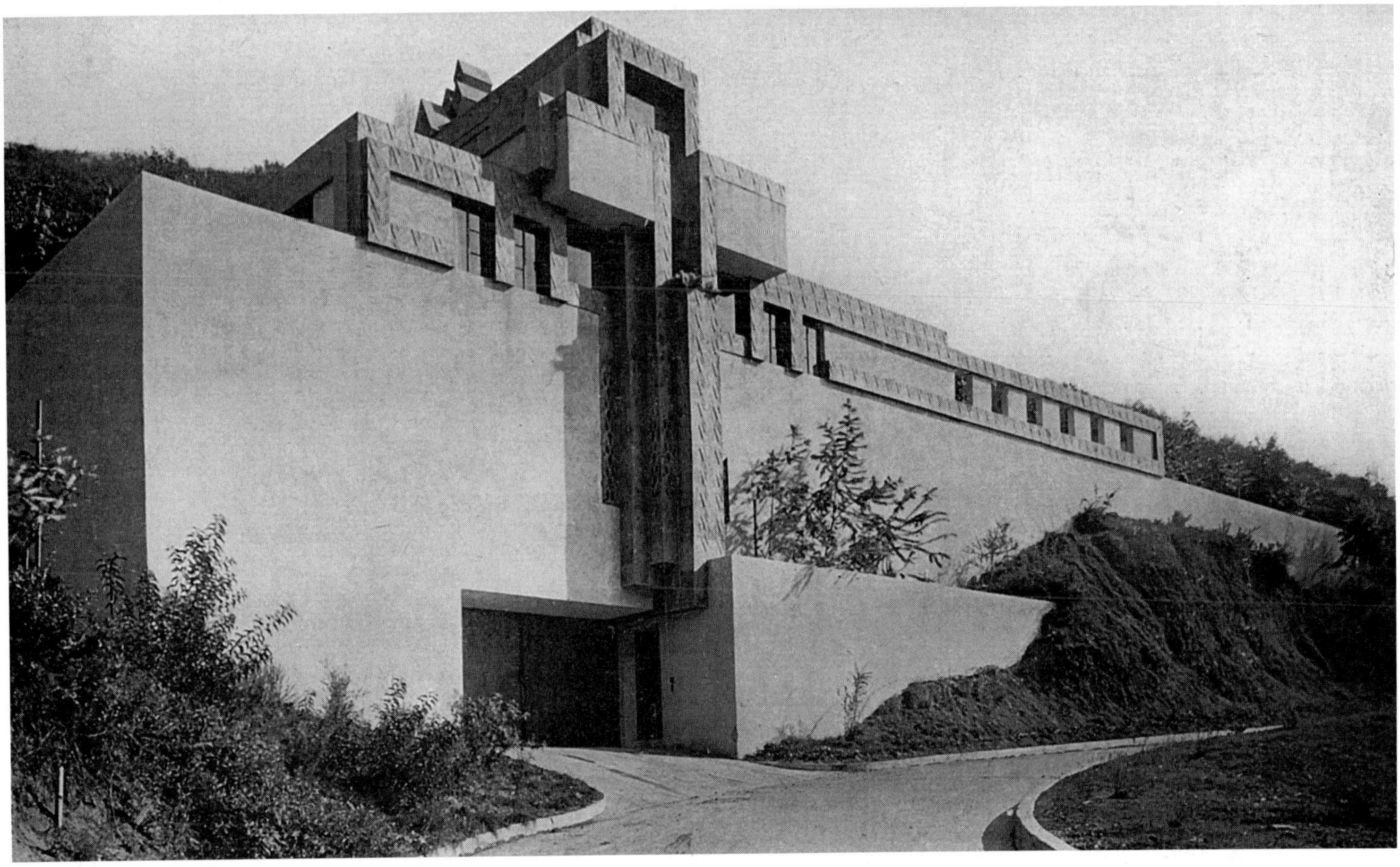

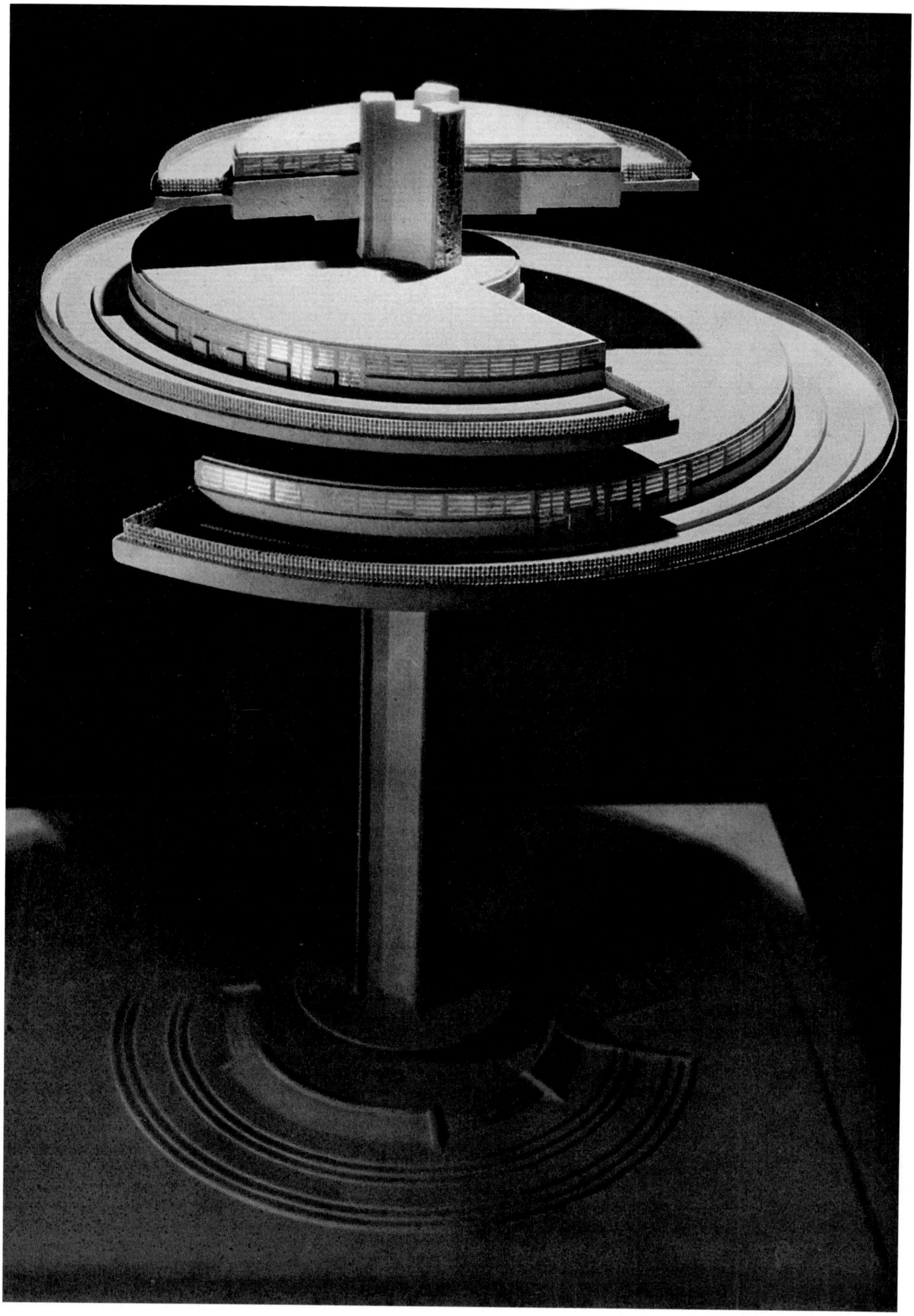

NORMAN BEL GEDDES

Model of cantilevered aerial restaurant designed for Chicago World's Fair 1933— Structure slowly revolves to give panoramic view at elevation of 25 stories.

# halls, walls and fittings

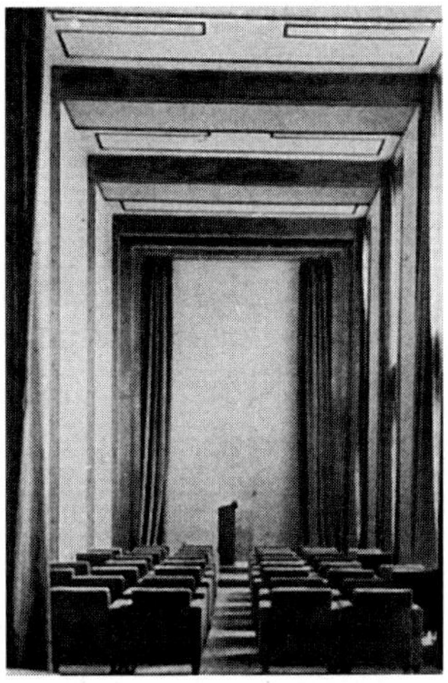

## NORMAN-BEL GEDDES BUSINESS INTERIORS

The last few years have seen the birth of a revolution in industrial design. Business leaders have admitted architects and designers to a confidence which formerly would have been, in their eyes, ridiculous. That the experiment has been successful may be readily deduced from a glance at the ever-growing list of artists who are engaging in industrial design. Of course it cannot be claimed that these alliances have inevitably been attended with success; they have not, but the percentage of success has been high. Those who have thus helped to annul the deep-seated prejudice of the business man against the artist have had one thing in common. They have been men who understood perfectly the principles of functional design, and furthermore let those principles govern their work. Thus, they have been able to demonstrate to the manufacturer that his product may be infinitely more beautiful and practical, and at the same time, cost less to produce than hitherto.

It is undoubtedly this large percentage of successful co-operation between Art and Industry, in actual production, that is responsible for what is really a natural corollary of it. I refer to the growing tendency, on the part of the commercial firms, to employ artists to design not only the product itself, but the factories in which it is made, the showrooms in which it is displayed and sold, and the offices from which its whole destiny is controlled and planned.

These business interiors are not only extremely interesting to plan, setting up, as they usually do, certain arbitrary conditions and limitations, but for that very reason they are extremely salutary in their effect upon the designer. In this field of creative art, while the designer may give, in fact must give, the fullest play to his imagination, he must focus on the ultimate purpose of his object so that it is first, last, and always efficient. There can be allowed him none of the latitude that is granted in the designing of dwelling houses for example. Here he is designing one unit in a vast scheme and his plans, to be successful, must reflect this realization.

Since the focus of interest in any manufacturing company, and the factor which colours and governs its very action is its product, it is fitting to consider first the place where that product is actually fabricated; the factory.

The factory of a big industrial concern presents, today, a very different set of problems to the architect, than it did even five years ago. No longer can he plan a more or less standardized structure and leave it to the company engineers to make it fit their needs. He must create something which is not merely a shelter, but which may, by the ingenuity of its design, be instrumental in solving some of the problems of production, for example the elimination of manufacturing wastes.

This naturally involves complete familiarity with the methods used, and with the nature of the product itself. Not only must these aspects be considered, but also the problem of employee welfare and their consequently greater efficiency.

Ventilation, heating, lighting and cleanliness are of the greatest importance. There are many industries in which the workers have to work with bright metals, shiny porcelain, and other substances which form brilliant reflecting surfaces. If, as often happens, it is also a precision industry, the problem of light becomes an acute one. The light must be strong enough for accurate work and yet must be so arranged that the worker does not suffer from dazzle and the consequent eye-strain, which would impair his efficiency. At the same time it is naturally desirable, for the sake of economical operation, to reduce the necessity for artificial illumination to a minimum.

All factors being taken into consideration, it may be said that cantilever construction will, in many cases, prove the most satisfactory. Since masonry piers may be eliminated in the exterior walls, this type of construction will permit the maximum percentage of window space, and consequently the greatest amount of natural light. Insulation and suspended ceilings, aided by built-in heaters, will maintain the necessary stability of temperature. High head windows will form a natural air siphon which will eliminate the need of costly fans, and which will allow the greatest penetration of light.

Since manufacturing methods are constantly changing under the influence of the almost daily discoveries in science and engineering, the architect must endeavor to maintain, in his design, such flexibility as will permit the easy and economical expansion, contraction or re-location of any department, or of certain machines within a department.

The use of movable partitions, which may be fitted to mullions provided for them in the exterior walls, aids materially in achieving this result. Since these partitions are made in several sizes, the architect may plan his structure so that it may be sub-divided, by their aid, into spaces of almost any size and shape.

While flexibility is of importance in a factory, in a showroom or display-window it must be a primary consideration. The display-window is the stage, the merchandise the players; the same considerations which govern the art of the theatrical designer, should in a measure govern those of the window-dresser and show-room designer. There is no doubt but that qualitative window-dressing is bound to be not only more attractive but more appealing than quantitative. Display-rooms and windows must rely on the fact that the greatest stimulus to buy is through the imagination; and it is obvious that the imagination is not stimulated by a confused and overloaded display of merchandise. Forms must be simple, ornamentation dispensed with, so that the eye can be guided to the focal point which must be arranged with such freshness, light and colour as to hold it. The product must be displayed in such a way that its beauty and its obvious utility are emphasized in equal proportion. Most utilitarian articles are susceptible of at least one arrangement which might be termed dramatic; that is the aspect which the display designer should endeavour to show.

The design of offices offers a very large scope, for the nature of the business to be transacted in them will naturally be the deciding factor in their planning. The designer must be prepared to allow the requirements of his client to outweigh all other considerations. An office must be machine-like in its efficiency, and its suitability for its purpose. It should be an example of functional design carried to the highest possible degree. The architect must consider whether it will be, for example, a work-room, or one whose primary purpose will be the reception of visitors.

Here again the problems of ventilation and lighting are of paramount importance. The noise of large cities make sound-proofing an absolute necessity, and the dust and dirt in the air are constantly emphasizing the desirability of a ventilation system which is independent of windows. In the modern office in a large city, windows should be considered solely as a means of admitting light. However well a room may be sound-proofed, its advantages will be lost entirely if the windows have to be opened to admit necessary air. It must always be remembered that anything which causes loss of concentration — such as noise or unsuitable temperature—also means loss of efficiency; an office should be like a good servant, never obtrusive but always anticipating the every wish of his master.

An office which is required primarily for the reception of visitors naturally sets up an entirely different set of problems. The visitor must be impressed, made comfortable and soothed, so that he is in a receptive frame of mind. Psychology is playing an ever-increasing part in business and the designer should not overlook this fact. Decoration and lighting must be applied to this one end, the creation of a certain impression upon the visitor.

In our day, the architect has all the elements at his command. His only limitation is that his creation be practical, designed always with its ultimate purpose in mind. In designing business interiors, he requires more than his knowledge of architecture and design; he must have imagination, flexibility and a knowledge of human psychology; he must be entirely of our time, ready to take the fullest advantage of the benefits our modern civilization has to offer.

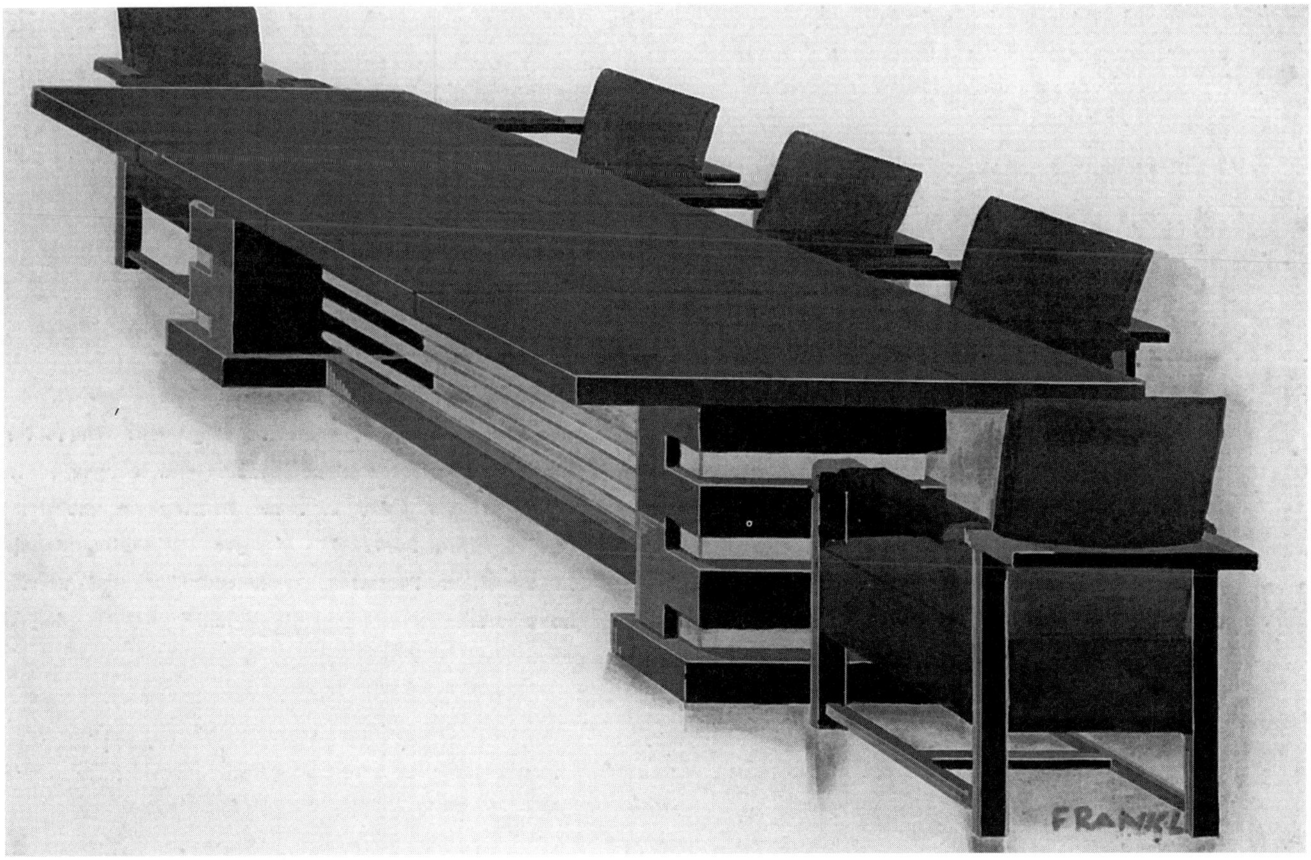


PAUL T. FRANKL
Conference table and chairs.

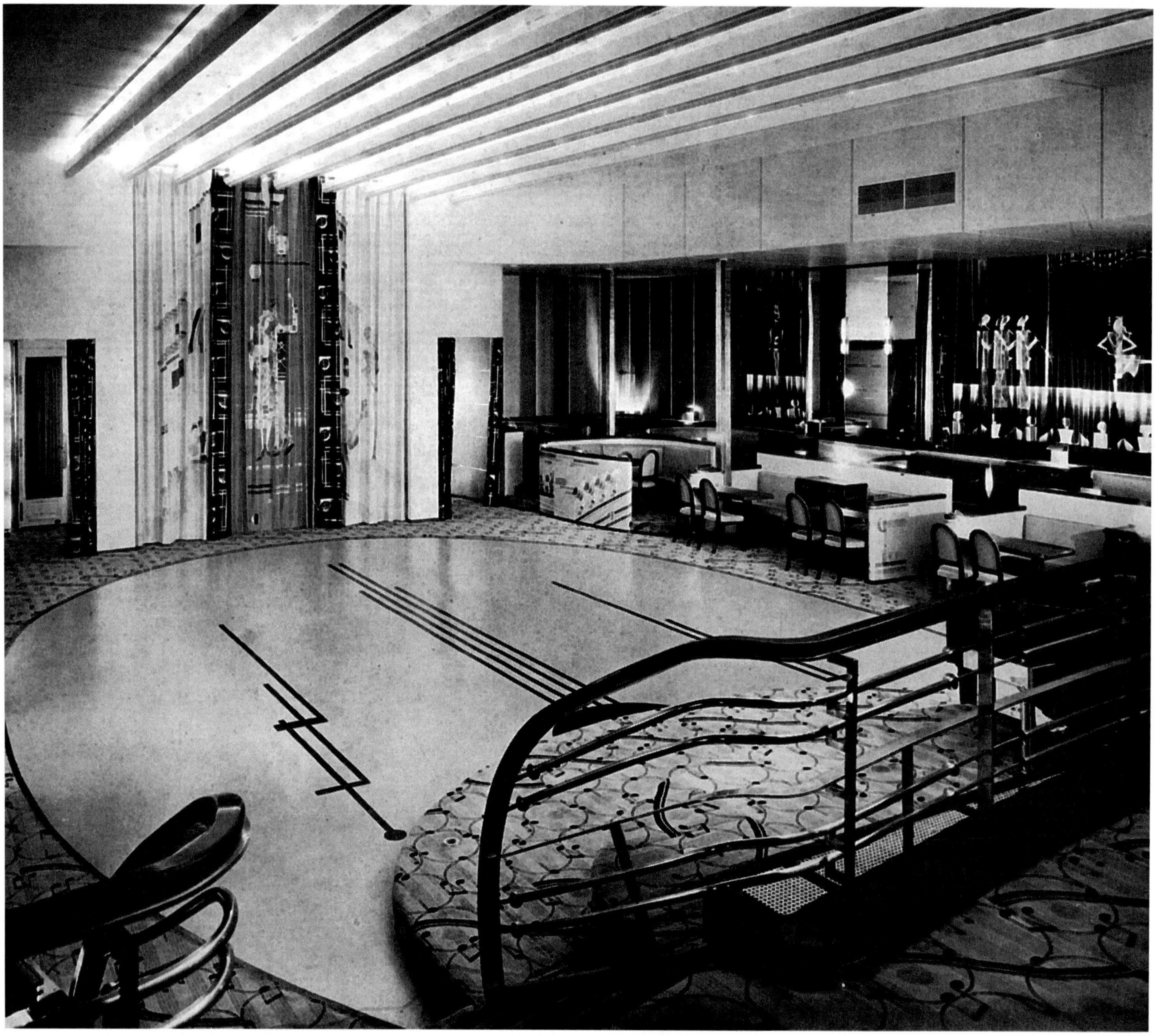

**Night Club—S. S. Leviathan.** The major elements of the plan are the dance floor, orchestra stage and alcoves for seating. Alcoves consist of stationary tables and lounges on two raised levels at both sides of room insuring an unobstructed view of the entire floor. The lounges and chairs are upholstered in vermilion Permatex. Refreshment and serving tables have each an individual lighting fixture in chromium.

E U G E N E   S C H O E N

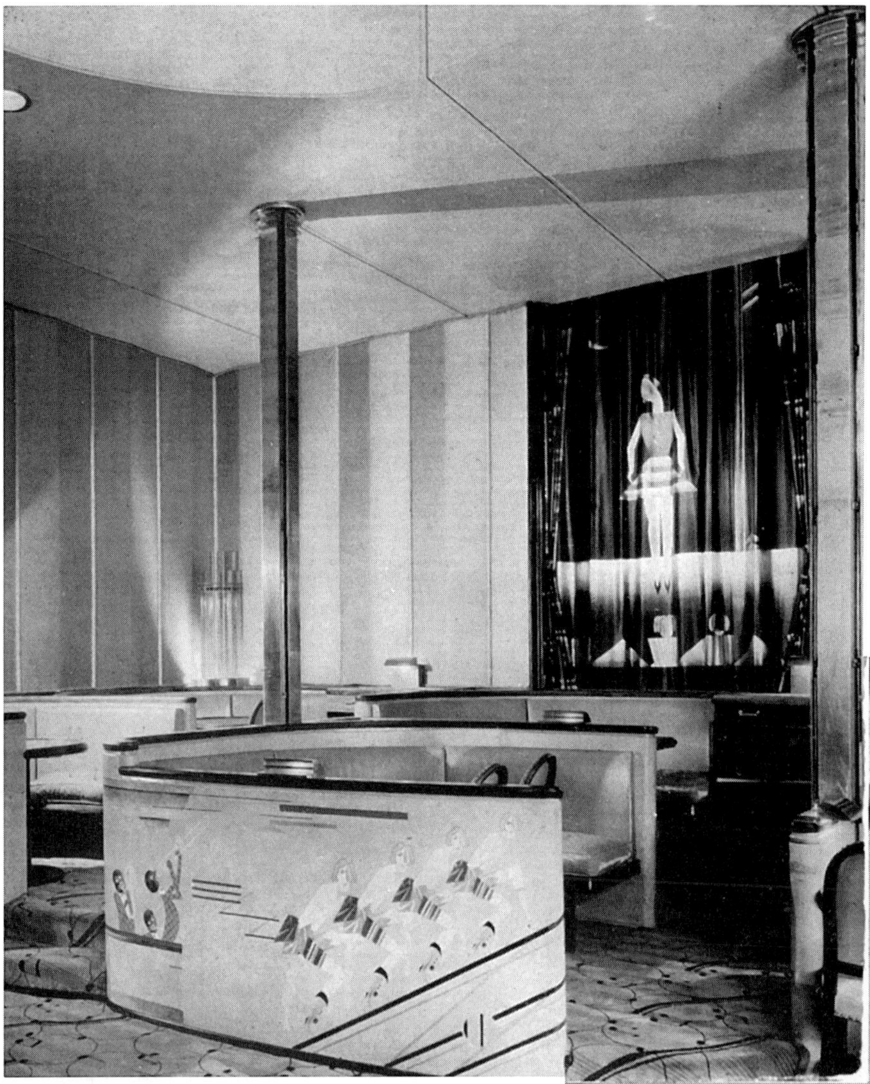

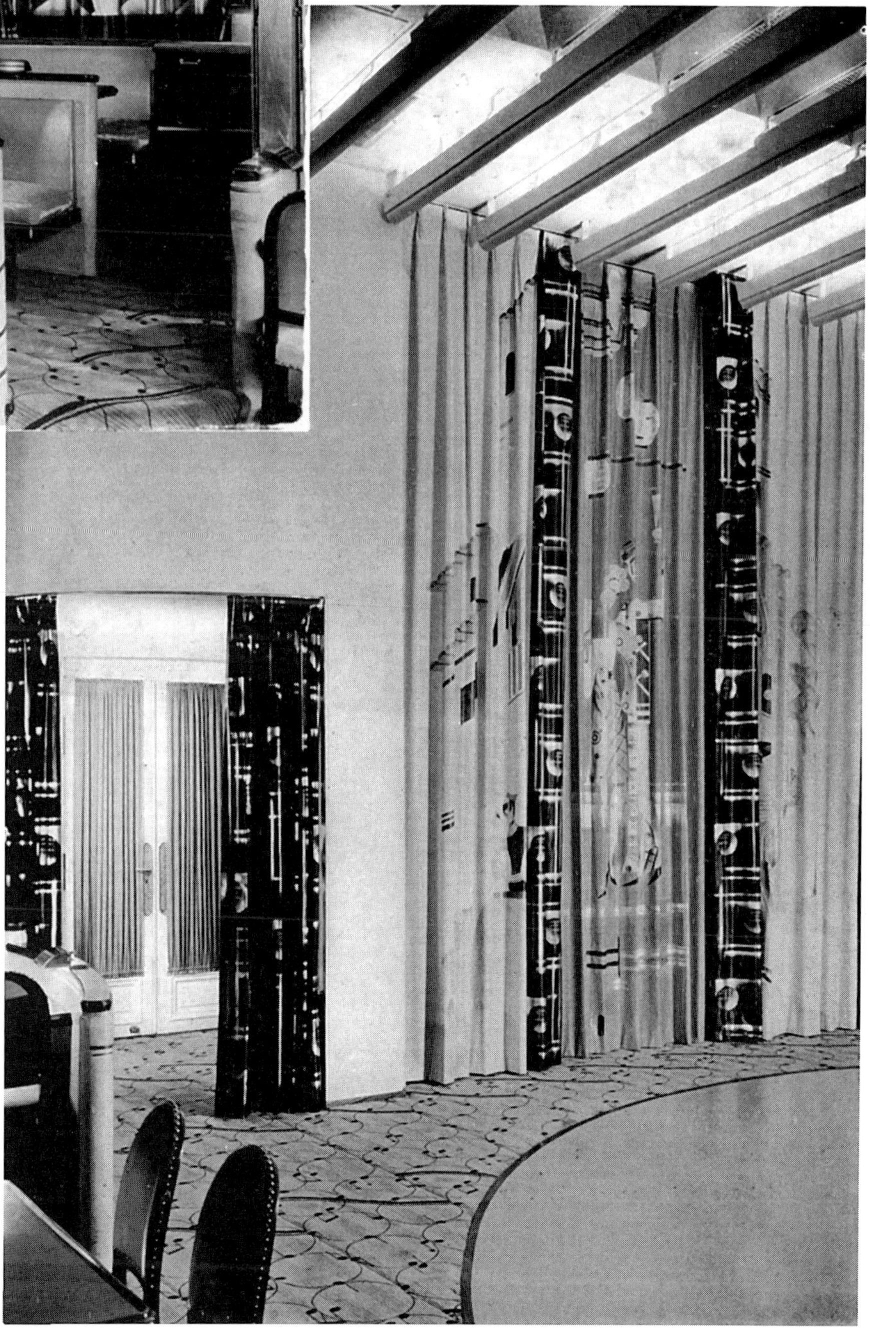

**The central portion of the ceiling is in the form of serrated planes which receive the light with varying intensity from continuous reflectors running the entire length of the room. This light can be varied at will by a combination manual and automatic control upon the orchestra platform producing any intensity or shade of light to suit the music. The dance floor proper is covered with an orange Armstrong Linoleum with a black striped design.**

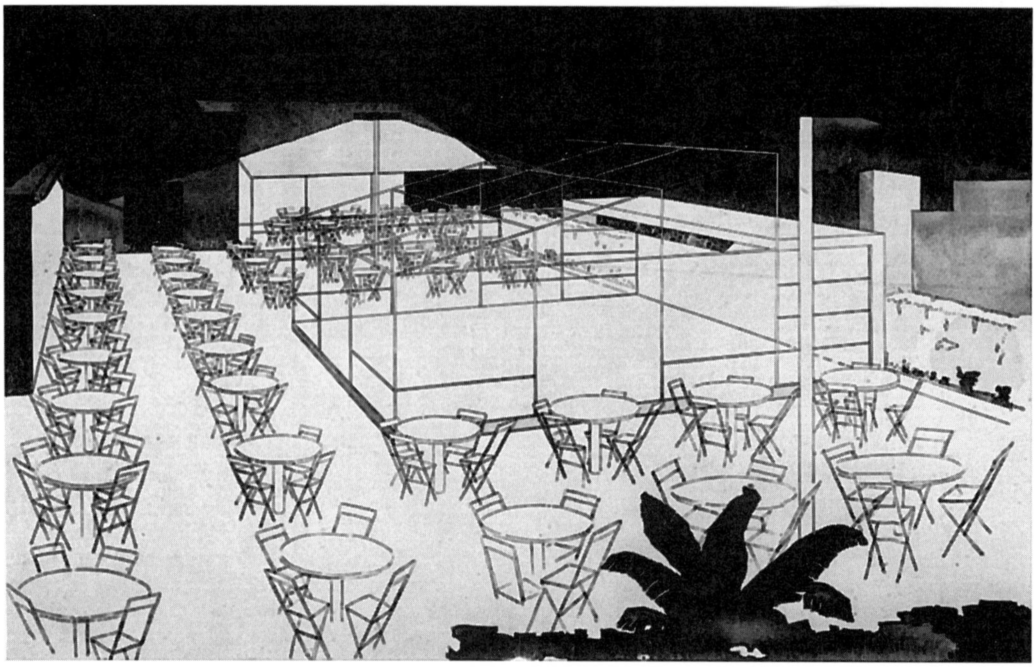

WILLIAM MUSCHENHEIM
Design of open air roof at the Hotel Astor, New York City.

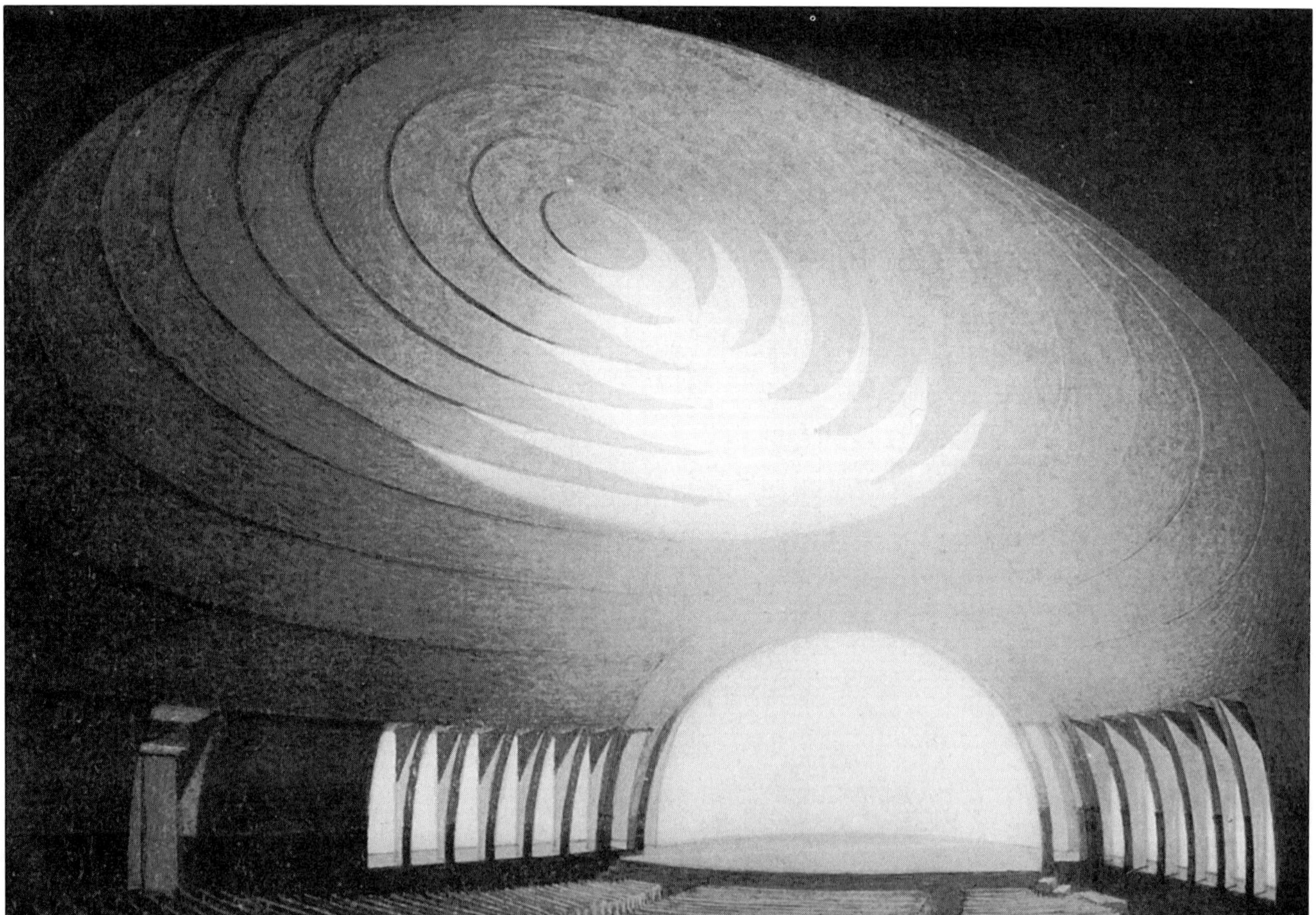

JOSEPH URBAN
Auditorium — New School for Social Research, New York City.

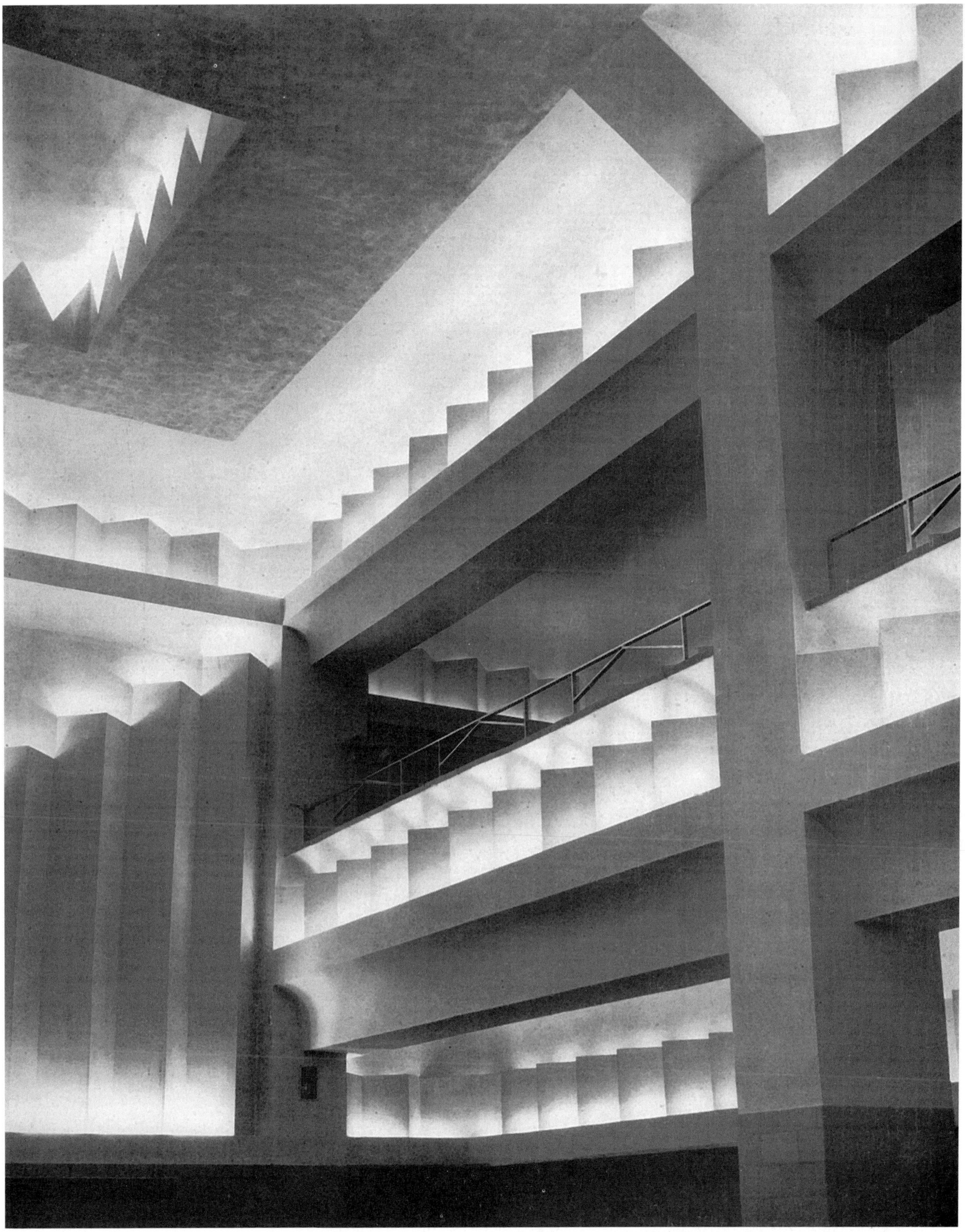

W I N O L D R E I S S

The Grand Ballroom of the Hotel St. George, Brooklyn, N. Y.

**The cloakroom and main foyer of the ballroom, Hotel St. George, Brooklyn. They have especial recourse to the newer composition materials. The Ballroom is lighted entirely by indirect illumination which, due to the forms of the recesses, throw interesting patterns upon the white walls and ceilings. An elaborate color organ controls the play of light and provides a varied and fluid decoration for the room. Fabricoid is used on the walls of the main foyer, the rails in brass;—vermilion, red, gold, and white the color scheme.**

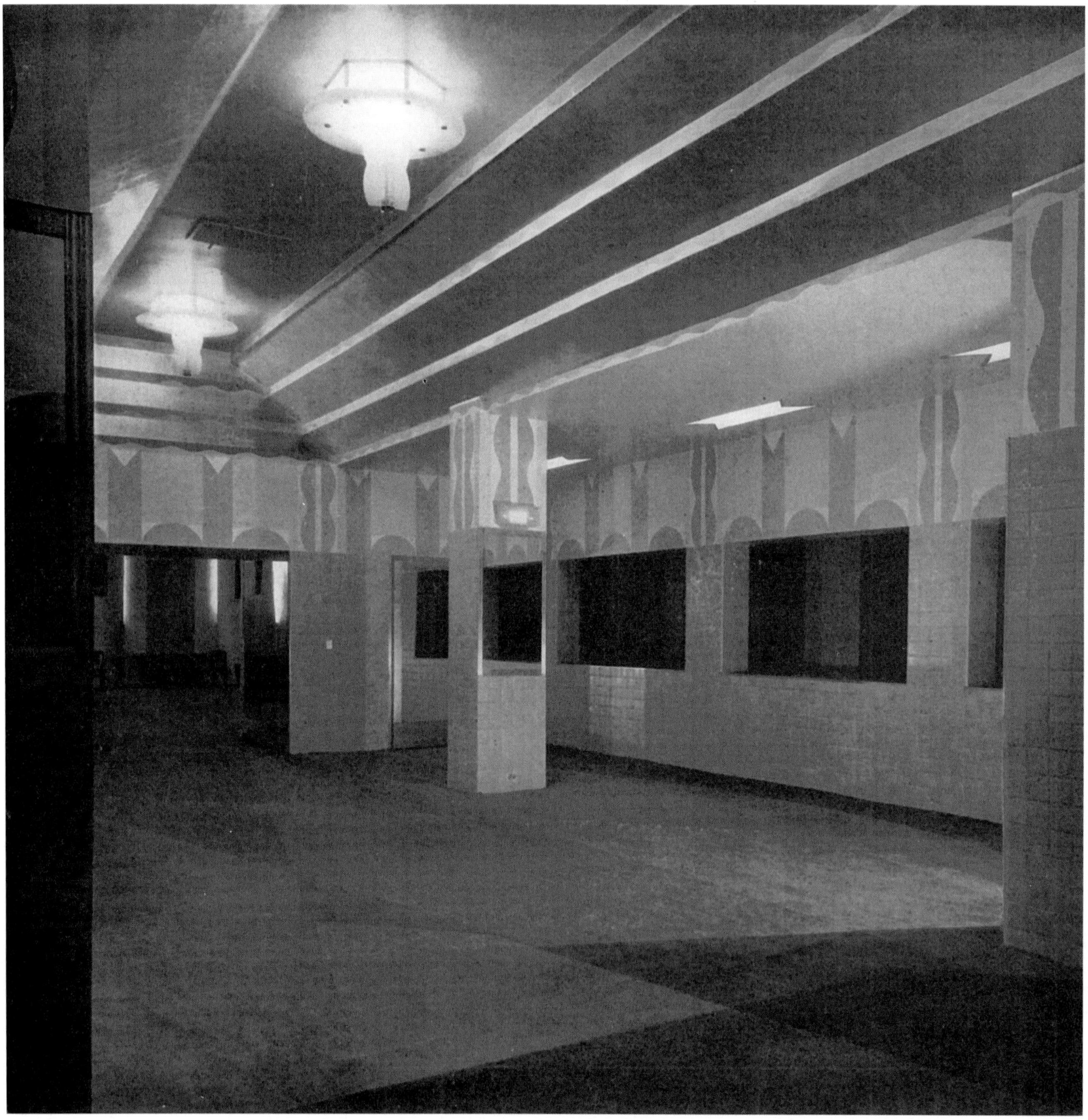

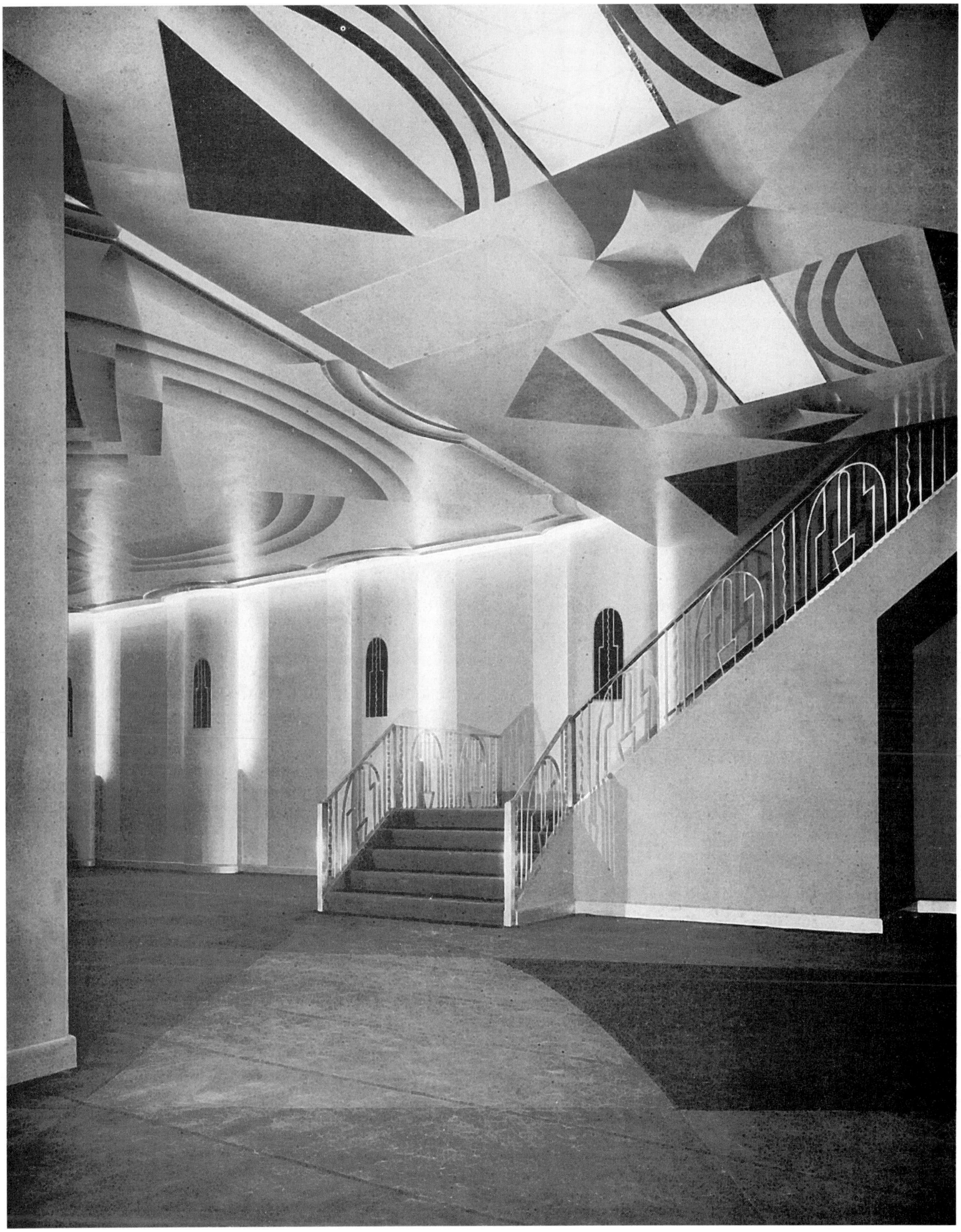

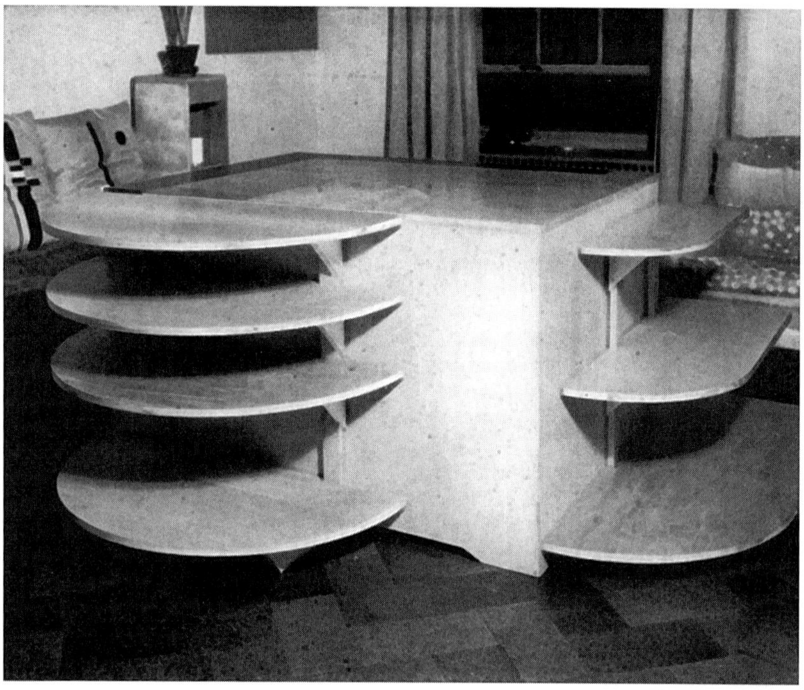

GEORGE SWITZER
Studio work table.

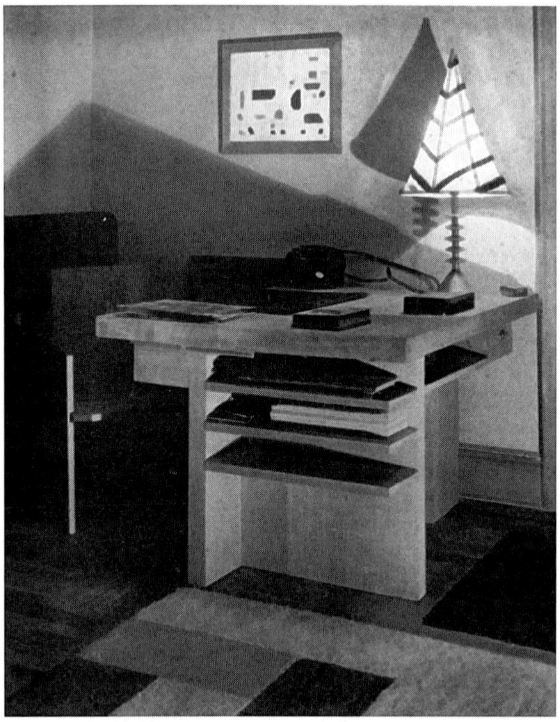

ILONKA KARASZ
Secretary studio table.

GEORGE SWITZER
An art director's supply case and reference shelf.

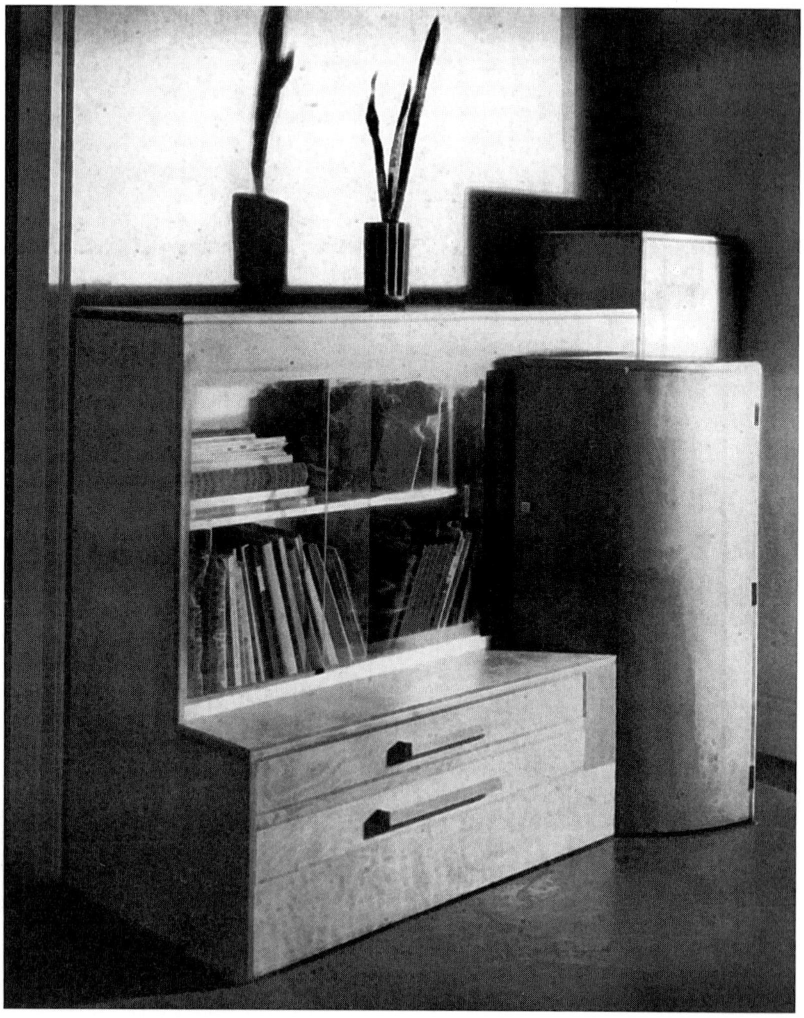

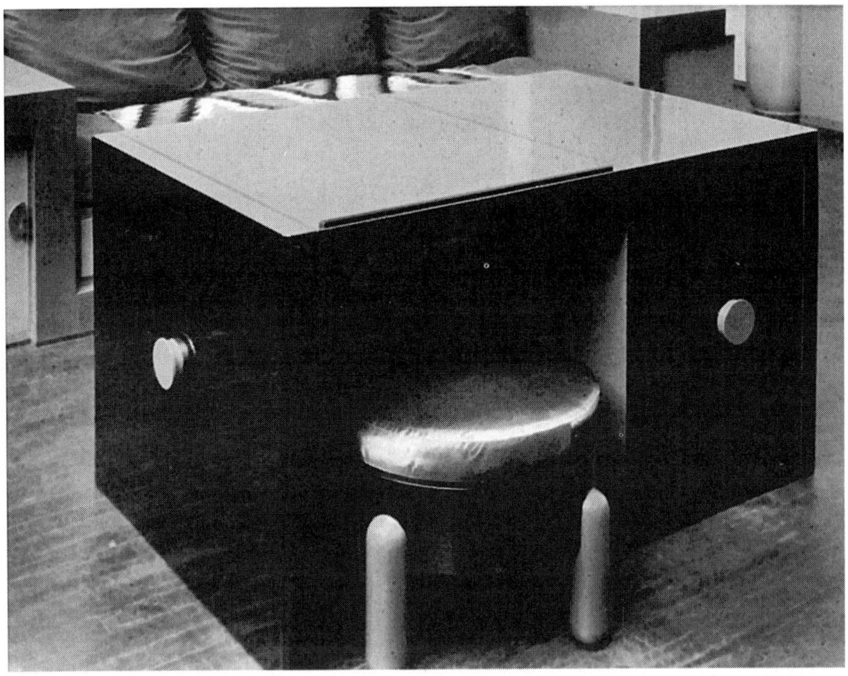

J O S E P H   S I N E L

An artist's desk, closed and open—drawing board elevates—paint cabinet pulls out—table extends to left.

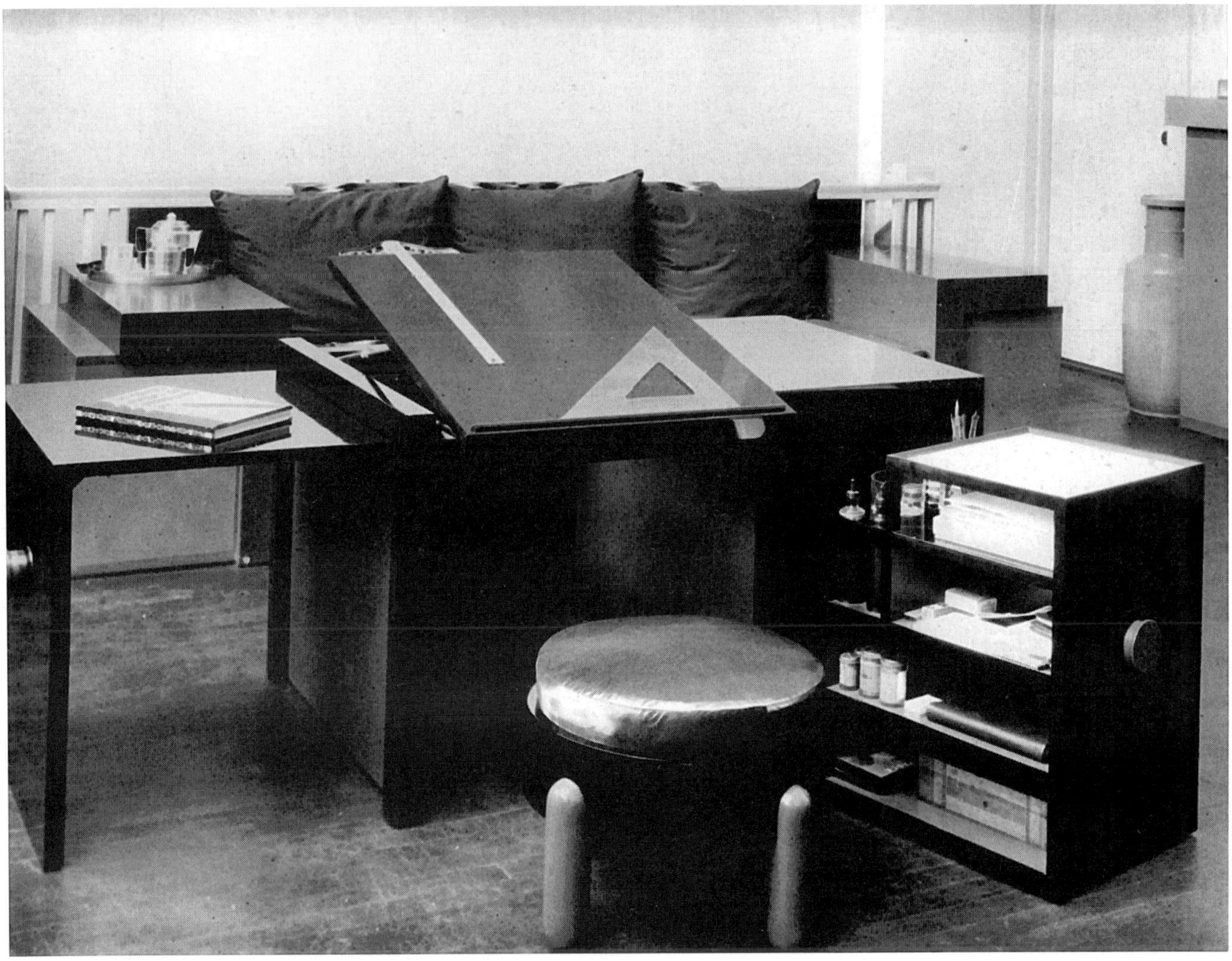

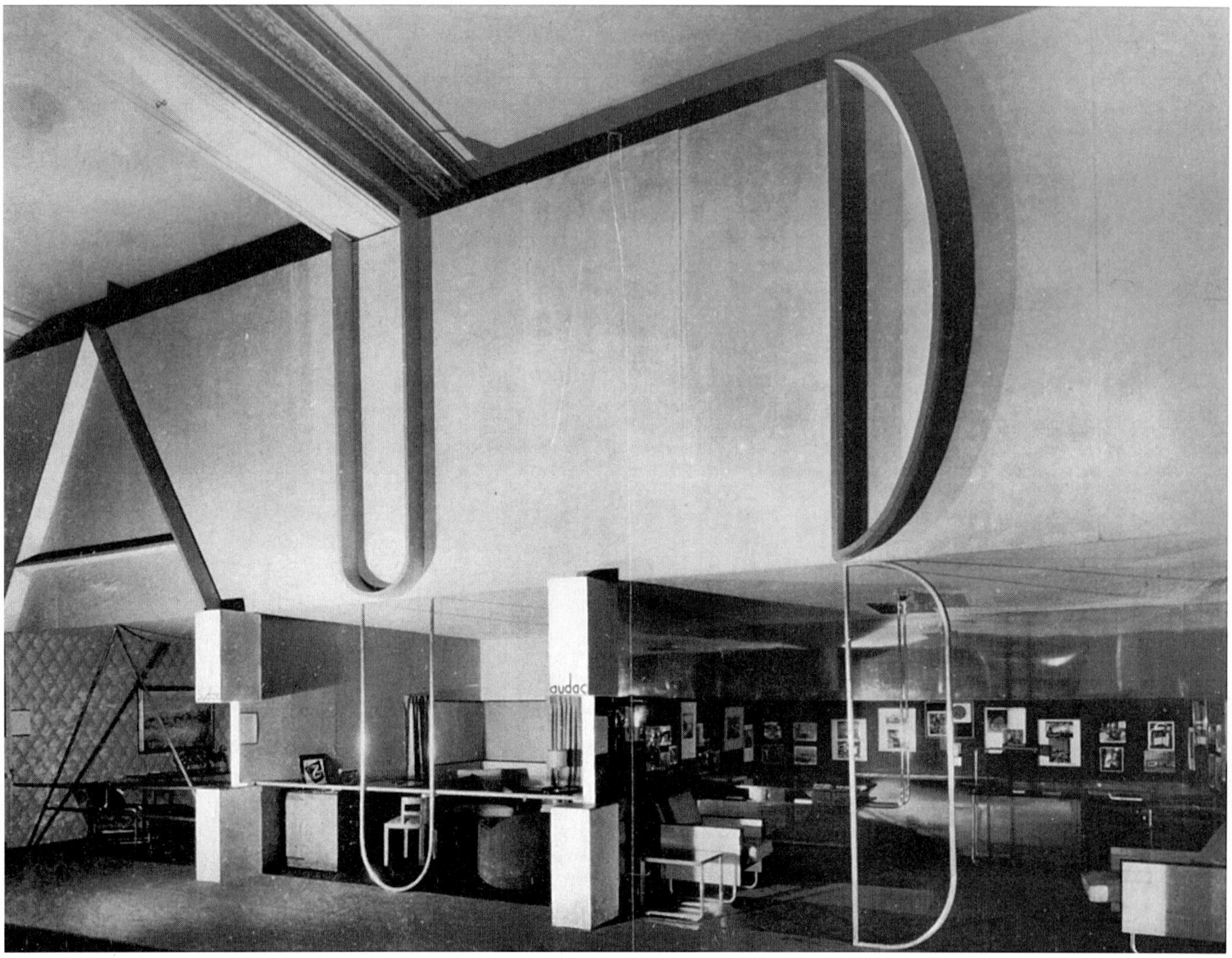


During the month of March, 1930, these five rooms designed by five members of AUDAC (American Union of Decorative Artists and Craftsmen) were exhibited at the Grand Central Palace. The plan was designed by Frederick J. Kiesler and the individual rooms were contributed by Donald Deskey, Willis S. Harrison, Frederick J. Kiesler, Wolfgang and Pola Hoffmann, and Alexander Kachinsky.

Although the complete ensemble was exhibited under the auspices of AUDAC, each room was the result of the individual effort of the five members of AUDAC represented. The attending public had the opportunity to see, in a very small way it is true, what accomplishments had been made in contemporary interior decoration in America within the past year. It is difficult to overestimate the value of such exhibitions for the creation of a vital and effective appreciation of the tendencies in design not only in the minds of the general public, but in the manufacturer as well, through the display of just such rooms as are illustrated in these two pages.

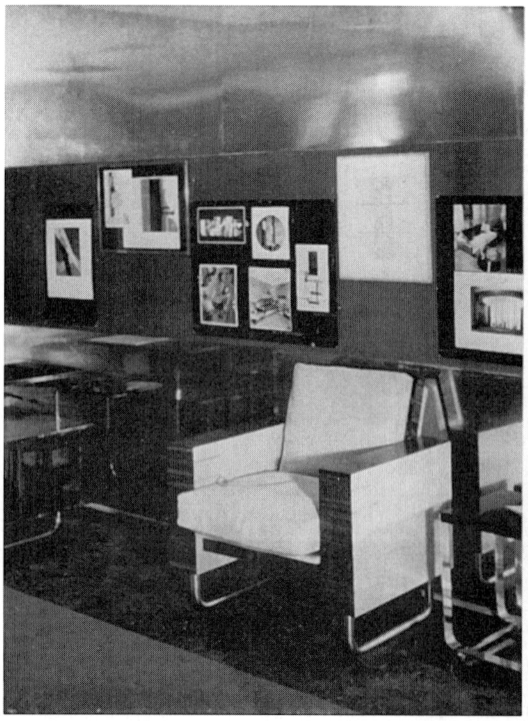

**A U D A C**

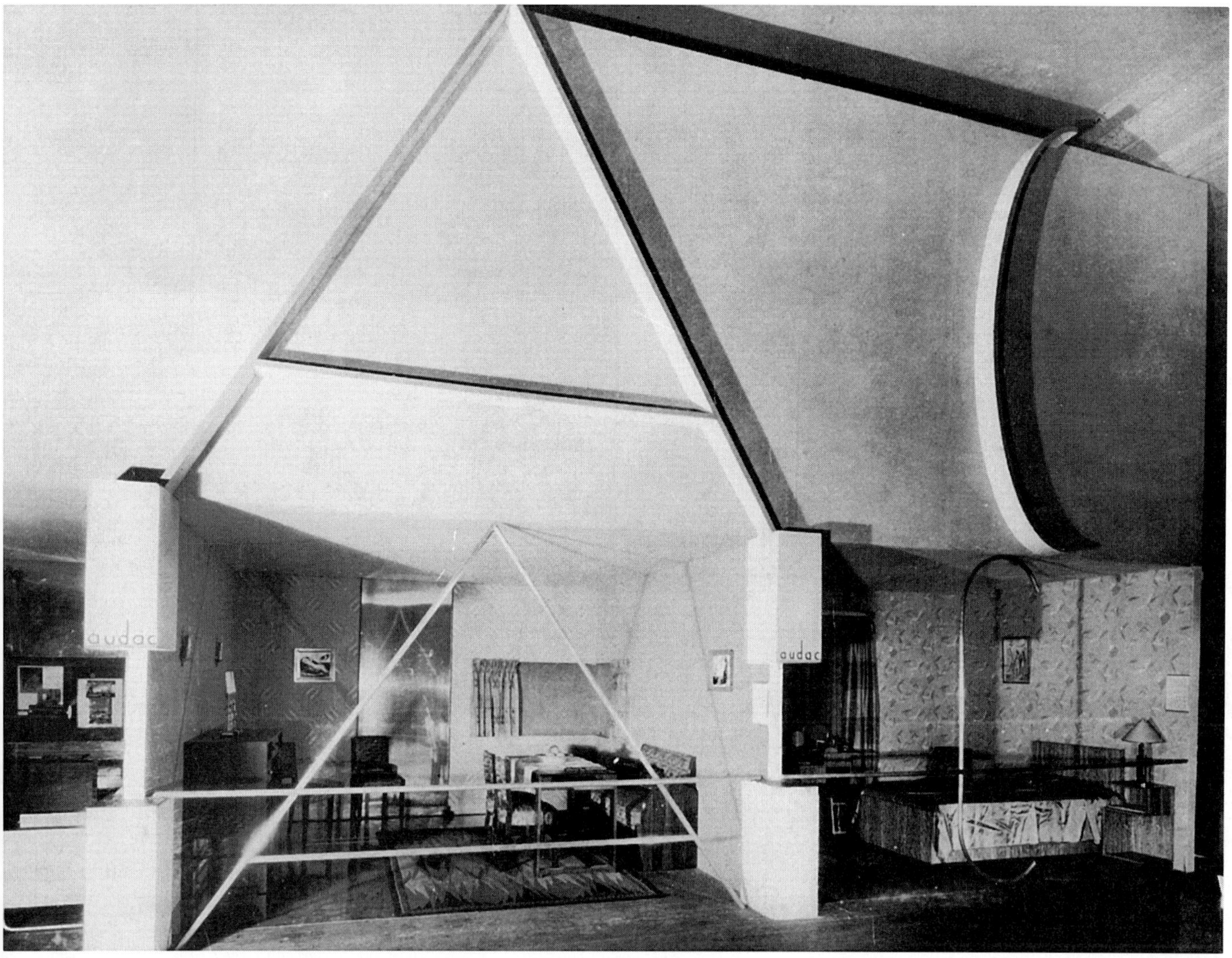


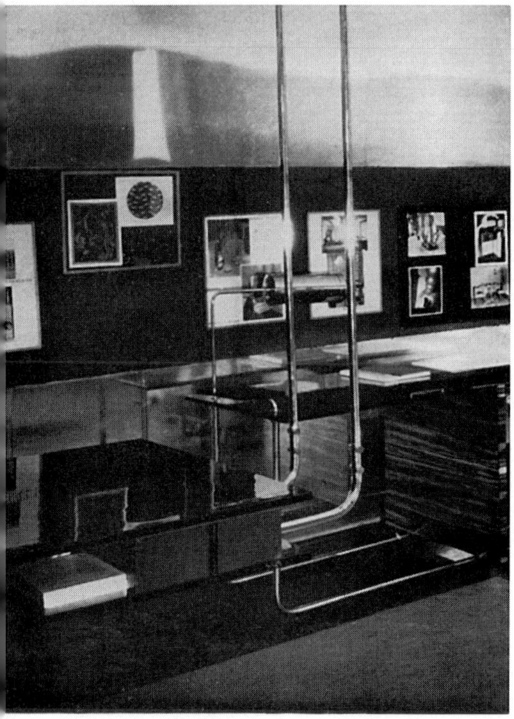

Perhaps one reason, and even the greatest, why the continental nations appear to be far more in consonance with the mechanization of contemporary life than our own very industrial nation is due to the very fact that the European countries are annually made acquainted through their expositions with the most significant accomplishments of their designers. When Mr. Hoover, then Secretary of the Interior, refused a request to gather an exhibit for participation in the Paris show of 1925 on the grounds that America had no modern decoration worthy of presentation, he did so with some justification. Till then, there had been no public exhibition of contemporary design by which he might have been informed of its presence.

But today conditions are different. There would be little difficulty in collecting a notable group of exhibits, for America is vitally engaged in forming a decorative art suited to present life.

E X H I B I T

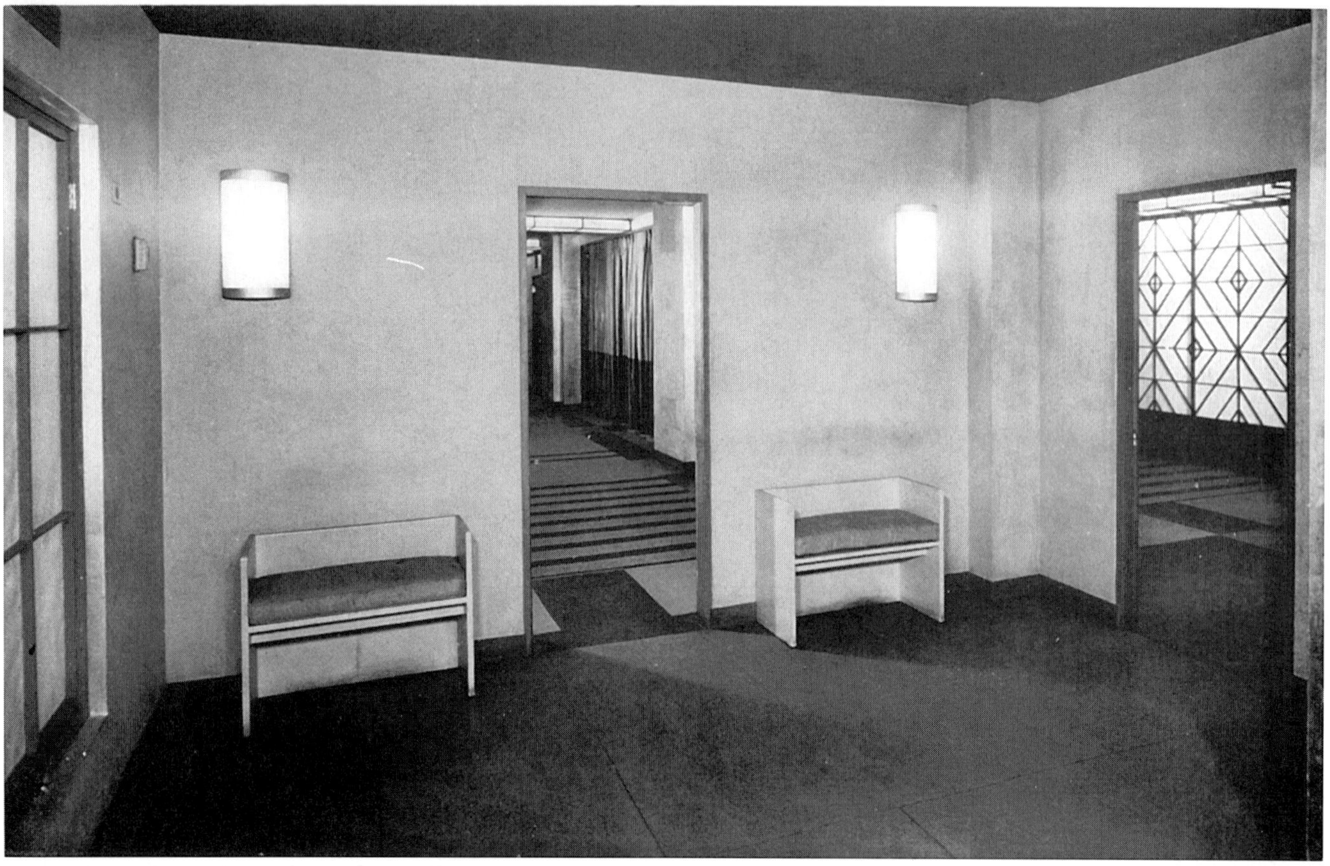

W I L L I A M M U S C H E N H E I M
Vestibule entrance to parlors Hotel Astor, New York City.

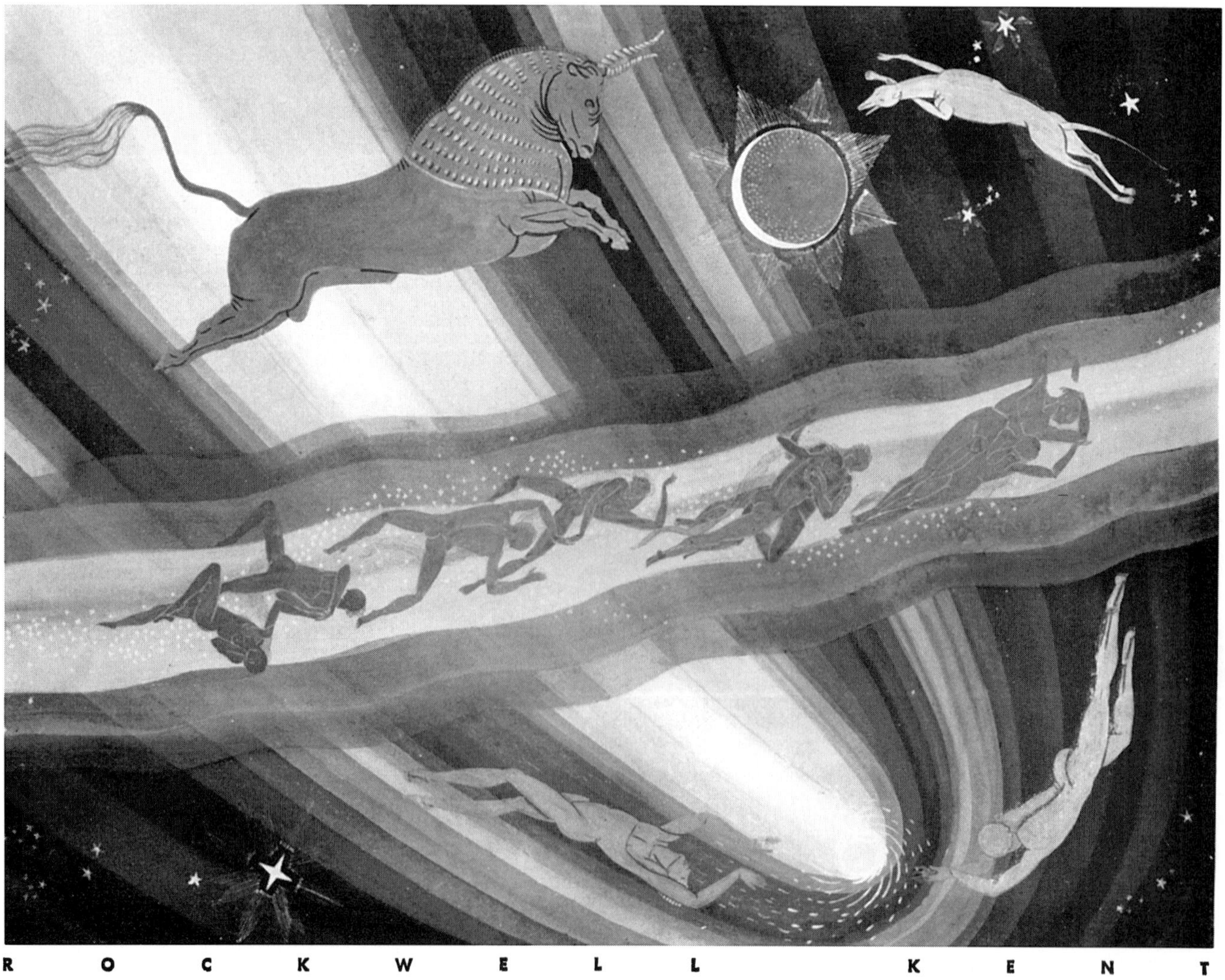

R O C K W E L L K E N T
Mural ceiling of Motion Picture House, Dennis, Cape Cod.

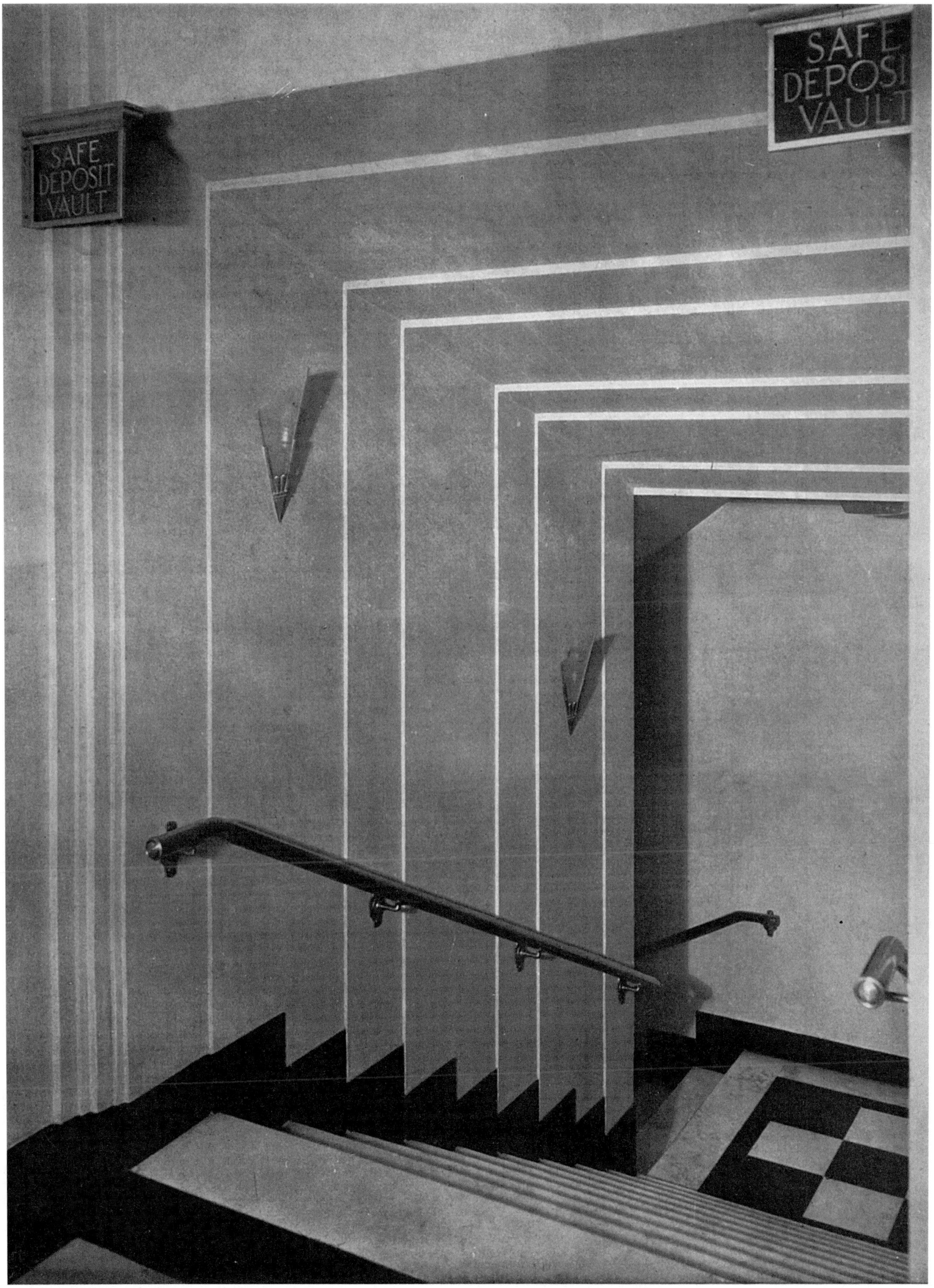


CORBETT, HARRISON & MACMURRAY
Entrance to Safe Deposit Vaults of Plaza Trust Co., New York City.

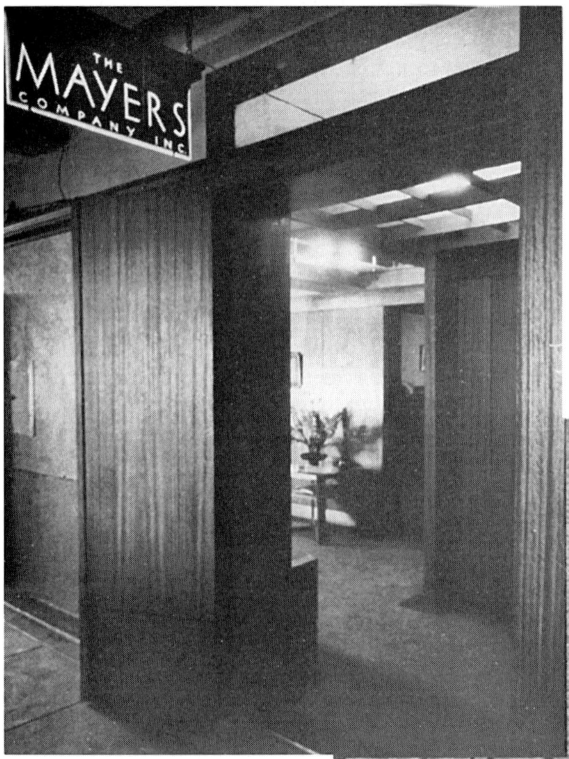


**K E M W E B E R**

**Entrance to offices of The Mayers Co., Los Angeles.**

**Private office of Max Sommer, Sr., San Francisco. Desk is of natural teakwood, chairs in blue leather. Furniture executed by Fink & Schindler Co.**

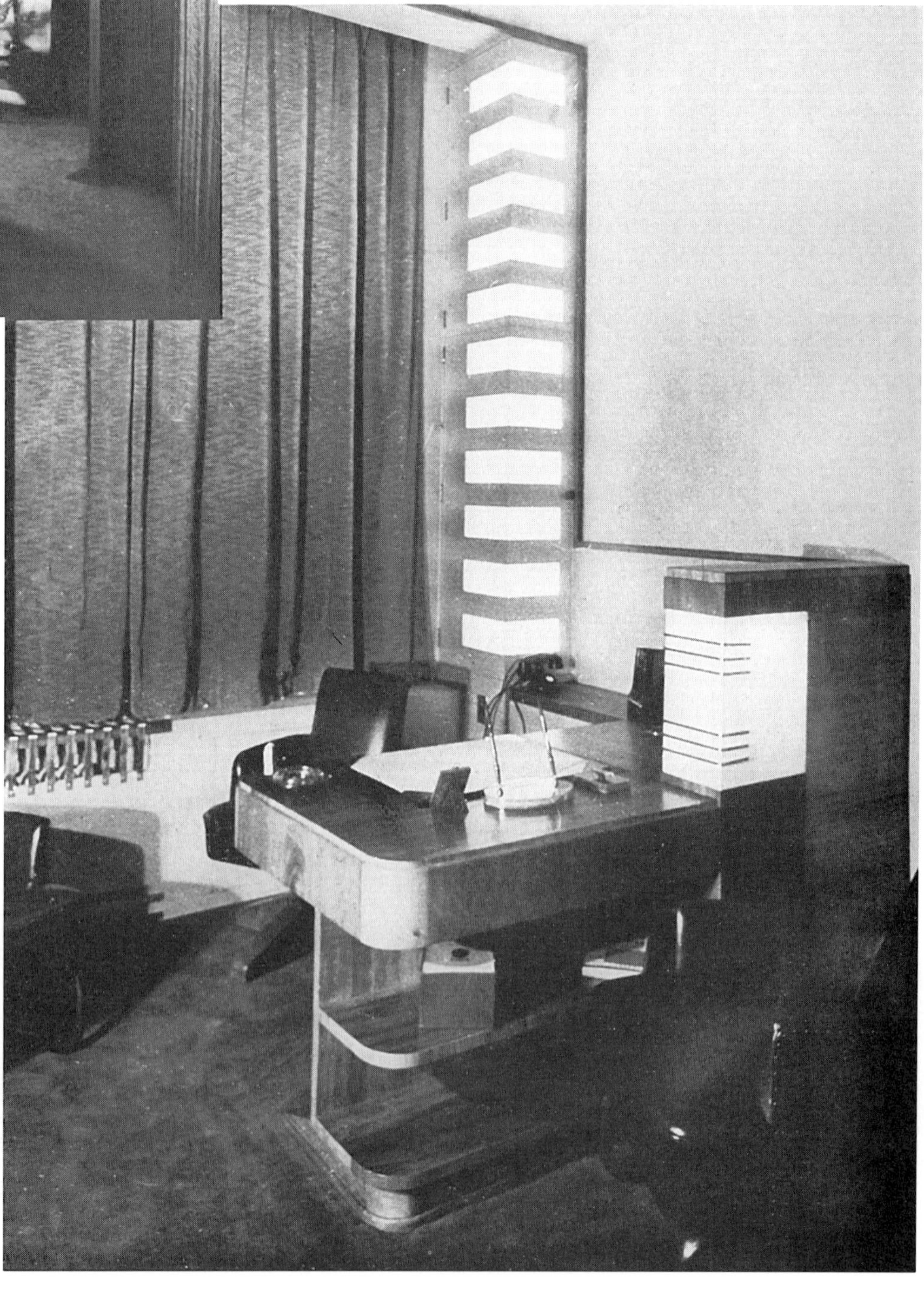

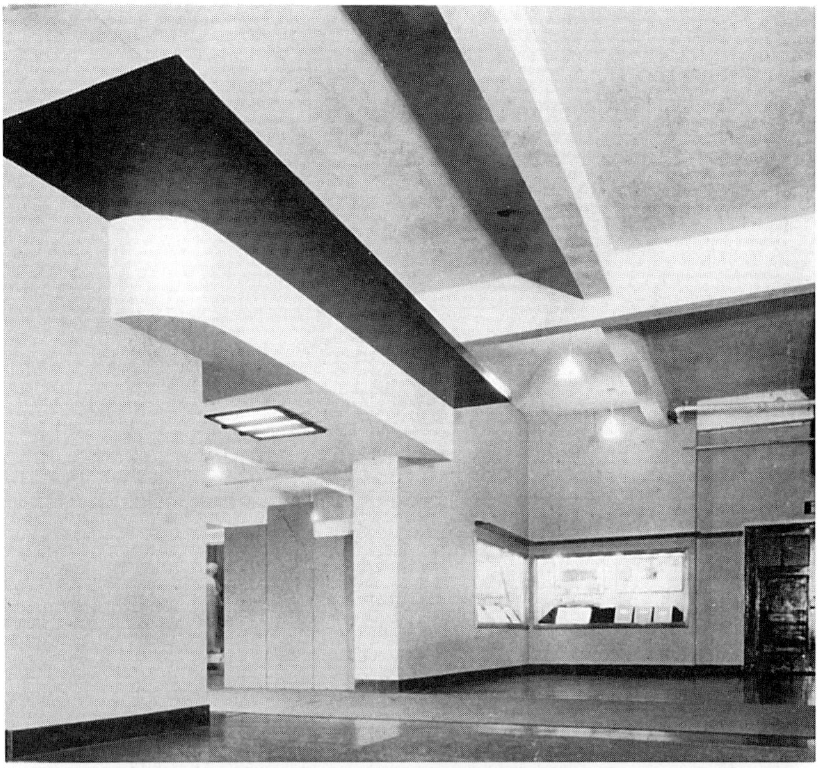

HOWE & LESCAZE

Entrance hall to the Home Making Center, Grand Central Palace, N. Y.

Mannequin's stage in Show Room of Nudleman & Conti, New York City.

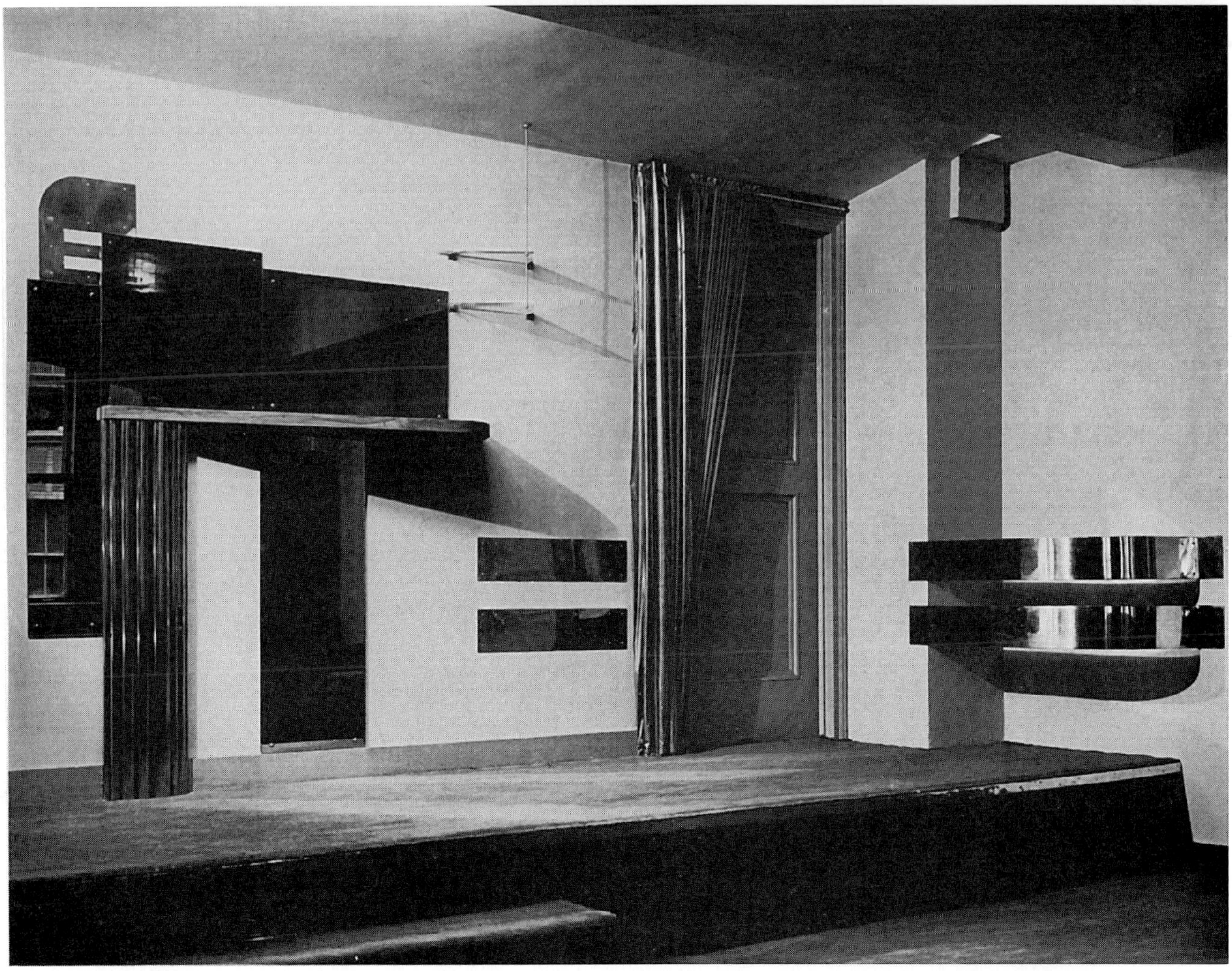

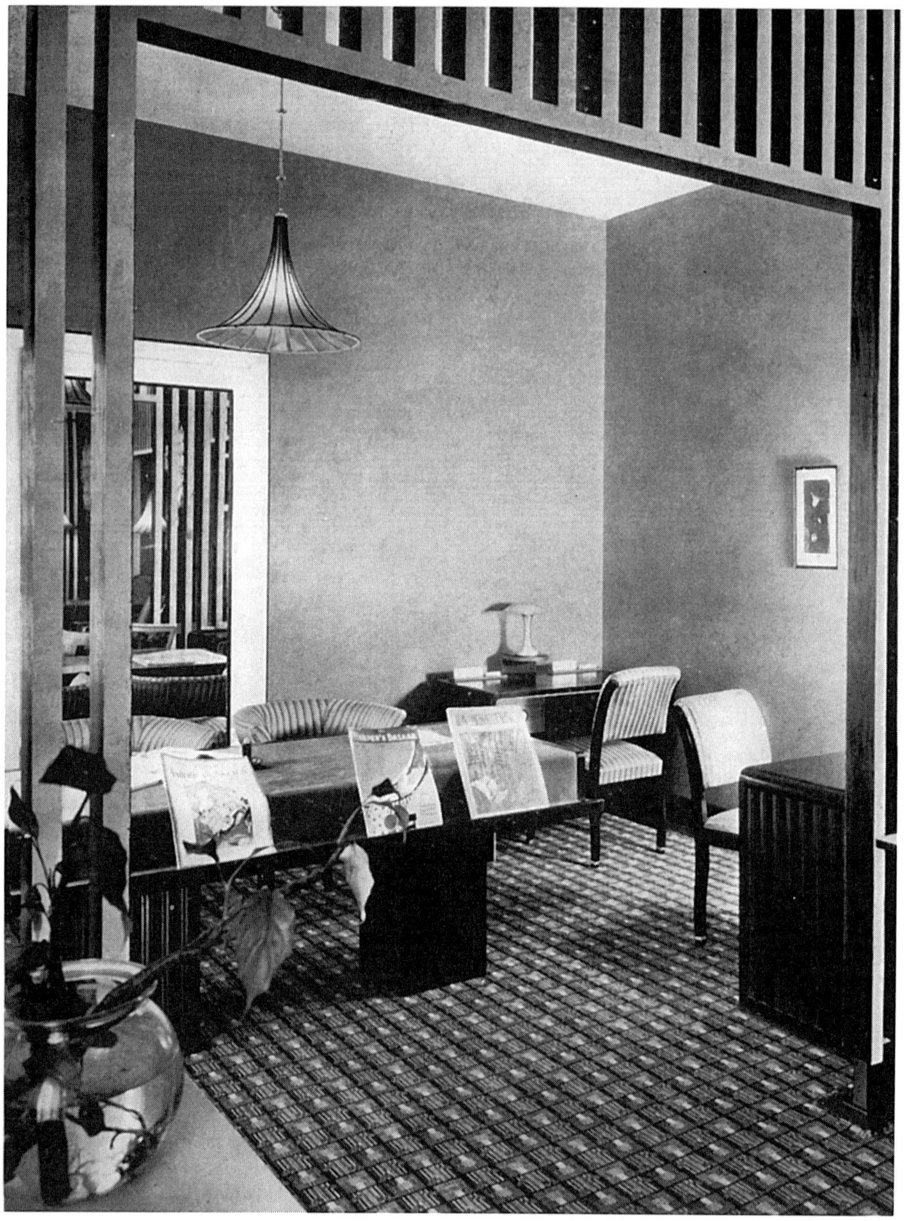

J O S E P H   U R B A N

Writing room of Atlantic Beach Club, Long Island. Red walls — blue to white upholstery — black lacquered furniture.

Central Park Casino, N. Y. C. — dining room.

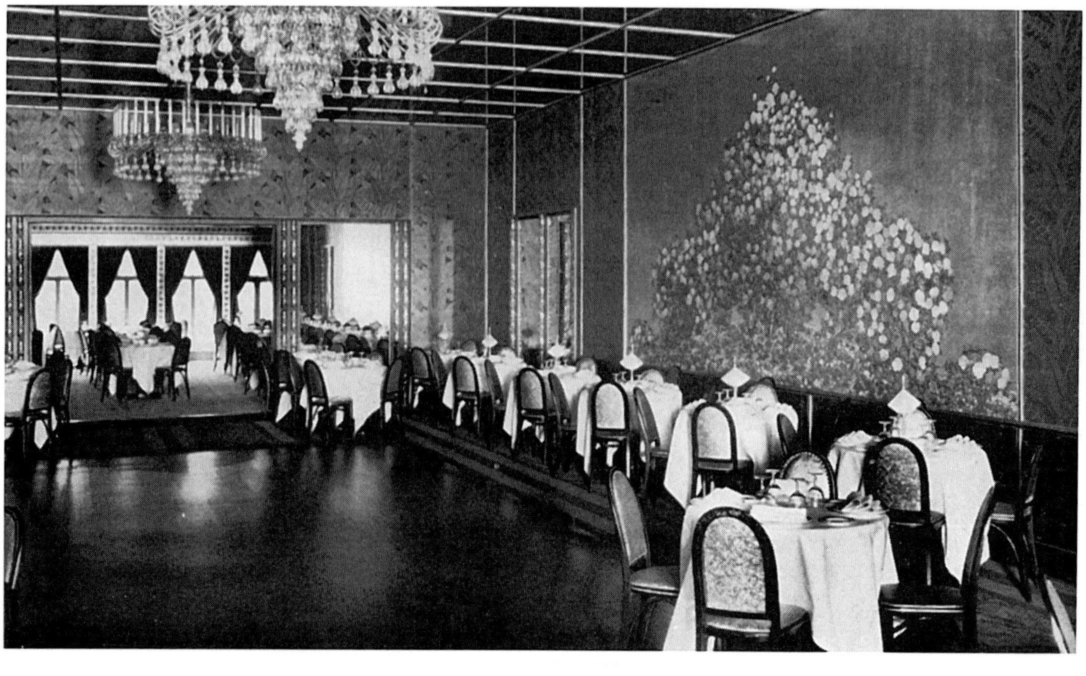

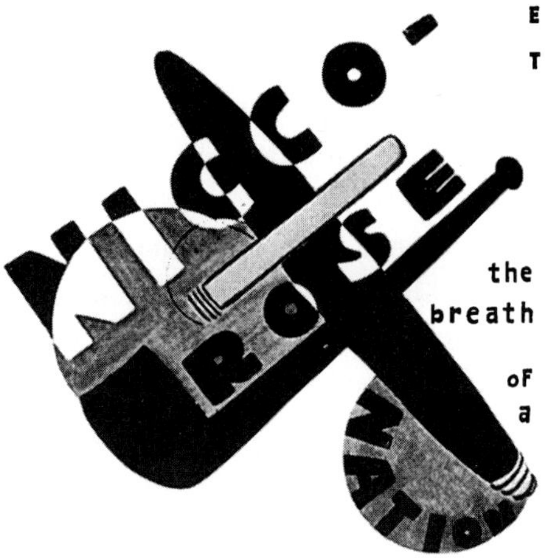


ELISE SEEDS
Trade mark for Nicco Rose.

# GRAPHIC ARTS IN ADVERTISING

## moderns and modernists

by M. F. AGHA

There is very little doubt that the sudden penetration of the Moderns in the sacred Temple of American "Graphic Arts" was due to the same complex of reasons that made Alcibiades cut off the tail of his dog.

The desire to be conspicuous and different is one of the normal aspirations of the advertising and editorial mind—and one which had been inhibited in American advertising for a long time. There, in a moment of giddiness the guardians of advertising and editorial dogmas allowed Attention Value in advertising to overpower Selling Points and items of Practical Information. And then, the thing happened: in dense herds the Moderns swarmed through the breach; there were all breeds of Moderns: from the most rosebud-covered Viennese to the extremely chromium-plated Dutchmen, from the white-haired domestic geniuses, who were Moderns before Picasso was born, to the juvenile converts with French-Line labels still fresh on their portfolios.

The arrival of the Moderns was not marked by any strong opposition; neither was it accepted with any particular enthusiasm. They were tolerated; they were such Attention Getters! They were treated well and fed every day; given the liberty, (and even encouraged) to produce Attention Value, Snap, and Wallop; while, in their spare time, they were allowed to indulge in innocent discussions about the machine age, fitness to function, and objectivity in art.

The boom in Modern picture collections and a few exhibitions of newly discovered modern furniture and decoration completed this idyllic picture. It seemed that a firm foundation had been laid for the triumph of modern art which in the industrial field later resulted, among other things, in the mass-production of turquoise-colored India-rubber overshoes and rainbow-colored skyscrapers. As far as the "Graphic Arts" were concerned the Sans Serif-types, little black dots, the liberal use of the air-brush and the famous dynamic symmetry appeared to be the forerunners of its brilliant future.

All this, of course, was too beautiful to last. The Moderns were weakened by the excitement of their apparent victory and by various fanatic creeds. Some were even bold enough to think that modern art was something more than one of fifty-odd ways to merchandise. Others, erring in the opposite direction, were firmly convinced that modern typography had no other god than practicality and was more Catholic than several advertising Popes.

Too much attention paid to Art, whether in the shape of worship or renunciation, is always pernicious in business. The Moderns were bound to degenerate, fall into decadence and be replaced by a new and stronger generation. It is this new transition that we are witnessing now. The successors of the Moderns call themselves Modernists (horribile dictu). Their chief characteristic is that they have thoroughly eliminated all the hesitations, errors, and uncertainties which are inherent in the activities of the creative artist. They are quite businesslike and professional about it. Their predecessors did not always originate, but they had the decency to take what is politely called "inspirations" from hidden and mysterious sources. They went to Van Dongen and Fujita for fashions, to Miro and Lurcat for posters, to Tristan Zara and Moholy-Nagy for typography. The Modernists go simply to their neighbor's last advertisement or the last page of a rival magazine; they receive their inspiration from each other. This closed and vicious circle of inspiration is, of course, one of the necessary conditions for the formation of a STYLE. But, unfortunately, the other conditions do not seem to be present. A real contact with life is not established. This mutual imitation does not transfer from one Modernist to another any real art values. The situation is comparable to that of the two proverbial Irish families, stranded on the desert island, and whose sole source of income was taking in laundry from each other.

Another point in which the Moderns differ from the Modernists is that the Moderns have carried Amateur and Dilettante qualities intact through the strenuous years of professional activities. This is especially true of the imported makes of Moderns. One of the German writers defined an Amateur as somebody who still loves his work and a Dilettante as one who still finds delight in his trade. We would not go so far as to say that all of the contemporary Modernists are only mechanical robots, accomplishing certain art work operations without knowing what it is all about, but it is certain that their horizons are narrower, while their theoretic background is almost non-existent. Of course, their professional training and the calm attitude of the specialist to whom all the styles are alike as long as they are marketable, help them to produce on the whole fairly good modern art work. However, some of the severer critics are inclined to feel that fairly good modern art is like fairly good eggs. All this does not diminish the importance of the Modernists in esthetic economy. They are the last link in the chain which connects the creative spirit of the few originators and the population at large.

We do not deny the important role that turquoise overshoes and navy-blue railroad engines play in the education of the public eye, (a role some have called, "visual hygiene.") Certainly the "Graphic Arts" presented a more painless way of making the masses acquainted with the simplest forms of Modern art. The work of innumerable assymetric layout men, of scores of photographers with cock-eyed perspective, and of the artists who know all about whirling squares—is accepted by the masses without any aparent revolt—and this in itself is a great accomplishment.

But herein also lies a danger. To the masters of the destinies of Commercial Art in this country the Moderns are attractive and the Modernists are useful only because they are conspicuous and different. If the public becomes too familiar with the Modern type of art to notice it or if the artists themselves become neutralized, tame, and repetitious in the vicious circle of mutual imitation—their usefulness will stop there and they will be forced to look for another country to modernize. In this respect, no difference will be made between Moderns and Modernists.

G E O R G E S W I T Z E R

**Typographic compositions for Kurt H. Volk, Inc. and designer's personal letterhead.**

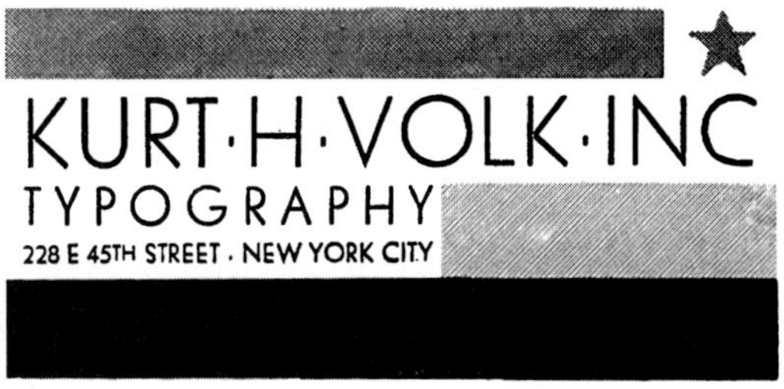


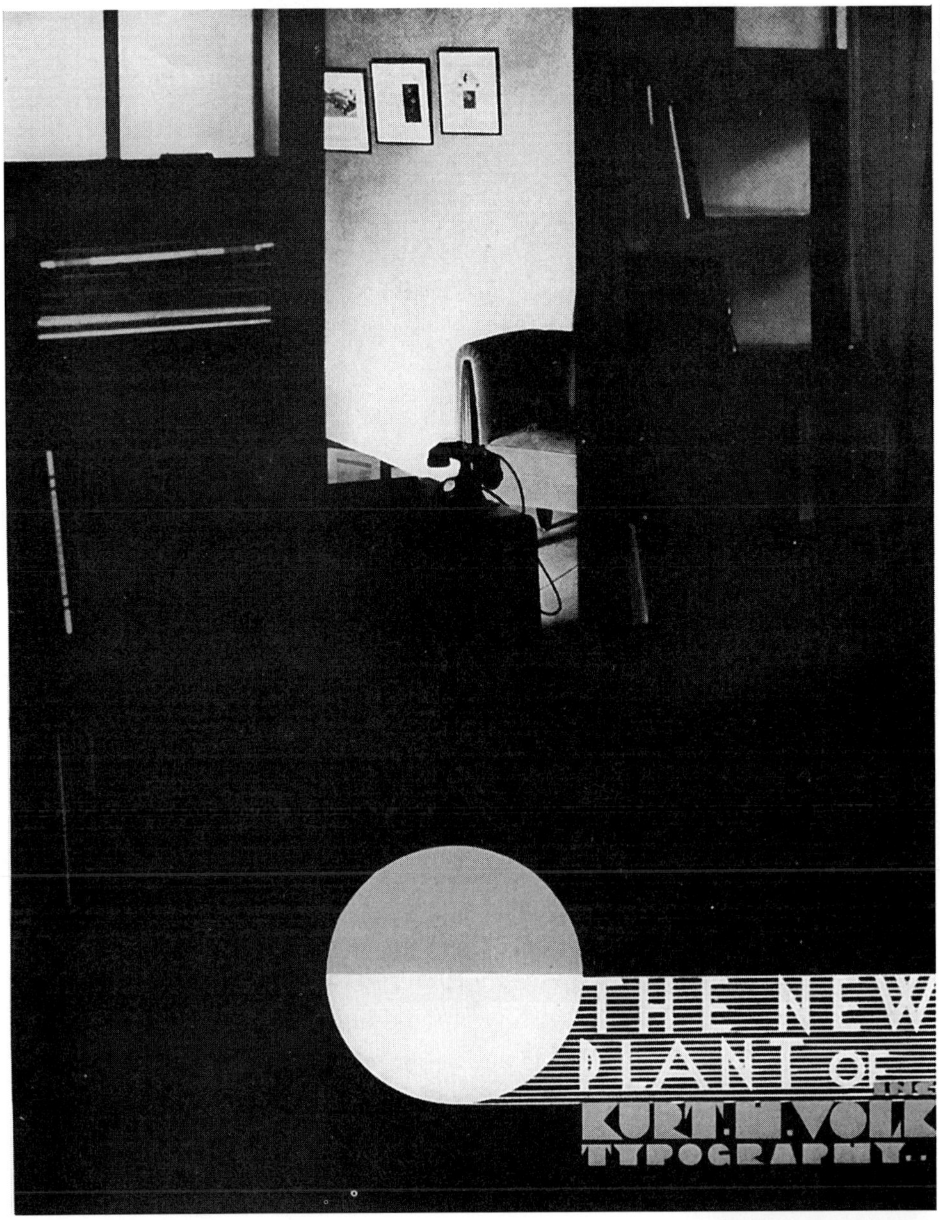


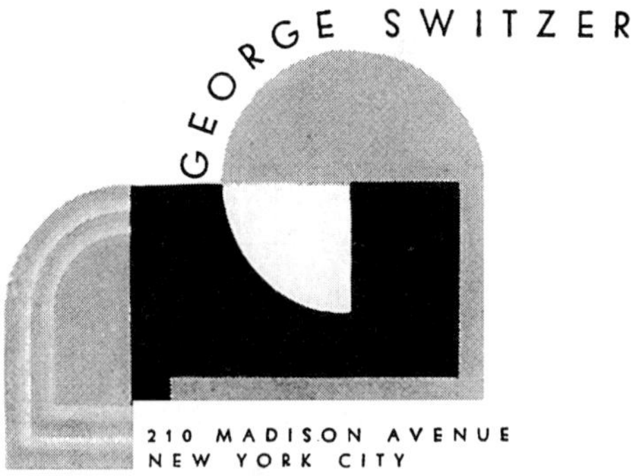


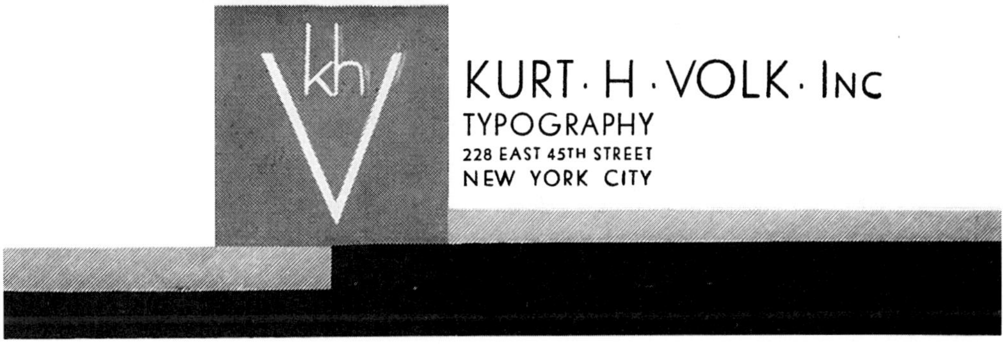

J O S E P H   S I N E L

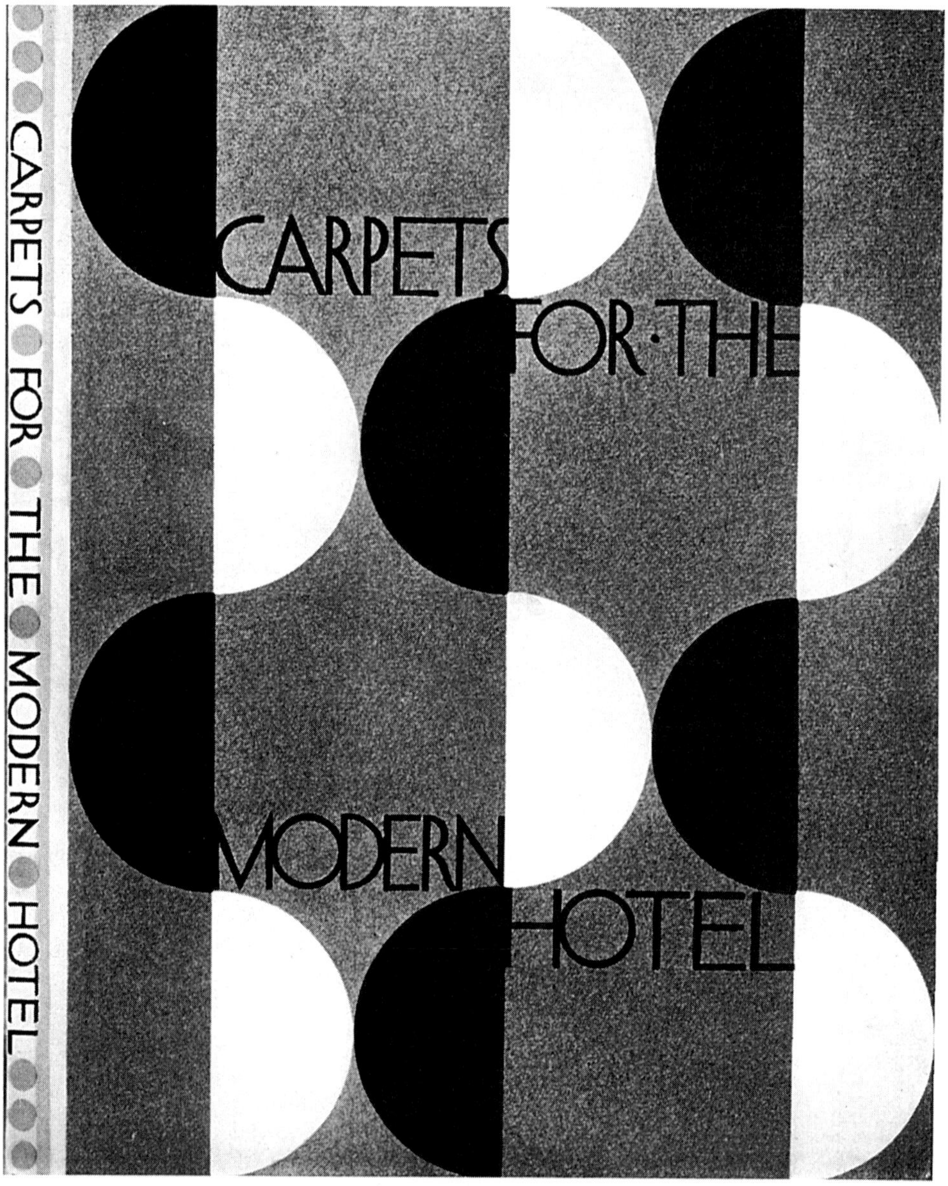


Commercial book cover for James F. Newcomb & Co.

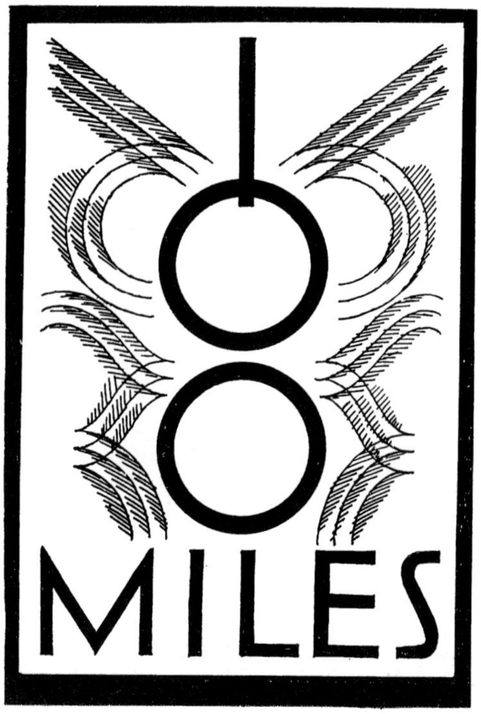


Cover for automobile booklet.

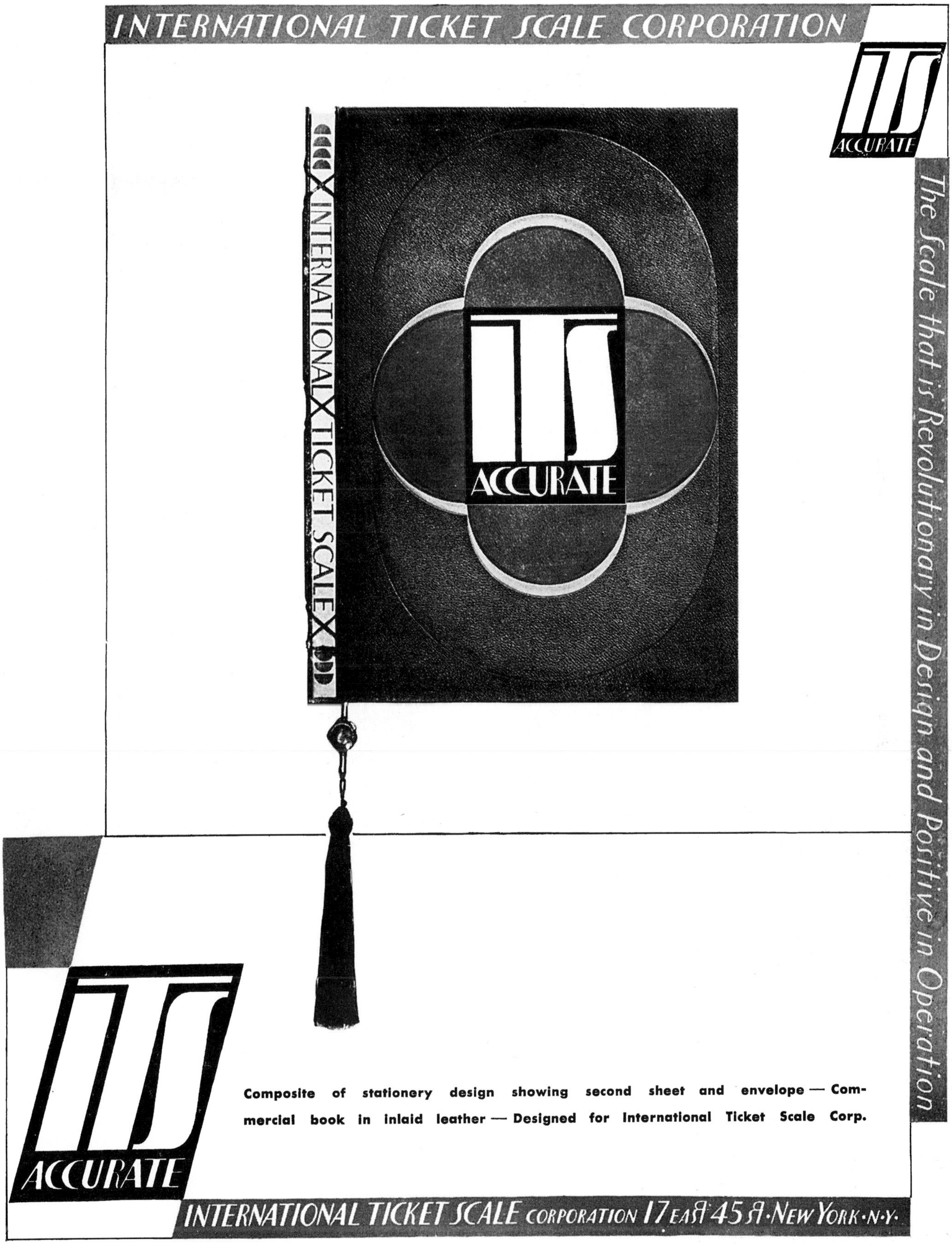


**Composite of stationery design showing second sheet and envelope — Commercial book in inlaid leather — Designed for International Ticket Scale Corp.**

W I T O L D   G O R D O N

**Magazine page made for Van Cleef & Arpels. Courtesy of McCready & Parks.**

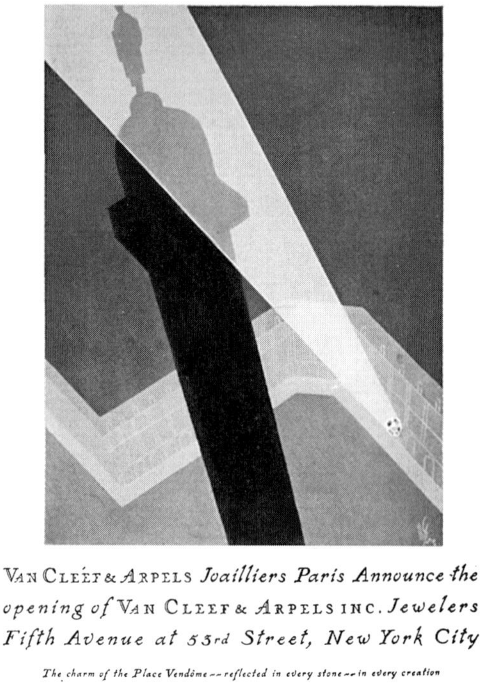


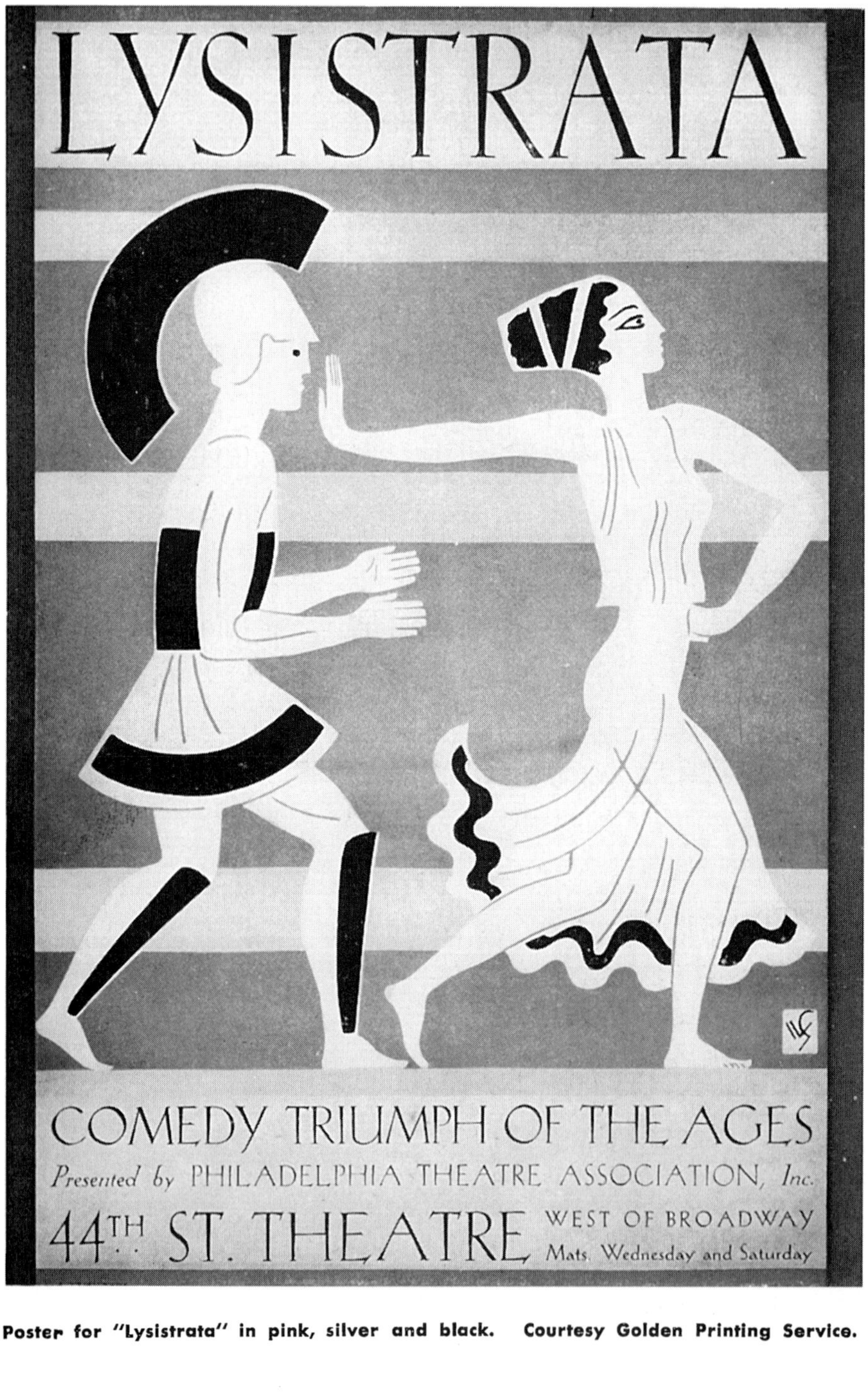


**Poster for "Lysistrata" in pink, silver and black. Courtesy Golden Printing Service.**

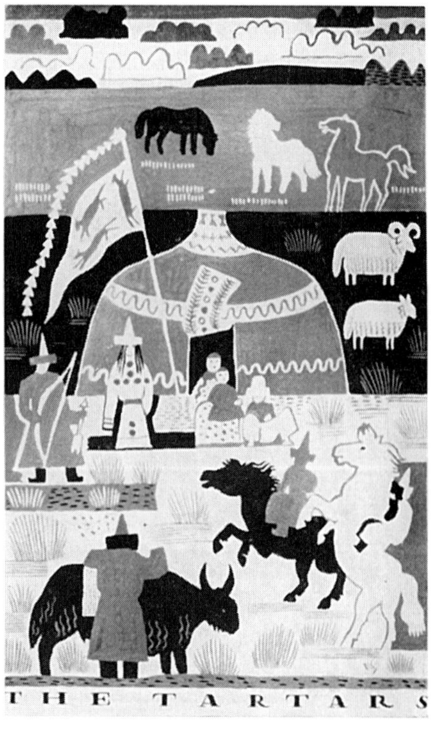

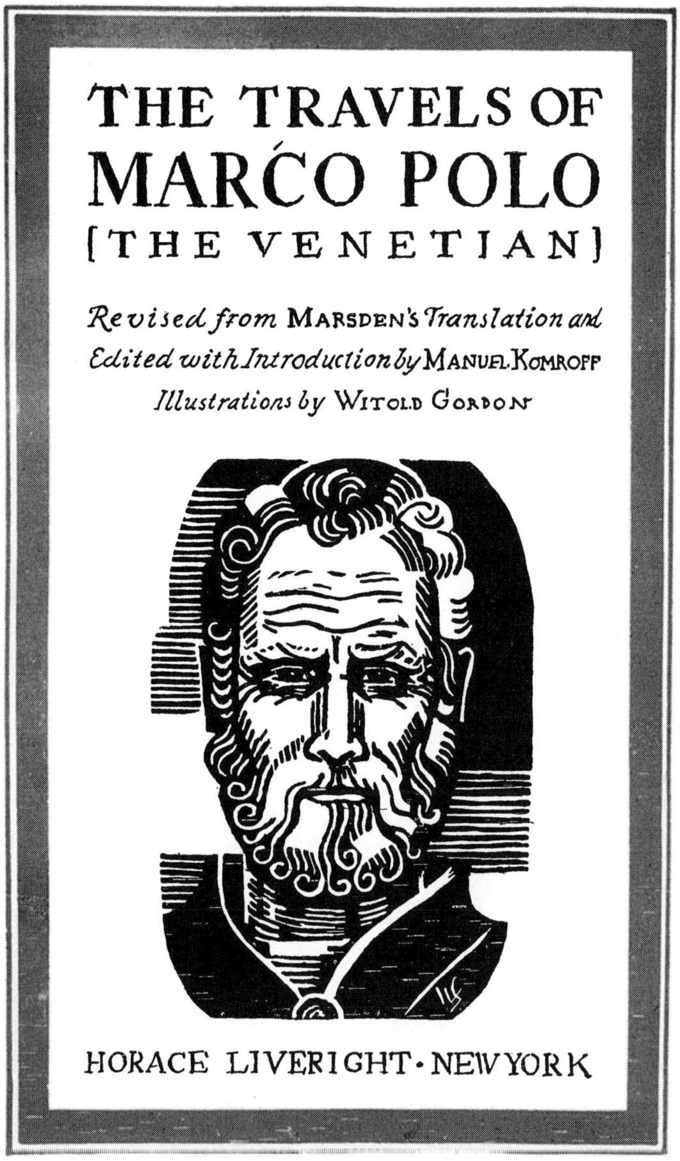


Title Page and illustrations for the Travels of Marco Polo. Published by Horace Liveright.

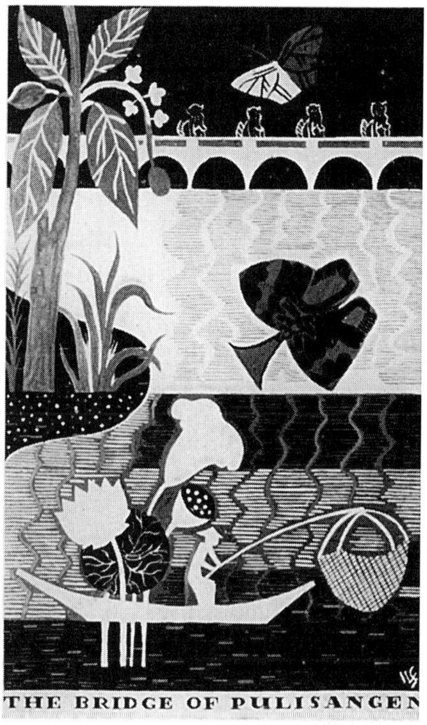


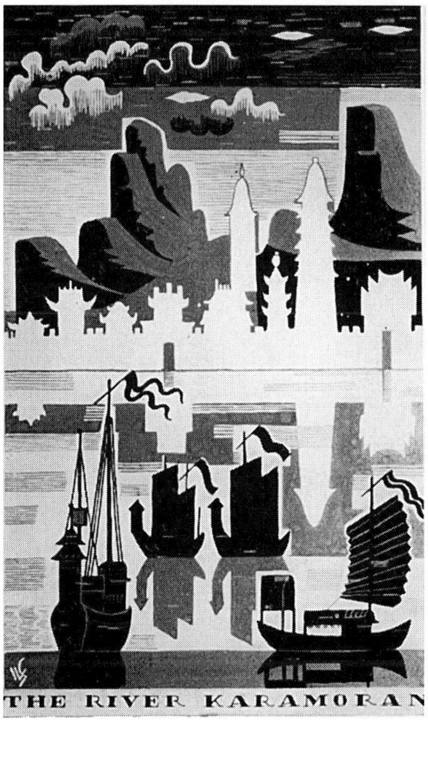


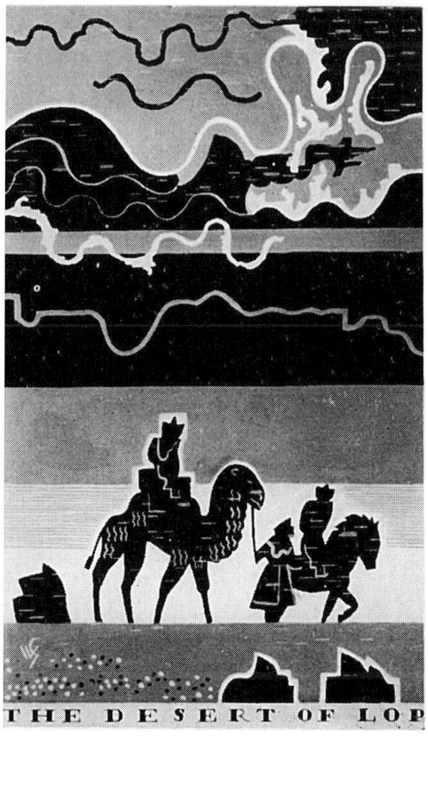

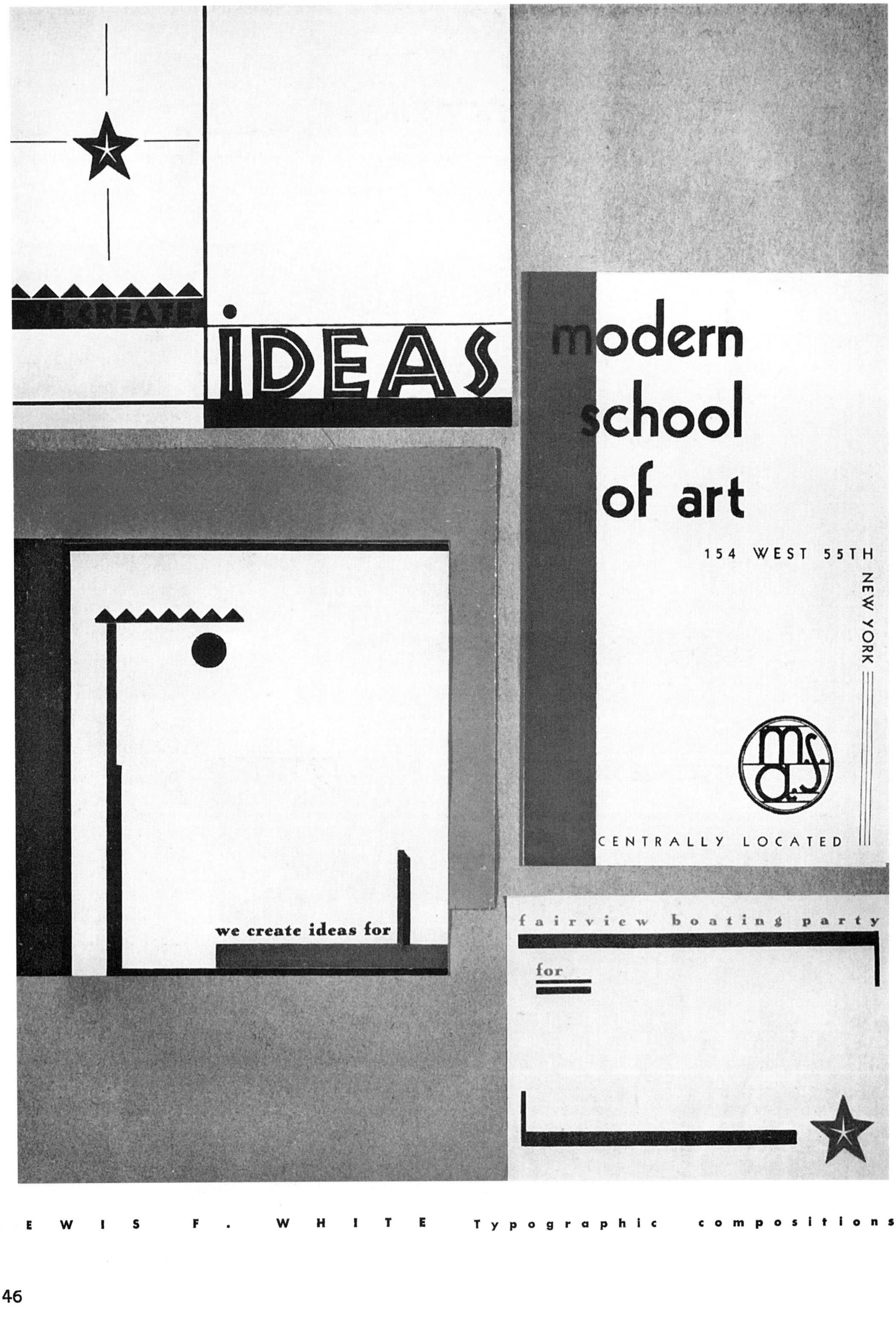


LEWIS F. WHITE Typographic compositions.

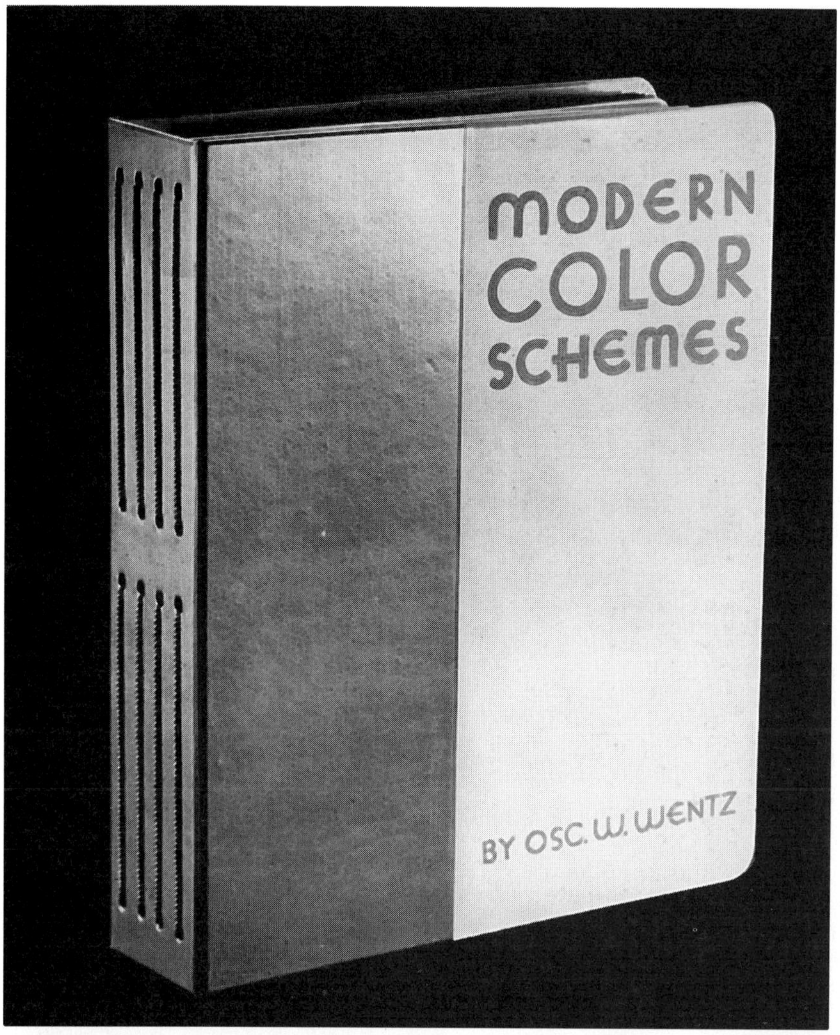


O S C A R W . W E N T Z

**A book of modern color schemes—bound in gunmetal and white DuPont Fabricoid.**

H E N R I E T T E R E I S S

**Paper book jackets designed for E. P. Dutton & Co., Inc. and G. P. Putnam's Sons.**

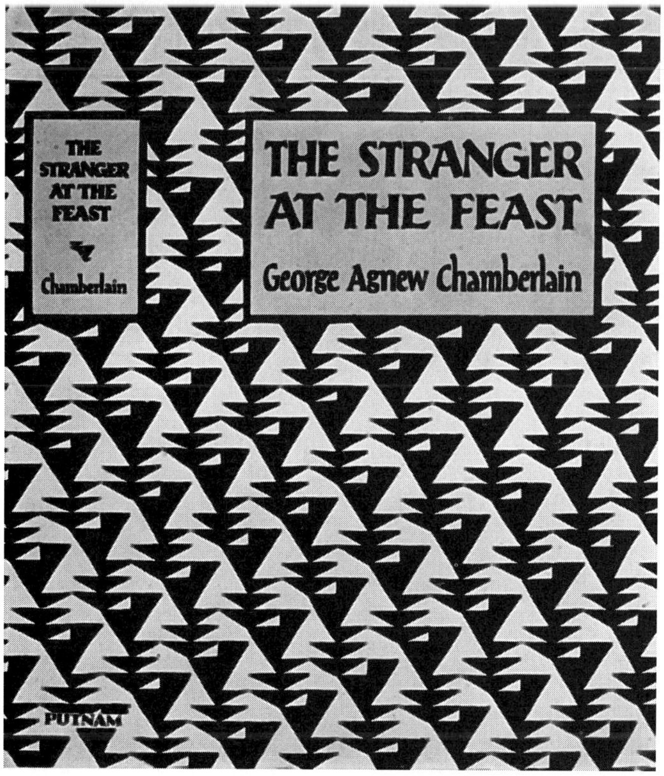


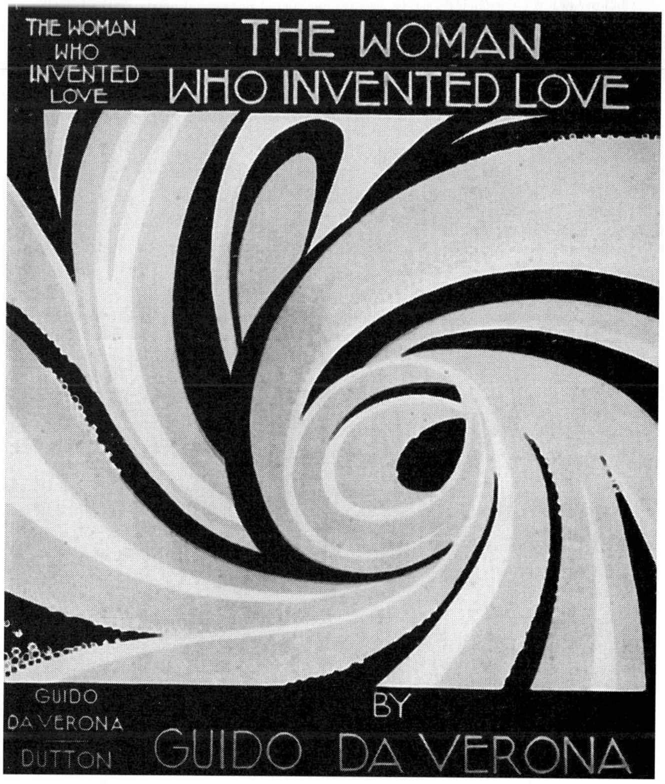

R O B E R T L . L E O N A R D

Colored drawing of advertisement for La Salle, General Motors. Courtesy MacManus, Inc.

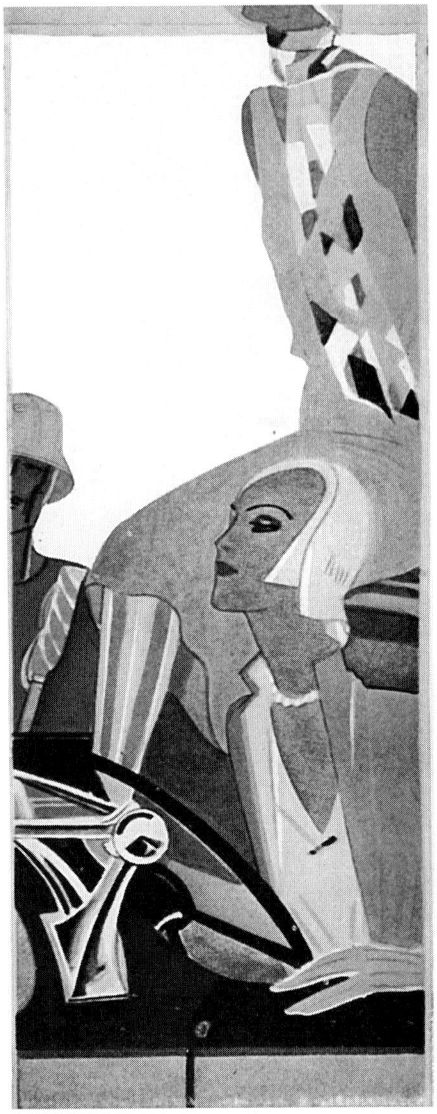

Cover for Du Pont Fabricoid booklet in 5 color offset.

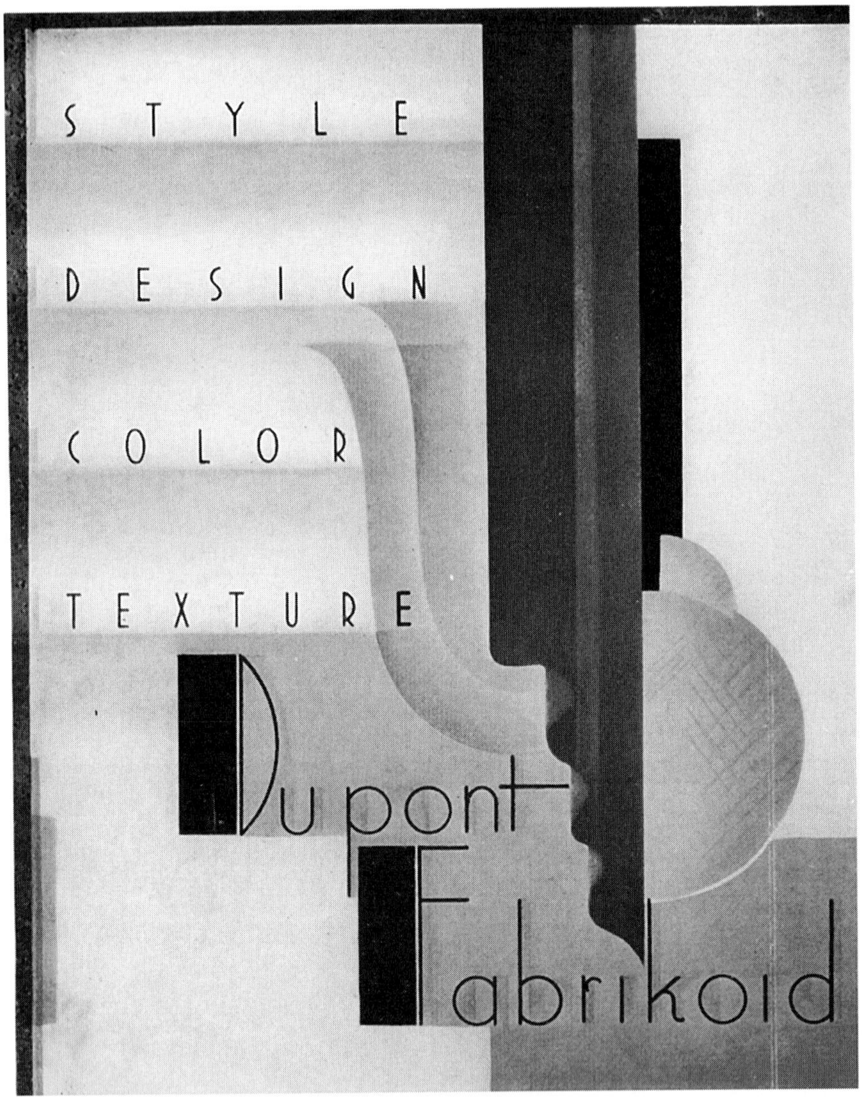


Advertising drawing for manicure product.

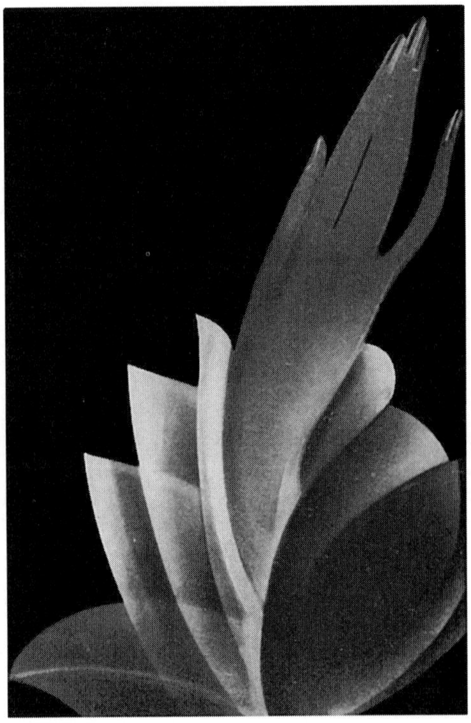

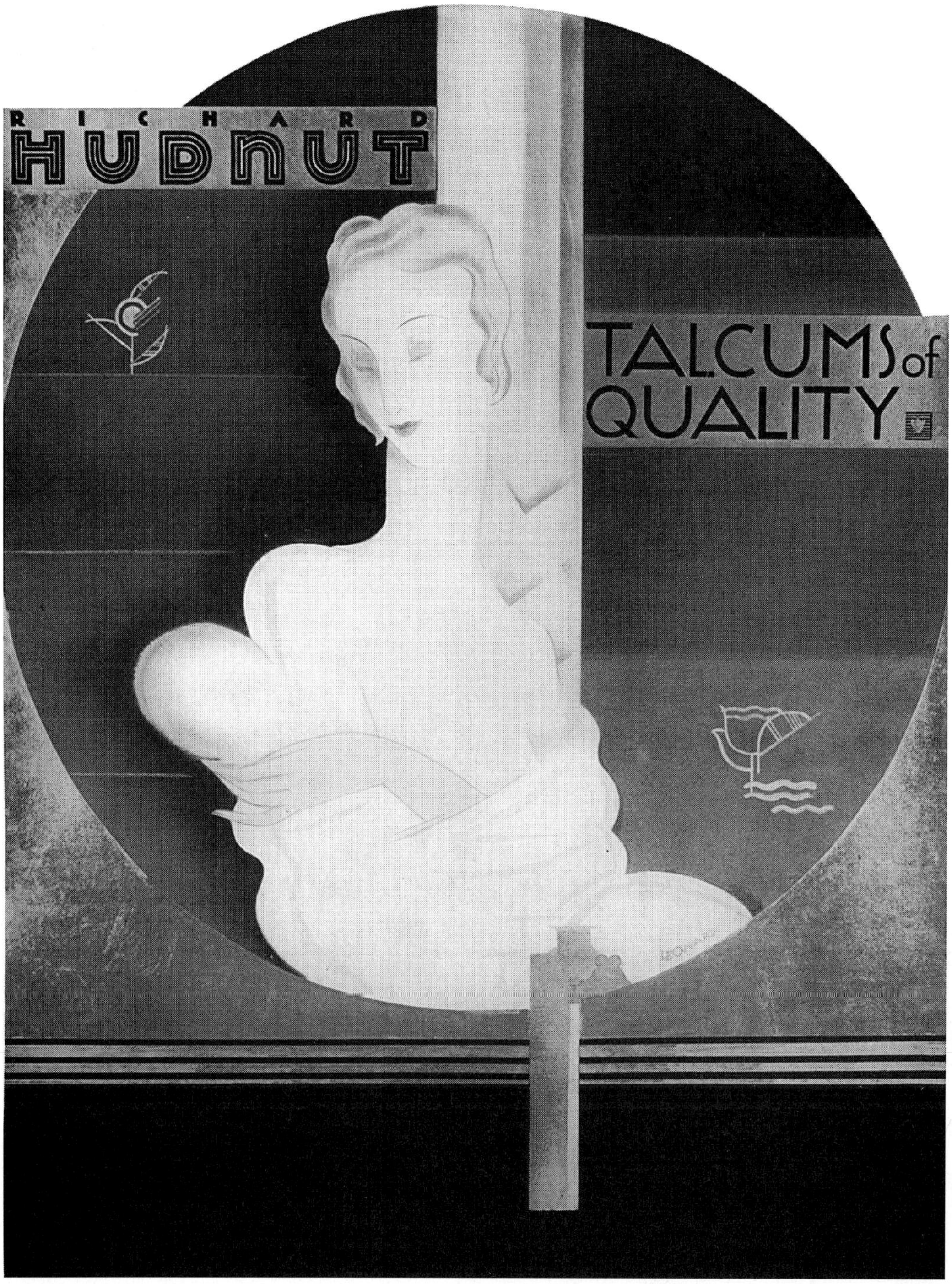


Center piece of window display for Richard Hudnut.

Bath salt labels for same firm.

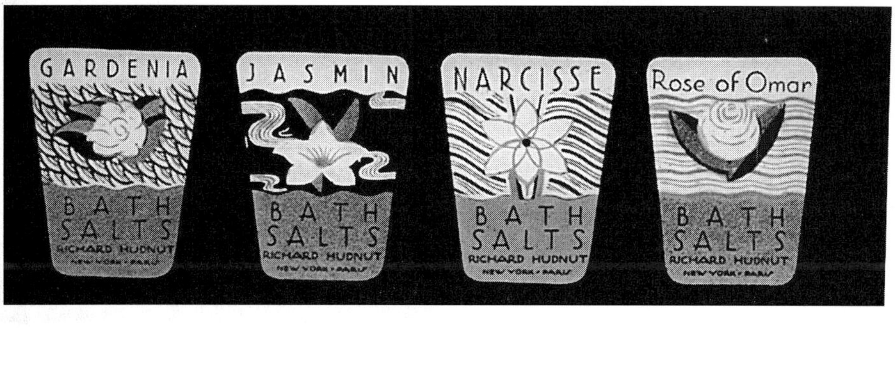

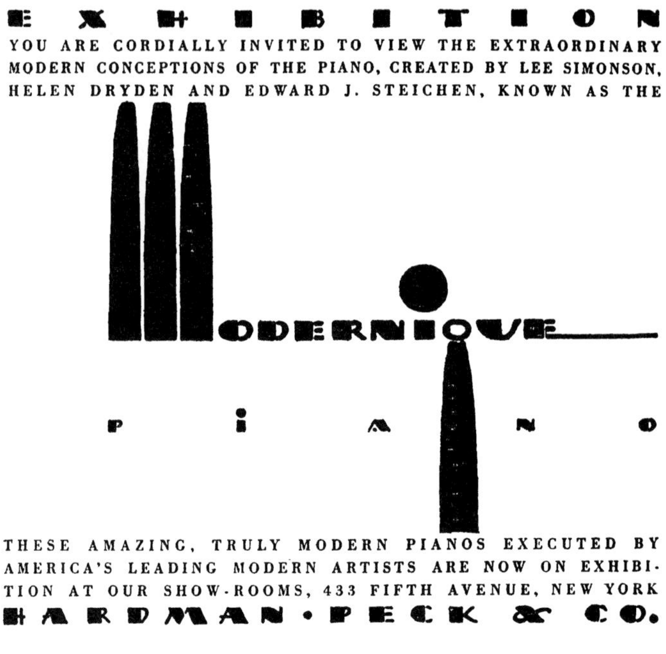


GUSTAV B. JENSEN
Magazine advertisement for Hartman, Peck & Co.

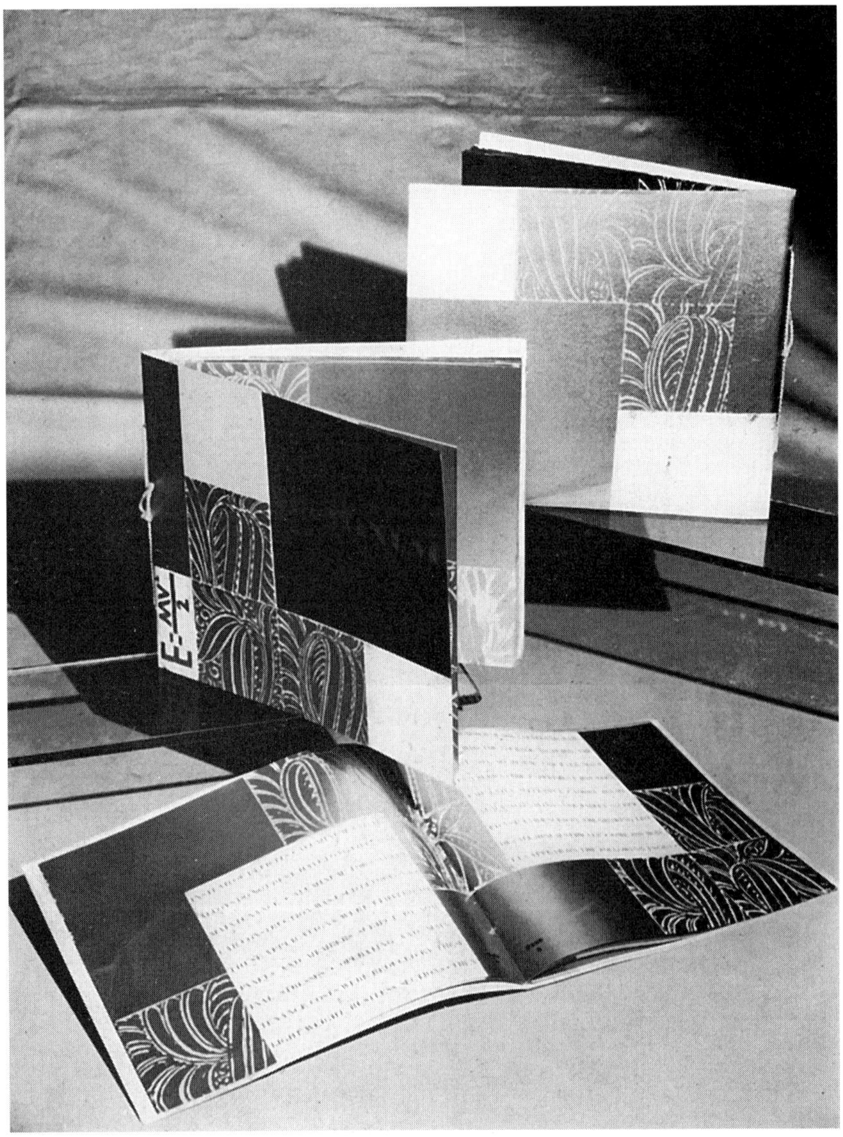

Booklets designed for the Aluminum Co. of America.

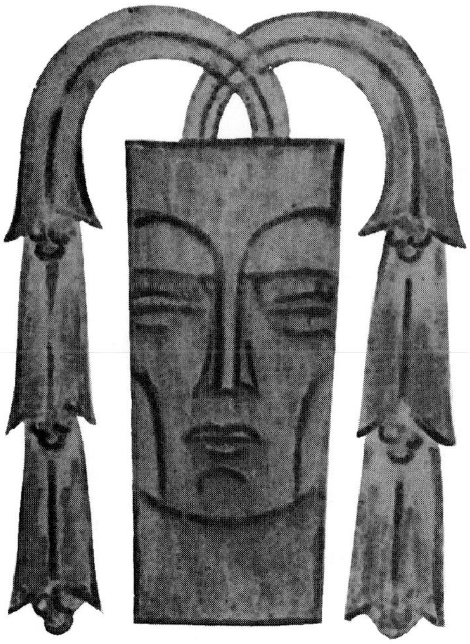

Personal trade mark

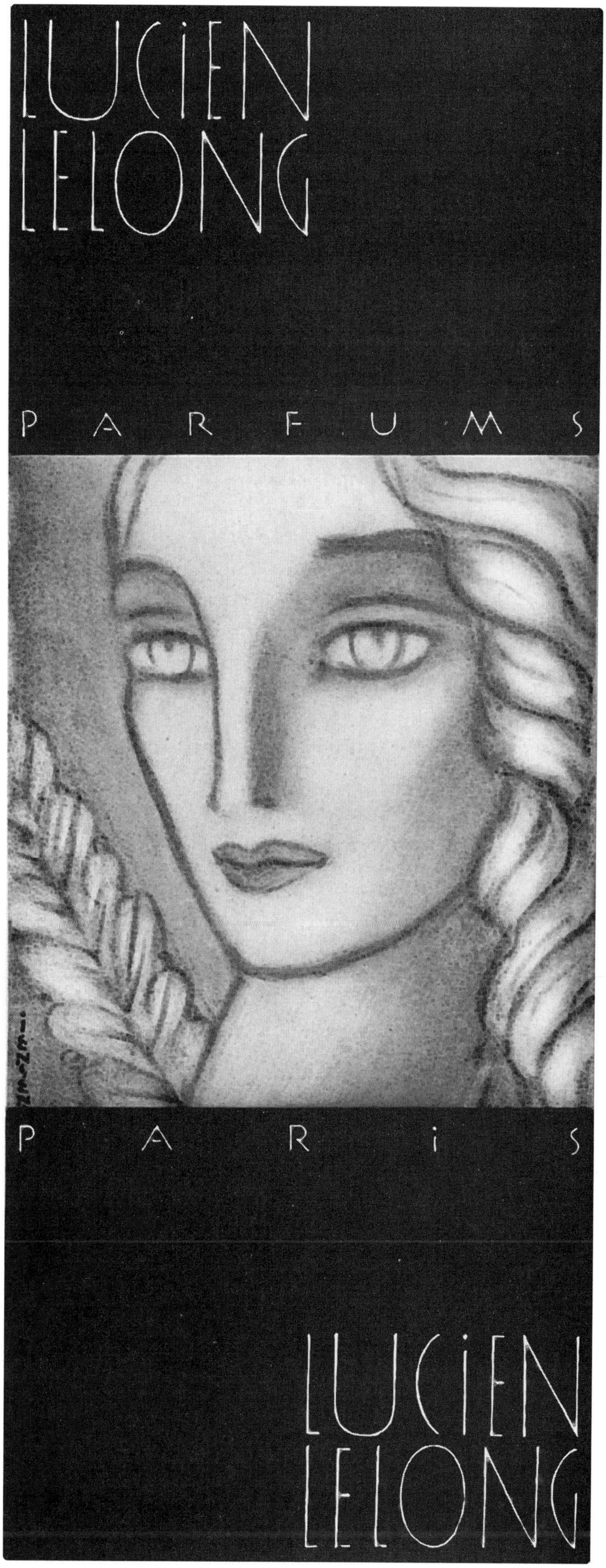


Magazine advertisement made for Lucien Lelong.
Courtesy of Earl Ludgin, Inc.

Cover design of Pierce Arrow booklet made for Bartlett-Orr Press.

Cover for magazine set in Bernhard Gothic and Ombree ornaments.

Cover and trade mark for Advertising Arts Magazine.

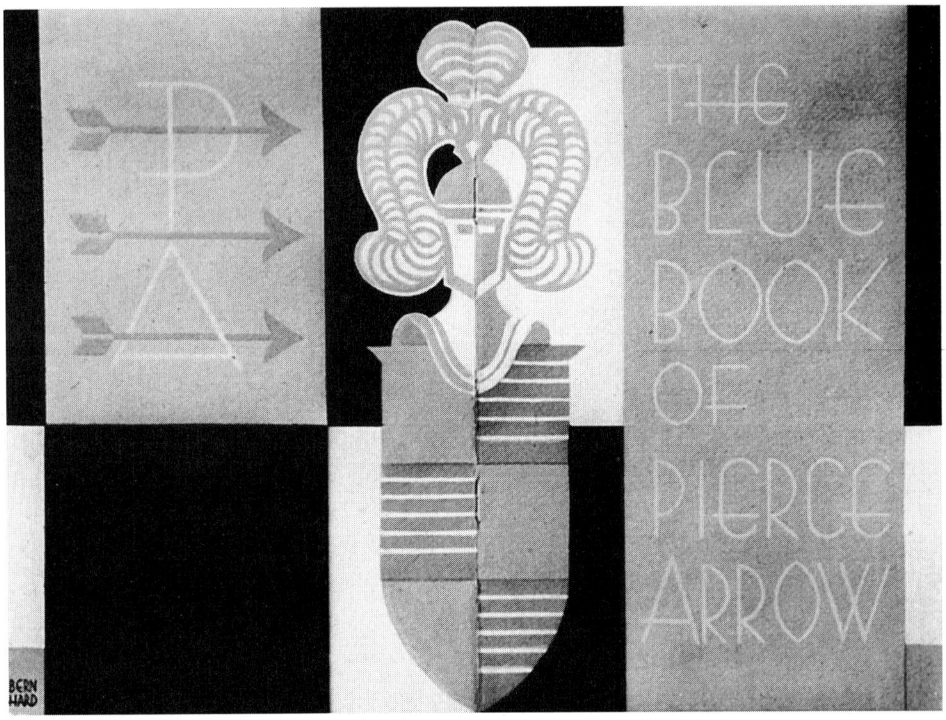


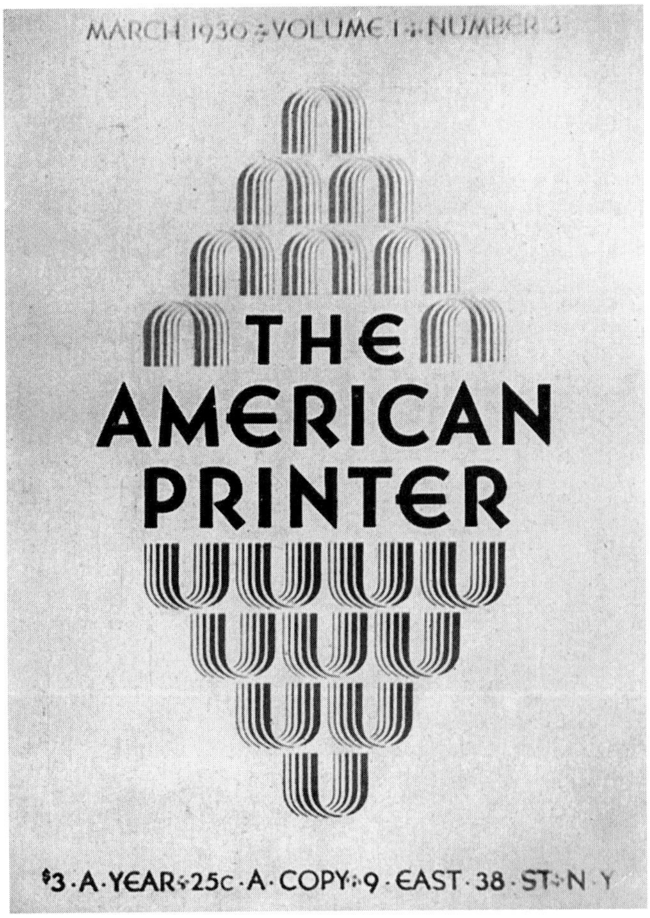


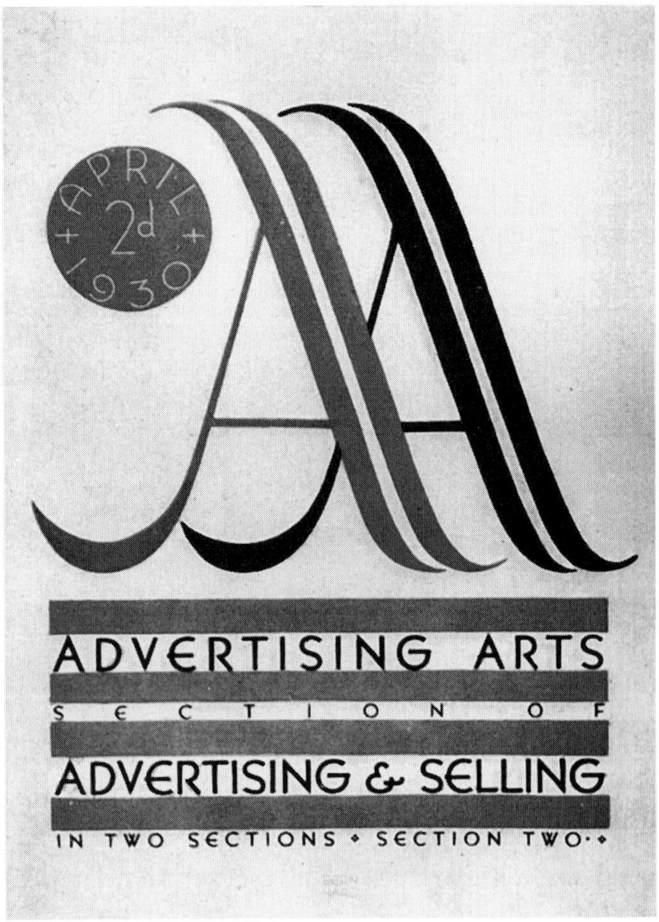

A variety of type faces designed for the American Type Founders Co.

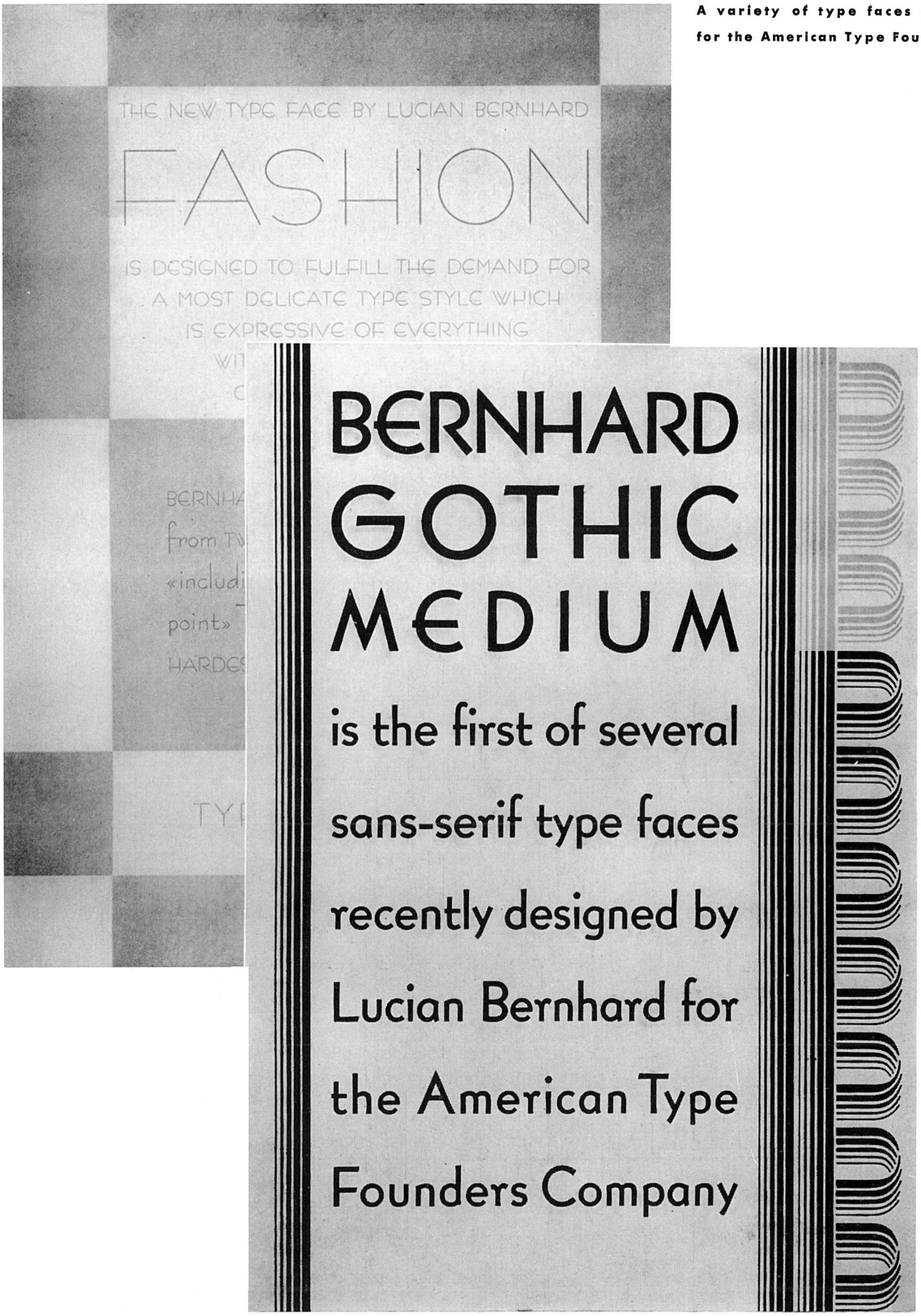

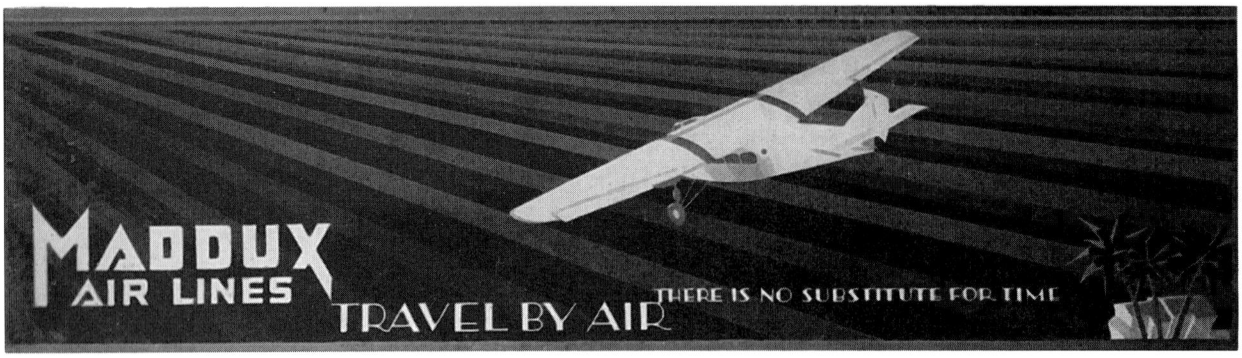


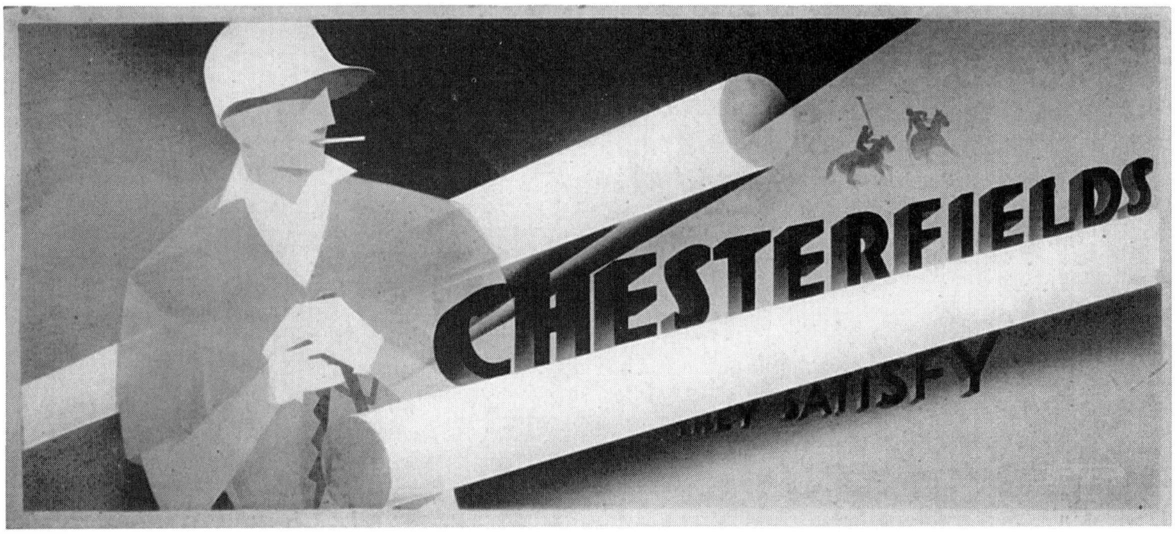


J A C O B   A S A N G E R

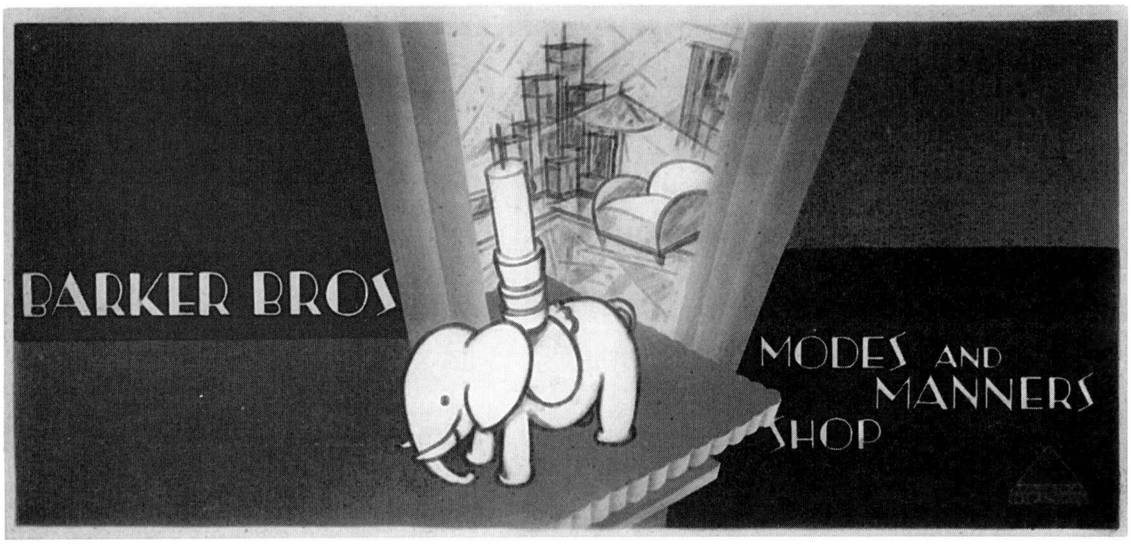

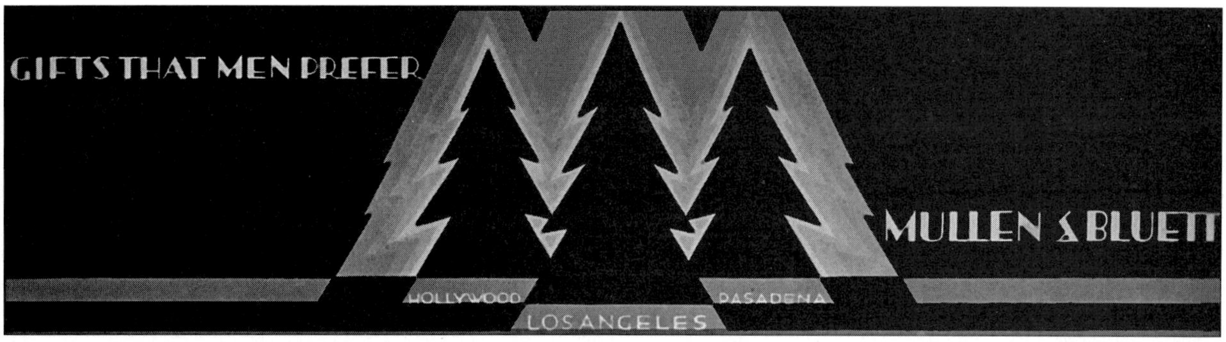


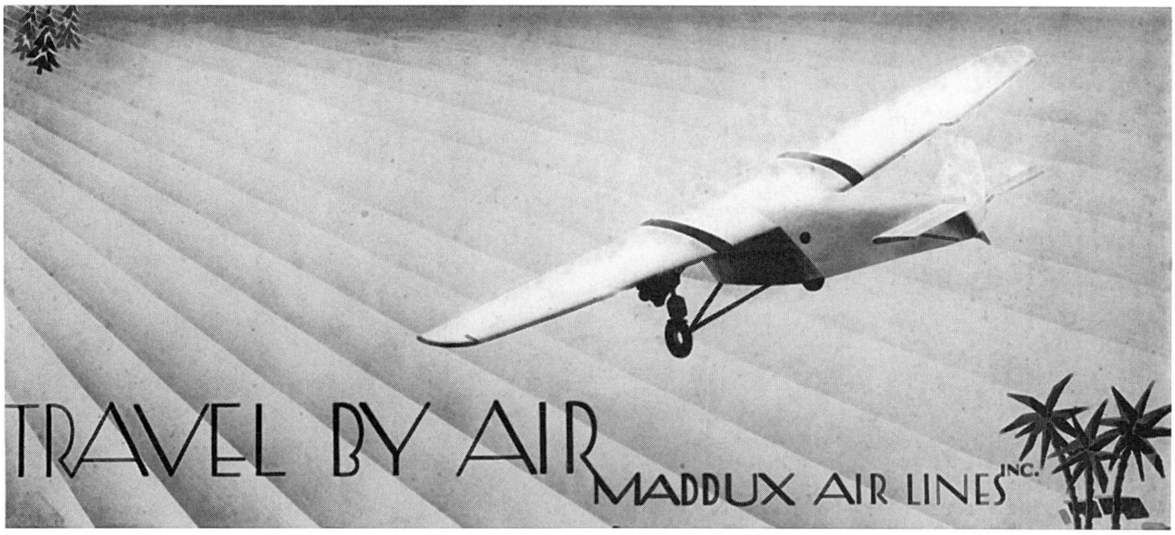


**A selection of posters displayed in the western part of the United States. Illustrating a definite departure from reproduced oil paintings and establishing a definite poster style — i.e. strong contrasts through flat colors, short copy, great simplicity.**

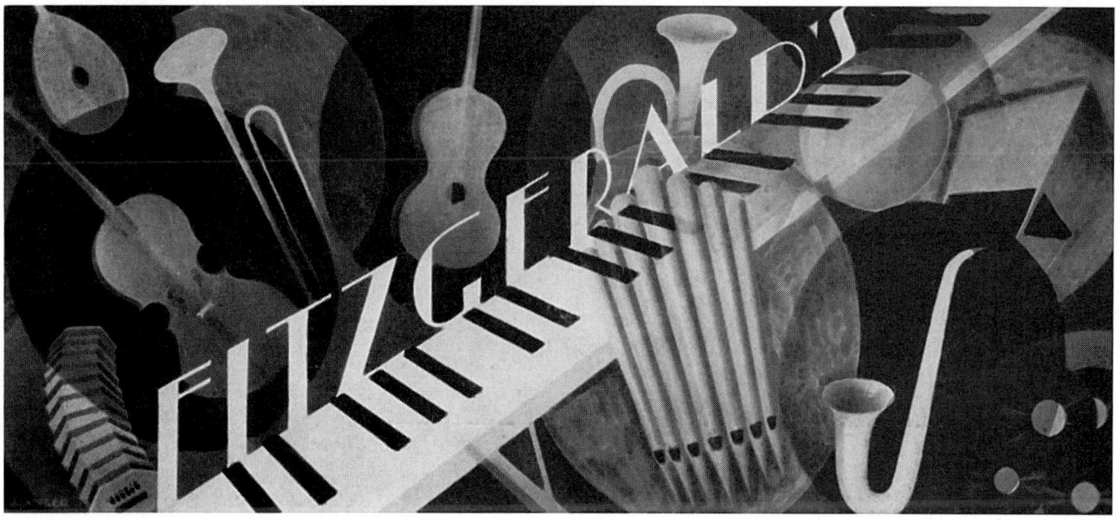

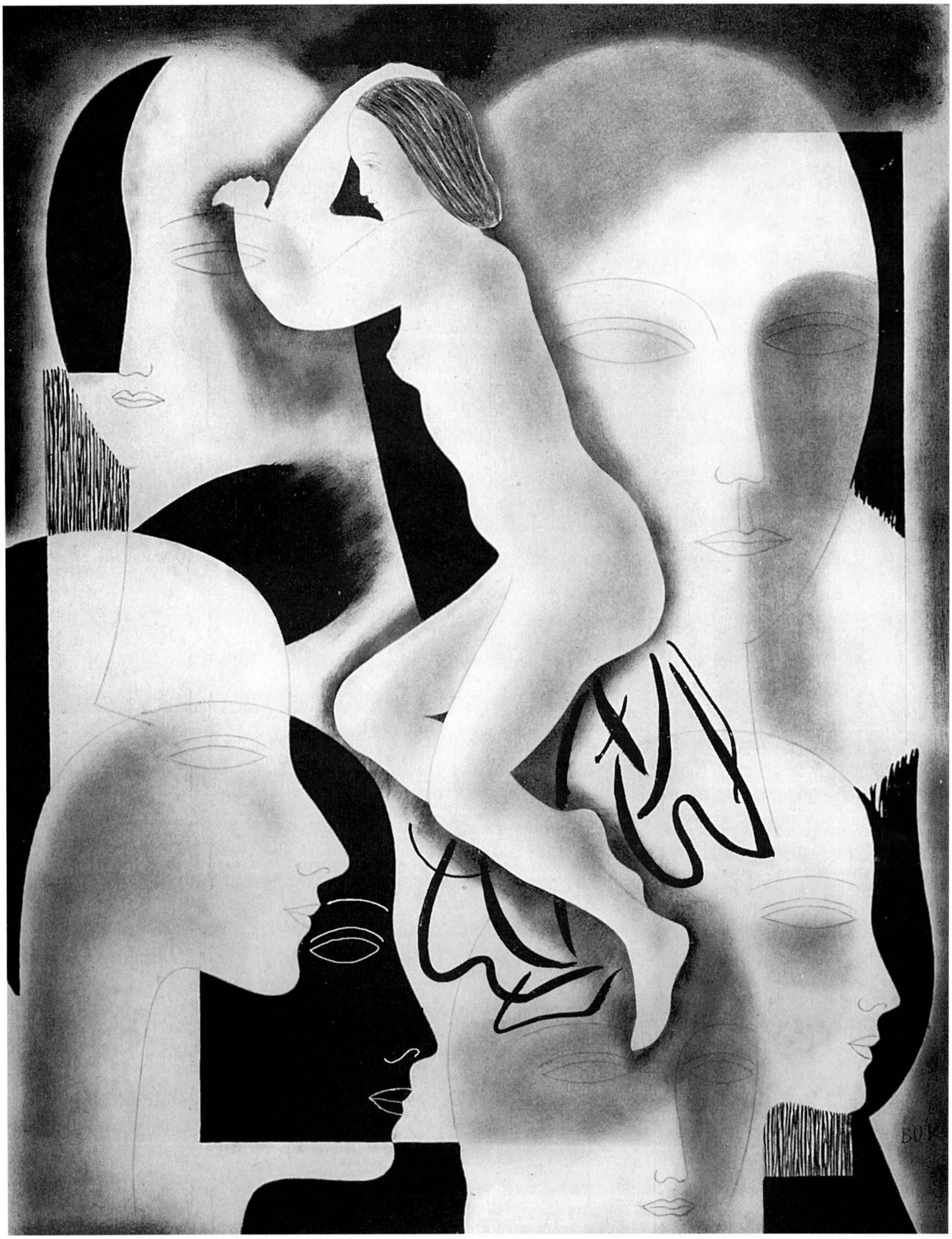


EDUARD BUK ULREICH 'Forms Femina'' — Page decoration.

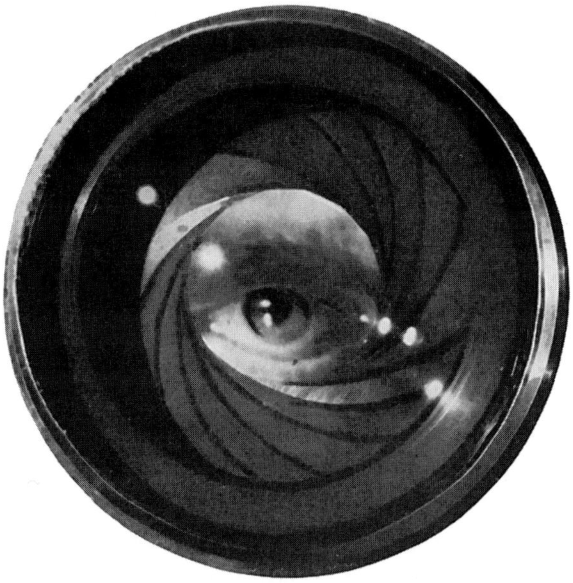

EDWARD STEICHEN

# COMMERCIAL PHOTOGRAPHY

Until recent years business and industry have been timid in their approach to the arts. The searching analysis made by great advertising agencies and magazines devoted to Fashion and the decorative arts have been active factors in the modern demonstration that the element of art was not necessarily limited to an article that is surrounded by a heavy gold frame. With characteristic swiftness, business sought to develop an inteligent collaboration with the artist, but the artist and his henchman, the art director, promptly began an active campaign to sell Art, the kind of Art known as the capital "A" brand. The business man was bombarded with the jargon and chatter of the art student:— "composition," "pattern," "spacing," etc.—The art director was usually of the type that harbored a secret ambition to be a painter of "arrangements of blue and silver." The artist was then merely going commercial because there was money in it. He really felt snobbishly inferior because he was not out in the green fields painting Corots or Monets.

During this formative period, a new medium quietly invaded places which had been held sacred to "handwork art." A glass eye fastened on a box that held sensitized material produced photographs of people and things. The original appeal that led to the use of photographs was that it was a cheaper way of getting pictures, but as the Camera Worker began to measure up to his medium and the job, it was often found to be a better way of doing such things.
The frank objectivity of the photograph found favor with the business man and with his client, the public. Here were pictures of a glass, a box, a bar of soap, or a person that told a simple, natural, convincing story. When the more skilled photographers who directed the searching objectivity of their cameras were also possessed of good taste and a sensitive understanding, the resulting pictures began to open up new directions and new fields. Photography thus brought fresh points of view into the realm of commercial art. The flat horizontal plane from which the painter regarded his models in the studio was changed. The camera looked at the pageant of modern activity from all angles and under all conditions of light. It reflected the perpendicular trajectory of the elevator as well as the horizontal one of a train. The automobile lifted people out of ruts woven by habits by taking them to new places. The camera changed standardized points of view. Age old things were revitalized when pictured from new angles and under new factors of illumination. From an airplane vast and distant stretches of the earth's surface were pictured;—through a telescope the camera found new

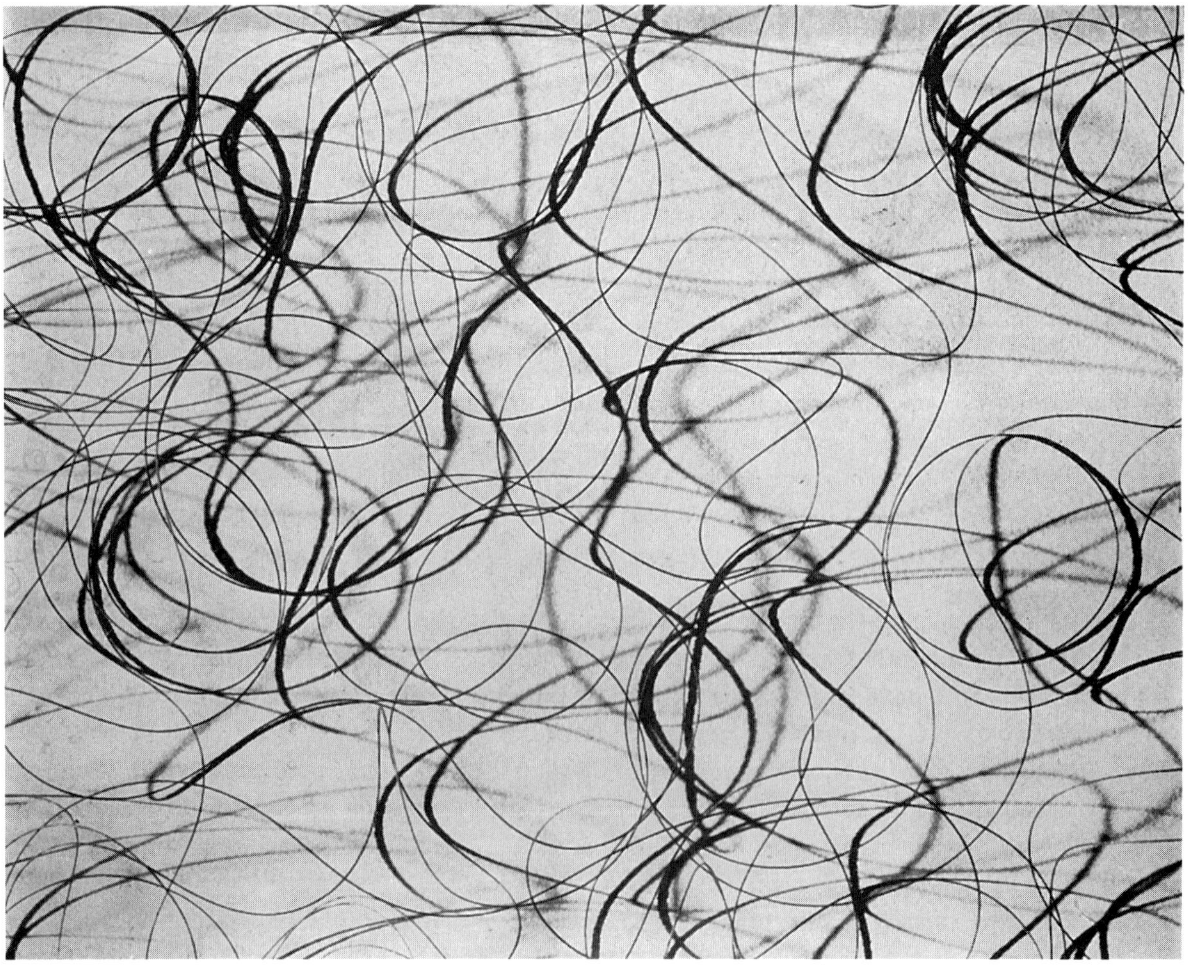

**E D W A R D   S T E I C H E N**

**Photographic designs for fabric. Stehli Silks Corporation.**

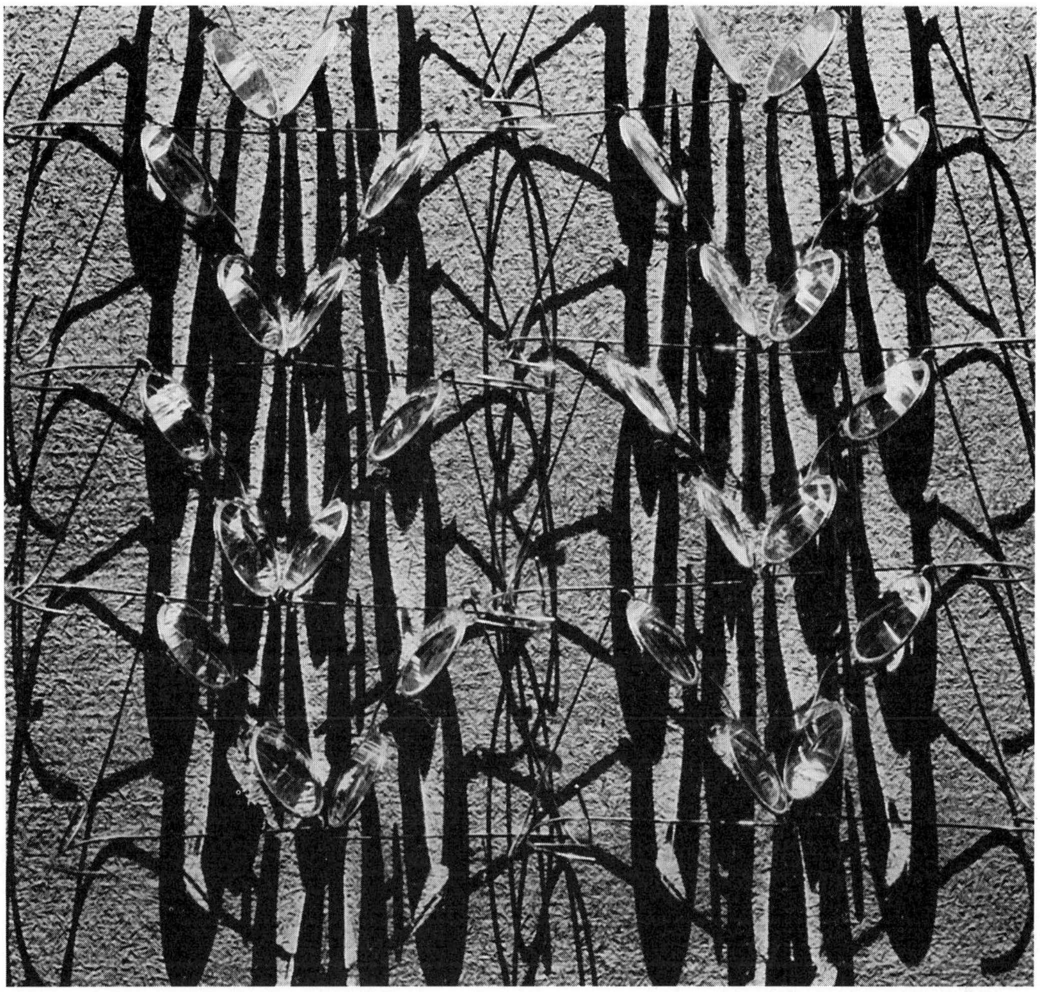

worlds;—through a microscope it recorded minute fragments of matter split into millionths;—by the X-ray photograph it made the medical diagnosis more certain. It brought the news events of the world vividly before the eyes of the world.

Today, Photography has a new momentum. As well as a collaborator, it is an invader, a discoverer, an iconoclast. The intelligent American photographer has definitely abandoned all petty trickery that made for imitation of the other arts. The meticulous detail, the biting precision with which a lens can draw an image is of such beauty that any arty blurring, or diffusion in imitation of bad painting becomes nonsense.

The modern European photographer has not liberated himself as definitely. He still imitates his friend, the painter, with the so called "Photo-montage." He has merely chosen the modern painter as his prototype. We have gone well past the painful period of combining and tricking the banal commercial photograph,—too far past it to be seriously tempted again into imitating even the brilliant technique or ideas of the Dadaists, or the Futurists by combining various and sundry photographs by pasting and retouching.

It is logical, therefore, that we find many modern photographers lined up with Architects and Designers instead of with painters, or photographic art salons.

Photography is a modern art because it is a factor in and a contributor to our time—and not because it imitates, or is subservient to any other medium.

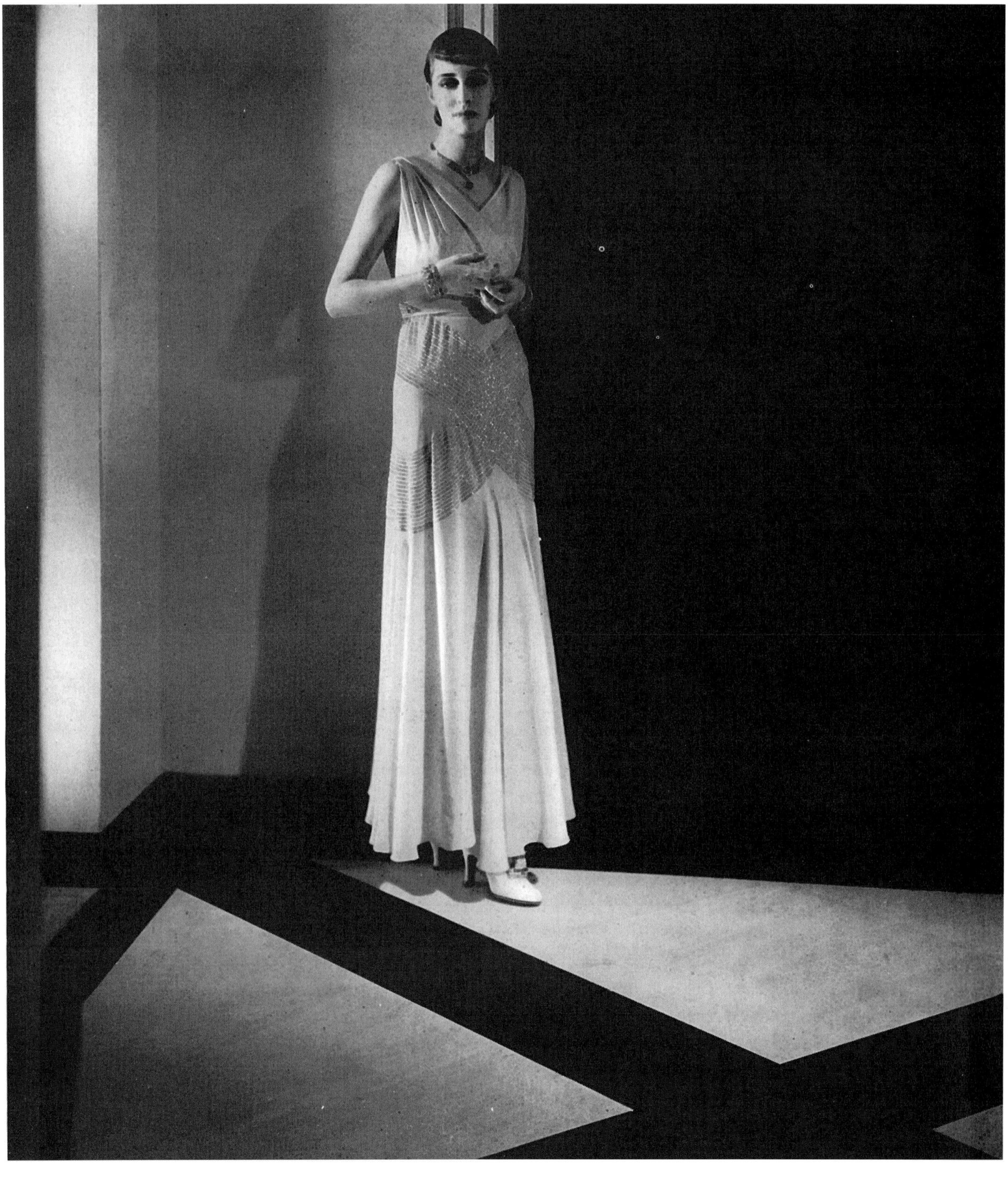

E D W A R D   S T E I C H E N

**Fashion photograph for Vogue. Courtesy Conde Nast Publications.**

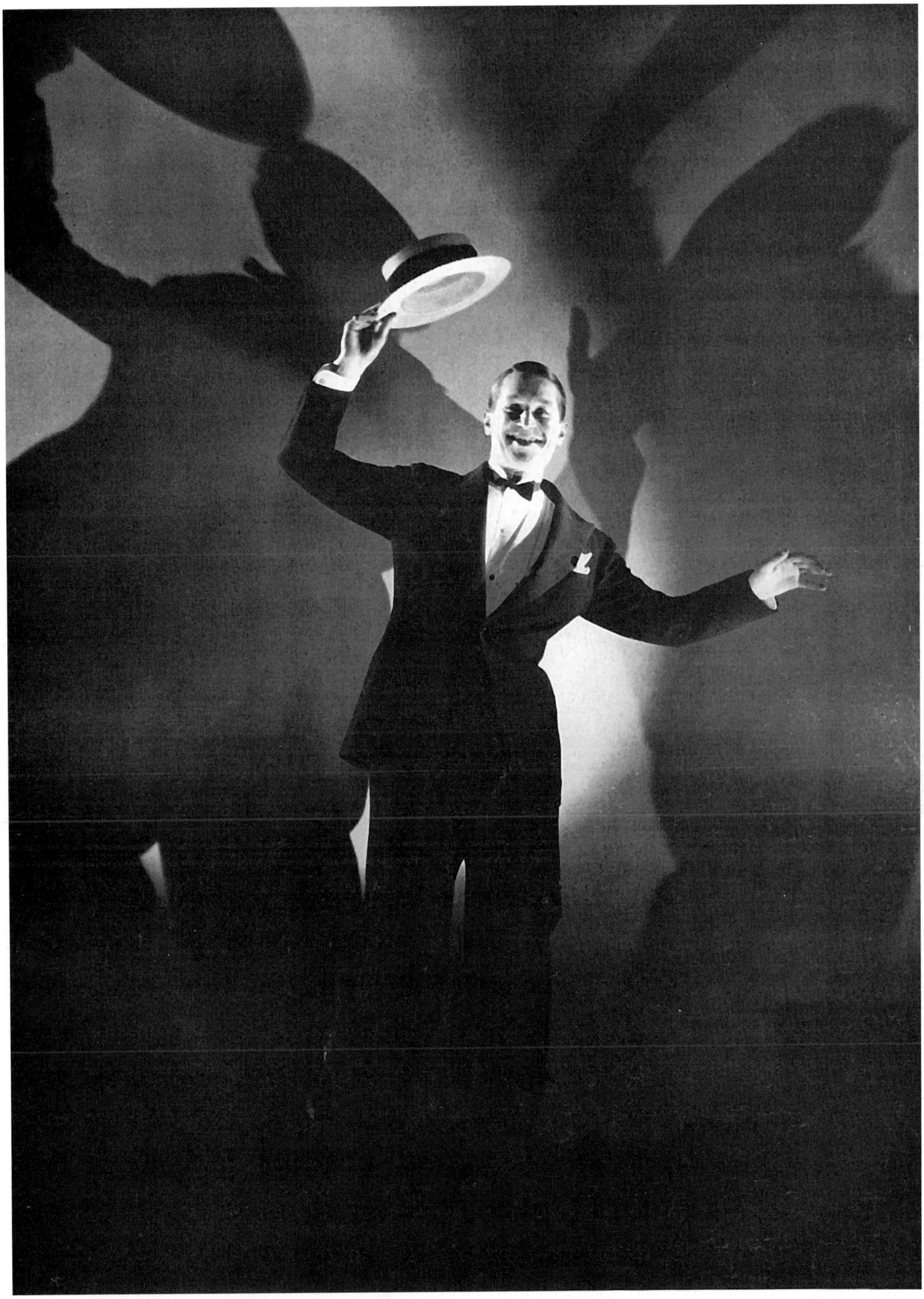

Photograph of Maurice Chevalier for Vanity Fair.
Courtesy Conde Nast Publications.

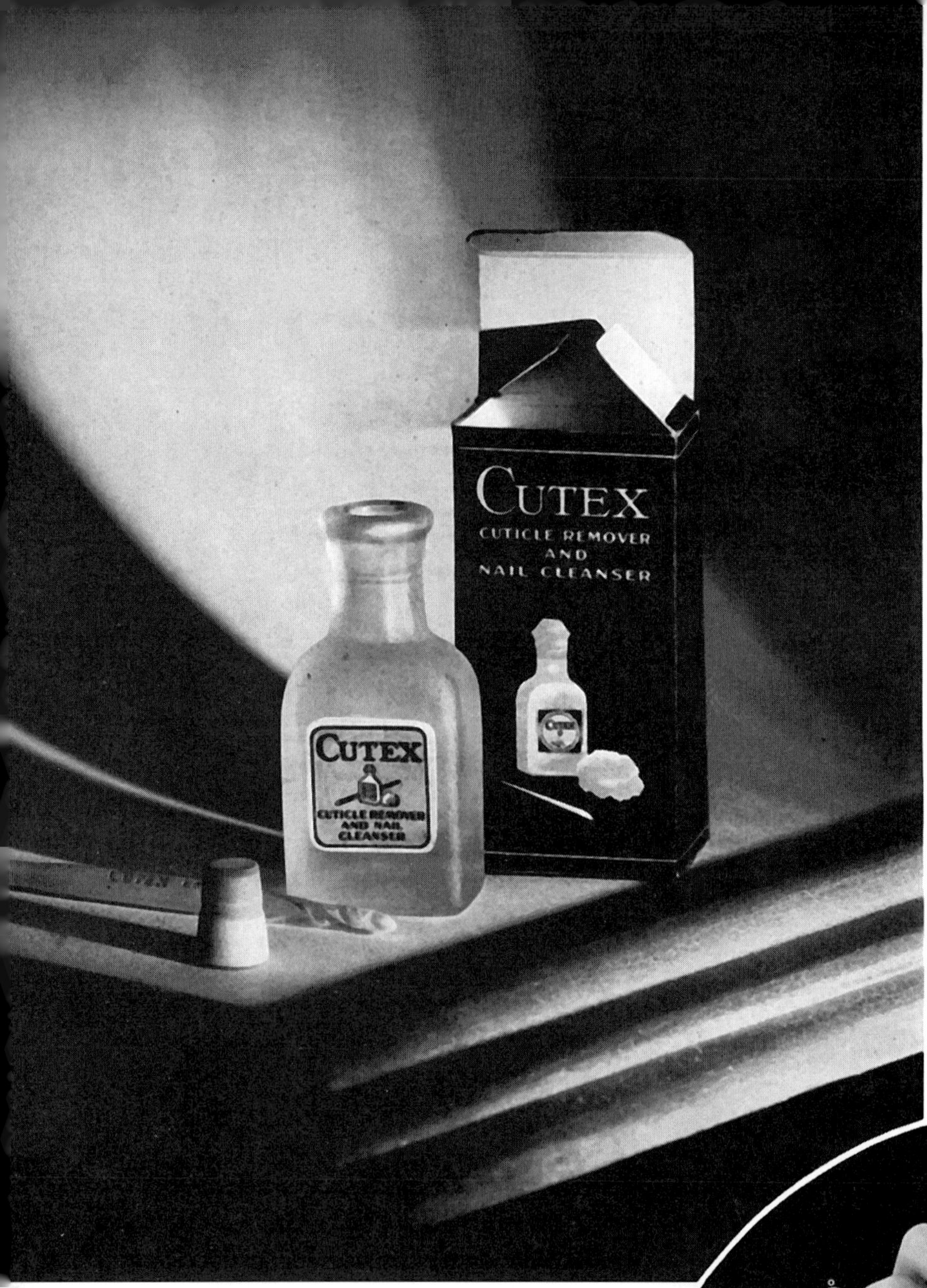


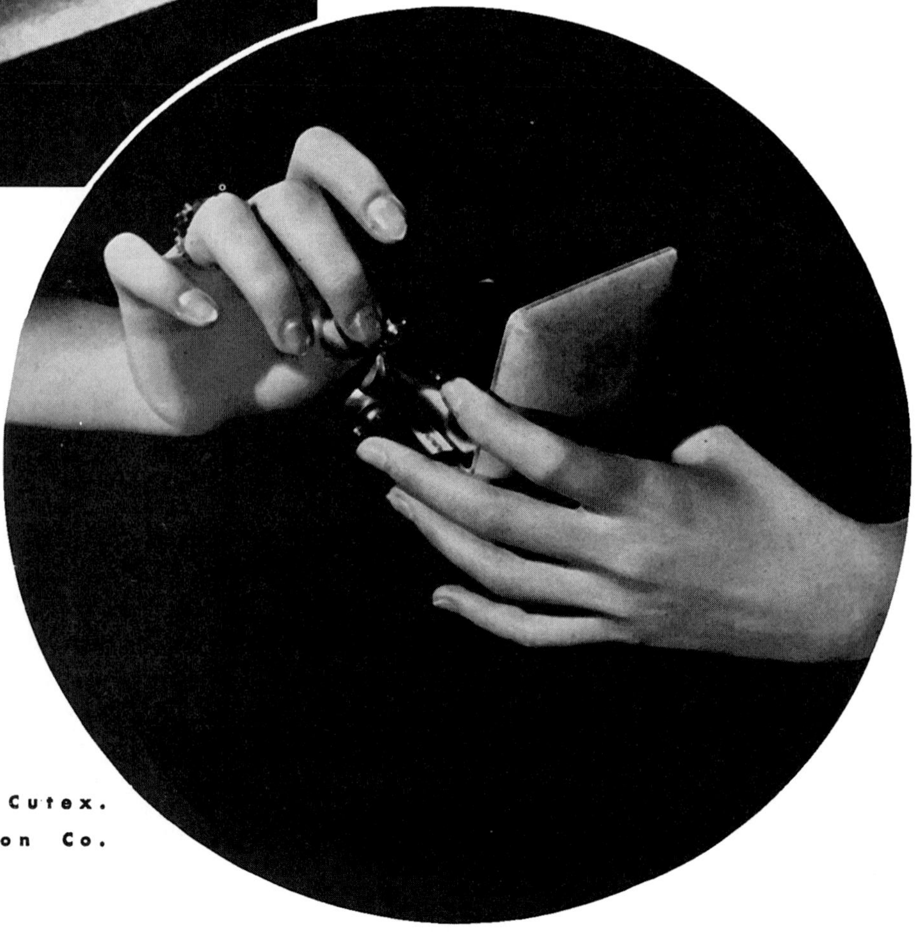

Two advertising photographs for Cutex.
Courtesy of J. Walter Thompson Co.

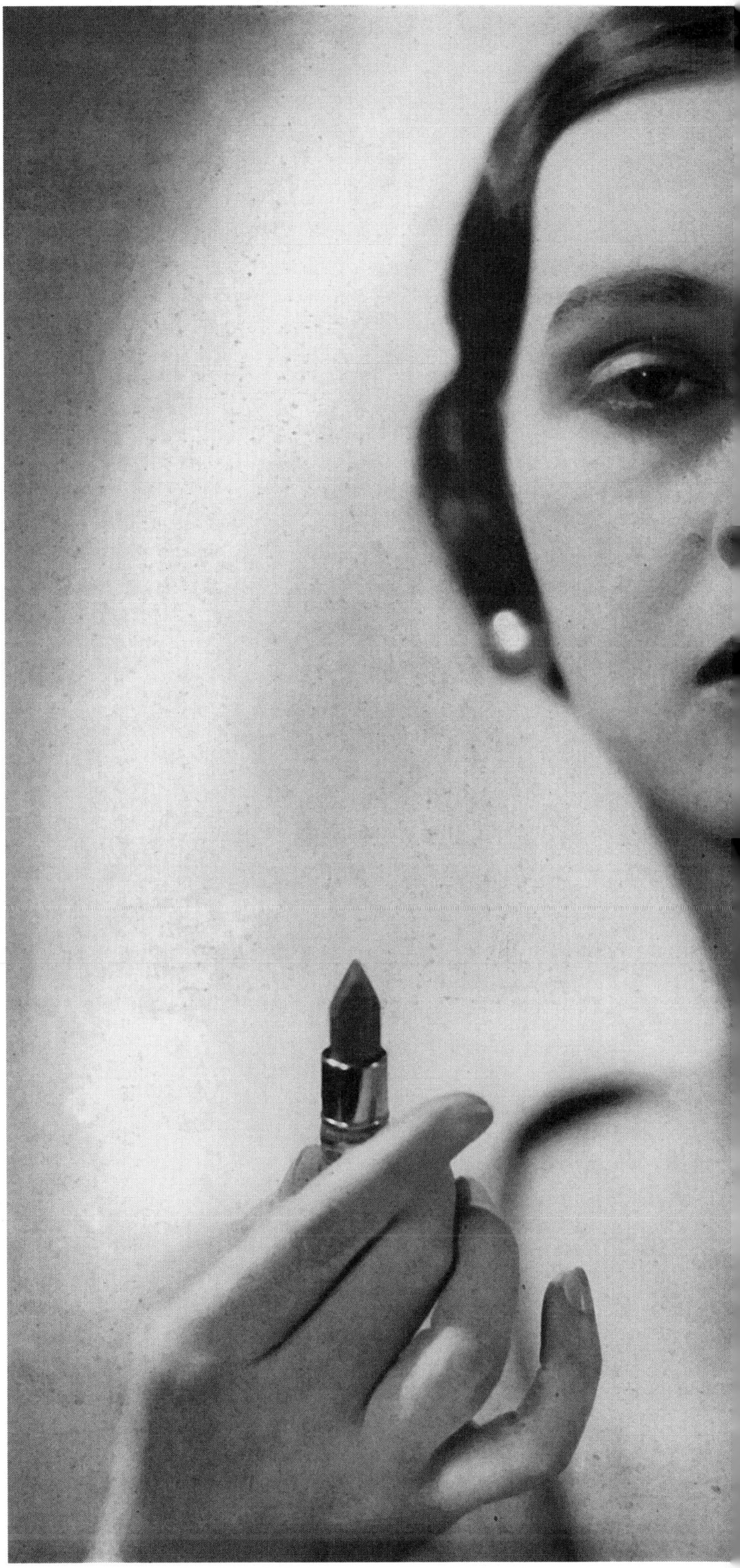

N I C K O L A S   M U R A Y

**Angelus Lipstick advertisement. Courtesy of Cecil, Warwick & Cecil.**

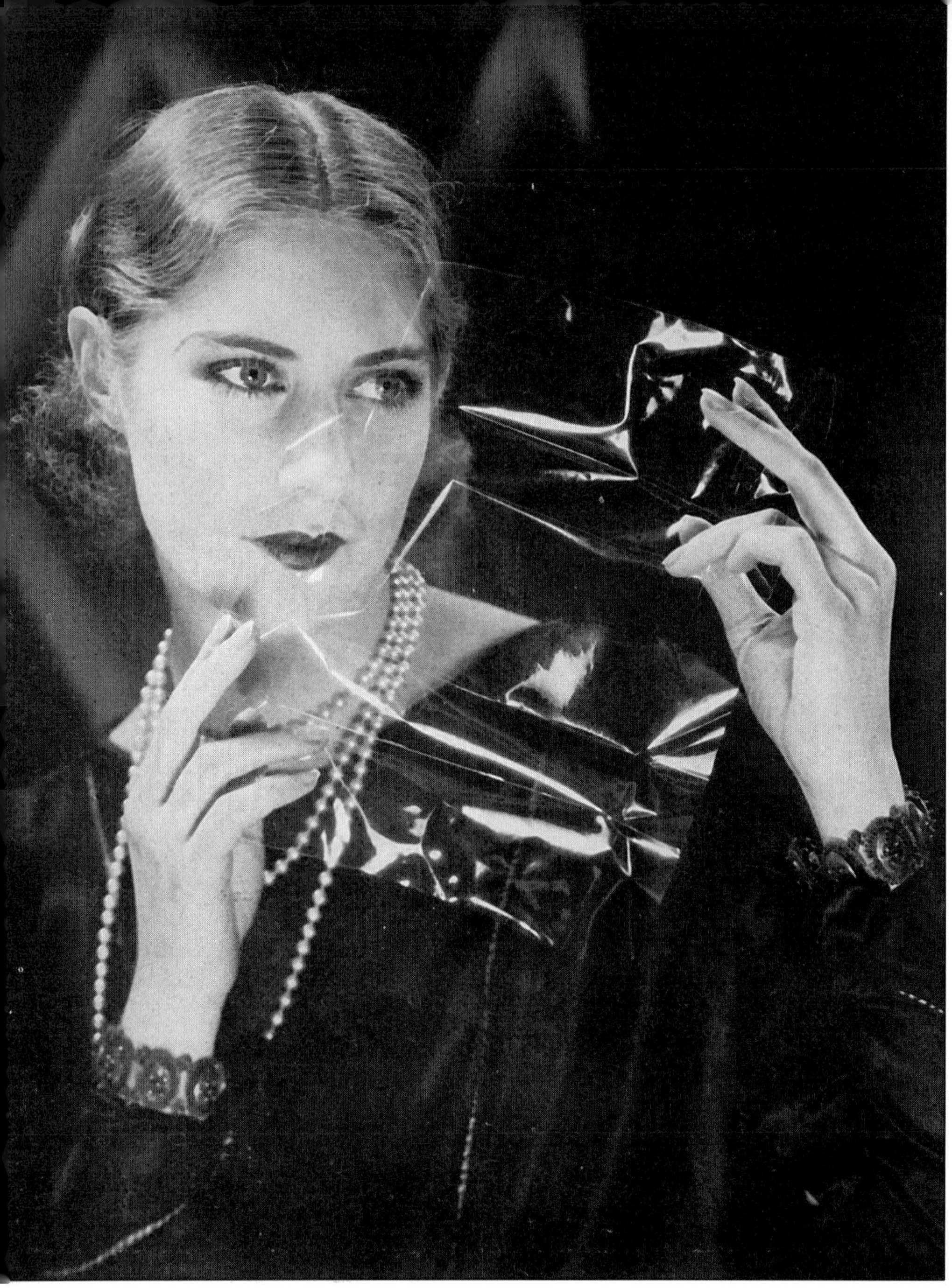

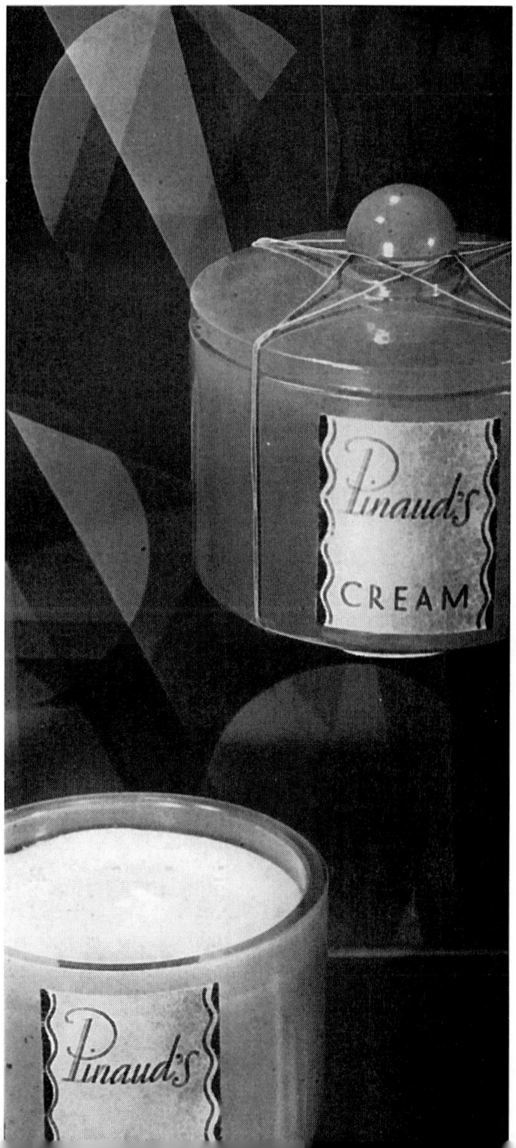


SARA PARSONS

**Advertising photographs featuring Cellophane and composition for advertising of Pinaud's Cosmetics.**

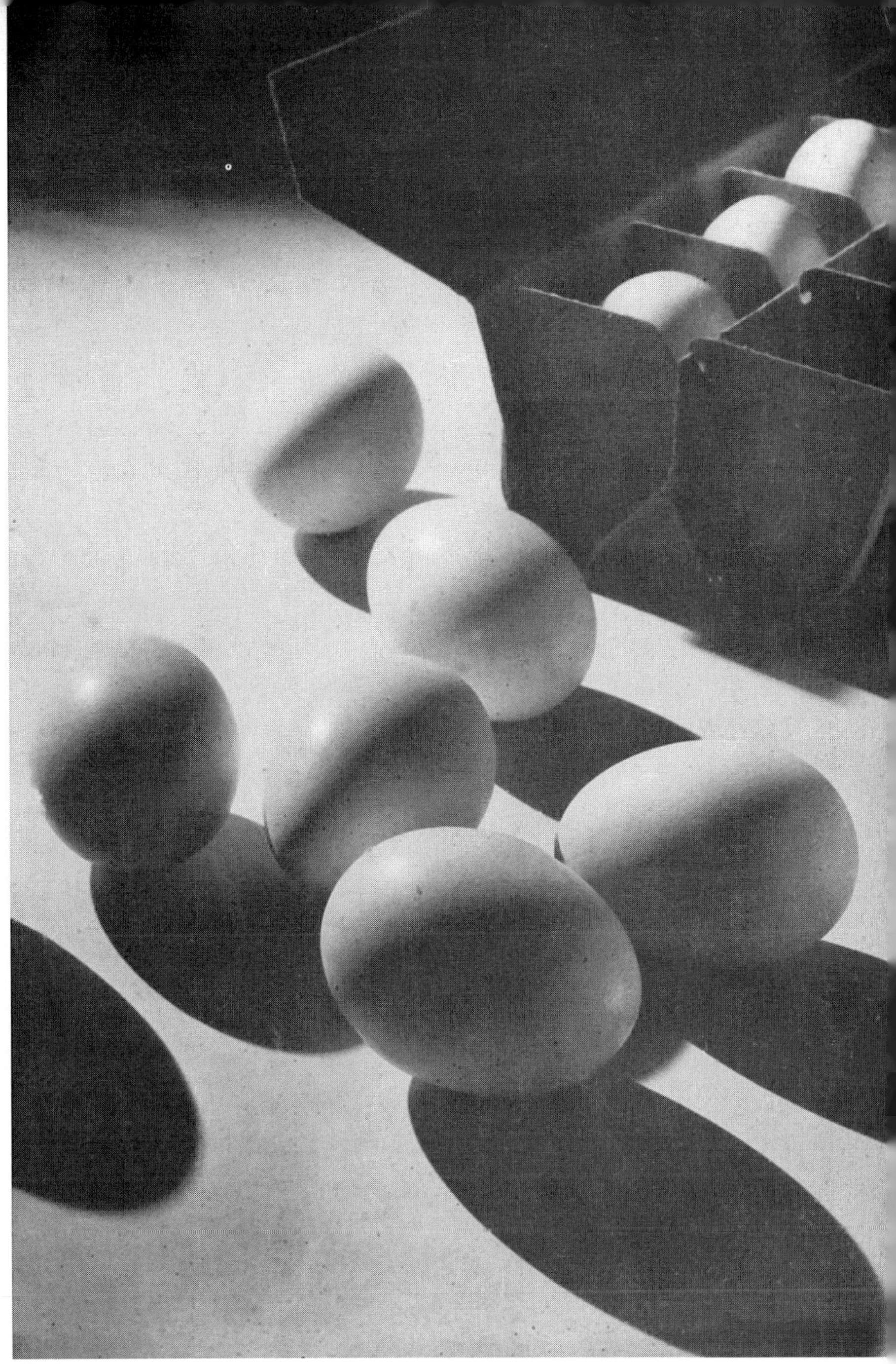

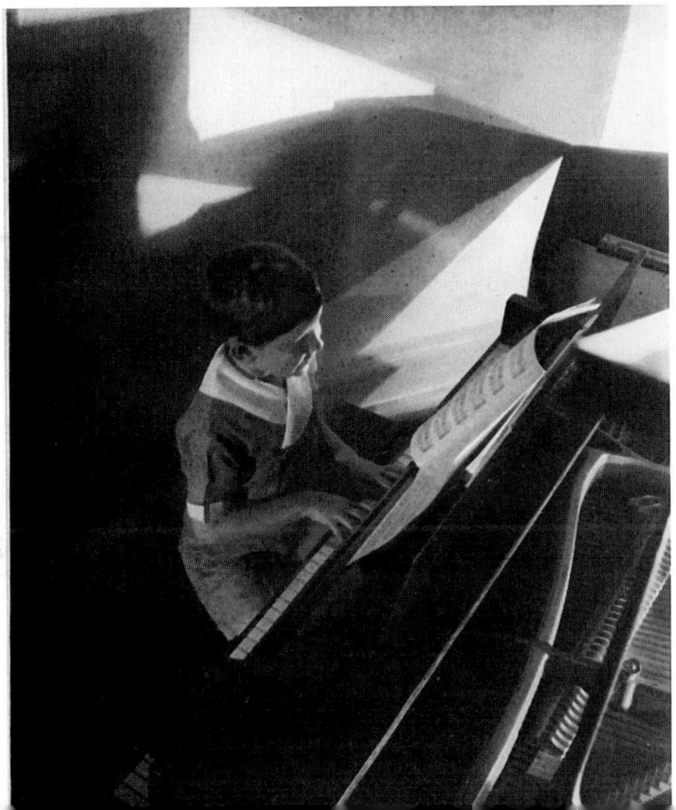

H I W I L L I A M S

Photographic Study made for Good Housekeeping Magazine.

Advertising of Ampico Piano. Courtesy of Erwin, Wasey & Co., Inc.

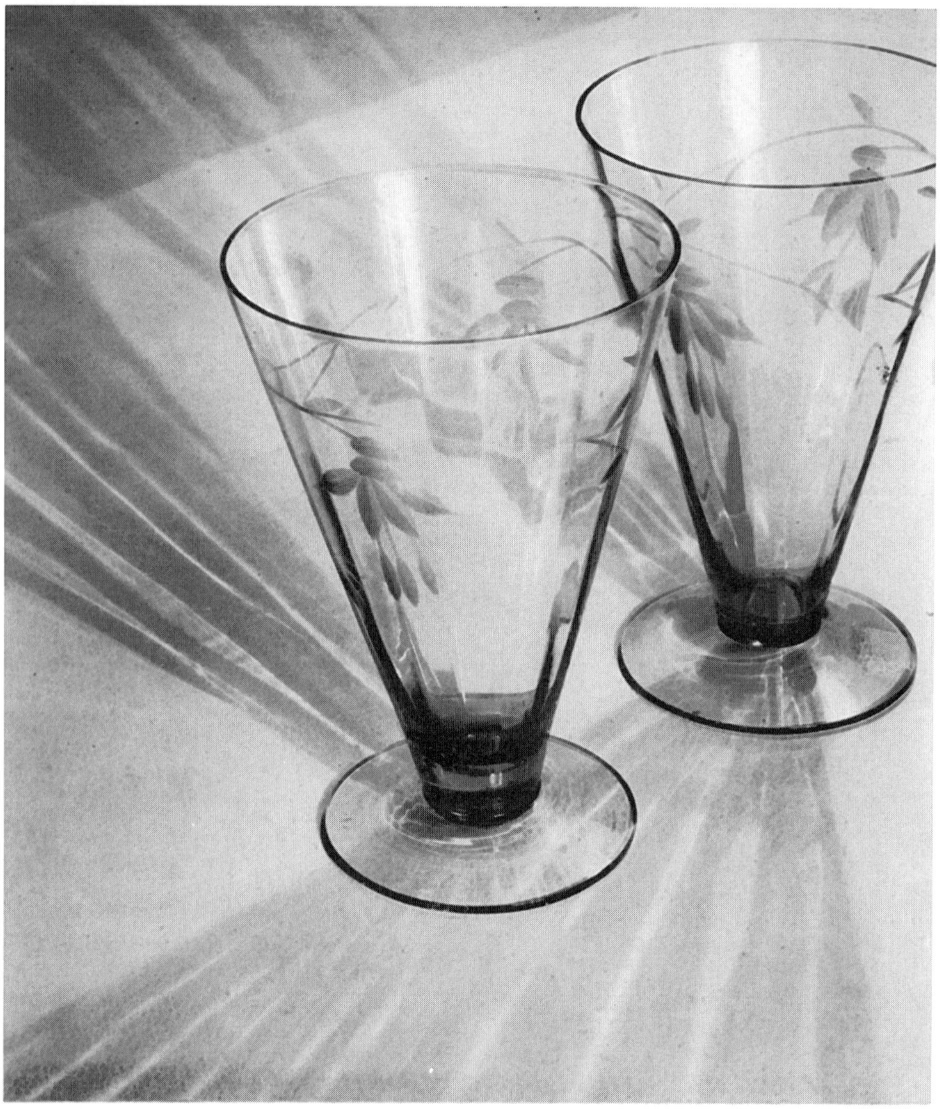

EMELIE DANIELSON

Two studies of glassware for Vogue.

Courtesy Conde Nast Publications.

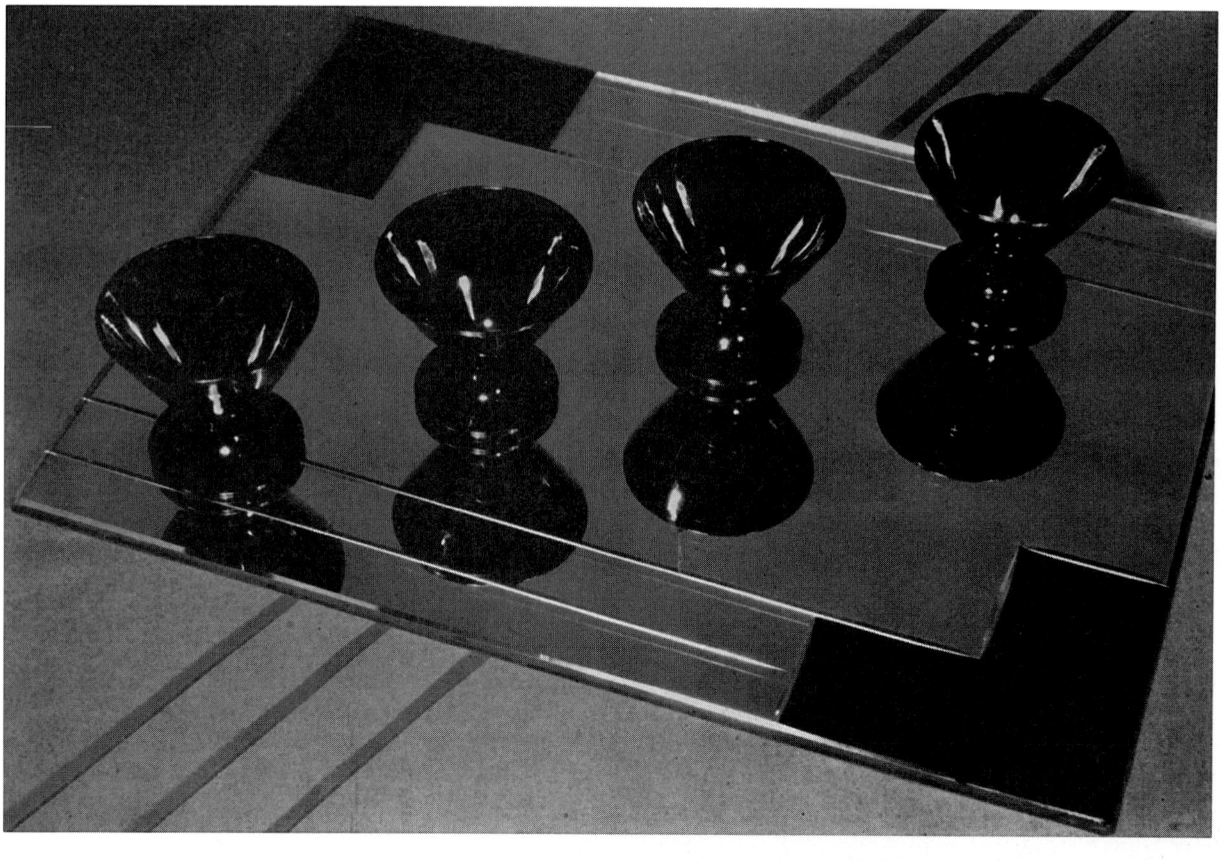

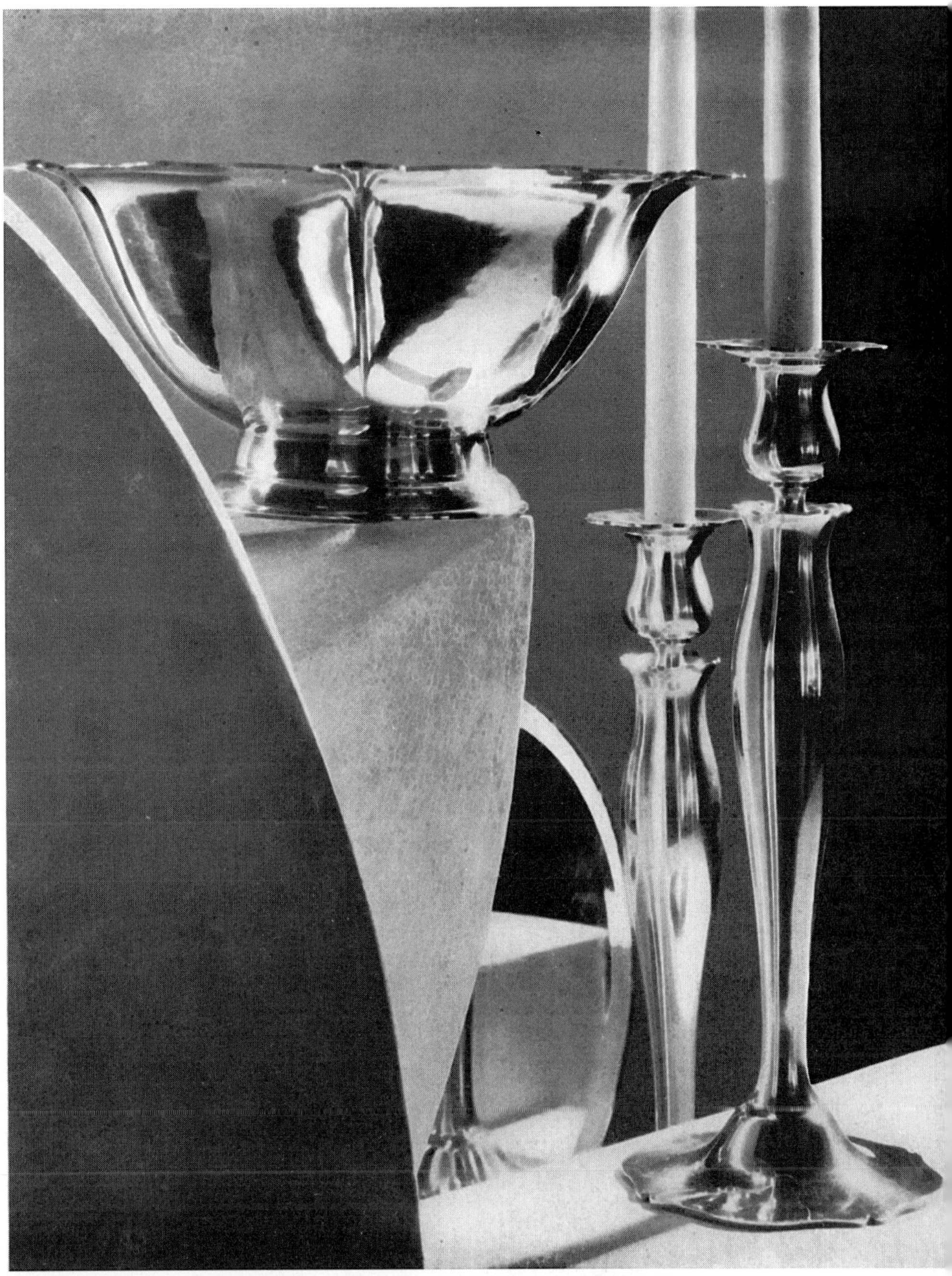

A R T H U R   G E R L A C H
Studies in silver and ceramics used in advertising by Marshall Field & Co.

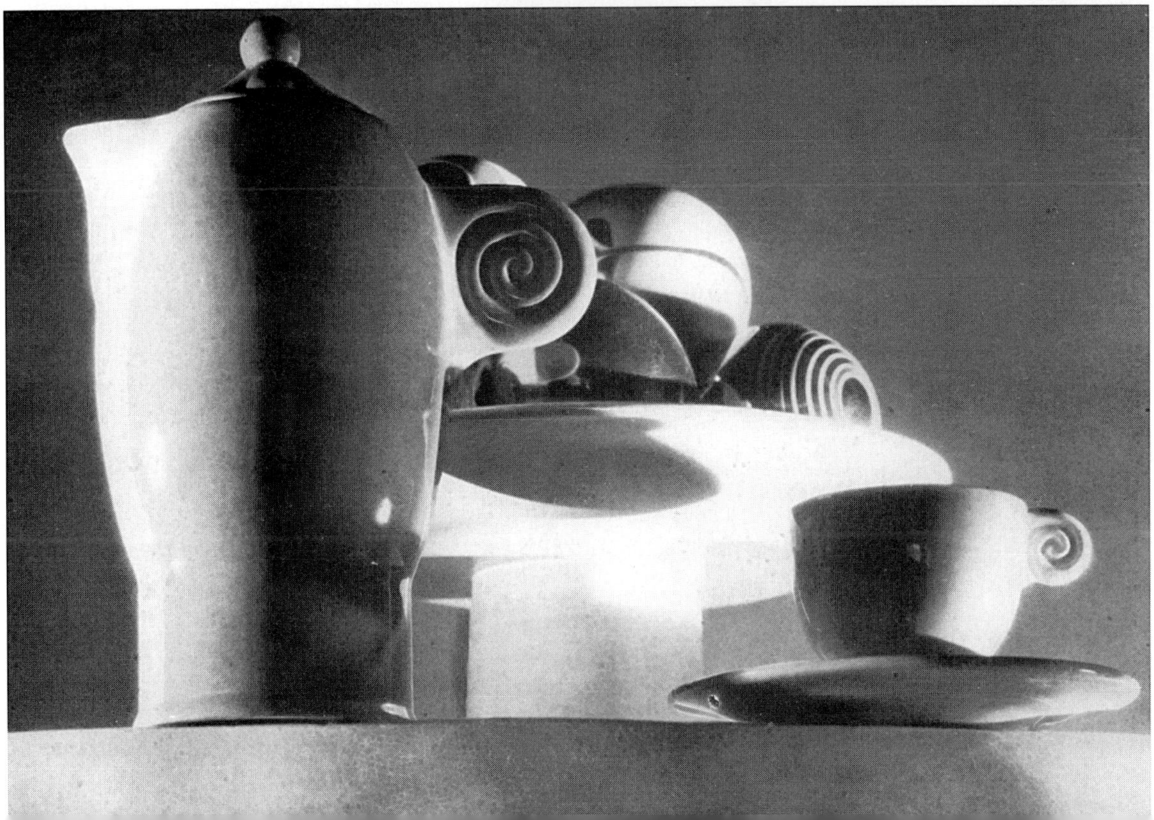

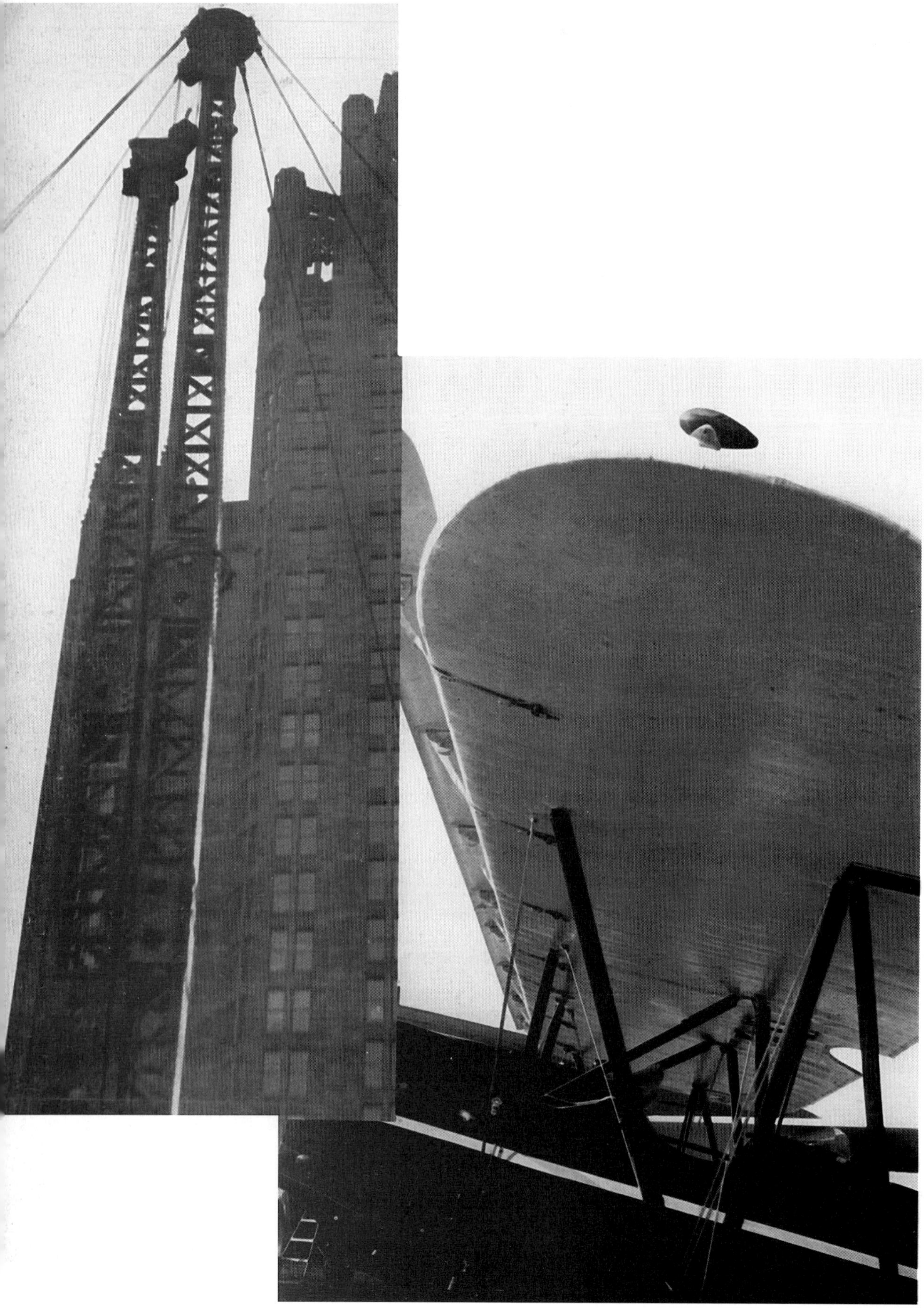

ARTHUR GERLACH
Symbols of Today

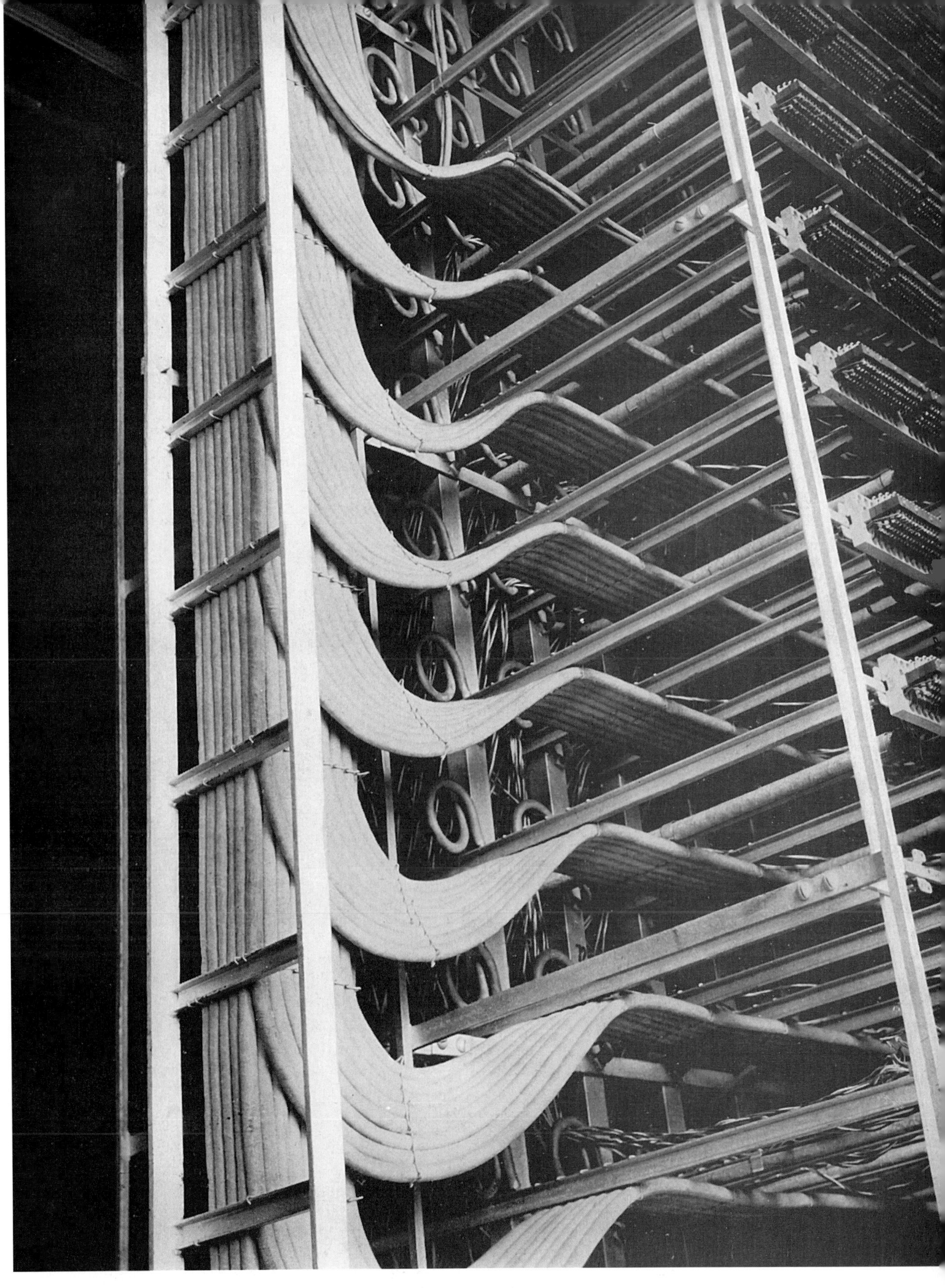

**Telephone Cables New York Telephone Co. Courtesy "Fortune."**

WILL CONNELL

Two pages of photographs made for advertisements of the ''Sunkist Oranges.''

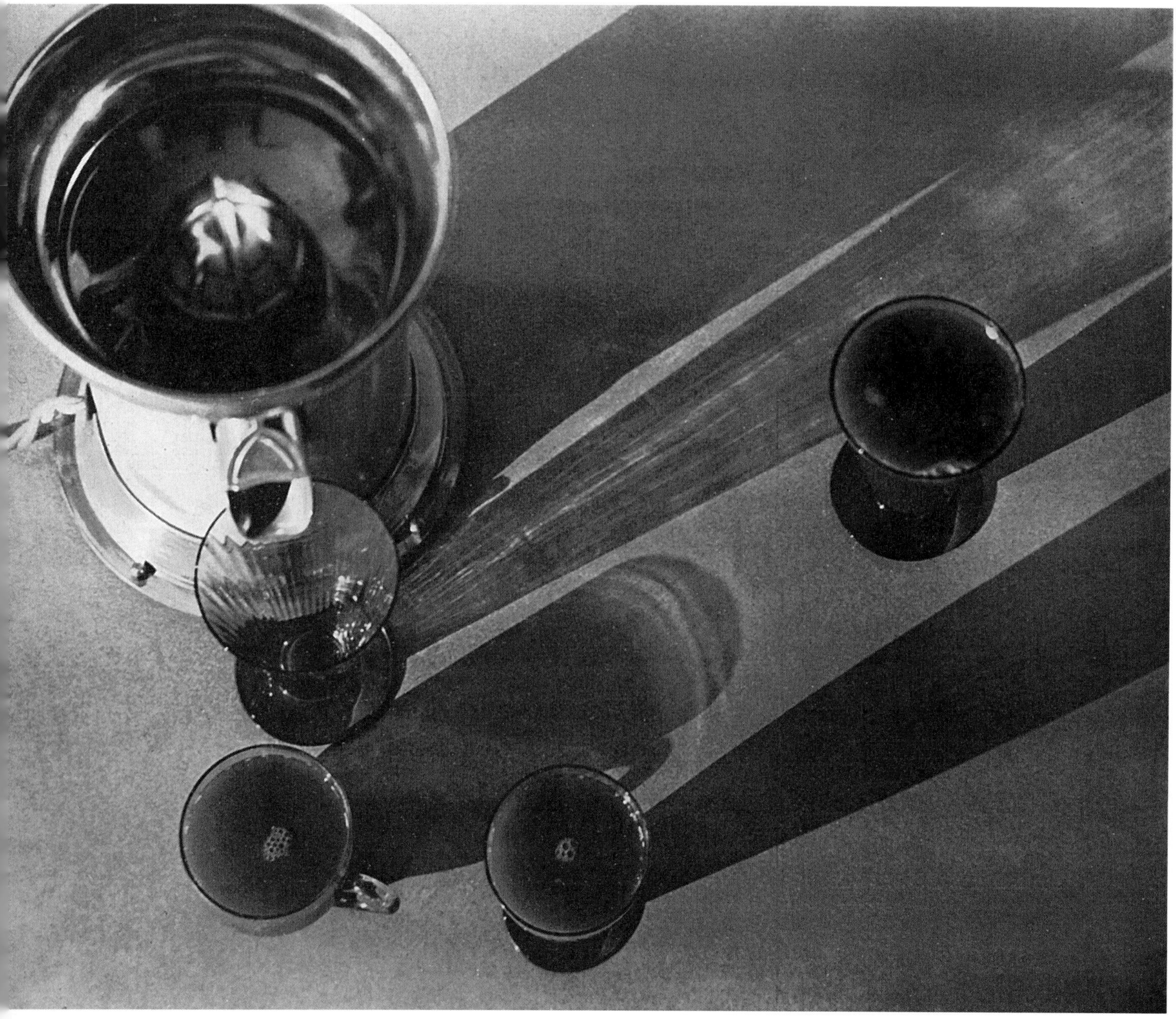

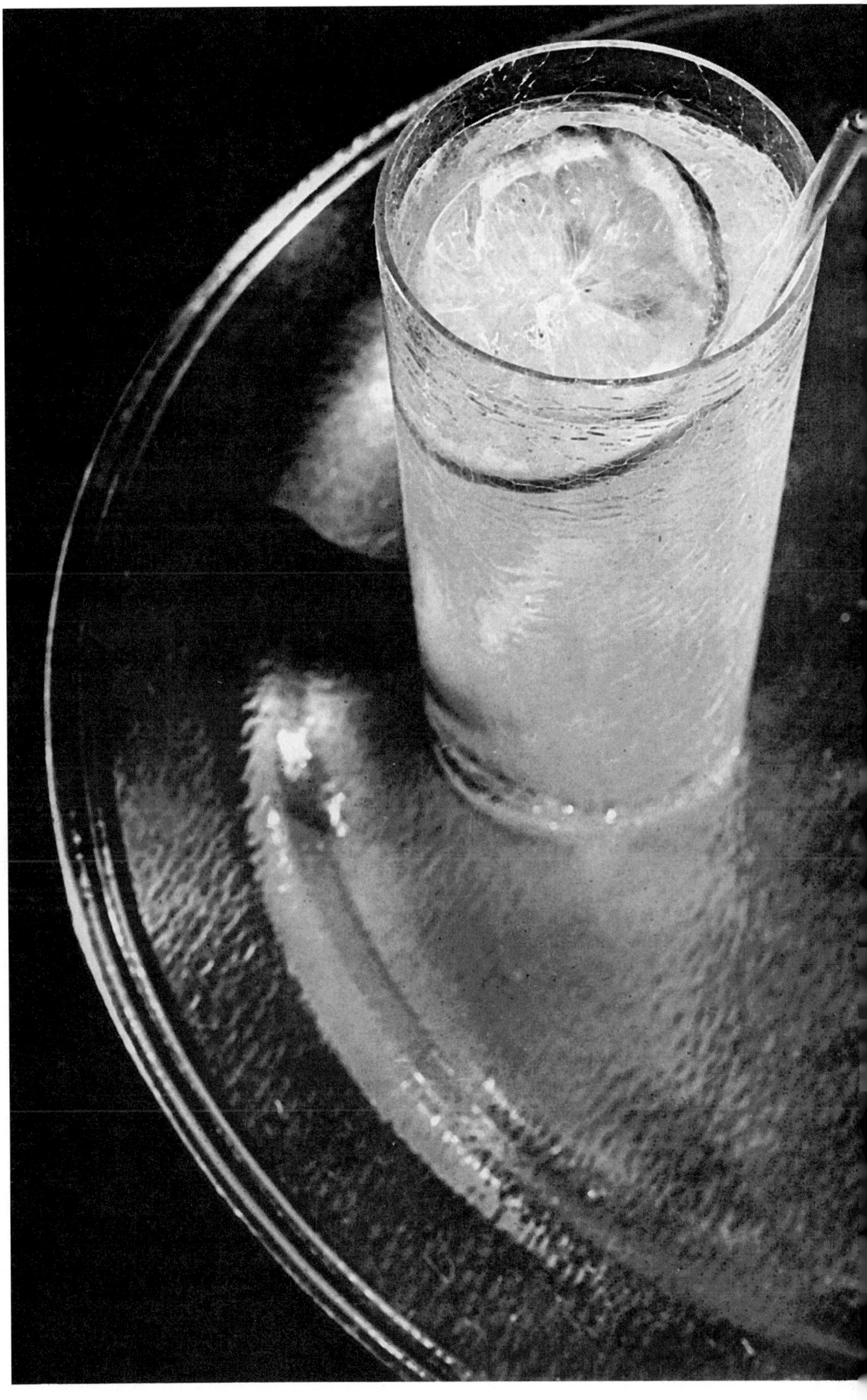

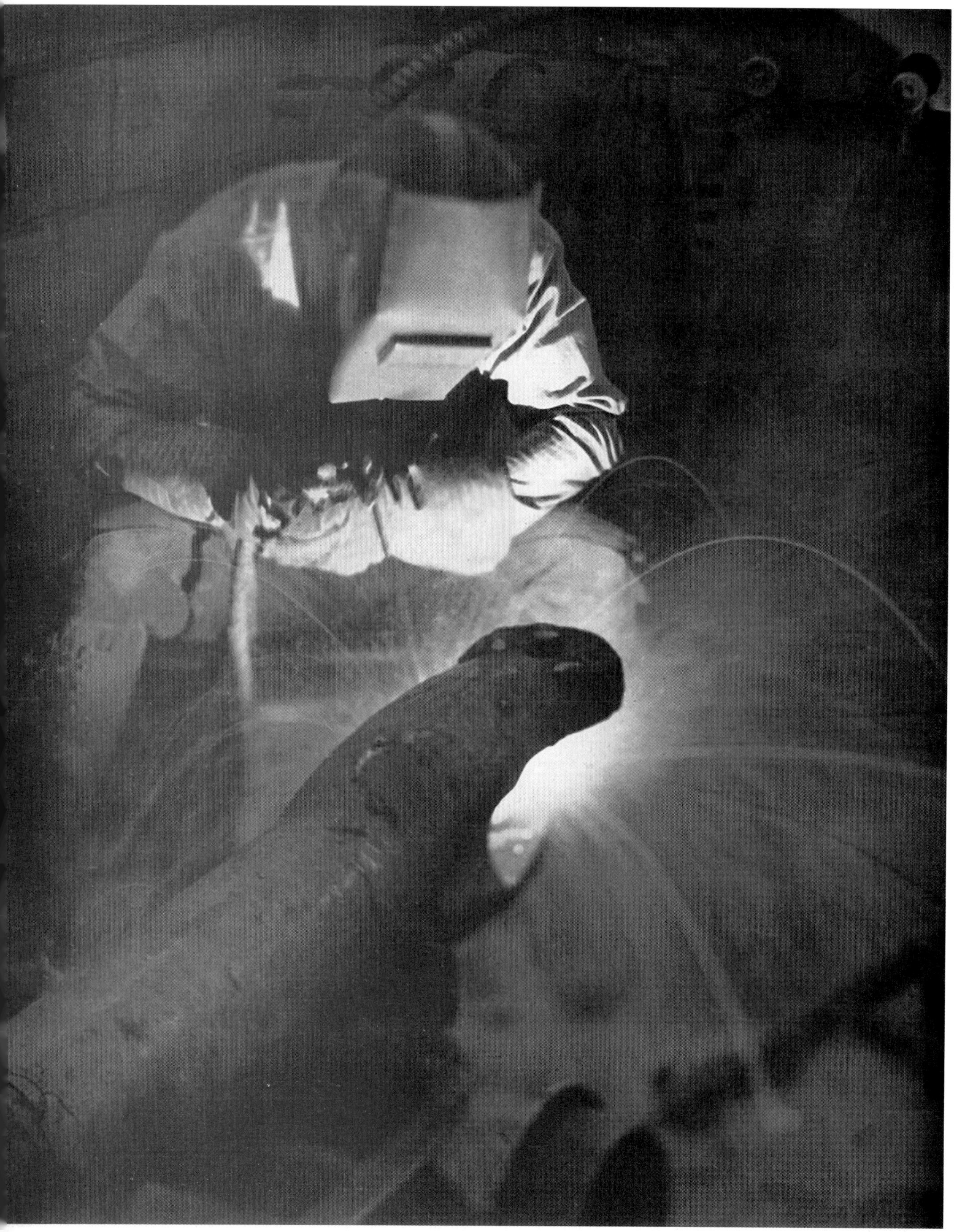

W I L L C O N N E L L — Torch Welding

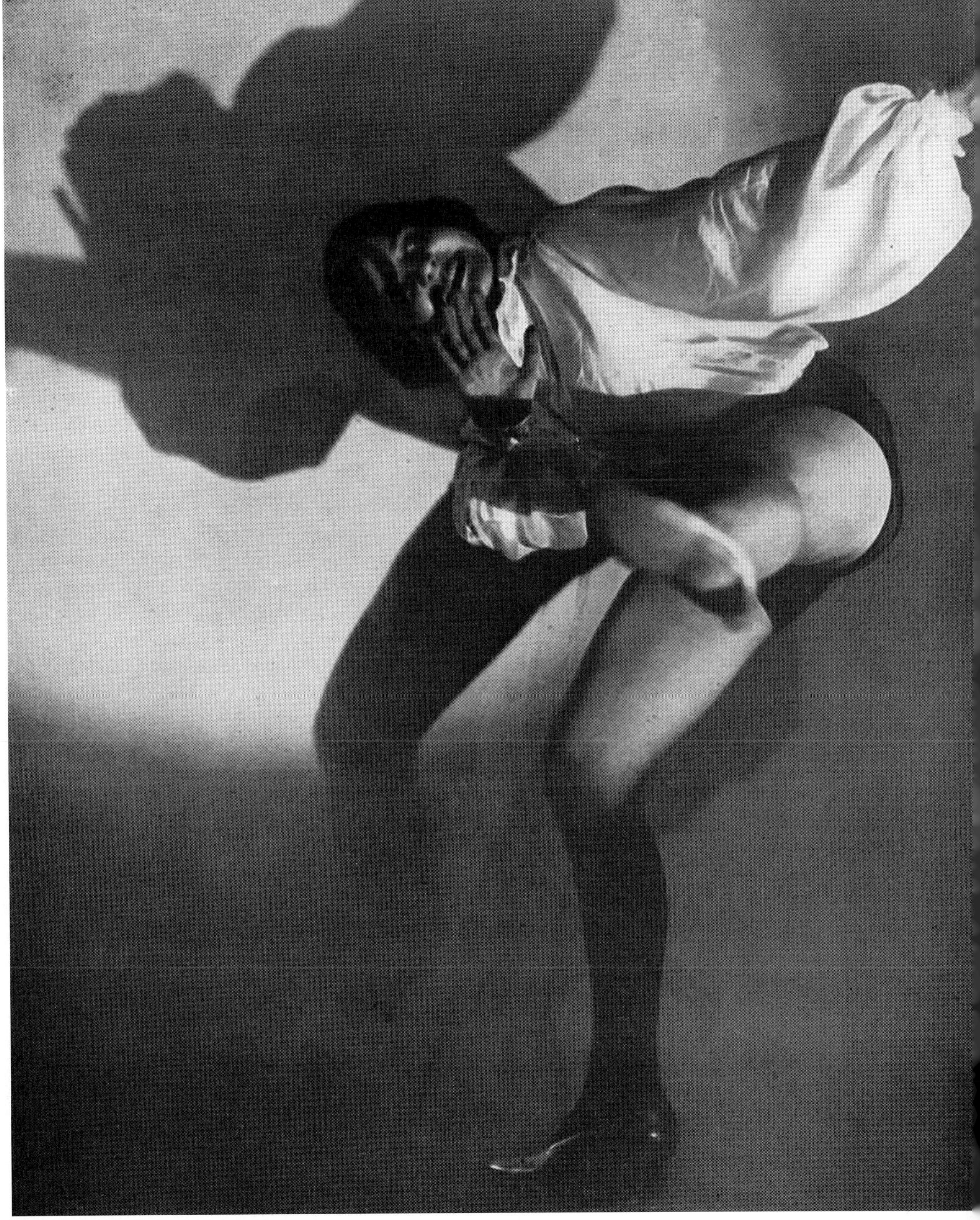

The Breakaway

C. A. GLASSGOLD

# DESIGN IN AMERICA

More than ever before in our country, because of widespread education, elevated standards of living, rapid communication, transportation and other social factors, there is an active and wide participation in the decorative and applied arts. The appreciation by the general public is, however, not equal to the inherent vitality of the decorative arts and it is this discrepancy which is a distinct problem in the cultural life of America.

We see ourselves immersed in a mechanical civilization and we fear lest the values of life be submerged beneath the inhuman weight of the machine. In some, this fear has tended to provoke a vigorous condemnation of the machine age and to arouse a nostalgic, yet vain longing for "the good old days." Nevertheless we must accept contemporary conditions. It is utterly impossible to undo what has already been accomplished by Taut, Le Corbusier, Van der Rohe, Wright, Gropius and others. Besides, and what is more important, by the exercise of intelligence we can force the machine into the service of beauty.

There are those who attempt to effect a compromise between their old allegiances and the dynamic forces of modern society. By running modern techniques down traditional channels they deceive themselves into believing that the ancient beauty of the world may be recaptured. It is they who erect steel skyscrapers adorned with medieval decorations, it is they who ornament the interior of a railroad car with the rococo garlands of French periods. The efforts to evoke the ghosts of the past is a futile delusion. Within the past thirty years it has become clear that only by giving the forms mechanically produced an appropriateness to contemporary life can the machine be kept in its proper sphere—a means to the full cultural development of man. For that reason, the more intelligent designers engaged in the decorative and applied arts, while striving to meet the needs of today by using methods and materials most congenial to their tasks, seek forms at once beautiful and functional. In fact, it is an irresistible process.

A few years ago it would have been impossible to predict any life for the modern movement of design in America. Now it is palpably absurd to maintain that it is just a fad. In the short space of six years, America has become acquainted with its international and sturdy character and although many Americans, who accept and admire the movement, are unaware of its long period of development on the continent, they are, however, able to realize its present maturity.

For thirty years or more, experiment, trial, error, manifestos, controversy and theorizing attended the slow but certain growth of the contemporary movement of design in Germany, Holland, France and Austria. Before the war Germany and Austria had established its basic forms to have them carried with meteoric brilliance by the French to the point of word-wide recognition thereafter. The Paris Exhibition of 1925 is for us, the significant date in the history of this movement for it brought clearly to us the realization that Europe had brewed a stimulating potion while we were pottering about in our own unsavory stew.

The effect upon American design was stupendous. Little wonder then that our first experiments should have been closely modeled upon French design to be followed later by translations from the German and Austrian. A more extenuating reason for our imitativeness during those first few years of apprenticeship is the international character of the basic principles of contemporary design. These principles are so universal that it seemed immaterial, at the time, whether they were expressed in forms derived from the French, Austrian or German. We have come to know better now—or should know better.

This summer, Stockholm held its Exposition of Swedish Arts and Crafts and Home Industries.

Not only was it an illustration of the prevalence of modern design but was equally illustrative of the distinctly national quality the movement may have. The peoples of the world have not yet become sufficiently alike to warrant the assumption that their music, literature, painting and practical arts are alike, and the elusive qualities that differentiate one nation from another are still productive of excellencies with which we cannot yet dispense.

Whatever is typical of Sweden, whatever goes to distinguish her from other countries went into her decorative and applied arts that were shown at the Stockholm Exhibition. True enough much of the work was akin to the works of Taut, Gropius, Le Corbusier, Djo-Bourgeois, Lurcat and others of France and Germany. But with rare exceptions the Stockholm Exhibition never relinquished the purely Swedish touch.

It is high time for the American designer to emancipate himself from European masters. From them he has learned the principles; he must now apply them to the solution of his own problems. The American designer working in the contemporary style may proceed with confidence for from Europe he has learned that modern design is no "fly-by-night" phenomenon but a condition destined to remain so long as the needs of our times are what they are. An exhibition of antiques, such as still held in the United States, is inconceivable in Cologne, Berlin, Vienna, Antwerp, or Paris today except as an historic curio. Our antique shows are the expiring gasps of unimaginative "decorators" and ensembliers and will soon be as anachronistic as a horse-car on Broadway.

This is no place to explain why the modern designer retains an admiration for the really beautiful antique objets d'arts or to fathom why the antiquarian sees red in a modern book-case. It is simply our duty to record the fact that the Victorian "what-nots" and fret-worked pianos have irrevocably used the back-stage exit. As yet we are still in a transitional period and we still have to consumate the battle begun with the Lord & Taylor and the R. H. Macy exhibits held in 1927 and 1928 in New York.

America has one alternative for contemporary design—to return to colonial interiors and encase its radios in grandfather clocks. The other so-called American periods were at all times both tasteless and inappropriate to the American scene and with no stretch of the imagination to be conceived as a source of inspiration for contemporary design. The eclecticism of the "brown-stone" age immediately preceeding our own was a hideous nightmare which we will do well to forget. Modern design, if intelligently employed, will help us do so.

The modern developments in the applied, industrial and decorative arts are indicative of recent and eventual changes in our social outlook. Their present significance lies not alone in substituting an appropriate style in the place of outmoded traditional ones, but also revivifying the esthetic appreciation of the public.

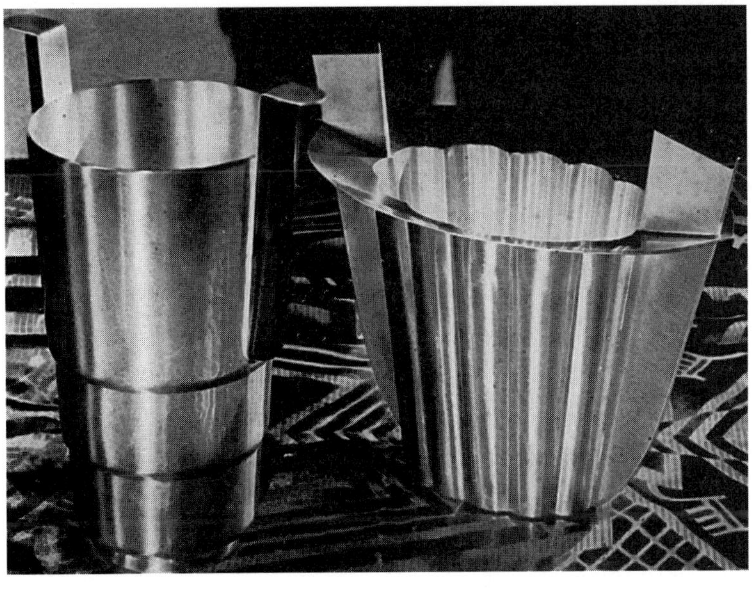

**K E M W E B E R**

**Flower baskets in silver and ebony. Executed by Friedman Silver Company, N. Y.**

## INDEX OF DESIGNERS



## CREDIT TO PHOTOGRAPHERS